THE DEVELOPING PRACTITIONER

This book provides a comprehensive overview of the professional development of counselors and therapists over the career lifespan. Drawing on their own extensive experience as psychotherapists, supervisors, teachers, and researchers, as well as from their own extensive study of the topic, previously published in their 1992 book *The Evolving Professional Self,* the authors aim to provide an update of their work that all counselors and psychotherapists will find valuable and useful. Readers are provided with empirically based conceptual knowledge that can increase their awareness of the central issues in professional development, allowing them to monitor their own development. The authors discuss the concept of development and review the research literature on practitioner development, and then provide detailed descriptions of its six phases. Aspects of each phase addressed include the developmental tasks unique to that phase; the sources of influence and the learning process which impacts therapeutic work and a sense of development; the perception of the professional role and working style; and therapists' measures of effectiveness and satisfaction. All of this is augmented with quotes and illustrative examples from participants in the authors' research studies. The book includes knowledge generated from research on master therapists and from the Society for Psychotherapy Research/Collaborative Research Network. The book also considers themes of professional development; struggles faced by novice practitioners; patterns of practitioner resiliency; and ways to improve training, supervision, and practice.

Michael Helge Rønnestad, PhD, is Professor of Clinical Psychology at the University of Oslo, Norway.

Thomas M. Skovholt, PhD, ABPP, is Professor of Counseling and Student Personnel Psychology at the University of Minnesota.

THE DEVELOPING PRACTITIONER

Growth and Stagnation
of Therapists and Counselors

Michael Helge Rønnestad
Thomas M. Skovholt

Routledge
Taylor & Francis Group

NEW YORK AND LONDON

First published 2013
by Routledge
711 Third Avenue, New York, NY 10017

Simultaneously published in the UK
by Routledge
27 Church Road, Hove, East Sussex BN3 2FA

Routledge is an imprint of the Taylor & Francis Group, an informa business

Library of Congress Cataloging in Publication Data
Rønnestad, Michael Helge.
    The developing practitioner : growth and stagnation of therapists and counselors / Michael Helge Rønnestad & Thomas Skovholt.
    p. cm.
    Includes bibliographical references and index.
    ISBN 978-0-415-88459-4 (hardback)
    1. Psychotherapists—Training of. 2. Career development. 3. Self-actualization (Psychology) 4. Psychotherapists—Psychology. I. Skovholt, Thomas M. II. Title.
    RC480.5.R6625 2012
    616.89'140023—dc23
    2012006274

ISBN: 978-0-415-88459-4 (hbk)
ISBN: 978-0-203-84140-2 (ebk)

Typeset in Garamond
by EvS Communication Networx, Inc.

We dedicate this book to the therapists in the 'Minnesota study', the study conducted by the Society for Psychotherapy Research/ Collaborative Research Network, and the Master therapist studies. Their generous participation made this book possible.

CONTENTS

LIST OF FIGURES AND TABLES

Figures

Tables

ABOUT THE AUTHORS

Michael Helge Rønnestad is a professor of clinical psychology in the Department of Psychology, University of Oslo, Norway. He is a Specialist in Clinical Psychology (Norwegian Psychological Association). Rønnestad received a PhD in counseling psychology from the University of Missouri-Columbia in 1973. For decades, he has taught workshops on the topics of psychotherapy research, professional development, and clinical supervision for the Norwegian Psychological Association. Rønnestad has lectured extensively and provided consultation on various topics within psychology and counseling in many countries. He is the principal investigator of an intensive process-outcome study of the interpersonal aspects of psychotherapy, in which highly experienced psychotherapists who are also teachers of psychotherapy participate as therapists. Rønnestad is the European coordinator for the Society for Psychotherapy Research/ Collaborative Research Network (SPR/CRN), which has organized the International Study of the Development of Psychotherapists. The SPR/ CRN has collected data from about 11,000 therapists and counselors from more than 30 countries. Rønnestad has published extensively (scientific articles and book chapters). He has also published and edited nine books, including Orlinsky and Rønnestad (2005). *How Psychotherapists Develop: A Study of Therapeutic Work and Professional Growth,* which was based on analyses of data from almost 5,000 therapists.

Thomas M. Skovholt is a professor of counseling psychology at the University of Minnesota, a Licensed Psychologist, Board Certified by ABPP, and a Fellow of APA. He has also taught in Turkey and Singapore, and at the University of Florida. Tom has been a part-time practitioner for many years and has found that knowledge from practice is of great value just as is knowledge from research and knowledge from teaching. His presentations have focused on professional resiliency, struggles of the novice, the path toward expertise and mastery, clinical supervision, and cultural factors in counseling. Books, as author or coauthor, include *The Evolving Professional Self* with current coauthor Michael Helge Rønnestad, *The Resilient Practitioner, Master Therapists, Voices from the Field: Defining Moments in Counselor and Therapist Development, Skills and Strategies for the Helping Professions,* and *Ethics in Small Communities.* Awards include University of Minnesota Morse Teaching Award, the Research Award of Association for Counselor Education and Supervision with Helge Rønnestad, the Lifetime Contributions to Education and Training by the Council of Counseling Psychology Training Programs, and the Susan T. Rydell Outstanding Contributions to Psychology Award by the Minnesota Psychological Association. He and Helge Rønnestad met as students in the 1970s at the University of Missouri and began their research collaboration in April 1985. He has been fortunate to have had this long association with Helge and, in the broader view, he feels fortunate to have found counseling and psychology as a career field. Tom often tells his students that counseling and therapy is one of the great inventions of the last half of the 20th century and that he and they get to use this invention to try to be helpful to others. He tells them that this is gratifying and meaningful work.

About the Contributing Authors

Michael Goh is an associate professor at the University of Minnesota in comparative and international development education, Department of Organizational Leadership, Policy and Development and affiliated with the Counseling and Student Personnel Psychology program, both in the College of Education and Human Development. Michael's teaching, research, and service are focused on discovering better ways to conceptualize, assess, and ultimately teach multicultural counseling and intercultural communication skills. His current research program includes cultural competence in mental health practice, cultural intelligence, multicultural master therapists, practice-based evidence, and global mental health policies.

Len Jennings is a professor at the University of St. Thomas, Minneapolis, Minnesota. Dr. Jennings balances his work among teaching, research, practice, and service. Dr. Jennings is a Licensed Psychologist and has a private practice specializing in men's issues, career development, and group psychotherapy. Dr. Jennings's research interests include psychotherapy expertise, international/multicultural counseling, and career development. He has coauthored (with T. M. Skovholt) *Master Therapists: Exploring Expertise in Therapy and Counseling* (2004).

Fengqin Lian is currently a PhD candidate in the Counseling and Student Personnel Psychology program at the University of Minnesota, Twin Cities. Her dissertation focuses on developing an inventory to measure master therapists' characteristics. She has practiced psychotherapy/counseling in various settings for 6 years and she is completing her predoctoral psychology internship at the Student Health and Counseling Services at the University of California, Davis.

David E. Orlinsky is a professor of comparative human development at the University of Chicago, where he has taught since 1960. He is the author of *Varieties of Psychotherapeutic Experience* (1975, with K. I. Howard), *How Psychotherapists Develop* (2005, with M. H. Rønnestad), and coeditor of *The Psychotherapist's Own Psychotherapy: Patient and Clinician Perspectives* (2005, with J. D. Geller and J. C. Norcross). He has published over 100 articles and chapters, and in 1968 cofounded the Society for Psychotherapy Research. In 2010, he received an honorary doctorate from the University of Oslo.

Oddbjørg Skjær Ulvik is an associate professor in the Faculty of Social Sciences, Oslo and Akershus University College of Applied Sciences. She has a PhD in psychology from the University of Oslo. Her research interests include cultural psychology, theoretical psychology, child care, and research methods. In addition to articles and book chapters, she has coedited (with Hedegaard, Aronsson, and Højholt) *Foster Families in Late Modernity: The Cultural Psychological Study of Children's and Adults' Narratives* (2012).

Michelle Trotter-Mathison is a Licensed Psychologist at Boynton Health Service, University of Minnesota. She teaches within the Counseling and Psychological Services Program at Saint Mary's University of Minnesota. Michelle completed an MA and PhD at the University of Minnesota in the Counseling and Student Personnel Psychology program. She is coauthor of *The Resilient Practitioner and Voices from the Field: Defining Moments in Counselor and Therapist Development*. She has a small private practice in St. Paul, Minnesota.

ACKNOWLEDGMENTS

We appreciate the contributions of so many people who have made this research project and the publication of the results possible. Our gratitude goes first to the students in training and the therapists in practice who made up the research participants for the N = 100 qualitative interview study. The second author and the research team at the University of Minnesota conducted the first and second round of interviews, 160 in all. Bill Cuff was the head research assistant. The research team included Charles Boudreaux, Kevin Harrington, Elisabeth Horst, Patti Neiman, Mohammad Razzaque, Janet Schank, and Kay Thomas. Both the first and second author did the third round of interviews with the senior therapists 10 years later.

Furthermore, the second author appreciates the contributions of so many people who have increased his understanding of therapist development and therapist effectiveness. These include clients who have taught him so much over the years of practice, and graduate students, who in interactions in theory and practicum classes and as part of dissertation projects, have been so instructive. During more than 50 oral exams, with the second author as an examiner, the candidates for Board Certification of ABPP, and the other examiners too, have been great teachers about therapist mastery. For helping him understand therapist development, appreciation is expressed specifically by the second author to: John Dagley, Tabitha Grier-Reed, Len Jennings, Mary Mullenbach, Susan Neufeldt, Jaquie Resnick, John Romano, Janet Schank, Norma Simon, Ronald Soderquist, Michael Sullivan, and Michelle Trotter-Mathison. Special thanks go to Lisa Yost for encouragement, perspective, and insights about this book project.

In Scandinavia, the first author wants to thank colleagues for stimulating discussions and for having taken the time to read and comment on the manuscript: Anna von der Lippe, Kirsten Benum, Hanne Strømme, Sissel Reichelt, Geir Kirkebøen, all colleagues at the University of Oslo, and Peter Elsass at the University of Copenhagen. Thanks also to colleagues in the supervision research network for insightful discussions and collaboration on supervision. They are, in addition to some mentioned above, Siri E. Gullestad, Geir Høstmark Nielsen, Jan Skjerve, Claus Haugaard Jacobsen, Bjørg Røed Hansen, and Anne Mari Torgersen. The regular lunch room discussions over the years with Eva Axelsen, Hanne Haavind, Nora Sveaass, Bjørg Grova, Svein Mossige, Odd Arne Tjersland, Wenke Gulbrandsen, Bjørn Killingmo, and some of the persons mentioned above, have been highly appreciated; it has been a good forum for personal and professional reflections.

A special appreciation is extended to members of the steering committee of the Society for Psychotherapy Research/Collaborative Research Network, who have made it fun and stimulating to study therapist development. Special mention to David Orlinsky, Jean-Francois Botermans, Robert Elliott, Jan Grant, Armin Hartmann, Margot Schofield, Thomas Schroeder, Hadas Wiesman, Ulrike Willutzki, and Sue Wheeler. Special thanks go to Oddbjørg Skjær Ulvik and David Orlinsky (again), who both have contributed as coauthors of chapters in this book and who have provided the support needed to finish this book project.

Michael Helge Rønnestad and Thomas M. Skovholt

PREFACE

For over more than 25 years, the primary authors of this book have collaborated in the study of therapist and counselor development. We have been fortunate to enlist the cooperation of students and practitioners in the Minneapolis/St. Paul, Minnesota area who have generously shared both their professional and personal experiences with us. The interviews with these students and practitioners constitute the primary database for our study. The first comprehensive publication of our work was Skovholt and Rønnestad, *The Evolving Professional Self: Stages and Themes in Counselor and Therapist Development*, published by Wiley in 1992. In this book, we presented our conception of practitioner development at three levels of abstraction: First, as an eight stage model of practitioner development (the conventional helper, transition to professional training, imitation, conditional autonomy, exploration, integration, individuation, and integrity); second, thereafter as 20 themes of practitioner development, and finally, as a more abstract process model of development and stagnation.

Since our first publication, we have been engaged in related research projects that have contributed to our understanding of therapist/counselor development. Rønnestad has collaborated with a group of researchers from many countries who are members of the Society for Psychotherapy Research/Collaborative Research Network (SPR/CRN), of which he is the European Coordinator. By 2005, The SPR/CRN had collected data from approximately 5,000 therapists from many countries (e.g., Orlinsky & Rønnestad, 2005a), and now the database contains data from approximately 11,000 therapists.

Skovholt, his students, and colleagues initiated studies of master therapists, selecting them not by charisma, fame, or publications, but by practitioner-oriented selection criteria. These criteria were either peer-nomination or membership via the practice competence method of ABPP. The Minnesota Master Therapist studies were first published in book form in Skovholt and Jennings (2004). The current chapter includes studies from five countries.

Almost 10 years ago, we were able to draw on these additional sources of knowledge in a reanalysis and condensation of our work published in the *Journal of Career Development* (Rønnestad & Skovholt, 2003). Here, the stage concept for describing changes across therapist life course was dropped and replaced with the concept of *phase*. To us, this was a major change in how we conceptualized therapist/counselor development. Furthermore, the number of phases was reduced from eight to six (the lay helper phase, the beginning student phase, the advanced student phase, the novice professional phase, the experienced professional phase, and the senior professional phase). And finally, a reanalysis led to reducing the number of themes of therapist/counselor development from 20 to 14. The 2003 formulation was a parsimonious one.

Through the years, we have wanted to pull together different sources of knowledge that have been available to us through the years, with the original interviews (Skovholt & Rønnestad, 1992) and the interviews with the most senior group about 10 years later (Rønnestad & Skovholt, 2001) as a the main empirical source. We are grateful that Routledge provided us with this opportunity to carry our collaboration one step further.

The present book differs from *The Evolving Professional Self* in substantial ways and warrants a new title, *The Developing Practitioner: Growth and Stagnation of Therapists and Counselors*. We have approached the empirical material with new eyes through our engagement in the projects described above. We have extended the initial review of the conceptual literature in chapter 1, by adding in chapter 2 contributions within topics such as the study of expertise, learning, decision making, and cognitive complexity.

Chapter 3 on cultural conceptions of helping is a new chapter and replaces a previous chapter on the conventional or lay helper. This chapter describes ways to understand the point-of-departure for professional training. However, given the variety of ways that discourses and practices of helping are conceptualized within and across cultures, we have chosen to present a more abstract and theoretical discussion on helping practices that we hope will make the reader better able to understand both the variability in helping practices, but also the reciprocal relationship between professional and nonprofessional helping discourses.

Chapters 4 through 8 (phases of therapist/counselor development) differ from the original formulations in several ways. First, the number of phases has been reduced to five. Second, some of the content has been kept, but new material has been added which to a larger extent relates the material to the contributions of others in the field. Third, we have aimed to sharpen the "story" by highlighting what has emerged as most salient given our learning experience with other projects and also by taking into account the feedback we have received by presenting and discussing our findings and perspectives with others through the years. Fourth, inspired by Havighurst (1972), for each phase we have formulated developmental tasks for the therapist/counselor. Fifth, we have organized the content of each phase according to the following structure: Introduction; Developmental Tasks and General Description; Sources of Influence and Learning

Process; Professional Role and Conceptual Ideas Used; and Measures of Effectiveness and Satisfaction.

Inspired by Rod Goodyear's (Rodney, Goodyear, Wertheimer, Cypers, & Rosemond, 2003) recommendation, in his commentary on the Rønnestad and Skovholt (2003) article in the special issue of the *Journal of Career Development* on therapist/counselor development, to collapse the number of themes, we have reduced the number of themes to 10 in chapter 9. Thank you, Rod.

Chapter 10 is a new chapter where we present a cyclical/trajectories model of therapist/counselor development. In this model, the root cause of development/stagnations is practitioners' experiences of difficulties encountered in their professional work. In this chapter, a distinction is made between *reflexivity* as a *capacity*, *reflective stance* as an *attitude*, and *reflection* as *activity*. Effective closure, inadequate closure, and premature closure are the central mechanisms that lead either to development or to the trajectories of stagnation (i.e., exhaustion and disengagement). The model is compared to a model of cognitive complexity (Owen & Lindley, 2010). A chapter appendix illustrates movements through the different trajectories.

Chapter 11 on implications for supervision presents a new supervision model which differentiates between general principles of supervision (i.e., principles assumed to be important regardless of the experience level of the supervisee) and principles that are important to consider in the supervision of supervisees at different experience levels. The general principles are stimulated by the conceptual analysis of psychotherapy research by Marvin Goldfried (1980, 2009). He has suggested that it is possible to reach consensus among different theoretical orientations on some common principles of psychotherapy. The way to do this is *not* to focus on formulations specific to different theoretical orientations, or on observable techniques, but on midlevel abstractions. This principle is used as a basis for formulating general principles of supervision.

Chapter 12 by Jennings, Skovholt, Goh, and Lin brings together main findings and perspectives from a research program on master therapists who were selected based on their expertise as practitioners. Research on master therapists gives us insight into characteristics of therapists at the expert level. Knowing the end goal can help us along the developmental path.

Chapter 13 is a new chapter by Skovholt and Trotter-Mathison on professional resiliency. The focus of this chapter is on how to prevent burnout and maintain resilience. In this chapter the reader is invited to assess his or her own resiliency and self-care through the "Skovholt Practitioner Professional Resiliency and Self-Care Inventory" (see chapter 13 appendix). The inventory may be used to stimulate self-reflection as one reads through the chapter.

Chapter 14 contains a brief summary of main findings, perspectives, models, and implications of the Society for Psychotherapy Research/Collaborative Research Network (Orlinsky & Rønnestad, 2005b). In this chapter the positive and negative sequential cyclical models of the SPR/CRN are compared with the cyclical/trajectories model presented in the preceding chapter. Suggestions are made for how to improve on both models. Chapter appendices present two self-administering scales, one for the assessment of therapist involvement styles and the other for the assessment of professional development.

Part I

THEORETICAL AND EMPIRICAL FOUNDATIONS FOR THE STUDY OF PRACTITIONER DEVELOPMENT

1

PERSPECTIVES ON PRACTITIONERS' PROFESSIONAL DEVELOPMENT[1]

Introduction

During the last decades of the 20th century and into the 21st century, the fields of psychotherapy and counseling have been progressively valued as important contributors to human well-being. These fields are increasingly commanding a central position in the solutions of many of the complex and important concerns that are faced by numerous people. Mental health services are steadily expanding and continued growth is expected over the decades ahead. Central to this rise in popularity are the positive responses from individuals who are receiving counseling or therapy. People usually value the professional help that they receive from therapists and counselors in such diverse areas as anxiety reduction, managing depression, coping with loss, resolving relationship conflicts, developing positive organizations, finding satisfying work, learning new interpersonal skills, stopping addictive behaviors, struggling with meaning and purpose in life, and addressing family problems.

Within the fields of psychotherapy and counseling, there is an ongoing debate regarding definition of the knowledge-base for practitioners. The policy statement of the American Psychological Association on Evidence-Based Treatment (2006) is one expression of necessary sources of knowledge for professional practice. As many will already know, the definition is as follows: "*Evidence-based practice in psychology* (EBPP) is the integration of the best available research with clinical expertise in the context of patient characteristics, culture, and preferences" (APA, 2006, p. 273). One of the components of clinical expertise in this definition is continual self-reflection and acquisition of skills. One rationale for the work we are presenting in the book is the "know thyself credo" of the therapy/counseling culture. We hope that this book will stimulate readers to explore broadly and deeply the different aspects of their professional and personal selves, their motivations for entering and staying in the profession, their assets and limitations in professional functioning, and how to ensure continued professional growth. For those who may feel that they are stagnating or experiencing a sense of decline, we hope that this book will provide a stimulus toward regaining a sense of vitality and enthusiasm for their professional work.

We feel that the knowledge reported in this book, knowledge generated from in-depth interviews, survey data, and from reflections and dialogues with colleagues, has a potential to enhance the professional development of therapists and counselors. When we add to this the recent summaries of psychotherapy research that have convincingly documented the impact of therapist/counselor effects on the outcome of therapy and counseling (Norcross, 2011; Wampold, 2011), we feel that we have compelling arguments for the continued study of therapists and counselors. The focus of our research is on the professional development of practitioners throughout their professional lifespan.

Many models of therapist and counselor development were formulated during the 1970s and 1980s. Following publication of our initial work on professional development (Rønnestad & Skovholt, 1991; Skovholt & Rønnestad, 1991, 1992), few studies have emerged that have provided empirically based models for professional development with the focus on the entire professional life cycle of the practitioner. Exceptions are our follow-up study of therapists/counselors (Rønnestad & Skovholt, 2001), reanalyses of our material (e.g., Rønnestad & Skovholt, 2003); the large-scale survey conducted by the Society for Psychotherapy Research Collaborative Research Network (e.g., Orlinsky & Rønnestad, 2005), and studies in related fields of expertise (Chi, Glaser, & Farr, 1988; Feltovitch, Prietula, & Ericsson, 2006). There are, of course, large bodies of knowledge within established areas of inquiry that are highly relevant for understanding professional development, like therapist/counselor training (both basic and continuing education), supervision, personal therapy, and motivation for becoming a professional helper. Typically, this research does not attempt to describe professional development over the course of the entire professional lifespan.

In this chapter, we present first some reflections on topics which converge in a need to combine the study of therapist effects with the study of practitioner development in order to better understand the contribution of the therapist to the therapy/counseling outcome. This is followed by a discussion of the concept of development, and a historical review of the professional development literature.

The Profound Importance of the Therapist's Contribution to Successful Outcome

The person of the psychotherapist is increasingly attracting the attention of those interested in understanding the processes and dynamics of changes in therapy and counseling. Over the years, we have come to appreciate the deeply personal nature of being a practitioner. The work by Skovholt and McCarthy (1988) documented the personal nature of therapeutic work in their investigation of critical incidents in the development of counselors and therapists. Also, the book edited by Goldfried (2001) offers a highly engaging series of 15 first-person accounts by seasoned practitioners of their own professional lives. Another recent contribution to this literature is *Voices from the Field: Defining Moments in Counselor and Therapist Development*, (Trotter-Mathison, Koch, Sanger, & Skovholt, 2010), a book also filled with deeply meaningful and engaging stories by 87 practitioners who share the defining moments that shaped their own professional lives.

Another recent and convincing contribution to the perspective of the person of the therapist/counselor is the formulation of the real relationship in therapy (e.g., Gelso, 2002, 2009). Gelso suggests not only that the real relationship is a viable and useful construct in the study of therapy/counseling process, but also that the personal qualities of psychotherapists contribute to the formation of the professional relationship. This is how Gelso (2009) defines the real relationship:

> In sum, we define the real relationship as the personal relationship existing between two or more people as reflected in the degree to which each is genuine with the other, and perceives and experiences the other in ways that befit the other. (pp. 254–255)

Carl Rogers's seminal contributions to the conceptualization of psychotherapy, and his emphasis on therapist genuineness (Rogers, 1957), is a testimony to how important therapists' personal qualities are for optimal professional functioning. Gelso brings genuineness and the real relationship together by stating that the two concepts are interrelated. He writes: "It is difficult for me to think of a real relationship in the absence of these two elements, realism and genuineness" (p. 255). Another professional who describes the personal aspect of professional practice is David Orlinsky, who on his home page states:

> Orlinsky views psychotherapy also as essentially [a] "personal relationship," but one that is offered professionally as a corrective or remedial experience for persons in modern societies whose subjective distress or behavioral problems are rooted in impaired, incomplete, or deviant development in "natural" personal relationships.

There is an ongoing debate in psychotherapy research about the relative contribution of the therapeutic relationship versus the technical factors for therapy outcome (see Duncan, Miller, Wampold, & Hubble, 2010; Norcross, 2011; Norcross & Lambert, 2011 for contributions to this debate). We will address this briefly, as the empirical results that contribute to this discussion are arguments for focusing more intensely on the study of therapists. While some argue that it is the quality of the therapeutic relationship that is of most importance for client change, others contend that it is the therapeutic methods or techniques that are of greatest significance. This debate is often framed within a related discussion; namely, that regarding common versus specific factors of psychotherapy. Those who have most confidence in the common factors perspective believe that elements that are most effective in therapy are shared by the majority of forms of psychotherapy; the researchers with this perspective, typically will not investigate in their research what differentiates one therapy from another, but will explore those characteristics that they share. In contrast, those who deem that it is the technical aspects that are most important for therapy outcome, will typically look for differences between treatment forms in their research, and they are likely to do so by studying those therapies that are manualized.

The debate about the relative contributions of common and specific factors is far from settled, and it may also be argued that the distinction is artificial, as we illustrate below. Possibly overstating the change in the editors' position in the revision of *The Heart and Soul of Change* (Duncan et al., 2010), Orlinsky (2010) writes:

> Implicit recognition of this new paradigm is reflected in the fact that the architects of this new edition have abandoned the traditional distinction between common factors and specific factors as an organizing framework (in which specific factors refers primarily to differences in therapists' procedures or techniques) and have replaced that with a simpler, more inclusive emphasis on therapeutic factors. (p. xxii)

More than 30 years ago, Goldfried (1980) proposed a strategy to arrive at a rapprochement between different schools of therapy through identifying common clinical strategies. He suggested conceptualizing the therapeutic enterprise at various levels of abstraction. Theoretical frameworks or accompanying theoretical stances were at the highest level of abstraction. According to Goldfried, focusing the discussion at that level provides little chance for agreement. Therapeutic techniques or clinical procedures were at the lowest level of abstraction. Some agreement might be found at this level, but likely not beyond trivial points of similarity. There was more promise at the midlevel. He wrote:

> I would suggest, however, that the possibility of finding meaningful consensus exists at a level of abstraction somewhere between theory and technique which, for want of a better term, we might call *clinical strategies*. Were these strategies to have a clear

empirical foundation, it might be more appropriate to call them *principles* of change. (p. 994)

And indeed, in a special issue of *Applied and Preventive Psychology* (Volume 13, 2009) devoted to a discussion of Goldfried's seminal article, it is documented that principles of change have an empirical foundation (e.g., Castonguay & Beutler, 2006). Goldfried highlights the following: (a) client's initial expectations that therapy can be helpful and client motivation, (b) the therapeutic alliance, (c) having clients become aware of what contributes to their current life problems, (d) client engagement in *corrective experiences*.

Increasingly, prominent psychotherapy researchers question the validity and usefulness of arguing for either the treatment method or the relationship having most impact for therapy/counseling outcome. Norcross and Lambert (2011) write: "But perhaps the most pernicious and insidious consequence of the false dichotomy of treatment versus relationship has been its polarizing effect on the discipline" (p. 4). With their overview of the field, we are wise to listen to their advice to study the patient, the therapist, their relationship, the treatment method, and the context if we want to improve psychotherapy outcome.

Although we are mindful of the complexity and interrelationship of "what works," our focus is on the therapists' perceptions of their work and development. It is reasonably certain that *therapist effects* contribute substantially to variations in therapy/counseling outcome (Lutz, Leon, Martinovitch, Lyons, & Stiles, 2007; Wampold, 2010; Wampold & Brown, 2005). Even though it is conceptually questionable to single out different "effects," the empirical findings on the topic cannot be ignored. Indeed, "therapist effects" are much more important than "methods effects," and therefore *who* the therapist is, is much more important than the therapeutic method used. While there may be some exceptions to this description, this is the general picture. However, we caution against the misunderstanding that methods and techniques are not important; it can certainly be argued that it is through the use of different techniques and methods that relationships are formed. Orlinsky (2010) expresses this point of view: "The therapist's procedures are important but become effective largely by contributing to the formation and development of this relationship in the patient's perspective" (p. xxi). Nevertheless, the bulk of the empirical findings indicate that the relative importance favors the relationship effects and therapist effects. Indeed, one recent finding is that it is the therapist's variability in alliance scores that predict outcome, rather than client's variability (Baldwin, Wampold, & Imel, 2007). The findings above provide a compelling argument for focusing more research on the therapist's contribution to the alliance, and also, by implication, on the study of therapist/counselor development.

If you assume an instrumental/rational view of science, in which the therapist is merely a vehicle by which the treatment is delivered, you may be disturbed by the findings outlined above. But, if you are a clinician or a counselor, and consider who you would refer your close friends and family to for counseling or therapy then you are likely to find such findings not only quite agreeable, but obvious. They simply make sense.

By combining two major conclusions from psychotherapy and counseling research: (a) that the therapeutic relationship is highly important for outcome, and (b) that therapist effects are substantial, it follows that it is wise to study the entire person of the therapist/counselor, including personal aspects, if one is to grasp important aspects of practitioner functioning and therapist/counselor development.

Although the psychotherapist is no longer a neglected variable in psychotherapy research, as Garfield (1997) stated, there is still a need to combine traditional research on psychotherapy with research on psychotherapists and counselors. Studying change and stability in practitioners across their professional lifespan provides one avenue for increasing our knowledge on therapist functioning. Through the lens provided by such a perspective, we have the potential to view possible constructive and nonconstructive movements within and among practitioners, and may be able to identify those processes that impact on therapist/counselor development.

The Knowledge-Base for This Book

The main source of knowledge for this book is our own work, over many years, on therapist/counselor development, from which we have been fortunate enough to accrue extensive in-depth data from interviews that we have analyzed qualitatively. However, we have also drawn from other sources. In particular, we have consulted results from The Society for Psychotherapy Research-Collaborative Research Network (SPR-CRN) and results from studies on master therapists by Skovholt and Jennings (2004) and colleagues. In addition, we have compared our information with that from other research perspectives, and this has assisted in focusing our views on the nature of professional development. Lastly, our findings and perspectives have been both presented to, and discussed with, large numbers of students and colleagues from various professions over many years. Interacting with others, and obtaining reactions to our work during classes, seminars, workshops, conferences, and informal discussions has provided valuable feedback. These responses have assisted us in reconceptualizing our findings, in bringing some material to the forefront, leaving some on the back burner, even dropping some material that seemed less meaningful. This has been an ongoing process.

The SPR-CRN study is a research network that was initiated by David Orlinsky in 1989 and which has collected survey data from almost 11,000 psychotherapists from more than 30 countries. The major results from this study are presented in the book *How Psychotherapists Develop: A Study of Therapeutic Work and Professional Growth* (Orlinsky & Rønnestad, 2005a), while a summary of major concepts and results, including theoretical models from this large research study, is described in chapter 14 in this book.

Another line of research concerns studies of master therapists. The first study by Harrington (1988) sampled 201 American psychologists who were Board Certified by ABPP. The next studies used a peer-nominated group of 10 therapists in the metropolitan area of Minneapolis-St. Paul. Jennings (1996), Jennings, Sovereign, Bottorff, Mussell, and Vye (2005), Mullenbach (2000), and Sullivan (2001) conducted qualitative interview studies with this group. This same methodology was used when studying master therapists in Korea (Kwon & Kim, 2007), Singapore (Jennings et al., 2008), Canada (A. G. Smith, 2008), and Japan (Tatsuya, 2010). A related study of multicultural master therapists was conducted by Goh, Starkey, Jennings, and Skovholt (2007). The master therapist studies are detailed in chapter 12 of the present work.

In our own qualitative study of Minnesota psychotherapists and counselors, interview data of 100 therapists and counselors (160 interviews initially) were collected. The research method, which is presented in detail in appendix A, was elaborate. Extensive procedures were included to ensure that the descriptions matched the narrations of participants. Inspired by grounded theory methodology (Glaser & Strauss, 1967), we used an inductive bottom-up approach and applied the principle of comparative comparisons in our analyses. In retrospect, our methodology can also be described as being influenced by constructivist grounded theory (Charmaz, 2005).

The research projects on professional development of therapists and counselors originated with our individual independent writings (Rønnestad, 1985; Skovholt, 1985). Realizing our common interest in the topic, a collaborative research project was begun in 1986, with the purpose of understanding those elements that comprise development over the career lifespans of therapists and counselors. We constructed a research-based model of professional development that was published in *The Evolving Professional Self: Stages and Themes in Therapist and Counselor Development* (Skovholt & Rønnestad, 1992/1995) and in a series of articles. In this process, a variety of questions were asked, such as: How does a person progress and improve her or his competence in this field? How is professional development enhanced? What is the value of supervision? As an initial question we decided to ask: What is normative development for therapists and counselors? By answering these questions, we hoped to enhance the professional expertise of therapists and counselors and, thereby, also contribute to increasing the usefulness of the field in alleviating human suffering. We believed then, and continue to believe now, that answering these questions may also advance counselor/psychotherapy education and improve the quality of supervision. A clearer understanding of the developmental process may be helpful in establishing realistic demands in graduate education. We assume that some of the theoretical controversies in therapy and in counselor education and supervision can be resolved through refining that which we know about professional development. Supervisor and supervisee will be able to establish more effective learning contracts if professional developmental paths are better understood. We also believe that there will be less risk of encountering the negative avenues of professional development, such as incompetence, impairment, burnout, and disillusionment, if a more accurate and comprehensive conceptualization of therapist/counselor development is attained.

Our developmental interests have been fueled by the inspiration of our dissertation supervisors, Norman Gysbers (supervisor for MHR) and Joe Johnston (supervisor for TS) at the University of Missouri-Columbia who have been experts for many years in the broad field of career development. Together with Heppner, they wrote: "First proposed in 1973 by Gysbers and Moore (1973), life career development was defined as self-development over the life span through the interaction and integration of the roles, settings, and events of a person's life" (Gysbers, Heppner, & Johnston, 1998, p. 7).

On the Concept of Development

We claim to study psychotherapist and counselor *development*. Can the empirical findings that we report be classified as development? To examine this claim, we will refer to some of the theoretical literature on development to see if this can assist us. Kaplan (1983) has suggested that if the preconceptions of a particular study are few and distinct, and if the empirical findings are simple and well-defined, then it is relatively easy to determine whether the changes under investigation can be labeled developmental. However, if the preconceptions are many and complex, and if the findings are similarly complex and diverse, then determining whether the changes can meaningfully be described as developmental becomes more difficult. From these perspectives, it may not be easy to define our work as a study of development. The preconceptions are certainly many and complex.

However, we may find some consolation in the work of Lerner (1986), who has provided a comprehensive review of the theory of psychological development. Although the theoretical nature of the concept of development allows for great variability in its attributes, Lerner (1986) has pointed out that there are certain fundamental features that are common to the concept of development, regardless of philosophical and theoretical orientation. These are: (a) development always implies change of some sort, (b) the change is organized systematically, and (c) the change involves succession over time. The elements of change, orderly structure, and succession are thus basic elements in the concept of development. In their definitions, developmental psychologists may specify further prerequisites. Examples include: changes must serve an adaptive function (Schneirly, 1957); changes must be organized so that systems change from a global to a more differentiated, integrated, hierarchical form (i.e., the orthogenetic principle, Kaplan, 1983); and, change must be of a qualitative, not only quantitative nature. Preempting the conclusion that we are studying development, it seems that many of the changes that we report do indeed satisfy Lerner's criteria of change, orderly structure, and succession. So, giving credence to Lerner's (1986) ideas, we conclude that we are indeed studying development.

Within the therapist/counselor development and supervision literature, a comprehensive body of perspectives and knowledge has been developed to answer the questions of what changes, how does it change, and why does it change (description/explanation). But, the bulk of this literature is conceptual, rather than empirical. More emphasis has been placed on the "what" and the "how" questions, which lend themselves more readily to empirical investigation and logical analysis, than on the "why" questions.

The Stage Perspective and the Concepts of Continuity/Discontinuity

One of the trickier theoretical questions within the development literature is whether to view changes as continuous or discontinuous. Again, we can refer to Lerner (1986) to assist us in addressing this point. He has provided an overview of the continuity/discontinuity issue, a subject that is relevant for understanding the nature of professional development. Loganbill, Hardy, and Delworth (1982) described changes in a stage format, which presupposes that transition between stages occurs in a discontinuous fashion. We also did this in our early formulation (Skovholt & Rønnestad, 1992/1995). However, looking back at our empirical material, we find that most of the changes that we reported did not occur discontinuously. It should be noted that here we are not referring to the sudden, critical incident, epiphanic-type experiences that many therapists report, but rather the characteristics of the change processes *between* the assumed "stages." If the variables under investigation remain the same in the ontogenetic development of the individual, continuity is the appropriate concept, while if variables change, *discontinuity* is the correct term. A distinction is sometimes made between descriptive and explanatory continuity/discontinuity (Lerner, 1986). If behaviors at two different time points can be described in the same way, then we say there is descriptive continuity. For example, if supervisors do not change the manner in which they supervise as they become more experienced, then their behavior is an example of descriptive continuity. Explanatory continuity denotes whether behaviors at different time points can be explained similarly. Explanatory discontinuity is relevant if behaviors, whether the same or different, can be explained by different reasons. In professional development, these concepts direct our understanding of those factors that impede change and those that encourage change. It is our understanding that the concept of explanatory discontinuity, in particular, focuses on the many different ways by which professionals can reach the same level of functioning.

The classical theories of development, as represented by Freud, Erikson, and Kohlberg, are generally termed *stage theories*. The richness of literature that entertains a perspective of qualitatively different functioning at different points in time, which is generally seen as a characteristic of stages (Lerner, 1986), provides us with similar and related concepts, such as phase, sequence, and level. The stage concept may be regarded as the most stringent concept which, from the classical perspective, denotes an invariant ordering of universal stages; that is, a hierarchical, sequential ordering of qualitatively different functioning/structures.

Critiques of the stage concept generally question the universality, the hierarchical nature, the invariance, or the qualitatively different nature of changes. However, qualitative difference can also be understood as discontinuity. This is important because there is a shift away from looking at the continuity/discontinuity issue as being primarily empirical, toward considering this issue as being principally theoretical. Lerner (1986) argued that the main reason why researchers interpret a given change in contrasting ways is that they maintain different theoretical positions. He stated:

> If one adopts a theoretical position stressing the progressive, hierarchical integration of the organism (e.g., Gagne, 1968), one will necessarily view development as essentially continuous. On the other hand, if one stresses the progressive differentiation of the organism, one will view development as essentially discontinuous. For example, a given theoretical position might lead one to interpret a given piece of empirical evidence in one way (e.g., as consistent with a continuity position), while someone with a different theoretical position might interpret that same empirical fact in another way (e.g., as consistent with a discontinuity position). (p. 188)

Models of Psychological Development: An Overview

We have been influenced by a number of influential developmental model builders. Although Freud's psychosexual stages are historically important, they are of limited relevance for contemporary views of development, while Erik H. Erikson's (1959) *Identity and the Life Cycle* is a massive contribution. His conception of psychosocial stages, each representing a developmental outcome (autonomy vs. shame and doubt; initiative vs. guilt; industry vs. inferiority; identity vs. role confusion; intimacy vs. isolation; generativity vs. stagnation; ego integrity vs. despair) is a major contribution to our understanding of human development.

Erikson's (1968) four adult stage-related tasks, individuation, intimacy, generality, and ego integrity, have been valuable expansions within the Freudian tradition. In addition, through a long-term study, Vaillant (1977) contributed the idea of a career consolidation task that lies between Erikson's intimacy and generativity concepts. Also, George Marcia's discussion (1966) of Erikson's identity development is a contribution worth mentioning.

In the area of cognitive complexity, Perry (1981) formulated a four-stage model of cognitive change, in which dualism progresses to multiplicity, which progresses to relativity, which progresses to committed relativity. Kohlberg (1979) and Thoma, Rest, and Barnett (1986) have charted growth and change in the area of moral development. Super (1980) and Levinson, Darrow, Klein, Levinson, and McKee (1978) have developed career-focused stage models that are driven by age. Super's (1980) five career stages, growth, exploration, establishment, maintenance, and decline, are described in greater detail below. Levinson et al. (1978) described five stages as follows: leaving the family, getting into the adult world, settling down, becoming one's own (person), making a midlife transition, and reestablishing and beginning middle adulthood. Gilligan (1982) has provided useful criticism and elaboration of many of these developmental models in her critique of them as being biased toward male development and neglectful of interpersonal connectedness as a critical adult development issue.

Career Development Theory and Models

In this section, we describe the following models: Blocher (1983), Fleming (1953), Grater (1985), Hess (1987), Hill, Charles, and Reed (1981), Hogan (1964), Holland (1997), Loganbill, Hardy, and Delworth (1982), Stoltenberg and Delworth (1987), and Super (1980). Other models of therapist/counselor development that are not described here, include: Friedman and Kaslow (1986), Herroid (1989), Jablon (1987), Littrell, Lee Borden, and Lorenz (1979), Patton (1986), Stoltenberg (1981), and Yogev (1982). Although not described in detail here, the work of Jablon (1987) is important because it contradicts the common assumption that experience and age tend to promote increased professional development. An overview of

Table 1.1 Selected Developmental Models

Super's (1953/1996) Developmental Self-Concept Theory				
Growth	Exploration	Establishment	Maintenance	Decline
Fleming's (1953) Supervision Models				
Jug-Mug Model		Potter Model		Gardener Model
Hogan's (1964) Psychotherapist Development Model				
Level 1	Level 2	Level 3	Level 4	
Hill, Charles, & Reed's (1981) Counseling Skills Change Model				
Sympathy	Counselor Stance	Transition	Integrated Personal Stance	
Loganbill, Hardy, & Delworth's (1982) Conceptual Supervision Model				
Stagnation		Confusion		Integration
Grater's (1985) Supervision Model				
Stage 1		Stage 2		Stage 3
Rønnestad's Supervision Focused Model (1985)				
Confirmation	Awareness of Complexity	Confusion	Exploration	Integration
Enthusiasm	*Anxiety*	*Depression*	*Hope*	*Realism*
Hess's (1987) Supervision Model				
Inception	Skill Development		Consolidation	Mutuality
Stoltenberg, McNeill, & Delworth's (1998) The Integrated Developmental Model (IDM)				
Level 1	Level 2	Level 3	Integrated Counselor Level	
Owen & Lindley (2011) Cognitive Complexity Developmental Model				
Phase 1		Phase 2		Phase 3

some models of counselor/therapist and supervisee development is presented in Table 1.1.

Below we will describe the developmental models presented in Table 1.1 in addition to the contributions by Holland (1997) and Blocher (1983).

The Developmental Self-Concept Theory of Super

Donald Super, a central career development theorist, began his work in the 1940s (Super, 1949). In a series of articles and books published during the second half of the 20th century, he described and developed his theory of career development. His contribution is massive. Inspired by economist Eli Ginzberg, he contributed to the transformation of the field of vocational guidance, from a narrow focus on career choice, to conceptualizations of career development throughout the lifespan. Central to his theory is the concept of the vocational self, and that people implement their self-concepts through work. A growth in self-concept is stimulated by a variety of sources such as physical maturation, the adult models in one's environment, and experiences in school, home life, and work.

This implementation of self-concept occurs through cycling and recycling of developmental tasks during stages of growth, exploration, establishment, maintenance, and decline (Zunker, 1998). For each stage, developmental tasks consist of crystallization, specification, implementation, stabilization, and consolidation. For example, exploration in the early work years may result in career options, which later in professional life may result in new choices in which subareas are identified that better match the person's self-concept. He described this implementation as a process, rather than something that happens at a single time. Super stated that work satisfaction relates directly to how much the individual has been able to implement her or his self-concept. A fine description of Super's contributions is found in work by Savickas (2004), who was Super's collaborator over many years.

In our work on the practitioner's evolving professional self, one of our main ideas is the movement that therapists and counselors undergo in strengthening, expanding, and solidifying their professional self. A major part of this process is negotiating the misalignment of the internal and external dimensions of both the personal and professional self. As we describe in later chapters, establishing congruence between these two elements of the self in which the dimensions are aligned, is a central developmental task that takes years to complete. We have also described this as movement from the fragile and incomplete practitioner-self to a solid and complete practitioner-self. Super delineates a similar process in his self-concept work (Fouad, 2003).

Holland's Career Typology Theory

Through his research, John Holland discovered strong evidence for career types. As his research progressed, his career theory evolved in scope and complexity. A first major publication was in 1962 (Holland & Austin, 1962). After much research activity over the next decades, expressed in articles, inventories, and books, a final edition of his core research and practical application ideas was published in 1997 in the book, *Making Vocational Choices* (Holland, 1997).

Holland construed the work world as consisting of six different personality types and six different occupational environments. The personality types and occupational environments have matching names. They are: artistic, conventional, enterprising, investigative, realistic, and social. The types are represented in a hexagon with the types that are similar next to each other on the hexagon, and with the most dissimilar farthest away from each other. These relationships are based on statistical correlations that have emerged from extensive research (Spokane, 1996). Examples of personality and occupational environment are:

- Realistic: electrician and electrical contracting shop;
- Investigative: chemist and science lab;
- Artistic: musician and band;
- Social: psychological counselor and mental health clinic;
- Enterprising: real estate agent and real estate office;
- Conventional: teller and bank.

Most individuals have a mix of personality types (with secondary and tertiary characteristics too), and are employed in occupational environments that also have multiple characteristics (codes). An example here being a university counseling center psychologist (mainly Social type), who is employed in a big research university (mainly Investigative type). According to Holland, people search for congruence between personality type and occupational type. If congruence is attained, work satisfaction ensues, while incongruence leads to career frustration.

Our work strongly confirms this fundamental characteristic of Holland's theory. As is shown in both the phase formulation and the theme formulation of our theory, the therapist/counselor searches for work environments in which there is congruence between self-perceptions (both professional and personal selves), and central characteristics of the work environment. The popularity of Holland's theory is easily understood because it reflects a conceptually sound, well-organized, and empirically based view of a zeitgeist, in which consistency and authenticity are valued above fragmentation and inauthenticity. Expressions of this are reflected in the literature, such as the Parker Palmer's (2004) book *A Hidden Wholeness: The Journey toward an Undivided Life.*

The Psychodynamic Learning Model of Fleming

A classic developmental model that has been influential within the domain of dynamic psychotherapy is that of Joan Fleming (1953). It is surprising that not more references are made to her model within the fields of counseling, psychology, and the human services. As outlined below, her model preempts modern conceptions of learning, articulated as the acquisition metaphor, the participation metaphor, and the knowledge creation metaphor (Paavola, Lipponen, & Hakkareinen, 2004). Fleming proposed three different models of supervision, the Jug-mug model, the Potter model, and the Gardener model, models that can be conceptualized as relevant for different levels of experience. Within each model, a particular form of learning takes place. They are: *imitative learning, corrective learning,* and *creative learning* respectively. According to the Jug-mug model, supervisors pour (their knowledge) from their jugs to the supervisees' mugs. Learning occurs primarily through imitating the supervisor. There is a teaching and didactic focus, in which emphasis is on suggestion and demonstration. The lack of professional self-confidence necessitates a supportive attitude from the supervisor. According to the Potter model, the supervisor assumes the role of a potter by forming the supervisee as an unfinished piece of clay. As the therapist attains greater self-confidence, emphasis is more on correction and less on support. According to the Gardener model, the supervisor assumes the role of a gardener, who prepares the soil and nurtures the seedling, metaphors which convey the facilitative function of the supervisor. This last supervisory model presupposes that the basic skills of psychotherapy have been mastered.

There are at least two weaknesses in Fleming's model. One concerns the image of supervisees/trainees, and the other is the outdated perspective of "providing conditions" for change, rather than assuming an interactional perspective of change and development. Although the Jug-mug model and the Potter model depict the supervisee as a more passive recipient of supervisor influence than characterizes modern trainees and supervisees, we think that the perspectives provided by Fleming nevertheless point to some important principles that have at least partial support in the empirical literature.

The Four-Level Model of Hogan

Hogan's model (1964) has been influential in therapist/counselor development. In his classic article, four stages (levels) of psychotherapist development are described.

During Level 1, the psychotherapists' approach is strongly influenced by the "method of choice," which was promulgated during training. At Level 1, psychotherapists are insecure, "neurosis-bound," and dependent. They have little insight into their own motivations for being a psychotherapist. However, they can be highly enthusiastic about their work, although they frequently rely on a single method, and they learn through imitation.

During Level 2, the psychotherapist "adapts this method to his own personality, his own idiom" (p. 139). At this level, the psychotherapists struggle with a dependency-autonomy conflict. In their quest to find their own adaptation, they vacillate between feeling overconfident and being overwhelmed. During this stage, motivation fluctuates considerably. Hogan recommended psychotherapy at this stage.

During Level 3, a stage likened to becoming a master of a trade, "the method-person balance is reversed, and his [the therapist's] approach to therapy is a reflection of his personal idiom through one or more methods "(p. 139). At this conditional dependency level, there is heightened professional self-confidence and more insight into the therapist's own motivation for the work. Motivation is also more stable than at the preceding levels.

During Level 4, the master psychologist stage, the psychotherapist has developed "that depth of artistry and intuitive judgment" (p. 140). At this level the psychotherapist "goes beyond method and his own personal idiom to develop creative approaches which are an outgrowth of both method and person" (p. 139).

At the master psychologist level, there is personal autonomy and a superior level of insight regarding one's own motivation, which remains stable. There is personal security at this level and a recognized need to confront personal and professional problems.

For each level, Hogan recommended different supervisory interventions such as teaching, interpretation, support, awareness training (Level 1); support, exemplification, and ambivalence clarification (Level 2); sharing, exemplification, and confrontation (Level 3); and sharing and mutual confrontation (Level 4).

In the supervision and professional development literature, it is no longer comme il faut to use clinical terms (like *neurosis-bound*) in describing supervisees/trainees. However, with that exception, the conceptual model of Hogan has endured the test of time, and appears rather modern, given today's knowledge of trainee development and supervision. The model has received considerable support from the empirical material in our study. In fact, in the original formulation of midlevel students, we used the term *imitation stage* to capture the strong preference among students for observing models. Also, the dependency-autonomy struggles of the advanced students that Hogan described is strikingly consistent with the reports from the advanced students who were interviewed in our study. We also chose "conditional autonomy stage" as the name for the last period of graduate study.

The Counseling Student Model of Hill, Charles, and Reed

As part of a more extensive study on the development of counseling doctoral students, Hill, Charles, and Reed (1981) described a four-phase model, in which *Sympathy* is the first phase. Sympathetic involvement with the client, consisting mostly of constant positive support, is an essential focus of counseling. If the client improves, the new counselor feels successful. *Counselor stance* is the second phase of the model. Here the search is for a method to use for understanding and intervening with clients. The focus is on mechanical mastery of the chosen method. *Transition* is the next stage. During transition, new input from theory, clients, and supervisors results in a move away from reliance on a single method. The last phase is *Integrated personal style,* in which techniques and theory begin to be combined into a consistent, personal style. Feedback from clients is now considered in a more objective way than previously.

Three aspects of the model of Hill and collaborators have been particularly supported by our study. The first is the prevalence of the experience of sympathy early in the career life cycle. We have described sympathy as being primarily characteristic of the conventional or lay helper. This is because our material suggests that the massive input of stimuli early in training quickly challenges students' conventional behavior. However, as the process of exchanging sympathy for empathy is relatively slow, the formulation by Hill and collaborators may be considered as being supported by our study.

Similarly, the breakdown of reliance on a single model that occurs during the transition phase described by Hill et al., finds a parallel in the disillusionment with self, the profession, and one's training that occurred following graduation in our material. Finally, the characteristics of the integrated personal style are similar to our findings. Nevertheless, despite supportive data and similarities with other models, the model of Hill et al. (1981) provides only a limited description of the process by which the therapist/counselor achieves an integrated personal style.

The Cognitive Developmental Approach of Blocher

Blocher (1983), who based his supervision model on the psychology of learning and behavioral change and on human cognitive development, regarded supervision as an instructional process directed toward higher levels of cognitive functioning. These increasingly higher levels of cognitive functioning provide a stagelike model. Blocher defined supervision as follows:

> Supervision is a specialized instructional process in which the supervisor attempts to facilitate the growth of a counselor in preparation, using as the primary educational medium the student's interaction with real clients for whose welfare the student has some degree of professional, ethical, and moral responsibility. (p. 27)

Blocher criticized model "straw man" categories, such as those described by Hess (1980); that is, lecturer, teacher, case reviewer, collegial peer supporter, monitor, and therapist. According to Blocher, these categories have limited utility as schema for categorizing goals, and he argued that the ultimate focus should be "on the acquisition of new, more complex, and more comprehensive schemas for understanding human interaction" (p. 29). He delineated relationship and communication conditions as process goals of supervision. He emphasized the importance of communicating trust and respect through clear and honest feedback, and in creating communication processes that allow for two-way, broadband channels of communication on a wide range of topics.

Blocher argued for a continually changing, contract-based interchange, in which goals and objectives are made explicit. He suggested that these goals frequently focus on interview skills, relationship conditions, personality constructs early in practicum, and on issues such as confidence, comfort, and authenticity. Later, the focus turns toward broader issues: implementation of process goals, overall case management, and clarification of professional roles.

A rich contribution from Blocher (1983) is his description of the developmental learning environment. He conceptualized this with the seven basic person–environment dynamics of challenge, involvement, support, structure, feedback, innovation, and integration.

The Developmental Model of Loganbill, Hardy, and Delworth

Loganbill et al. (1982) hypothesized three stages of supervisee development: *Stagnation, Confusion,* and *Integration.* For each stage, a description of characteristics, attitude toward the world, attitude toward the self, attitude toward the supervisor, and value of the stage, was elaborated. They perceived the counselor as cycling and recycling through the stages at increasingly deeper levels.

Some central characteristics of their model are outlined below. Stage 1, *Stagnation*, is characterized by being unaware of one's own deficiencies in professional functioning or by an ignorance of the issues regarding supervision, or one's own "stuckness" or stagnation. There is typically a limited and constricted view of the world, and thinking tends to be all or nothing. The student may have a low self-concept and be dependent upon the supervisor, or the student may think he or she is functioning well and regard supervision as unnecessary. In Stage 2, *Confusion*, primary characteristics are "instability, disorganization, erratic fluctuation, disruption, confusion, and conflict" (Loganbill et al., 1982, p. 18). This involves a liberation, an "unfreezing" of attitudes, emotions, or behaviors. There is realization that something is wrong and feelings fluctuate between a sense of expertise and a sense of failure and incompetence. Attitudes toward the supervisor often change from positively toned dependency to disappointment and anger, a shift that can be quite uncomfortable for both parties. This stage is perceived as being very positive, as it entails the abandonment of old ways of thinking and behaving, and provides the opportunity for new learning to occur. Stage 3, *Integration*, "is characterized by reorganization, integration, a new cognitive understanding, flexibility, personal security based on awareness of insecurity, and an ongoing continual monitoring of the important issues of supervision" (p. 19). Assessment is more realistic, and this results in acceptance of the world as it is, and of oneself, together with shortcomings and undeveloped areas. The supervisee has more pragmatic expectations in terms of supervisory goals, is able to perceive the supervisor more rationally, and is capable of assuming responsibility for the content and process of supervision.

Although some of the descriptions for the different stages of counselor development such as that of Loganbill and collaborators find support in other models, the term *stagnation* does not fully capture the intensity of the quest to learn what characterizes the student and novice therapist.

A Professional Developmental Model Focusing on Supervision by Rønnestad (1985)

A conceptual work that serves as theoretical hypothesis, it dates back to a publication in the *Journal of the Norwegian Psychological Association* (Rønnestad, 1985). An "empirical background" for this work was the first author interacting with colleagues over many years discussing supervision in a development perspective in numerous workshops on supervision for Norwegian psychologists organized by the Norwegian Psychological Association. Here, a cyclical five-phase model was formulated that suggested two tracks, *development* and *stagnation*. Each developmental phase was characterized by an accompanying emotion/attitude.

In the original formulation these were: Phase 1, *Confirmation/ enthusiasm*; Phase 2, *Awareness of complexity/anxiety*; Phase 3, *Confusion/ depression*; Phase 4, *Exploration/hope*; and Phase 5, *Integration/realism*.

Development was conceptualized as *cycling* through these phases when confronted with different *challenges* and with the recognition of the therapist's own limitations and inadequacies

Some further central perspectives/components in this theoretical model were:

1. The central role played by experiencing challenges and recognizing and experiencing the complexity of therapeutic work, with the accompanying or ensuing anxiety for professional development.
2. The primary role played by premature closure as an entry into stagnation, with therapist defensiveness as a central characteristic. It was suggested that if the therapists had little tolerance for uncertainty and felt uncomfortable about "not knowing," these characteristics would contribute to premature closure.
3. Introduction of the term *pseudodevelopment* with rigidity as a primary characteristic.
4. Relating premature closure and pseudodevelopment to possible therapist characteristics such as Adorno's authoritarian personality as

a prototype of a person who is not able to experience uncertainty (Adorno, Frenkel-Brunswik, Levinson, & Sanford,1950), and to Rokeach's (1960) concepts of the open and closed mind to understand the dynamics of entering stagnation. It is recognized that the percentage of therapists who would score high on Adorno's dogmatism scale is probably quite low.

The Supervision-Focused Model of Grater

Based on his extensive experience as a psychotherapy teacher and supervisor, Grater (1985) created a four-stage model of therapist development with particular application to supervision.

Stage 1: Developing basic skills and adopting the therapist role. The focus here includes the replacement of social patterns of interacting with therapeutic responses. Trainee anxiety is extensive and an important focus for the supervisor. Specific skills include learning about the nuances of client statements, the use of body language, and adjusting the pace of an interview.

Stage 2: Expanding the range of therapy skills and roles. Here client assessment takes a more prominent position. The trainee must learn to assess clients in two ways: (a) in terms of the problem areas, and (b) in terms of the expectations of the therapy process. Increased therapist flexibility is an important learning goal here.

Stage 3: Using the working alliance to understand the client's habitual patterns. Here the focus is on recognizing how the client brings habitual, and often maladaptive, patterns into the therapy. At this level the trainee is taught to recognize these patterns and to respond in a way that produces growth, rather than client stagnation. The trainee must learn about the interactions between the client, the problem, and the techniques.

Stage 4: Using the self in assessment and intervention. Building from the three preceding stages, at this stage the therapist learns to use the self as a powerful tool for both assessment and therapy. For example, the therapist learns to use the experience of being challenged as a source of information and as a vehicle for a therapeutic response, rather than as an occasion for self- protection. Sensitivity to therapy process issues is a focus of this stage.

The Supervision Focused Model of Hess

After reviewing the major stage theories, Hess (1987) provided a synthesis formulated into four superordinate stages. In Hess's formulation, the professional can recycle through these stages in an ascending spiral fashion. The stages are:

1. *Inception stage*: central characteristics are role induction, demystification of therapy, skill definition, and setting of boundaries.
2. *Skill development stage*: this entails being increasingly able to adapt the didactic and experiential materials that are being mastered to the client's particular needs. Other stage characteristics include assuming an apprentice role and beginning to identify with a particular system of therapy and philosophy of human nature.
3. *Consolidation stage*: primarily characterized by integrating the knowledge that has been previously acquired. At this level, the therapist may have been recognized by others for particular talents, and thus realizes that one's professional identity is, in part, defined by skills. There is refinement in adeptness and competence, and the role of therapist personality becomes recognized.
4. *Mutuality stage*: the therapist emerges as an autonomous professional who engages in the give and take of peer consultation, and is able to create unique solutions to problems. Potential concerns of professionals at this stage are burnout and stagnation.

The Three-Stage Model of Hess

Hess (1986) also formulated a three-stage model for supervisor development.

1. The novice supervisor typically lacks formal training in supervision, and therefore frequently focuses on the concrete. Such a supervisor has a teaching focus and is technique-oriented during supervision as a means of coping with any difficulties experienced.
2. The exploration stage supervisor regards supervision as a professional activity that is to be safeguarded and protected from interruption. There is a shift in focus toward truly assessing and addressing student learning needs, a shift towards informal power, and an attention to the supervision literature.
3. In the third stage, confirmation of the supervisor's identity, supervisor and student both experience learning as exciting. Hess is particularly observant of the impact of evaluation in the supervisory relationship.

The Integrated Developmental Model (IDM) of Stoltenberg, McNeill, and Delworth (1998)

The reformulated model of Stoltenberg, McNeill, and Delworth (1998) is based on the models of Hogan (1964), Stoltenberg (1981), Loganbill et al. (1982), and Stoltenberg and Delworth (1987). In the 1987 formulation, four levels of development are described, three of which are trainee levels (Levels 1, 2, and 3 are trainee) and one level as the integrated counselor.

In the IDM-model the trainee is described as progressing, in terms of awareness, motivation, and autonomy, in a continuous manner through the levels. This progression is assumed to proceed in a relatively orderly fashion through various domains of functioning relevant to professional activities in counseling and psychotherapy (p. 35). According to their model, there is a structural shift across domains in each stage. The eight domains are: intervention skills competence, assessment techniques, interpersonal assessment, client conceptualization, individual differences, theoretical orientation, treatment goals and plans, and professional ethics. According to the model, the levels are perceived as irreversible structural changes. However, their conceptualization allows for temporary lapses and returns to familiar territory. Movement through the levels is seen as occurring through Piaget's (1972) processes of assimilation and accommodation.

Within each stage, the IDM suggests changes in three overriding structures. These are: self–other awareness, motivation, and autonomy. Specific challenges within each stage have implications for these structures. For example, the Level 1 supervisee's anxiety, evaluation apprehension, and self-focus has implications for the structures of motivation and autonomy (Stoltenberg, 2005). As Level 1 is characterized by a supervisee focus on self, there is a shift in focus toward the client at Level 2:

> Development to Level 3, according to the IDM, is characterized by a change in the self–other awareness structure where the supervisee retains the ability to focus on the client, setting the stage for understanding and empathy, while also being increasingly self-aware of his or her own thoughts, emotions, and behavior in relation to the client. (p. 859)

Important features of the IDM model are the use of supervisory interventions, some of which are considered useful across developmental levels (such as facilitative interventions), while others (i.e. prescriptive, conceptual, confrontive, and catalytic interventions) are typically most useful at specific levels. Another important feature of the IDM model is the formulation on domains of practice. The model suggests that supervisees can be at various levels of development in different domains of practice. For example, a supervisee can be functioning effectively at Level 2 transitioning to Level 3 in individual counseling, while functioning at Level 1 in couple's therapy (Stoltenberg, 2005).

Owen and Lindley's (2010) Development of Therapists' Cognitive Complexity Model

We will describe some of what we see as the most central characteristics of their three-phase model. In the context of therapeutic practice,

Owen and Lindley (2010) differentiate between three levels of cognitive/metacognitive complexity: (a) session thoughts (basic cognitions); (b) metacognitions, the "ability to monitor their progress when engaging in session thoughts, or to evaluate their own thoughts and reactions as they occur in the session cognitions while engaging in session thoughts" (p. 131); and (c) epistemic cognitions (therapists' view of the nature of knowledge and learning). A theoretical assumption in their model is that therapists go through three developmental phases of increasing cognitive complexity.

Phase 1. The model suggests that during the first phase, therapists typically focus on knowledge identification (i.e., acquisition); session-thoughts and the metacognitive attention may be on self-monitoring. Therapists may "exhibit a blend of dualistic and relativistic epistemic cognitions" (p. 132), which is expressed by a belief that authorities can provide the answers, while also questioning the expertise of authorities.

Phase 2. During the second developmental phase, Owen and Lindley (2010) describe a movement where therapists become better able to differentiate the information they receive. This means, for example, that they are better able to "discern commonalities and unique features of the information" (p. 133), and also that they should be better able to develop a differential diagnosis. The model also suggests that therapists at Phase 2 are better able to monitor multiple aspects of the therapeutic process. Another feature of Phase 2 is movement toward being more occupied with the application than with the acquisition of knowledge. Also, in contrast to the first developmental phase "therapists are now faced with selecting counseling theories, interventions, and empirical evidence that most appropriately fit their cases" (p. 133). Furthermore, their model suggests that therapists at this phase may ignore or discount evidence that contradicts their experiences, thus making them susceptible to errors of decision making.

Phase 3. During the third phase of development, Owen and Lindley describe several changes. Some of these are: Therapists are better able to integrate knowledge, which is expressed in their ability to sort irrelevant from relevant information; there have been changes in metacognitive stance, which is expressed in various ways such as in the ability to know which experiences are generalizable and which are not, and they are more reflective of their counseling abilities. In addition, during this phase, the epistemic approach to knowledge is also more coherent and thoughtful. They also describe therapists during this last phase of development as follows: "In contrast to relying on idiosyncratic decisions and justifications of beliefs, they are reliant on careful analysis of their previous experiences and empirical evidence" (p. 133).

General Comments on the Models

These models have provided many useful constructs. Aspects of some have been validated, either conceptually by similarity to other conceptual models, or by empirical analyses. There is some evidence that beginning therapy/counseling students compared to more advanced practitioners experience considerable anxiety in their meeting with clients (e.g., Rønnestad & Skovholt, 1992a, 2003; Stoltenberg, 2005; Strømme, 2010). However, results from a recent large scale study suggest that anxiety is mastered by most after relatively little therapy/counseling experienced (CRN). It is proposed that anxiety level has implications for how supervision is conducted, either in the form of, for example, providing support (Rønnestad & Skovholt, 2011) or facilitative interventions; Stoltenberg, 2005). It also seems that beginning counselors/therapists, compared to more advanced practitioners, prefer structured and didactic supervision (Bernhard & Goodyear, 2009; Rønnestad & Skovholt, 1993; Worthen & McNeill, 1996). However, this does not mean that beginning students want only supervision to be structured and didactic. Many appreciate that the supervisor also focuses on relationship issues (both within therapy/counseling as well as outside it) and on the personal aspects of being a therapist/counselor. This will be discussed in more detail in chapter 11 on the implications of our findings for supervision.

However, the developmental models presented above are limited because they provide little information regarding how change occurs, or knowledge of the developmental process. They are also restricted in their emphasis on understanding early development. In addressing later development, they tend to lean on general theories regarding adult development, and empirical investigations of what actually happens after graduation are considered to only a limited extent, if at all.

Note

1. A previous version of this chapter was published in *The Evolving Professional Self* (pp. 22–41), by T. M. Skovholt and M. H. Rønnestad (1992).Copyright is reverted to authors. Chichester, England: Wiley. All quotes are from *The Evolving Professional Self.*

2

MODELS AND CONCEPTIONS
OF LEARNING, EXPERTISE,
AND DECISION MAKING

Highly relevant for the study of professional development, are the related fields of expertise, learning, and decision making. These fields of knowledge can be defined as distinct, and can be studied separately, but can also be regarded as being highly interrelated. For this section some models and perspectives have been selected that we believe are particularly important for understanding the professional development process. We start out by presenting some of the perspectives by Tversky and Kahneman, thereafter some perspectives from a group of Finnish researchers (e.g., Engestrøm, 2001), and from Glaser and Chi (1988) and Dreyfus and Dreyfus (1986) that collectively seem to suggest a common structure of learning that has emerged from different authors, in different countries, and at different periods. If there is a common structure for learning in the helping professions, it is important that we capture it. A proposed schema for organizing types of learning expression is presented in Table 2.1.

Kahneman and Tversky

In this section we will briefly refer to some of the extensive work conducted by Kahneman and Tversky on human judgment and choice (decision making). Their work addresses an important topic relevant to the understanding of novice and expert decision making. The Nobel Prize laureate Kahneman (2003) describes "The Two-System View" (p. 698), in which the distinction between intuition and reasoning is made. The studies of judgment under uncertainty are of particular relevance, as our research has sensitized us to the challenges that therapists/counselors face in continually maneuvering in a complex and ambiguous terrain. "The operations under System 1 are typically fast, automatic, effortless, associative, implicit (not available to introspection), and often emotionally charged; they are also modified by habit and are therefore difficult to control or modify" (p. 698). System 2 operations are quite different; they are "slower, serial, effortful, more likely to be consciously monitored and deliberately controlled; they are also relatively flexible and potentially

Table 2.1   Learning Types and Perspectives

Bateson (1972)	Type I	Type II	Type III
Sfard (1998)	Acquisition	Participation	
Engestrøm (2001)	Acquisition	Participation	Expansive/Creative
Fleming (1953)	Imitation	Corrective	Creative
Dreyfus & Dreyfus	Rules	Aspects	Use of Maxims à Post Maxims
Bandura/Skinner	Modeling & Conditioning	Operant & Conditioning	
Rønnestad (1997)	Modeling	Feedback	Experiential

rule governed" (p. 698). Intuition, a System 1 operation, is associated with both poor and good performance. We can draw on the work by Dawes (1994) who documented that experience in itself did not guarantee superior performance unless accurate feedback was provided. Thus, it may be inferred that if experienced practitioners have not received quality feedback on their performance, the quality of decision making based on intuition alone may be poor. Even though therapists/counselors may not necessarily enlist feedback from colleagues, supervisors, and other external observers, they continuously receive feedback from their clients. But can we be sure that they pick this up? It seems plausible that the quality of therapists/counselors' interpersonal sensitivity (or reflective functioning) impacts on whether they notice the feedback, the accuracy of what they comprehend, and how they process the information (also with the client) if they do perceive the feedback.

Kahneman (2003) documented that intuitive thinking can be powerful and accurate, and that skilled decision makers often perform better if they do not engage in detailed analysis, but rather trust their intuition. At their best, intuitive thoughts arise spontaneously and effortlessly. In order to understand why some thoughts arise readily and others do not, Kahneman introduced the concept of accessibility, which is adapted from memory research, and described it as being on a continuum between System 1 (rapid, automatic, effortless) and System 2 (slow, serial, effortful). But which factors determine accessibility? It is not surprising that the actual properties (salience) of an object of judgment determine accessibility. Possibly more important for understanding the development of intuitive thinking in the therapist/counselor is that salience can be overcome by deliberate attention. There is reason to believe that the extensive experience of proficient therapists/counselors results in better abilities regarding the recognition of relevant cues. Kahneman (2003) also refers to the Gestalt principle of perceptual grouping for influencing accessibility.

Here a conceptual link may be made with Boreham's (1988) memory storage template model, which suggests that knowledge is stored in the form of schemata or stereotypes. The process of arriving at a diagnosis involves comparing a particular case with previously stored data patterns until a match is identified. This model may be used to explain the processes by which therapists/counselors assess a particular case. An experienced therapist in our study said:

> With a new client I think about cases I've had. I think about how they have gone. Themes come in a case and this stimulates a memory in me. The memory is in the form of a collection of vignettes, stories, and scripts. It isn't fully conscious, but new cases do kick off the memory—the memory of how things went before provides a foundation to begin the current case.

Some of the perspectives and findings on learning and expertise first formulated by a group of Finnish researchers will be described, before we present the perspectives provided by Chi et al., Dreyfus and Dreyfus, and other selected contributors.

The Finnish Researchers' View of Learning

Various Finnish contributions have been published that are relevant to understand the expertise and learning of therapists and counselors (e.g., contributions by authors such as Engeström, Laitila, Tynjälä, and Paavola and colleagues). Paavola, Lipponen, and Hakkarainen (2004) described three views or metaphors of learning, that can serve as analytical tools for studying differences between novices and experts. The influential article by Sfard (1998), "On Two Metaphors for Learning and the Dangers of Choosing Just One," in which she proposed that there are basically two ways of conceptualizing learning, formulated as the acquisition and participation metaphors. According to these authors, the basis for this distinction is the debate on learning and human activity as being either cognitive or situated and they draw on the work by Anderson, Reder, and Simon (1996, 1997) and Greeno (1997) for describing the background for this debate. About the acquisition view, Paavola et al. (2004) write:

> [T]he mind is a kind of container of knowledge, and learning is a process that fills the container, implanting knowledge there.... Hence knowledge is understood as a property or capacity of an individual mind, in which learning is a matter of construction, acquisition, and outcomes, which are realized in the process of transfer (that is, the process of using and applying knowledge in new situations). (p. 57)

As will be described in chapter 4, "The Novice Student Phase," our data suggest that how the novice students view their learning process is captured well by the acquisition metaphor. On the participation metaphor, Paavola et al. (2004) write,

> In contrast, adherents of the participation metaphor examine learning as a process of participation in various cultural practices and shared learning activities. In this view, the focus is on activities ("knowing") more than on outcomes or products ("knowledge"). Knowledge does not exist either in a world of its own or in individual minds, but is an aspect of participation in cultural practices (Brown, Collins, & Duguid, 1989; Lave, 1988; Lave & Wenger, 1991). (pp. 557–558)

Paavola and collaborators suggest that there is room for a third model, a knowledge-creation model that emphasizes collective knowledge creation, which they suggest would soften the distinctions between the two prior models. They analyzed three models of innovative knowledge communities: (a) Ikujiro Nonaka and Hirotaka Takeuchi's (1995) model of knowledge creation; (b) Yrjö Engeström's (e.g., 2001) model of expansive learning; and, (c) Carl Bereiter's model of knowledge building (e.g., Bereiter, 2002).

Engeström's (2001) model, most relevant for our purpose, was anchored in sociocultural theory and, more specifically, in cultural-historical activity theory. It is heavily influenced by Vygotsky (1972, 1978), is particularly relevant for the analysis of learning, focusing both on the organizations and on the individuals. The sequential cyclical model is complex and can be summarized as a matrix consisting of four questions. One dimension consists of the questions:

1. Who are the subjects of learning?
2. Why do they learn?
3. What do they learn?
4. How do they learn?

The other dimension consists of five central principles of activity theory. A premise in this theory is that human activity is mediated through cultural artifacts that people use. Engeström and collaborators have developed an intervention method called "the boundary-crossing laboratory" where they, with the assistance of researchers, assist members of a workplace community to reflect upon their joint activities, thus creating the opportunity for innovative and creative learning.

This approach is similar to that of the reflecting team method that the late Norwegian psychiatrist, Tom Andersen (1987), developed for family therapy. In the reflecting team method, a group of therapists observe a family talk about a topic of their choice through a one-way mirror. Thereafter, should the family members give their permission, the team of therapists discusses their observations, first among themselves, and afterwards, if acceptable to the family members, with the family members.

Engestrøm also draws on work by Gregory Bateson (1972), specifically on Bateson's distinction between three levels of learning. Learning I refers to acquisition (conditioning) of responses that are considered appropriate in a given context. Novice students who learn by modeling themselves on an expert therapist/counselor may be an example of Learning 1. Learning 2 occurs when more deep-seated, complex rules and patterns, which are appropriate in different contexts, are learned. Learning II occurs in counseling and therapy when the advanced counseling/therapy student learns the rules of academia, of how to please supervisors, pass exams, and so on. Bateson adds a special twist to this form of learning by introducing the concept of the double-bind, a consequence of the contradictory demands that different contexts may provide. Learning 3 occurs in an interpersonal context such as group supervision, and is less precisely described by Bateson. Engestrøm builds on Bateson's concept of Learning 3 in order to articulate his view on expansive learning activity, which produces culturally new patterns of activity and novel forms of work activity.

Complex and nuanced perspectives on learning and expertise are needed in order to conceptualize the evolution of expertise within the fields of counseling and therapy. This way of categorizing learning captures the variations in tasks that the counselor/therapist undertakes when interacting with clients, and also when maturing or declining professionally. Although the models aspire to providing concepts that are relevant for the task and behaviors of professionals in general, and are formulated to provide analytical perspectives at an abstract level, the various models appear to be particularly relevant for understanding the learning that occurs in different educational contexts. These are hypotheses only. The situated cognition perspective may be especially pertinent in studying the more boundaried decision-making processes; for example, diagnostic assessment or case formulation. The participation view of expertise may be germane for the study of the highly complex processes of interaction between professionals (not necessarily within the same fields) and between the professional and client/patient. In contrast, the knowledge-creation view is an analytical approach, which, from our perspective, provides the most advanced expression of expertise, and therefore best describes the advanced professional. The latter is addressed in our description of themes of therapist/counselor development, where our findings are also described in relation to the model formulated by Belenky (1986; see chapter 9).

In the description of the expertise literature by Laitila (2004), the review by Tynälä, Nuutinen, Eteläpelto, Kirjonen, and Remes (1997) appears to make good sense when the focus is on the expertise of therapists and counselors. According to the review by Tynälä et al. (1997), experts are characterized as follows:

1. They perceive larger meaningful patterns within their own domains.
2. They are able to focus on the relevant cues of the task.
3. They represent problems at a deeper level than novices are able to achieve.
4. They have better self-monitoring skills than novices.
5. They have knowledge structures that are hierarchically organized and they have greater depths in their conceptual levels compared with those of novices.
6. They categorize problems within their own domain according to abstract, high-level principles.
7. They have more coherence in their knowledge structures than have novices. (p. 477)

This way of describing expertise in many ways converges with the descriptions of expertise provided by Chi and Ceci (1987) and Dreyfus and Dreyfus (1988).

The Glaser and Chi Model of Expertise

In their description of the general characteristics of experts, Skovholt, Vaughan, and Jennings (2011) present a summary on expertise formulated by Glaser and Chi (1988) and related to their own studies on master therapists and also to the conceptualization of expertise by Feltovich, Prietula, and Ericsson (2006). Some overlap can be noted between the Glaser and Chi formulation and that of Tynjälä et al. (1997).

Central characteristics of the Glaser and Chi model are as follows:

Experts Tend to Excel in Their Own Domain. Feltovich et al. (2006) also describe experts as having developed complex cognitive representations within a domain and that these representations enable experts to access and integrate information quickly. In addition, Tynälä et al. (1997) limit the context to their own domain when they describe experts' abilities to categorize problems according to abstract, high-level principles.

Experts Perceive Larger, More Meaningful Patterns in Their Chosen Domain. Skovholt et al. (2011) draw attention to the work of Feltovich et al. (2006) in contrasting descriptions of novices and experts in their abilities to identify meaningful patterns and profiles within the fields of architecture, radiology, and computer programming. One conceptual foundation for an expert's ability to perceive larger and more meaningful patterns is the classic paper by Miller (1956), "The Magical Number Seven, Plus Or Minus Two: Some Limits On Our Capacity For Processing Information." "Chunking" can be described as an assembly of elements with strong similarities to each other; experts can conceptualize larger chunks.

Experts Are Faster Than Novices in Performing Domain Skills. Feltovitch et al. (2006) differentiate between weak methods and strong methods of problem resolution. These two differ from each other by the extent to which the knowledge utilized is only general and superficial (weak) or is more integrated (strong). The description of the work by Kahneman and Tversky is also of relevance within this context. Experts' unconscious and effortless execution of various tasks (System 1 operations) enables them to process information rapidly.

Experts Have Superior Memory. Feltovich et al. (2006) describes automaticity as being central in the development of expertise. It seems to us that highly experienced therapists/counselors "free up" their memory capacity for the next step of the work.

Experts See and Represent a Problem in Their Domain at a Deeper (More Principled) Level. The extensive experience of experts enables them to visualize the complexity and context of problems in their domain. Experts are capable of analyzing a specific problem from different perspectives, and do this before reaching a decision. However, the nature of the task apparently can determine the speed at which an expert reaches a decision.

Experts Spend a Great Deal of Time Analyzing a Problem Qualitatively. As previously stated, experts' decisions, which are based on intuitive judgment, can be made more quickly than by nonexperts. However, in the study of "literary expertise" (Scaramalia & Bereiter, 1991; cited in Skovholt, Vaughan, & Jennings, 2011) expert writers used more time in planning and writing the first sentence, and completing a simple essay than novices.

Experts Have Strong Self-Monitoring Skills. Self-monitoring can be conceptualized as a metacognitive processing of their problem-solving activity. The quality of the self-monitoring process is influenced by the degree to which the individual is capable of recognizing their strength and limitations relevant to the task. The American Psychological Association has included the related concept of self-reflection as one of the characteristics of clinical expertise (APA, 2006):

Clinical expertise requires the ability to reflect on one's own experience, knowledge, hypotheses, inferences, emotional reactions, and behaviors and to use that reflection to modify one's practices accordingly. Integral to clinical expertise is an awareness of the limits of one's knowledge and skills as well as a recognition of the heuristics and biases (both cognitive and affective) that can affect clinical judgment (e.g., biases that can inhibit recognition of the need to alter case conceptualization that are inaccurate or treatment strategies that are not working). Clinical expertise involves taking explicit action to limit the effects of these biases (p. 277).

Now we move from the Chi model of expertise to Dreyfus and Dreyfus.

The Dreyfus and Dreyfus Model

A developmental model that focuses on increases in expertise has been formulated by Dreyfus and Dreyfus (1986). This model hinges on experience as well as education, and differentiates between levels of skilled performance. This model was formulated as a reaction against the rationalist tradition of analytical reasoning and against the predominant view of artificial intelligence. In this model, Dreyfus and Dreyfus argued against what they call the "Hamlet model" of decision making, which they described as "the detached, deliberative, and sometimes agonizing selection among alternatives" (Dreyfus & Dreyfus, 1986, p. 28). Instead, the importance of intuition was emphasized, and the "tacit knowing" in the strategies used by experts when solving problems. Thus the emphasis of the model was on knowing how, not on knowing what.

The model consists of five professional development levels (novice, advanced beginner, competent, proficient, and expert). A central feature of the model is that functioning varies across levels on two general dimensions: (a) the shift in time to using one's own work experience rather than abstract principles to guide one's performance, and (b) perceptual changes in the use of only certain elements of a complex situation, rather than many equal parts.

The Novice is described as one who must rely on context-free rules due to lack of experience with which to guide practice. Tasks are decomposed into context-free features, "which the beginner can recognize without previous experience in the task domain. The beginner is then given rules for determining actions on the basis of these features, and so acts like a computer following a program" (H. L. Dreyfus, n.d., p. 2). The fact that a novice pays minimal attention to the context in which observations are made, results in behavior that can be interpreted as being rigid. Løvlie-Schibbye (2011) has described the process of exaggeration, which typifies the inexperienced supervisee. This occurs when a novice supervisee interprets a supervisor's advice on how to act in relation to a client in a literal way, a way that is not context-sensitive, and that appears to be "out of place." The Novice can become lost when encountering exceptions that the "rules" do not cover.

The Advanced Beginner has accumulated some experience with which to guide practice. This enables some degree of "aspect recognition."

Aspects are overall, global characteristics that can be used for decision making. They differ from rules and can be described as "new situational aspects" that are recognized from experience, but which also take into consideration the less advanced nonsituational features. Aspects presuppose that the individual has some experience with the domain in question. Although there is greater awareness of context, context sensitivity is nevertheless still relatively limited compared with the more complex decision-making processes that are characteristic of higher levels of expertise. The advanced beginner does not order aspects in terms of importance; that is, crucial information is not ordered ahead of less important information.

The Competent individual functions at the highest level of performance using textbook rules. Sufficient work experience has been accumulated so that events can be anticipated and relevant clues can be sought. Individuals at this level can process information from many sources simultaneously and can execute hierarchical decision-making skills. The focus no longer needs to be limited to the present, but can be adapted toward conscious planning ahead. At this level, some procedures have become standardized.

The Proficient individual has replaced "aspects" with "maxims," characteristics of a situation that, to a Novice, are only unintelligible nuances. The individual is now able to assess situations holistically, and this also contributes toward the decision-making process becoming more fluent, more rapid, more intuitive, and less strained. Maxims provide direction regarding what is important in a situation, and can be used as guidance in a range of situations. The Proficient individual is also able to discriminate between usual and unusual patterns.

The Expert individual has the richest experience-base, and this enables functioning from an intuitive level, regarding the important elements of a demand situation. Rules, guidelines, and maxims are no longer used, and understanding is tacit. The Expert operates from an experience-base that is so embedded, that it is often difficult for the expert to explain why a particular action was the correct one.

One important element of the Dreyfus and Dreyfus (1986) formulation is that the essential guide for practice entails replacement of the theories of experts with one's own relevant experiences. Many of the findings from our study fit well within the Dreyfus and Dreyfus model, such as the Beginning Student's reliance on textbook knowledge as a guide to practice, the Novice Professional's increasingly taking context into account when assessing clients, and the Senior Professional's use of integrated experience-based tacit knowledge. Many of the descriptions of the Proficient individual fit with the Experienced Professionals. However, it seems that the ability to organize knowledge hierarchically, a characteristic of the Proficient individual, also fits the Novice Professional in our study, which suggests a possible uncertainty in the Dreyfus and Dreyfus model.

The Dreyfus model is a major contribution to the study of expertise. However, it has been criticized for many reasons. For example, the differences between laypersons' and experts' modes of decision making are exaggerated by formulating questionable assumptions about everyday behavior; considerations of the metaprocesses involved in controlling one's own behavior are neglected; the problem of expert fallibility is underestimated; and the conditions or proportions of professional work that the model is supposed to encompass are not specified (Eraut, 1994, p. 128). In spite of these limitations, their formulations are an impressive contribution to the study of expertise.

Some Comments

In the chapters that follow, we will first present reflections on cultural conceptions of helping. Thereafter follows descriptions of phases and themes of therapist and counselor development, before we present our cyclical/trajectories model of professional development. A chapter on the supervisory implications of our joint work is presented thereafter. In the final chapters, a chapter on the resilient practitioner and master therapists are presented, followed by a summary of the work done within the SPR/CRN study.

We have aimed at constructing a model of therapist/counselor development that is transferable to therapists/counselors in different contexts. However, we fully realize that it is impossible to describe each individual's developmental path with detailed accuracy. Therefore, the validity of this study rests partly upon you, the reader, in recognizing our descriptions and finding our analyses to be meaningful. Finally, although the phase model is empirically grounded, it can still be viewed as a series of hypotheses to be examined, confirmed, or disconfirmed by other qualitative studies and also by precise quantitative studies. As collaborators in two other empirical studies on therapist/counselor work and development—SPR/CRN study (e.g., Orlinsky & Rønnestad, 2005), and the Master Therapists Studies (e.g., Skovholt & Jennings, 2004)—we are fortunate to have been provided with a variety of input with which to understand therapist/counselor work and professional development from other perspectives.

In the next chapter on cultural conceptions of helping, we draw on theoretical knowledge from cultural psychology and psychotherapy to provide perspectives on helping others in distress. We also refer to studies which have explored similarities and differences between how people in general view what is helpful when seeing a psychologist versus seeing a friend. The intention with the chapter is to provide frames of references to understand what the coming therapist/counselors bring with them when they start training in one of the helping professions.

3

CULTURAL DISCOURSES OF HELPING

Perspectives on What People Bring with Them when
They Start Training in Therapy and Counseling

Oddbjørg Skjær Ulvik and Michael Helge Rønnestad

Introduction

When students enter professional training in counseling or therapy they should not be regarded as a "clean slate" or tabula rasa. As cultural participants in a specific society at a given historical time, they bring with them into training experiences, beliefs, and everyday concepts of how to help others. The students will have had previous experience of helping others in roles such as friend, family member, colleague at work, neighbor, or school classmate. How they view helping practices when assisting people in distress is formed by their personal histories as well as by the cultural discourses of helping that exist in the society in which they have grown up and now live. During training, the students are socialized into a specific professional culture of psychotherapy and counseling with shared beliefs and technologies.

In the chapters that follow, the phases of professional development that the person goes through during training, and after graduation, are described. In this chapter, we present some perspectives on cultural discourses of helping, and reflect upon the ideas that those entering training bring with them. We will also explore and discuss possible distinctions between professional and nonprofessional conceptions of helping. By making the culturally embedded helping discourses more transparent, we hope to better understand the expectations and challenges of the new student when he or she enters training.

Helping as Cultural Practices

All cultures have theories of what it means to be human, what causes suffering, and how suffering can be relieved. These theories vary across cultures. Only a minority of the world's population lives in societies that share the Western concept of psychology and psychotherapeutic practices. According to Kleinman (1988), it is only in the Western world that this kind of professional help is appropriate for psychological problems.[1]

Indeed, the custom of individual (person to person) contact in a "closed room" is a form of practice that is shared by only one third of the world (Elsass, 2003). While Western cultures tend to regard disease as an individual phenomenon, localized in the patient, in some other cultures disease may be a collective phenomenon that requires political and social action, rather than individual treatment. Symptoms which in one culture are referred to as "disease," might in other cultures be regarded as having moral or religious causes (Elsass, 2003).

Anthropological studies have found varied patterns of sufferings, "culture bound syndromes" (Simon & Hughes, 1995, cited in Elsass, 2003). In accordance with this perspective, Philip Cushman (1995) specifies cultural and historical variety to configurations of a self. He writes:

> Each era has a predominant configuration of the self, a particular foundational set of beliefs of what it means to be human. Each particular configuration of the self brings with it characteristic illnesses, local healers and local healing technologies. (p. 3)

Healing practices are embedded in the culture in which the practices take place. Cultural embeddedness, or contextualization of practices, is a fundamental principle in cultural psychology. Inspired by anthropological studies, Jerome Bruner (1990) introduced the concept *folk psychology*, which he suggested could also be understood as "common sense." He writes:

> All cultures have as one of their most powerful constitutive instruments a folk psychology, a set of more or less connected, more or less normative descriptions about how humans "tick," what our own and other minds are like, what one can expect situated action to be like, what are possible modes of life, how one commits oneself to them, and so on. We learn our culture's folk psychology early, learn it as we learn to use the very language we acquire and to conduct the interpersonal transactions required in communal life ... a system by which people organize their experience in, knowledge about, and transactions with the social world. (p. 35)

As psychotherapeutic discourses of helping are part of a late modern society, persons entering professional training will have access to those ideas, and probably share them as part of folk psychology. But according to Bruner (1990), those ideas might not be recognized as cultural ideas, rather they might be taken for granted as "natural." This may even be the case for those who are professionally trained.

Cushman (1995) argues for the central role played by psychotherapy in our culture. He refers to psychotherapy as a cultural artifact and writes: "When social artifacts and institutions are taken for granted, it usually means that they have developed functions in the society that are so integral to the culture that they are indispensable, unacknowledged and finally invisible" (p. 6). About psychotherapy he writes: "... psychotherapy, somehow, is so accurately attuned to the twentieth-century cultural frame of reference that it has developed an intellectual discourse and provides human services that are crucial, perhaps indispensable, to our current way of life" (p. 6). He underscores the integral part of the intellectual discourse of psychotherapy as follows: "Psychotherapeutic practices and ways of understanding could be discussed and criticized, but analogous with the weather, they are part of what culturally is taken for granted." Cushman (1995) goes on to describe the cultural embeddedness of psychotherapy:

> We do not often question the assumptions of many of its theories, such as the underlying ideology of individualism or the valuing of "inner feelings" or the unquestioned assumption that health is produced by experiencing and expressing these feelings. (p. 18)

Psychotherapeutic discourses permeate modern cultures and are implicit in our part of the world, and may thus be regarded as part of folk psychology (Bruner, 1990). Several concepts are offered to demonstrate this embeddedness. One of them is "therapeutic culture" (Furedy, 2004; Imber, 2004; Madsen, 2010). *The Psy complex* is another concept that demonstrates the pervasiveness of psychological discourses within contemporary modern society. The concept refers to theories, practices, and techniques within psychology, psychiatry, psychotherapy, and psychoanalysis (Ingleby, 1985; Rose, 1979, cited in Roald, 2010).

In his seminal book *Persuasion and Healing*, Jerome Frank (1961) presents an abstracted concept of healing practices across cultures. There are four components in his model:

1. A *healing context*, that is, helping takes place in a setting that communicates that a positive change is likely to take place.
2. An *emotionally charged relationship* that communicates hope for change.
3. A set of procedures for how the helping practice is carried out, which he also called a *ritual.*
4. A set of explanations for the root of suffering and how it can be relieved, which he also called a *myth.*

If Frank's model is read as a contentless abstraction and not as a claim of universality, it may be compatible with the cultural psychological contributions presented above. The model can serve as a tool for analyzing particular healing practices.

A Dynamic Relationship between Culture and Professional Discourses of Helping

It seems more complicated than ever to draw definite boundaries between professionals and nonprofessionals with regard to how helping practices are conceptualized. There is a dynamic reciprocal relationship between professional discourses of helping and ideologies, and ideas in the general culture. Society is permeated by professional discourses of helping, and varying zeitgeists with their ideologies influence professional practice. Let us look first at some channels of transfer of psychological discourses into the general culture, before we briefly consider how ideas and perspectives (zeitgeists) in society may transfer to the professional world.

In a late modern society, the population is quite well educated and is well informed of changing scientific paradigms. Popular scientific journals, newspapers, and magazines continually present a variety of psychological themes. Therapeutic discourses are also available through literature, plays, and various media, and therapeutic discourses are often presented in the popular culture. For decades, written texts in various literary genres have described therapeutic practices and human suffering in great detail, and have informed the public about professional therapeutic practice. Many of the popular books have also been filmed. Irvin Yalom's numerous books about therapeutic cases are amongst the most read. With sophistication, Yalom has transformed and communicated advanced professional knowledge into highly readable texts that have reached large audiences throughout the world.

The public's fascination with understanding the phenomenology and dynamics of psychological distress and therapeutic practice has also found its expression in numerous popular films such as, *The Three Faces of Eve, I Never Promised you a Rose Garden, Dibs in Search of Self, Equus,* and *Antwone Fisher.* Numerous films by Woody Allen have painted vivid pictures of psychotherapeutic practice. Television series like *Sopranos* and *In Treatment* present therapeutic practices and concepts that reach a large international audience. In addition, bookstores are filled with self-help literature based on the same therapeutic discourses.

From a professional point of view, the quality of the knowledge presented in such sources ranges from excellent, with accurate and sophisticated insights into the professional world, to caricatures and vulgarized examples of professional attitudes and practices. This melting pot of professional perspectives, communicated through the channels mentioned above, constitutes part of the fabric of Bruner's (1990) folk psychology and contributes to the fact that professional discourses that Cushman (1995) described are taken for granted.

Therapeutic/professional knowledge is not only communicated through the arts, written texts in various formats, film/DVD, and TV. In addition, the public's knowledge of the therapeutic culture is acquired through real-life actual encounters with professional helpers. The professional services of various kinds of helpers (e.g., psychologists, psychiatrists, social workers, nurses, counselors) are increasingly valued by the public. Within the school system, students see counselors and school psychologists. Increasingly, professionally trained consultants contribute within the public and private sector. New professions emerge, such as coaching, which, at its best, introduces professional psychotherapeutic-type concepts and procedures to individuals and groups in various contexts. A large proportion of the population has gradually become quite familiar with concepts from professional therapeutic/counseling practice because of their *personal experiences* with therapy. All of these sources, working together, have increasingly provided the population with a variety of conceptual tools for understanding themselves and others, and have given a direction for helping practices in everyday life.

The Influence of General Cultural Discourses on the Professional Culture

We will now change perspective, and reflect on the impact that past and current cultural ideas and societal tendencies may exert on professional practice. To do so, we will provide a few examples. In the Cushman (1995) quote on page 39, the underlying ideology of individualism in psychotherapy was mentioned. We suggest that the sociohistoric process of individualization in modern societies (Z. Bauman, 2001; Beck & Beck-Gernsheim, 2002) is a historical precondition for the expansion of psychotherapeutic practices. Individualization refers to the process of deinstitutionalization of modern society, with expanded freedom for the individual. Zygmunt Bauman (2001) succinctly states that the process of individualization changed identity from being "given" to being a "task." Modernity has also brought cultural ideals like the right of individuals to freely form their own lives. Ulrich Beck (2000) characterizes individualization as an enforced institutionalized individualism, where individuals gradually become more responsible for their choices and actions, and also for the results of those. This process, may again lead to new patterns of suffering.

Dominant ideas in a society may serve as cultural tools. This is a concept that was introduced by James Wertsch (1991, 1998) for analyzing how mental functioning is related to cultural, historical, and institutional contexts. Each sociocultural environment supplies the persons within that setting with a cultural toolkit. The tools provided will simultaneously both enable and limit practices. Cultural tools, which can be both symbolic and material, are a legacy from earlier generations, and they are usually transformed and developed by new generations. Language, concepts, ideas, and artifacts can be conceptualized as cultural tools that are in a state of continual change. One example of a powerful cultural tool is information technology, which enables people to engage in new practices. Advances in information technology have contributed to new treatment modes such as Internet therapy and Skype psychoanalysis.[2]

The concept of development is an example of a cultural tool that we now take for granted in our self-understanding. It is an example of what we now consider as part of being human and has become a concept that permeates our understanding of professional helping. The concept of development serves as a tool both for our self-understanding and for professional practices. The concept of development dates back to the Age of Enlightenment in the 18th century. The concept denotes a progressive [pro=forward and gradi=go forward] change in human functioning (Oxford English Dictionary, 1997).

As suggested by Oddli (2011), we might also ask if the ideology of New Public Management,[3] in its early phase, has provided a context that may have influenced the formulation and operationalization of the working alliance concept (e.g., Bordin, 1979, 1983; Hatcher & Gillaspy, 2006). The version of the alliance, with the components of *goals* and *tasks,* in addition to the *bond* (Bordin, 1979), may reflect a zeitgeist that values goal-directedness, rational differentiation of roles and responsibilities, and evaluation. Oddli (2011) wrote:

> At that time, the research paradigm had adapted to the medical model, which emphasizes predictability and control (Goldfried & Wolfe, 1998; Wampold, 2001).[4] Another marker of the zeitgeist is the introduction of New Public Management to the field of Mental Health Care, which stresses contracts, benchmarking, results and evaluation (Bergin, 2009; see also Morreim, 1990). The view of the therapeutic alliance as a contractual relationship, favoring explicit negotiations and agreement on tasks and goals, may be a natural implication of the zeitgeist, resulting in a rational and instrumental perspective of the technical aspects which constitute the [working alliance] model. (p. 66)

The postulated relationship between the zeitgeist and the contractual relationship of the working alliance may be an example of what is *taken for granted* (and, as such, not necessarily easily available for explicit reasoning). The "alliance case" may demonstrate the dialectics between psychology and society.

To sum up, there is a dialectical relationship between psychology and culture; psychological discourses are pervasive cultural tools (Wertsch, 1998), as well as products of the society in which they exist. From this perspective, psychotherapy is a cultural practice. The boundaries between professional and nonprofessional conceptions of helping are blurred, in the sense that professional discourses are both part of, and formed by, general cultural discourses, and students who enter professional training do so as cultural participants. The students, at different levels of sophistication, bring with them, more or less consciously, elaborated conceptions of helping practices. These practices are fueled both by general cultural discourses and also by professional discourses of helping.

How People View Being Helped by a Friend in Comparison with Being Helped by a Psychologist

Drawing its data from a representative sample of Norwegian citizens, an investigation was conducted that included the assessment of the helpfulness of different healing practices for individuals seeing a psychologist for anxiety and depression (Rønnestad & Tjersland, 2009). These healing practices may also be conceptualized as mechanisms of change. The study represents an empirical exploration of contemporary Norwegian folk psychology, to use Bruner's (1990) term. The questions posed in the study were based on knowledge of psychotherapy research and derived from focus groups. The questions in the focus groups explored the public's attitude to psychologists, including the public's view of what they considered to be helpful when seeing a psychologist. Some examples of healing practices that were assessed by the participants were: "to get assistance in thinking and behaving in new ways; to have the opportunity to express one's emotions, to understand oneself in new ways," and to obtain concrete advice. The informants were asked to indicate how important the different alternatives were on a scale from 0 (does not help at all) to 5 (helps very much).

Given that all alternatives have at least partial empirical support in psychotherapy research, the overall results suggest an overlap between what psychotherapy research has documented as being effective and what a layperson considers as effective. In other words, in this specific cultural context, folk psychology coincides with scientific psychology. The alternatives that were endorsed by most participants as being very helpful were: to have the opportunity to talk with someone; to get assistance in thinking and behaving in new ways; to have the opportunity to express one's emotions; the communication of hope for change; and to see the situation from a new perspective. These are all common denominators of helpfulness for seeing a psychologist as well as for seeing a friend.

Let us look a little more closely at the results for two of the items, the opportunity "to get the opportunity to talk with someone" and "to get the opportunity to express one's feelings," which may serve to illustrate the similarity in perception of professional and nonprofessional concepts of helping. "To talk with someone" is certainly not a "mechanism of change" reserved for therapy or talking with a psychologist, even though the "talking cure" formulation was first used in the famous work by Freud and Breuer (1892), *Studies on Hysteria*. "The opportunity to talk with someone" is an idea that occurs repeatedly in several historical and cultural contexts as an approach to change. Persons entering professional training share with people in general the view of potential for change through talking with other people. We can regard this as part of what is taken for granted in Western culture.

The potential for change through "having an opportunity to express one's emotions" is a cultural idea also shared by Aristotle, who described catharsis as purification or purgation and as relief from tension. In modern society we can recognize the concept in verbal expressions such as "it is important to get it all out" or "to get things off one's chest." As we know, psychoanalytic theory adapted the term *catharsis* both as a central personality concept and as an important concept in psychoanalytic practice.

In a follow-up of the study above (Rønnestad & Ulvik, 2011), the same questions were asked, but "when seeing a psychologist" was replaced with "when talking with a friend." The results from this follow-up study basically replicated the results from the study described above, which suggests that, in this specific cultural context at least, and with the alternatives investigated, "helping is helping."

It is worth noting that only about a fifth of the men and a third of the women rated "to obtain concrete advice" as being highly helpful when talking with a friend. This seems to run counter to previous formulations, in which rapid problem identification and "giving advice" were seen as being typical characteristics of the conventional helper (e.g., Rønnestad & Skovholt, 2003; Skovholt & Rønnestad, 1992). These recent results indicate that people are generally quite divided on this issue of the helpfulness of "giving advice." However, it seems that professional therapists are divided on this issue as well.

A psychoanalytically oriented therapist, who typically will structure therapy in ways that facilitate and encourage projections, may be less likely to give advice than a cbt-therapist who is working with parents of a child with a behavioral disorder. On the other hand, the idea that advice is illegitimate could be found in some forms of family therapy (see the "not knowing position" by Anderson & Goolishian, 1992). The variabilities on the issue of giving advice may be equally distributed among people in general and professionally trained therapists. Thus, we may assume that persons who have not yet started training are probably quite divided on whether giving advice is an appropriate thing to do when you are helping people. There is no clear empirical answer from psychotherapy research regarding whether giving advice is an effective "intervention" for people in distress. Indeed, a review of research on the relationship between advice (and related prescriptive therapists' interventions) and therapy outcomes over a 50-year period, showed that "this approach was generally unhelpful (except perhaps with highly disturbed patients who might be at risk with use of 'uncovering' techniques)" (Orlinsky, Rønnestad, & Willutzki, 2004, p. 341). On the question of whether advice is helpful, it is probably wise to contextualize the issue; that is, by asking when, where, from whom, in which mode, in which situations, and by which people is advice experienced as helpful.

"Being challenged" was an item endorsed as being "very helpful" by few respondents. This was so for seeing a psychologist as well as for seeing a friend. A few valued it highly, however. But generally, the results indicated that "to be challenged" was not considered to be a very helpful way to relieve suffering.

Gender and Developmental Optimism

In many countries there is a marked movement of more women than men seeking training in some of the relationally oriented helping professions. In this study, gender differences were noticed in the responses obtained for seeing a friend and seeing a psychologist. With one exception, a significantly higher proportion of the women rated all change mechanisms to "help very much." An intriguing question is whether these results may be replicated for professional therapists. As therapists' communication of hope is important for therapy outcome, there might be some subtle gender differences in therapists as change agents that can be attributed to gender differences in "developmental optimism."

The three mechanisms endorsed by more than half of the women as helping *very much* when seeing a psychologist, were: to have the opportunity to talk with someone; to have the opportunity to express one's emotions, and the communication gives hope for change. It seems that the women in this study, more so than the men, saw a potential for change (hope) foremost in the relationship/emotional aspects of a "talking cure." This finding is supported when we shift our view toward considering which mechanisms of change demonstrate the largest gender differences. "To get assistance in thinking and behaving in new ways" received the highest endorsement score (helps very much) from more than half of the men in the study, twice as many as from the women, and was the mechanism receiving the highest proportion of endorsement for the men. Thus, in combination, the two findings above suggest that the men, more so than the women, recognize a potential for change foremost in the cognitive/

behavioral aspects of therapy, while the women, more so than the men, believe that the potential for change is most associated with the relational/affective aspects of therapy.

The gender differences in this study are on a descriptive level, and are congruent with widespread gender stereotypes; namely, that women are more relationally and emotionally oriented than men. The findings give no explanation for the small, although statistically significant, differences reported, and the study results do not warrant claims of "essential" gender difference. Nevertheless, these results do provide some ideas for reflection on the gendered experiences that trainees bring with them into training, and how these experiences may possibly impact on the decision to enter professional training in one of the helping professions.

How Can We Articulate Possible Distinctions Between Nonprofessional and Professional Helping Knowledge and Practice?

In the previous sections of this chapter, we have presented some reflections on the complexity of the relationship between professional and nonprofessional discourses of helping. We have described perspectives that underscore the reciprocal influence between professional and nonprofessional conceptions of helping people in distress. Distinguishing between what could be labeled "professional" and "nonprofessional" concepts is not simple. However, the legitimacy of the helping professions rests upon the assumption that professionals have something unique to offer, something that goes beyond what laypeople can provide. Below we suggest some lines of reasoning that might be useful in articulating these distinctions. The discussion is primarily a conceptual one, and the aim is not to present empirically based knowledge claims about group differences between trained professionals and nonprofessionals.

The British philosopher, Gilbert Ryle (1949/2000), distinguished between *knowing that* and *knowing how*. Setting aside his discussion on the complex relationship between the two, this distinction can be reduced to a distinction between conceptual knowledge and procedural knowledge. We might ask the question: what differentiates the pretraining person from the professionally trained practitioner in how they conceive and practice "helping"?

We suggest the following three characteristics are necessary conditions to be fulfilled in order that the definition of a professional practitioner be met:

1. That the person has acquired a highly differentiated and scientifically based conceptual frameworks that are necessary in order to understand what causes human suffering and concerns.

46

2. That the person has an integrated competence in using themselves as instruments, which also includes the application of a wide range of established therapeutic procedures for helping another person.
3. That the person has sufficient background knowledge in the natural, social, and humanistic sciences that is necessary for flexible and ethical assistance to be provided; assistance that is contextualized and adapted to the needs of the individual client.

The term *nonprofessional* implies that, in all their variety, this group is defined by *what they are not*; that is, they are not meeting the criteria listed above. This is an important point. As we have indicated in the first part of this chapter, there are large variations in helping conceptions and procedures in the general culture, and thus it is not possible to provide a precise definition or description of the nonprofessional helper. However, we will suggest some possible distinctions between professional helping and nonprofessional helping that ensue from the above criteria. The first three follow directly from the necessary conditions that are formulated above, while the fourth addresses the issue at a different conceptual level.

First, we suggest that by *not* having acquired a highly differentiated conceptual framework necessary to understand what causes human suffering and concerns, the nonprofessional helper has less ability to analyze what it is that the other person needs in order to be helped efficiently.

Second, we suggest that by *not* having an integrated competence in using themselves as instruments, which also includes the application of a wide range of therapeutic procedures, the nonprofessional helper is less likely to be able to establish an optimal helping relationship, and will have fewer procedures to apply in the helping practice.

Third, the nonprofessional helper may not necessarily have as wide a background in many sciences as a professional helper will have, and may be less likely to be able to adapt their helping practices to the specific needs of the other person. Further weight is added to this argument by reference to the last element in the definition of Evidence Based Practice as defined by the American Psychological Association (2006). This definition specifies that the best available research and clinical expertise is integrated *"in the context of patient characteristics, culture and preferences"* (p. 2).

In order to accentuate further the need for breadth in the knowledge base, Levant (2005) (in the report from APA's Task Force on Evidence Based Practice), listed which patient characteristics should be considered in maintaining a treatment relationship and in implementing specific interventions. He wrote:

These include, but are not limited to, a) variations in presenting problems or disorders, etiology, concurrent symptoms or syndromes, and behavior; b) chronological age, developmental status, developmental history, and life stage; c) sociocultural and familial factors (e.g., gender, gender identity, ethnicity, race, social class, religion, disability status, family structure, and sexual orientation); d) current environmental context, stressors (e.g., unemployment or recent life event), and social factors (e.g., institutional racism and health care disparities); and e) personal preferences, values, and preferences related to treatment (e.g., goals, beliefs, worldviews, and treatment expectations). (p. 15)

To the above knowledge necessary for competent professional practice, Levant adds more. Reading it, one realizes the comprehensiveness and depth of knowledge that are necessary for optimal helping. This suggests a distinction between nonprofessional and professional helping conceptions. Levant writes;

A wide range of relevant research literature can inform psychological practice, including ethnography, cross-cultural psychology (e.g., Berry, Kagitcibasi, & Segall, 1997), cultural psychiatry (e.g., Kleinman, 1977), psychological anthropology (e.g., LeVine, 1983; Moore & Matthews, 2003; Strauss & Quinn, 1992), and cultural psychotherapy (Sue, 1998; Zane, Sue, Young, Nunez, & Hall, 2004. (p. 16)

To include the suggested perspectives of what constitutes the knowledge base for professionals as mentioned above, may help professionals to analyze their own approaches as cultural practice, as we have argued for above.

The third distinction is that of having, or not having, a wide scientific background, which is required for a helping practice that is contextualized and adapted to the needs of the individual client. This point is important. It is a fundamental perspective on what differentiates therapy/counseling as a professional practice from therapy/counseling as a technical intervention, and thus differentiates a professional from a technician.

As a fourth distinction between professional and nonprofessional helping, we want to address the ability to fluctuate between being in the experiencing and observing mode when relating to clients. Observations and experiences from collaboration with nonprofessionals are likely shared by many supervisors/professionals. Analyzing such experiences may provide insights into the difficulties and challenges of the nontrained or minimally trained helper. We will do so while also recognizing that some nonprofessionals appear to be "natural helpers" and may not experience the difficulties described below.[5]

As a fourth distinction between professional and nonprofessional helping, we want to address what we see as another important criterion in the definition of professional helping practice; that is, the ability to fluctuate between being in the experiencing and observing mode when relating to clients. In order to reflect on the challenges involved in the above task, we will reflect on experiences working and collaborating with nonprofessional helpers in varying treatment contexts. An analysis of these experiences may inform us of the difficulties and challenges encountered by the nonprofessionally trained helper. A common difficulty for the nontrained helper is not being able to shift from being *empathically involved* with the client, to *observing* the client, oneself, and the interaction. We may call the former being in the *experiencing mode* and the latter in the *observing mode*. It is our experience that moving flexibly between the experiencing and observing mode is a demanding professional skill that takes years of training to master. There are at least two reasons why these flexible shifts are hard for the nontrained helper to accomplish. First, the nontrained helper has insufficient theoretical and conceptual knowledge to perceive and organize the experiences. Second, the nontrained helper may be more likely than the professional helper to engage in overidentification with the client. There is a subtle but important distinction between identification and overidentification. Therapists/counselors' identification with clients, expressed as an empathic involvement in clients' experiential world, is an important ingredient in alliance formation. Overidentification, however, entails the loss of being in the observing mode, and prevents the helper from effectively providing the new and different perspective that is needed for effective change (challenging, interpreting. etc.). Overidentification may also be conceptualized as lacking in metacognition and may stimulate an urge to act, rather than continuing to engage in the reflective activity that is needed to provide the client with optimal assistance. The crucial role played by reflection is discussed in chapter 10.

Another way of addressing the limitation above, that of not being able to shift between the experiencing and the observing mode, is to compare the concepts of empathy with sympathy.

One of the more consistent findings in psychotherapy research is how important client- rated therapist empathy is for therapy/counseling outcome (e.g., Bohart, Elliott, Greenberg, & Watson, 2002; Norcross, 2011; Orlinsky, Rønnestad, & Willutzki, 2004. The challenge associated with this fundamental therapist capacity can be better understood if we compare sympathy with empathy.

Sympathy and Empathy

Consideration of the difference between sympathy and empathy may add to our knowledge of the difficulty in fluctuating between being in the observing mode and the experiencing mode.

Sympathy can be characterized by the helpers directing their attention toward their own experiences, and also the experiences of others (Nerdrum, 2011). Nerdrum writes:

> She [the helper] is continuously comparing the experiences of the other person with her own. The comparison becomes the reference point for how to understand, and the "understanding" of the other person is mediated primarily through how things have been for her. She expresses her understanding of the feelings of the other person by referring to something that she herself has experienced. (p. 64; author's translation)

Referring to Bohart et al. (2002), Hoffmann (2000), and Ickes (2009), Nerdrum (2011) states that most empathy researchers will agree that there are three elements in the empathy process. Empathy is experienced as: (a) feeling in the same way that the other person is feeling (an emotional component); (b) taking the perspective of the other person (a cognitive component); and (c) sensing or understanding that the empathic experience has its origin in the other person, a structural (self-other differentiation) component (Nerdrum, 2011, p. 57).

In contrast with sympathy, empathy is defined not by the inclination to compare experiences of another person with their own, but by a consistent focus on the experience of the other person. "The basis for understanding the other person is not oneself. Empathy is thus a deeper way to understand the other person than by sympathy" (p. 64).

During the 1960s and 1970s, empathy was typically measured by external raters (not the client) (Nerdrum, 2011). By this method, research on empathy training had long concealed how difficult it is to learn empathy at a deep level, thus obscuring an important distinction between professional and nonprofessional helping. An empathy-training program for experienced milieu therapists, aimed at this deep level showed the difficulty and the extent of exertion that is demanded when engaging in a deep empathy learning process (Nerdrum & Rønnestad, 2003).

Some Concluding Comments

Further differentiation between the professional and the nonprofessional helper may be located in many of the developmental tasks that are presented in the subsequent chapters. In a shorthand form, the Beginning Student needs to acquire the basic and general knowledge of the field; the Advanced Student needs to begin to learn the more complex picture of taking context and individual differences into account when conceptualizing clients and planning therapy/counseling; the Novice Professional needs to handle constructively the disillusionment that may set in some time after more fully recognizing the complexity of therapeutic work. Furthermore, the Novice Professional will also intensify the quest to integrate personal characteristics with the conceptual knowledge that guides the conception and the performance of the professional role. A major task for the Experienced and the Senior Professional is to continue to refine his or her competence and to integrate and consolidate the individual's personal self, not only into a professional role, but into a professional self.

When people enter training, their knowledge is transformed, changed, and developed. The distinctions that we have provided may serve as tools for understanding the challenges that nonprofessionals and new trainees will face. In the following chapters, the empirical data will be used as the basis to describe this process, the transformation from "nonprofessional" to "professional" within the fields of psychotherapy and counseling in a late modern society.

Notes

1. This seems to be changing. Documentation from various sources has shown that psychotherapeutic practice is being carried out in non-Western cultures such as China, India, Japan, and South Korea. See, for example, research within the Society for Psychotherapy Research/Collaborative Research Network (Orlinsky & Rønnestad, 2005).

2. *Skype psychoanalysis* is a term used for the practice in which psychoanalysts "psychoanalyze" long distance by using Skype technology.

3. New Public Management is a management philosophy that emphasizes efficiency, goal attainment, benchmarking, and evaluation. It was introduced around 1980 to modernize the public sector

4. See, for example, Goldfried and Wolfe (1998) for an account of the development of different research paradigms in psychotherapy research (see also Wampold, 2001).

5. *Natural helper* is a term we apply to a person without professional training, whose practice resembles that of a professionally trained person. A natural helper is one who has a talent for helping without having acquired the conceptual knowledge of a professional person. Teachers of psychotherapy and counseling have observed that some new students, at the very start of their therapy/counseling training, demonstrate an interpersonal skillfulness that, in many ways, matches that of a more experienced professional. They ask open questions, follow up with appropriate probes, check to see that they have understood what the client is saying, allow the client to tell their story without interruption but structure the session if necessary, listen respectfully and empathically, and communicate hope and encouragement. They are able to create a reflective atmosphere. The interpersonal sensitivity of these students is high.

Part II

A QUALITATIVE STUDY OF THERAPIST AND COUNSELOR DEVELOPMENT

4

THE NOVICE STUDENT PHASE[1]

There was so much self-awareness. Every issue seemed to be mine. It got really intense for me.

At times I was so busy thinking about the instructions given in class and textbooks, I barely heard the client.

Introduction

We define the Novice Student Phase from the beginning of a graduate training program in one of the helping fields through the second year of training, which normally encompasses "the beginning practicum" or its equivalents. This definition is partly determined by a common structure of graduate training programs in therapy and counseling.

For all phases of professional development and for this phase in particular, there is variation among therapists and counselors in terms of the parameters we describe. Age, previous therapy/counseling training or experience, impactful personal suffering or personal stress, and previous professional work experience contribute to this variation. For example, a 35-year-old mother with three children, or a 40-year-old with many years of experience in the human services and a personal stress history will experience this phase in different ways from a 22-year-old new college graduate with a low personal stress history. The phase description we provide is more representative of the younger, less experienced individual who has not suffered from extensive personal stress. To a certain degree, the older, more experienced person will have already confronted many of the issues addressed here.

Developmental Tasks and General Description

The Novice Student Phase is challenging. From the analysis of our data, we have extracted the following developmental tasks for this phase, which are: (a) to make preliminary sense of an extensive amount of new information which the individual is primarily acquiring from graduate classes and professional literature; this means to meet the criteria for conceptual knowledge set by the educational system; (b) to demonstrate in practicum sufficient procedural competence; that is, sufficient mastery of assessment and therapy/counseling skills; (c) to handle the intense emotional reactions that ensue from seeing their first clients in practicum; and (d) to maintain an openness to information and theory at the meta-level, while also engaging in the "closing off" process of selecting therapy/theories and techniques to use.

Although some beginning students feel assured that they have made the right choice in entering a therapy or counseling graduate program and feel confident in their ability, this is not the rule. Typically, students feel threatened and anxious when confronted with the tasks of mastering theory and applying it in practicum. A common question that students ask is: "Am I suited for this kind of work?" One student expressed it this way, "Could I really pull it off?" A female in this phase who had done some volunteer work said the big issue was, "How did it feel to be sitting with a person and being the professional responsible for improvement?"

For most, student anxiety also seems to be very present among therapy students across countries and cultures. From the survey research of the International Study of the Development of Psychotherapists (Orlinsky & Rønnestad, 2005), we know that inexperienced therapists frequently feel overwhelmed and highly challenged in client sessions. We also know that compared to later phases, beginning therapists report more frequently to experience difficulties in their work. With data from many countries, factor analyses of a high number of difficulty items[2] yielded three factors (Professional Self-Doubt, Negative Personal Reaction, and Frustrating Treatment Case); see Chapter 14 for a description of these concepts. There was a significant decrease in frequency of experienced difficulties across experience cohorts. As we will return to later (chapters 10 and 11), therapists need not be alarmed if they experience some doubt in their self-confidence because the results of a study by Nissen-Lie, Monsen, and Rønnestad (2010) showed that therapists who doubted their professional skillfulness (Professional Self-Doubt) obtained higher client rated alliance ratings (Nissen-Lie et al., 2010). A possible explanation for this is that such experiences may indicate that those therapists have respect for the complexity of therapeutic work.

Recent analyses of data from the Society for Psychotherapy Research/Collaborative Research Network (SPR/CRN) indicate that during the first 6 months of practice therapists are particularly prone to experience stressful involvement with their clients (Rønnestad & Orlinsky, 2010). Similarly, Melton, Nofzinger-Collins, Wynne, and Susman (2005) found four themes of inner experience for beginning counselors:

Anger/frustration
Disappointment/regret,
Anxiety/fear,
Happiness/excitement.

Also, research on supervision within therapy confirms that training experiences can be threatening for students (e.g., Gray, Ladany, Walker, & Ancis, 2001; Moskowitz & Rupert, 1983; Nielsen et al., 2009; Reichelt et al., 2009; Skjerve et al., 2009; Strømme, 2010).

The intensity of student reactions can be illustrated as follows: A licensed Scandinavian psychologist who was looking back at her training years, stated recently that she and a friend had been throwing up for 2 hours before their first practicum client appointments (personal communication to MHR). In addition, a college friend of the second author said that the night before his first client in counseling practicum in 1967 that he was in the bathroom throwing up (personal communication to TS). These two stories across continents and decades well illustrate the performance anxiety experienced by the beginning student when facing an unknown task, which in this phase is a task also experienced as diffuse and ambiguous.

However, the stories can be different. The experience of being a new graduate student can also be exhilarating and intellectually stimulating. Since being successful with their first clients is so important, students will devote an enormous amount of energy to these clients. From the perspective of therapeutic impact, the commitment and positive expectations of the beginning student may compensate for the lack of experience-based ability. Yet, overinvolvement, which often accompanies the commitment of the younger beginner with no experience, can also be a reality at this point.

The Novice Student is trying to move as quickly as possible from the known of the conventional helper role to the unknown of a future professional role. To know that conventional ways of helping are not appropriate and insufficient, and *not* know what the alternatives are, is disconcerting. As we will describe below, the beginning student is typically trying to fill the void by learning a series of discrete, highly pragmatic therapy/ techniques. There is a certain intensity in the learning process at this phase. We will present the supervisory implications of our findings in chapter 11, but want to emphasize here that there is a need to create a constructive "holding" learning environment in which the student is provided with appropriate and clear feedback and is allowed, within certain boundaries, the privilege of being a student and not being fully competent.

At this phase, the practitioner focuses intensely on trying to become a competent therapist. The long term goal is to be able to use the ideas and methods of seasoned practitioners, who have used acknowledged conceptual systems (schools, methods, approaches), as a standard for their performance. Since completing this task naturally takes years of effort and the influences that the beginning student is being exposed to are many, students typically try to manage the immediate challenge in various ways. One is to search for a simple therapy approach that is considered easy to learn and apply, while another is to search for competent practitioners that they can imitate. These approaches, which are not compatible and may add to the experience of bewilderment for the novice student, will be described below.

Sources of Influence[3] and Learning Processes

Analogous to the researcher collecting and analyzing data to generate knowledge, the Novice Students also draw their data from varied experiential and theoretical/empirical "databases" to increase their knowledge and competence. We have organized the "databases," which we can also call "sources of influence" into six categories: theories/research, clients, professional elders (professors/supervisors/mentors/therapists), one's own personal life, one's peers/colleagues, and one's social/cultural environment. All sources of influence now impact the beginning student. It is experienced as overwhelming. One student said: "There was too much data, too many conflicting ideas...." By itself, data from just one of these sources (i.e., a fascinating article, one's first real client, a comment from a classmate about one's personality) can be very intense and stimulating and the students' attention can quickly move from one arena to the next. One Novice Student said that "something grabs you and you run with it for a while." Another called it the "disease of the week phenomenon." Information from all sources of influence is typically combined to create information overload. One student expressed this as follows: "At times I was so busy thinking about the instructions given in class and textbooks, I barely heard the client."

Imitation as a Preferred Way to Learn

At this phase, imitation is a favored learning method. Local experts, admired peers, national and international experts may become inspiring models. Students want to perform like an acknowledged contemporary expert, such as, Leslie Greenberg, Judith Beck, Irving Yalom, Mary Pipher, and Derald Wing Sue or like historically renowned psychotherapists such as Sigmund Freud, Carl Rogers, Victor Frankel, Aaron Beck, or a local expert (e.g., one's supervisor in practicum). The classic *Three Approaches to Psychotherapy* films with Rogers, Perls, and Ellis (edited by Shostrom, 1965), although dated now, are excellent examples of prominent early models. Although these models can provide direction for the students' learning, it is of course unrealistic for beginning students to perform like those highly accomplished experts. Unrealistic goals may fuel performance anxiety.

The preference for learning by observation was also expressed in a study of personal therapy among Danish psychology students (Paulsen & Peel, 2006). At Aalborg University, personal group therapy is mandatory. Consistent with the strong desire to learn by observation in this study, these authors found that the *pedagogical* outcome, what students learned about therapy through observing the therapists, was assessed to be more valuable than *personal* outcome (e.g., insight, self-esteem).[4]

Analyzing the reports of therapists at different levels of experience has sensitized us to the different forms that modeling can take. Modeling can be differentiated along a continuum from *imitation*, which may be seen as an external, mechanical repetition, to *identification*, which may be conceptualized as an internalization of the characteristics of the model. At this phase, the modeling process may best be described as imitation, although the process for the internalization of attitudes and behaviors starts early. A male student at this phase expressed his undertaking this way, "I wanted to absorb from counselors I observed." At this point, the person wants to know how experts act, think, and feel in clinical practice. A female intermediate student was in group therapy to learn both about herself and to learn about being a therapist through observation of the therapy process. In the group, she could watch two therapists with their own styles working with a variety of other group members, and she said it was invaluable as a learning experience. The Novice Student with much life experience may not search as intensely for models to imitate.

Interacting closely with a dogmatically oriented senior therapist, professor, or supervisor may accelerate the modeling process. However, such interaction may impede the opportunity to maintain an openness to information and theory at the metalevel. As a consequence, the individual's epistemological search may be inhibited for the benefit of short-term gains.

An Attitude of Openness

An attitude of curiosity, openness to experience, and commitment to learn and develop is imperative to enhance professional competence; we will return to those issues in several chapters throughout the book. The simplification process favored by many beginning students may impede professional development in the long-term perspective. An ability and willingness to recognize the complexities of professional work are also crucial for professional growth. The simplification process that many engage in may involve choosing therapeutic approaches or methods that are seen as easy to learn. An open attitude facilitates professional development, while a restricted or closed attitude fosters professional stagnation.

We differentiate between a developmental and nondevelopmental approach to master the complexities that students/counselors encounter. The developmental approach has an active, searching, exploratory, trying-out quality, and is an expression of attempting to reach long-term developmental goals. The nondevelopmental (stagnant) approach has a defensive, experience limiting, anxiety reducing quality and is not an expression of a long-term developmental goal, but rather may be understood as impression management (Goffman, 1967), a face-saving maneuver. The achievement orientation of the academic culture, the power differential between professor/supervisor and student, and the magnitude of challenges encountered all fuel such maneuvers.

The structuring and organizing strategies that the beginning student uses to handle the complexities and challenges of work, whether developmental or nondevelopmental in nature, tend to reduce feelings of chaos and incompetence. Usually, the use of modeling at this phase will provide the student with direction and structure, which eventually gives the student a sense of calm and temporary security.

Supervision

Supervisors have a major impact in the Beginning Student Phase. The dependence and vulnerability of the beginning student, in combination with the intense need for confirmation and guidance, combine to make supervision an important learning arena. There are many reasons why the supervisor has such an impact. Supervisors are powerful gatekeepers, a role that adds to the student's emotional investment in the supervisory relationship. Supervisors are more often than not seen to be competent and are thus viable models, and for many they are the only more senior person who interacts closely with the student in the work setting. They not only evaluate the clinical performance, but sometimes also the student's academic performance, so they have a direct, powerful impact when they give feedback to an individual (e.g., Rønnestad, 1977).

Supervisors are most valued for their enthusiastic support and encouragement. Looking back at the early student years, one experienced female practitioner recalled being observed by her supervisor through a one-way mirror while working with a difficult client. The supervisor's positive feedback was very important to her. She said, "I can still remember how needed that was."

Novice Students express the wish for honest and clear feedback from their supervisors. But many feel vulnerable, and negative supervisory evaluations in practicum are feared and can be experienced as traumatic. Students who receive negative evaluations react to this in different ways ranging from using the evaluations constructively to attempting to invalidate them by searching for opinions that contradict the supervisor's evaluation. Sources for this search are peers, other seniors in the field, and indirectly, clients. If students are receiving strong negative feedback, they may initiate a search for alternatives within the field or also drop out of training. The movement out of therapy/work may be a lateral one into research, career advising, teaching, administration, or some other role.

Research within the SPR/CRN indicates that overall, supervision is a favored learning arena at all phases of development, and particularly so for the novice student. Analyses of data from approximately 5,000 psychotherapists from more than 20 countries showed that therapists with less than one year of client experience ranked supervision as the most important source of professional development (Orlinsky, Botermans, & Rønnestad, 2001). For those with more than one year of experience, direct client work was ranked first while supervision was ranked second or third.[5] These results were consistent across profession, nationality, therapist's theoretical orientation, and gender.

The Social/Cultural Environment

The social/cultural environment provides an impactful learning context for the beginning student. Prestigious areas of study within the training institution, or the predominant professional zeitgeist attract the attention of the novice student who may be "imprinted" by the popular contemporary topics. Examples of salient social/cultural topics for our total sample that entered graduate school between 1950 and 1986 include civil rights, anxiety and meaninglessness, sexism and women's issues, helping skills training for paraprofessionals, Gestalt therapy, cognitive theory, Holland's typology, family systems, and alcoholism. As we will see later in this chapter when we describe the role and working style of the novice student, the topics have changed.

Peers

At this phase, classmate support is highly valued. Classmates are credible, approachable, present, safe, more spontaneous and social equals, and are believed to have an accurate awareness of issues. Essential questions for feedback from one's classmates are: How do you see me? What are my personal strengths and weaknesses? Do I have the personality to be an excellent therapist? The answer to these questions may come informally, in social interactions with other students, or formally, when interacting with students in a graduate course offered by some training programs that focuses on personal growth. Whether the feedback is very supportive, very critical (which seldom happens) or mixed, it is of great importance to the individual and is taken very seriously. Admired peers are particularly influential.

Supervision research focusing on what students do not disclose to their supervisors (Ladany, Hill, Corbett, & Nutt, 1996; Reichelt et al., 2009; Yourman & Farber, 1996) has confirmed the essential role played by peers in providing feedback to students. The issues that students do not disclose to their supervisors were typically brought up and processed with peers, who can provide a safer environment in which to discuss sensitive issues.

Personal Life

In one's personal life, the stress of the early graduate school experience is often buffered by the social support of family and friends. In addition, the lives of significant others, and most of all, oneself, are constantly being understood through newly acquired psychological concepts. These psychological concepts provide a lens through which many observations and experiences are viewed. Much of this personal process is strongly internal and introspective in nature.

We have been describing younger, less experienced beginning students who have gone directly from high school, through undergraduate studies, into graduate school. Novice Students who are older and have had one or more previous careers, maybe a family on their own, or possibly also gone through crises as adults, may experience the Novice Student Phase differently from what we have described. When addressing a draft description of the younger student with little experience, a 40-year-old female Novice Student said:

> I don't fit all parts of this phase description; perhaps part of this is a function of being older and already having had two careers which have been rewarding and engrossing for me: teacher and mother. From these, I have brought the knowledge that I could work effectively with people and that I could not solve their problems for them without at least an equal effort on their part. I think I also have the notion that in any field there are many theories and that I can comfortably pick and choose and combine elements from any or all of them as they seem appropriate and helpful for me. I have also done extensive reading on the subject. I think this has served to cushion me from many things that you describe in Stages 1 and 2 of the draft copy, such as feeling a need to solve all my clients' problems and not understanding my personal issues and their relation to choosing a career field.

Intensive Psychologizing

At the Novice Student Phase, the student engages in intensive psychologizing. It is an introspective process that engages the student at a deep, meaningful level. From their research, Farber and Golden (1997) also described psychotherapists, including nondynamically oriented therapists, as highly introspective. They were also described as psychologically minded, characteristics which are expressed in the students' quest to understand how theoretical concepts relate to themselves and to significant others.[6]

One male student expressed some of this in the following way: "There was so much self-awareness. Every issue seemed to be mine. It got really intense for me." Since few graduate programs formally process this data, the graduate student is usually left to him- or herself or with peers to process it. Deeply personal questions, are asked such as: What motivates me to be in this occupation? Am I suited to be a therapist? Yet, because the individual is so intensely involved in academic survival and socialization into the field, and also so intent on getting though all the mazes of required experiences, academic work, and evaluations, the questions are not fully answered. Also, when the evaluations of others and meeting the requirements of the system are pressing concerns it seems too difficult and painful to ask the harder questions, such as: Why do I want this? The verbalized reasons expressed in response to the question of why they are studying to become therapists/counselors seem not much different from what students entering training say (e.g., they often contain elements of altruism, interest in the behavioral sciences, and liking to be with people and helping them).

Acquisition-Application-Validation

According to one learning paradigm, the student studies the research and theories (e.g., counseling/psychotherapy, developmental psychology, psychopathology) and then directly applies the newly acquired knowledge in practice. If it works, the knowledge is validated. We may call it the paradigm of acquisition-application-validation, which is so widely accepted in academic psychology. Although all narrations of our participants do not fit such a paradigm, many do.

As stated before, there are six different sources of influence that the individual is drawing from for therapy/work at this phase: theories and research that are read and presented in classes, direct and indirect feedback from clients, feedback from professional elders, and modeling of elders (professors, supervisors/mentors/therapists), one's own life experiences (for some this includes one's experiences as a therapy client), one's peers/colleagues, and the social/cultural environment. We are reminded of Sfard's (1998) distinction between the acquisition and participation metaphors of learning and the extension of knowledge creation perspective (Paavola, Lipponen, & Hakkarainen, 2004) presented in chapter 2. The two first metaphors (acquisition and participation) capture the different nuances of the beginning students' learning process.

Through the process of acquisition, application, and validation, the typical beginning student processes information in many contexts. The student will apply what is acquired not only to clients, but also to his or her life and the lives of friends and family. If the conceptual idea or framework makes sense in the application to people's lives and is validated, then one becomes more committed to it. Reacting to this section of the draft paper, one female in this phase said:

> I'm putting together a jigsaw puzzle. First I pick up a piece to see how it fits with another. I turn it around to try and get it to fit. I try lots of different combinations. If a piece fits, I keep it and it becomes a natural part of the puzzle. If it doesn't fit, I keep trying to find a place for it. Eventually, with no place, it gets dropped.

If theoretical ideas are not validated, they tend to gradually lose acceptance and use by the therapist. However, if a particular conceptual idea or framework is promulgated within the culture of the graduate program or practitioner's agency, the individual may persist with this approach at this point irrespective of disconfirming personal data. The popularity within a smaller or larger culture of a specific method can powerfully derail the application to oneself and other's validity process.

It is important to note that many qualified therapists experience frustration and disappointment in this phase because of a lack of direct positive feedback from clients, supervisors, or peers. The strong feelings of insecurity, coupled with little positive feedback while attempting to succeed at a nebulous task, can lead to strong discouragement and a search for other career options. It is likely that many potentially successful practitioners in the helping, healing, and teaching professions have probably left their field at this point in their careers because of feelings of discouragement and despair. Yet if they had continued things may have improved. As we will discuss further, the ability and willingness to endure hardships and to continually reflect on the challenges encountered is a prerequisite for professional development. We will elaborate more carefully on this important perspective in chapter 6 on the "Novice Professional Phase," in chapter 9 on "Themes of Professional Development," and also in chapter 10, where we present an integrative model for professional development.

Professional Role and Conceptual Ideas Used

In this phase, the professional role is unclear. Without sufficient time to learn the concepts and behaviors characteristic of professional functioning, the Novice Student is torn between known conventional helping roles and stereotypical images of professionally conducted therapy/counseling. There is an eagerness to learn what the professional role is like. One male student expressed it this way: "I was very motivated to be in the right saddle, but didn't know what that saddle felt like."

The conceptual maps that students use in their work directly impact how they define the professional role. Conceptual maps vary in their differentiation and complexity.[7] Some are highly complex and require extensive education to master, whereas other maps are simple and can be learned in a relatively short time.

As Novice Students typically experience from moderate to high performance anxiety when interacting with their first clients, many are drawn to learn one easily mastered conceptual system (model, method, school, approach) which they attempt to applied to all clients. The Novice Professionals preference for choosing one approach is in line with Hogan's (1964) description of the Level 1 psychotherapist.

We may use the analogy of a funnel (see Figure 4.1) to describe the transformation of complex and differentiated data into manageable and more understandable concepts. By using a few ideas from theory, students can transform the unmanageable complexity of trying to understand the client's life into a comprehensible simplicity of concrete and specific instructions for how to act. To illustrate our point, we will create a method here that could be called the Seven-Things-to-Do-Method: show interest, listen, ask a few good questions, avoid quick advice, absorb the client

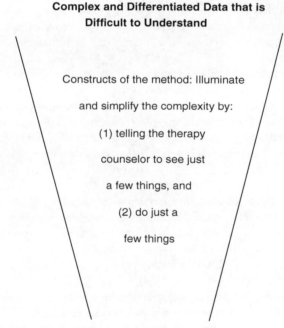

**Complex and Differentiated Data that is
Difficult to Understand**

Constructs of the method: Illuminate

and simplify the complexity by:

(1) telling the therapy

counselor to see just

a few things, and

(2) do just a

few things

Figure 4.1 The Conceptual Funnel

affect (but not too much), do not get ahead of the client, and try for a good ending.

Other examples of instructions are: use the interaction between yourself and the client for the data of the work (Teyber), focus on responsible behavior (Glaser), reflect empathically (Rogers), recognize interlocking triangles (Bowen), teach what normal is (Adult Children of Alcoholics) and look for faulty cognitions (Beck). The use of motivational interviewing (Miller & Rollnick) with four principles is a prototypical example of preferred simple methods (for example: Express empathy by reflective listening, develop discrepancy, roll with the resistance, and support self-efficacy by affirming the client's self-direction). Clara Hill's Helping Skills (Hill, 2009), which emphasizes open questions and probes, restatements, and reflection of feelings also provides a structure that is comprehensible and therefore popular with beginning students.

One male student illustrates the principle of "one approach for all." When reflecting on previous substance abuse counselor training, he said, "At my drug abuse practicum, I used one way with everyone." We are reminded of Maslow's (1966) famous saying: " If the only tool you have is a hammer, [you tend] to treat everything as if it were a nail" (p. 66).

Complex approaches are typically avoided because they do not provide specific recommendations and guidelines for how to act and cannot be quickly mastered. Since consumers of workshops are often novices, workshops which focus on new, single ideas (i.e., newer codependency or shame) tend to be much more successful in enrollment and profit than workshops that focus on the complexity or interaction of various concepts.

How strongly the individuals in the Novice Student Phase endorse the approach/method and become a "true believer" (Hoffer, 1951) depends on many factors such as pressure from the training program or field placement institution, the preferred approach of a supervisor or faculty member, the student's assessment of the competence of the faculty member or supervisor, and the personal characteristics of the student. One beginning male student said:

> Early on I was trained in a particular model and when people came in, I tried to fit them in. I quickly found out it did not work. I became disenchanted and began to look around. I grasped at another approach and felt more in control. I felt I was doing something here. I was earning my pay.

In this phase, the focus is not on critiquing the approach, but on mastering it. One student working in a psychiatric unit said, "Patients were my workshop. I would practice theories on them." Another said, "You don't want to shoot it down because you need something to hang onto."

Novice Students are frequently trying out aspects of the professional role with friends and family. To reflect on feelings and ask open questions are examples of typical role-content tried out by the beginning therapist. This can add a positive dimension to the person's interpersonal relationships; at other times the boundary between roles is inappropriately crossed. One female said, "It was powerful to see how you could get friends to talk while trying out being a counselor." Another said, "What I am learning is helpful, much to the chagrin of my family."

Given the emerging professional title of *therapist*, other people sometimes relate in new and unexpected ways to the person. One female said her mother invited her, the new psychology student, to give advice concerning the mother's relationship to other family members. The daughter/ new graduate student was uncomfortable with this request. In essence, the trying out of the role with friends and family seems to be an attempt to validate what is learned and also to represent a step in the development of a professional identity.

An intense crisis about the role is avoided most possibly because the Novice Students generally do not allow themselves to experience disabling complexity. By sticking to a few ideas/procedures/techniques and foreclosing on any other data disabling confusion is avoided.

Recognizing Complexity

Over time, the beginning student becomes increasingly aware of the complexity of human nature and the change processes. This awareness initiates a search for a conceptual system that will assist in organizing the data and provide guidance for how to act as professional. A female later in the Beginning Student Phase said:

> I see more than I used to and am looking for more parts of the professional role. I'm now trying to find ways to get to the underlying problems and therefore long-term solutions, rather than a short-lived quick fix of feeling better because of counselor support.

The search for a way to conceptually organize the complexity experienced becomes a major task involving vigilance and preoccupation. As mentioned earlier, the conceptual systems of respected professional elders within the training institution (i.e., professors and supervisors) play a major role in this selection process, as does the conceptual system used at the site or work setting where the individual may be working as a practicum student.

Contemporary issues endorsed by the training institution influence the definition of the work role. Within the popular professional focus, there is often a specific focus on (a) *certain client concerns*, for example, shame, career decision making, domestic abuse, cognitive impairment, attention deficit disorder, eating disorders, stepfamilies, attention deficit disorder; (b) *populations of individuals,* for example, depressed adolescents, violent adult males, individuals from other cultures, adult children of alcoholics, adolescents with eating disorders, adults who lose their jobs because of a company restructuring, child victims of intrafamilial sexual abuse; or (c) *specific counseling/treatment forms,* such as mindfulness, mentalization based therapy, short-term therapy, or motivational interviewing. The beginning student may prefer to focus on one or two of these topics in order to feel competent, but increasingly Novice Students embrace the opportunity to explore multiple client concerns and various approaches to therapy and counseling.

Attitude to Theory

After we analyzed the research participants' interview data about the beginning students' attitude to theory, we differentiated between four attitudes to theory, which are: laissez faire, one-dominant "open," true believer, and multiple attachments. In chapter 10, we discuss how an open attitude to theory facilitates professional development while a restricted or closed attitude may lead to stagnation. It is likely that students' affective functioning (in particular capacity to modulate affect) and cognitive capacity (in particular capacity for cognitive complexity) combine to impact formation of the students' attitude to theory.

1. *Laissez faire* refers to an attitude of not valuing theory or not being invested in any conceptual system. For the few students with this attitude to theory, previously held notions of common sense coexist with a variety of ideas from theory/research, clients, supervisors, peers, and one's personal life. Some of the students in our study claim that experience is the primary knowledge base (practice-based knowledge). Typically, these students seem not to be highly reflective on the epistemological base of their practice, and we may hypothesize that these students may typically not be strong in tasks that require high cognitive complexity to be completed successfully.
2. The student with the *one-dominant "open"* attitude to theory, which was the one most frequently endorsed, has given priority to learning one conceptual system, but has maintained an openness to other systems.
3. The student with the *"true believer"* orientation has focused intensively on learning one method and actively rejects other viewpoints. As was hypothesized for the laissez-faire therapists, the "true believer" may also not be strong in tasks requiring high cognitive complexity.

4. The student we described as having the *multiple attachment* attitude to theory is typically a serious student with many ideas, but one who gives no priority to any one system.

In our view the one dominant "open" and the multiple attachment attitudes are expressions of an inquisitive, curious, and exploring stance, which we interpreted to be conducive for optimal professional development. The laissez-faire and true believer attitude however, may restrict learning and developmental potential and students with that view may be candidates for later stagnation.

Measures of Effectiveness and Satisfaction

The young, inexperienced Novice Student asks him- or herself a crucial question: I may be able to do all the academic work, but am I any good at really helping people with their personal problems? The new graduate student with paraprofessional experience often asks a slightly different question: Am I going to get any better at doing this? To answer these questions, the beginning student looks eagerly for client improvement and acknowledgment of this improvement by the client. Effectiveness is primarily assessed by the degree to which the client simply returns for sessions, tells directly and explicitly that constructive change has taken place, and that the therapy/counseling is responsible for the change. Work satisfaction is directly related to client improvement. Indications of appreciation from the client, whether they are verbal, written, or gifts are greatly appreciated and sometimes subtly sought. A lack of improvement and acknowledgment of the helpful ways of the therapist are stressful for the beginner and direct client hostility toward the therapist is experienced as being very aversive.

Typical Novice Students are constantly monitoring their performance. They do so in various ways. In practicum, the arena where they have the most direct access to how their classmates are doing, is an arena for comparisons. In supervision, they get and enlist feedback from their supervisors which is used to gauge their performance from a professional perspective. Feedback from clients, which may also be discussed with peers, assists Novice Students in evaluating their performance.

If Novice Students master the developmental tasks for the phase, that is, have met the criteria for conceptual knowledge and procedural competence set by the training institution, have reasonably well handled the emotional reactions that ensue from the challenges encountered, and have managed to maintain an attitude of openness while also "closing off" sufficiently to select therapy approaches to use, the scene is set for a constructive movement into the Advanced Student Phase.

Notes

1. Previous versions of this chapter were published in *The Evolving Professional Self,* by T. M. Skovholt and M. H. Rønnestad (1992). Copyright has reverted to the authors. Chichester, England: Wiley, and in "The Journey of the Counselor and Therapist: Research Findings and Perspectives," by M. H. Rønnestad & T. M. Skovholt (2003), in *Journal of Career Development, 30,* 5–44, 2003. Adapted with permission from Sage. All quotes are from *The Evolving Professional Self.*

2. Examples of difficulty items in the *Development of Psychotherapist Common Core Questionnaire*: A lack of confidence that you can have a beneficial effect on a client; unsure of how best to deal with a client; [feeling] in danger of losing control of the therapeutic situation to a client; distressed by the powerlessness to affect a client's tragic life situation; troubled by moral or ethical issues that have arisen in work with a client; irritated with a client who is actively blocking your efforts; guilty about having mishandled a critical situation with a client.

3. We are not using the term *sources of influence* in a positivist causal sense, but as a retrospective construal of experiences.

4. We know that therapists/counselors seek therapy for various and interrelated reasons (Orlinsky, Rønnestad, Willutzki, Wiseman, Botermans, & the SPR Collaborative Research Network, 2005), and that the outcomes are varied but generally positive (Orlinsky, Norcross, Ronnestad, & Wiseman, 2005a). A British study of therapists with between 4 and 7 years of experience suggested that therapist attachment styles and capacity for reflective functioning may impact the outcome of therapists' personal therapy (Rizq & Target, 2010). The results suggested that insecurely attached therapists with low levels of reflective functioning reported that therapy was not valuable for managing complex process issues, but was valuable for behavioral modeling. Securely attached therapists with ordinary levels of reflective functioning found therapy to be helpful in processing feelings that were evoked by difficult or challenging clients.

5. *The Development of Psychotherapists Common Core Questionnaire* used in this research contained the following items to assess sources of influence: experience in therapy with patients; getting formal supervision or consultation; getting personal therapy, analysis, or counseling; experiences in personal life outside of therapy; having informal case discussion with colleagues; taking courses or seminars; reading books or journals relevant to your practice; giving formal supervision or consultation to others; working with cotherapists; observing therapists in workshops, films, or tape; the institutional conditions in which you practice; teaching courses or seminars; doing research; other.

6. Medical students tell a similar story. When studying the human body, medical students apply their new knowledge to themselves in a parallel way.

7. See the generic model of psychotherapy formulated by Orlinsky and Howard for a description of the relationship between the input (including therapists' conceptual models) and the processes of psychotherapy (including the contractual aspect and the operational aspect, i.e., what therapists and clients do; Orlinsky, Rønnestad, & Willutzki, 2004, pp. 307–389).

5

THE ADVANCED STUDENT PHASE[1]

I've learned that the basic stuff of active listening and support suffices at many times and this really helps. But it is also true that there is so much to know about specifics. I have to learn, but don't have time!

Definition

The modal student is in the last part of graduate training and is working as a therapist or counselor in a setting such as a practicum, internship, clerkship, or field placement, and is receiving regular and formalized supervision. For this chapter, we will use the terms *Advanced Student* and *intern* interchangeably.

Developmental Tasks and General Description

There are five developmental tasks during this phase. The first three are similar to the developmental tasks of the beginning student:

1. To learn more complex conceptual knowledge that meets the criteria set by the training institution.
2. To demonstrate procedural competence; that is, sufficient mastery of assessment and therapeutic skills as assessed by supervisors in particular.
3. To maintain an openness to information and theory at a metalevel, while also engaging in the "closing off" process of selecting therapy/counseling theories and techniques to use.
4. To modify unrealistic and perfectionistic images of psychotherapy and counseling and of the role of the practitioner.
5. To manage the bewilderment that comes from seeing psychotherapy/counseling as increasingly complex.

The first two developmental tasks, that is, to meet the criteria for conceptual knowledge and procedural competence set by the educational system, including the supervisor, entail "filling the gaps" of knowledge and competence before graduation. Both tasks generate a tension in the Advanced Student because they are increasingly defining what types of conceptual knowledge are seen as most relevant. There is often an eagerness, but not necessarily readiness to work independently. Many Advanced Students have high aspirations for their functioning and want not only to avoid making mistakes, but also to excel in their work. The tension is increased as the intern feels pressured to do things more correctly than ever before. A consequence of this is that interns usually behave conservatively and cautiously. They are typically not relaxed, risk taking, creative, or spontaneous, and there is little natural playfulness or sense of humor in their work. This more constrained style is driven by an external evaluation system that is constantly monitoring the intern's performance.

When comparing one's professional competence to that of beginning students, the Advanced Student appreciates that professional training has made an impact. As one intern said, "I have gone from being petrified to being comfortable," or, as another said:

Now I'm more self-assured, more firm, and less chameleonlike, more assertive and direct without being directive, and less afraid. It used to be that I was terrified before sessions … I'm less afraid of losing patients than in the past.

When the reference point for evaluating one's competence changes to that of the professional practitioner, the Advanced Student realizes there is still much to learn. As a practitioner, the Advanced Student may still feel vulnerable and insecure and actively seek confirmation and feedback from seniors and peers. Lacking confidence in their counseling or therapy skills is still reported by Advanced Students. As one said, "There weren't many times I felt highly competent. I questioned, am I in the right place, is this what I should do?" This questioning documents the external dependency still present at this phase, but as we will see, the Advanced Student also expresses self-confidence and agency. The professional self is still fragile.

Sources of Influence and Learning Process

The Advanced Student phase is a highly engaging period of training. Socialization and enculturation processes into the field are intensified, processes that peak during the next phase. The Advanced Students judge their competence by three benchmarks: the assumed competence of the experienced practitioners in the field, the skill level of other interns, and the skill level of less experienced beginning practicum students.

Interns continue to process data from all sources of influence mentioned earlier. Acquisition-application-validation sequences described in the previous chapter summarize a learning heuristic for the intern as well. As one intern said, "For me, this (active experimentation) applies both to experimenting with myself (i.e., deepening my affective reflections) and with techniques (making my interventions on the spot by acting on hunches)."

Methods and techniques that seem to work, and are used again, are reinforced by positive responses or positive movement of clients.

Modeling

Now, there is a refined use of modeling in the sense that the Advanced Students can accept or reject parts of what a senior is demonstrating. As the interns have already gone through several acquisition, application, and validation sequences with models, they are now more active than before in selecting and rejecting model components. A male intern said, "I take what I like." A female intern said that, "One's own counseling [or personal therapy] exerts a powerful influence, there's always the, 'What would my therapist do in this situation?' to fall back on." Another female intern said of models, "My God, I don't want to be like that!"

Often, therapists in training are frustrated by the lack of opportunities to observe senior practitioners in their work. One female intern said, "I wanted more opportunities to watch experienced practitioners at work." Another female intern said:

> I had very little opportunity to observe experienced practitioners even after repeated requests of a supervisor. The only model of an experienced person I had was the Gloria films. Supervisors and experienced people were unwilling to demonstrate skills.

Since many Advanced Students have so few live models to observe, students who are in personal therapy emphasize how important this experience is as a source of learning. The pedagogical value of personal therapy is thus emphasized by both the Novice Student and the Advanced Student.

The modal intern is now more critical than before toward the educational system, and toward professors, supervisors, and assumed experts. "The extreme trust I had in experienced counselors as people to copy is not so true now because I have seen so many different styles," said one female intern. They may argue that renowned therapists are not living up to the high standards of professional competence that they set. This can be illustrated by a recent experience that the first author had when first showing an APA demonstration DVD of a well-known and skilled therapist to a group of highly reputed therapists (many had received nominations by peers as expert psychotherapists), and thereafter to a group of advanced psychology students in psychotherapy training. The two groups evaluated the DVSs differently. The "expert group" rated the quality of the work demonstrated as very high and had few negative comments. The Advanced Student group rated the quality of the work lower, and pointed to what they saw as weaknesses and limitations in the therapist's way of functioning.

How can we understand the difference between how these groups evaluated the quality of the therapist's work? One hypothesis is that the Advanced Student group assessed the demonstration DVD using highly perfectionistic and idealistic criteria in their evaluation of therapist functioning. This hypothesis is consistent with typical characteristics of the Advanced Students. It is also possible that despite all they had learned during therapy training, the Advanced Students were not able to detect the high quality of the therapists' functioning. The critical comments may also reflect that the Advanced Students were saying to themselves and to me, Helge, as their teacher that they have learned a lot and are getting ready to graduate. Along this last line of reasoning, the Advanced Students may be expressing the part of their professional self that is self-confident and assured. In the original formulation of the stage model of professional development (Skovholt & Rønnestad, 1992/1995), the name of the stage covering the Advanced Student phase was *conditional autonomy*, thus indicating tentativeness in the students' self-efficacy.

The Influence of Personal Therapy and Other Arenas for Personal Exploration

Throughout their training, students have been wondering how their personalities influence their work. We reported previously on the psychologizing of the beginning student. At the Advanced Student phase, the issue is placed on the front burner. The intensive psychological course work, the active discussions with classmates, the stimulation of personal issues brought about by working with clients, and supervisory experiences have all been sources that have stimulated personal exploration. For example, one male in this phase said, "Counselor training made me powerfully aware of things I was blissfully unaware of before."

Some seek personal therapy or counseling now and if personal growth and professional development groups are not provided for within the framework of the training program, students may start such groups on their own initiative. In addition, if supervision is regarded as a safe learning environment, the intern may also want to discuss more personal issues with the supervisor, like, for example, how personal characteristics influence their work with clients.

We know that students as well as postgraduate therapists seek personal therapy for different reasons (Orlinsky, Norcross, Rønnestad, &

Wiseman, 2005; Orlinsky & Rønnestad, 2005). This research has shown that the majority of therapists who have been in therapy, including those in training and beyond, have done so for more than one of the following reasons: growth, training, personal problems. A potential effect of personal therapy was illustrated by one of our male interns, who said, "I did not like emotions, and this made it easy for me to develop technique-oriented approaches. But after participating in group therapy, I turned my focus more to the affective."

The Influence of Supervision

At this phase, the student invests much energy in the supervisory experience. As for the preceding phase, supervision rates as a highly impactful source of influence and nonconfirming supervision experiences can be highly detrimental, possibly even more detrimental than for the Novice Student. More is at stake now, as the students are further along in their training and are supposed to master professional tasks with more proficiency. Although it seems that the Advanced Students experience supervision as mostly positive, conflicts in supervision may nevertheless peak at this phase of professional development. The dependency of the intern and the need to meet the expectations of the graduate program, in combination with the aspirations to be autonomous, may contribute to the ambivalence that many Advanced Students report. These dynamics may also increase the tension and constant self-evaluation reported by the Advanced Student during the internship.

In a retrospective view, a therapist in the next phase of development (The Novice Professional Phase) reflected on her critical assessment of her supervisors while at the Advanced Student Phase. She said: "I wanted to believe that supervisors knew more than I did. It was disappointing to discover that they didn't. It reminded me of an earlier realization that ministers make mistakes." Interns want to be on their own, while also needing to meet the requirements of the gatekeepers. As mentioned earlier, the Advanced Student's struggle with dependency–independence issues, which led us to formulate initially the advanced student stage as "Conditional Autonomy," is highly consistent with Hogan's (1964) description of Level 2 therapists, which we repeat here: "At this level, the psychotherapists struggle with a dependency–autonomy conflict. In their quest to find their own adaptation, they vacillate between feeling overconfident and being overwhelmed" (p. 139).

In chapter 1, we also referred to the model of counselor development by Loganbill, Hardy, and Delworth (1982). The description of their second stage, "Confusion," converges with the reports from our participants; for example, students' fluctuate between a sense of expertise and a sense of failure and incompetence. Furthermore, their attitude to supervisors often changes from "positively toned dependency to disappointment and anger, a shift that can be quite uncomfortable to both parties" (p. 18).

It is also interesting to see these findings in light of the work that has been done on supervisee nondisclosure. The studies on the topic by Yourman and Farber (1996); Ladany, Hill, Corbett, and Nutt (1996); as well as by a group of Scandinavian researchers (Nielsen et al., 2009; Reichelt et al., 2009; Skjerve et al., 2009), have all documented high levels of non-disclosure in supervision for graduate students in counseling and psychotherapy. Since more than half (57%) the participants in the original study by Ladany et al. (1996) were in an advanced practicum or internship, and all of the participants in the Scandinavian studies were advanced graduate students, the results of these studies are relevant for understanding the paramount importance that the supervisor plays for the intern. The convergence of many of the results across countries also confirms the generality of findings.[2]

The overall story is one in which the students invest themselves intensely in the learning experience that supervision provides. Although students are vulnerable, they are also agentic. They consistently scrutinize the reaction of the supervisor and continually evaluate the quality of the supervision they take part in and the qualifications of the supervisor. But in spite of this continual assessment of the supervisors, the Advanced Students generally want more honest and direct feedback from their supervisors than they get. In a later discussion on supervisory implications from our findings (chapter 11), we will address the topic of supervisor feedback.

Since the Scandinavian study investigated not only supervisee nondisclosure, but also supervisor nondisclosure in group supervision, it was possible to explore convergence/divergence across observational perspectives. The results are a testimony to the lack of intersubjectivity between participants in supervision. Specifically, students believed that the supervisor was not communicating to the supervisee his or her assessment of the work that the supervisee was doing, and that the supervisor was not providing the feedback the students needed. The supervisor was concerned with providing feedback in a pedagogical way, and told of indirect strategies to influence the supervisee, which were quite different from what the supervisee wanted.

Although supervisors are a powerful source of influence at this phase, we see from our own research and from the research presented above that this influence can be moderated by the intern's perception of the supervisor's competence. Additionally, the intern's peer and senior level support system and the intern's age and experience base moderate the influence of the supervisor.

We see a gradual movement in students as they progress through training in that they become somewhat less dependent on constant positive feedback from clients. Even so, the Advanced Student still wants and appreciates positive feedback from clients. However, statements such as the following affect the student less than before: "I'm sorry I can't come to counseling tonight. I have too much on my mind." It is typical for messages such as this to be highly unsettling to a beginning student who would be likely to interpret such a statement as a devaluation, and would be less capable of judging the meaning of such communication. Now, as interns, they have a wider repertoire of perspectives for understanding the possible dynamics that may be in play, and thus are better able to respond therapeutically.

The Influence of Peers

Working in a setting with other interns is generally highly appreciated. Peers are an important resource for the Advanced Student; they are on the same "wavelength" in terms of experience and status, and are usually trustworthy. The work on supervisee nondisclosure is also a testimony to the important role played by peers because the material that students did not disclose to their supervisors was often discussed with their peers (Ladany et al., 1996).

The Influence of Theories and Research

To the intern, general theories and research in the broad academic sense are of diminished interest, much to the frustration of some teachers, although specific therapy/counseling issues are of heightened interest. One intern level person summed up the point when she said, "Client issues define what I read about and explore in the literature." The intern who feels unprepared for a specific client issue (e.g., depression, phobic anxiety, eating disorders), may expend much energy in reading, discussing, and attending workshops on this topic. But it is not only academic literature that attracts the attention of the Advanced Student. A female in this phase said, "I stopped reading textbooks and started reading self-help books. I thought the faculty in my department would die if they found out." The focus is on quickly learning what is needed. Accompanying this expenditure of energy may be anger directed toward the training program for not sufficiently preparing the intern on topics that relate directly to working with clients.

The Influence of Clients

Clients continue to be a very strong source of influence. How clients react and evaluate the therapist directly impacts the intern's sense of confidence, and is a valuable source of learning. As we will see below when we discuss how the Advanced Student assesses the effectiveness and satisfaction of work, clients' evaluations of therapy intensively attracts the intern's attention. The feedback that clients provide is filtered and enhanced by the supervisor's interpretation of the student's work. Research within the Society for Psychotherapy Research/Collaborative Research Network (SPR/CRN) has convincingly demonstrated that the quality of therapists' involvement styles with clients is the strongest predictor of professional growth and stagnation (Orlinsky & Rønnestad, 2005). This will be described in more detail in chapter 14.

The Influence of Being a Supervisor

Some interns supervise beginning practicum students, and those who do typically report this to be a significant source of influence. One student, reflecting on her experience as a supervisor while an intern, said: "It was a concrete realization of what I had learned. It was really valuable. The contrast between them and me helped me see my own style and how far I had come in my development." The first author was fortunate to have had the experience of supervising master practicum counseling students as an intern. The experience of being supervised on one's supervisory skills (*supervision on supervision*) emerged as one of the stronger learning experiences while in graduate school.

Professional Role and Conceptual Ideas Used

The Advanced Students see the therapy process as being increasingly more complex. The sympathetic friendship role (for example, the use of common sense and being a friend) is no longer valid. Compared to the entry level students, the Advanced Students feel they have a better grasp of what the professional role is like. At this point, the student may be embarrassed about early definitions of the role such as all that is needed is for the therapist to be a person who understands and accepts the client, or as one said, provide "a shoulder to weep on." The simplicity of the pretraining helper is largely gone and former ideas seem to be naive notions in comparison with newer ideas suggested in graduate school. Yet, some of the old skills seem to fit because empathy and related concepts such as the therapeutic bond are appropriate descriptions for the therapist role, and also have much empirical support. Nevertheless, the students keep asking questions such as: "Is this all, or is there more, and if so, what is it?" The Advanced Students find it cognitively challenging and emotionally taxing to explore these questions.

A student expressed her awareness of the complexity of human nature and the change process this way:

I see more than I used to and am looking for more parts of the professional role. I'm now trying to find ways to get to the underlying problems and, therefore, long-term solutions, rather than a short-lived quick fix of feeling better because of counselor support.

Contributing to this change is the experience of the Advanced Students that to help friends, family, and acquaintances is not as easy as previously thought. The less difficult aspects of the work may still not be fully mastered, and the Advanced Student may also struggle with relating competently to client problems which require therapist responses that go beyond providing emotional support. This includes specific problems that need specific solutions (e.g., panic attacks, career indecision, assessment of alcoholism, suicidal prevention steps). A male at this phase said, "I've learned that the basic stuff of active listening and support suffices at many times and this really helps. But it is also true that there is so much to know about specifics. I have to learn, but don't have time!"

An intensive study of psychotherapy training in Norway confirms how difficult it is, even for the Advanced Student, to supplement the nonprofessional ways of helping, such as merely providing support, with more advanced therapeutic behavior that demonstrates strategic and purposeful actions (Strømme, 2010). These struggles are likely common across cultures.

As with the beginning student, the Advanced Students are also searching for ways to manage the complexity and concurrently form a professional role that is manageable given their level of expertise. These become major tasks that involve vigilance and preoccupation. The Advanced Student is inspired by various sources of inspiration, such as the role performed by respected professional elders within the training institution (i.e., professors and supervisors), and by the popular foci of treatment in the training institution and larger professional community as well. As is true for the Beginning Student, dominant issues of the training institution, such as specific client concerns (e.g., career decision making, eating disorders), populations of individuals (e.g., depressed alcoholics, violent adult males), and specific treatment forms (e.g., mindfulness, motivational interviewing) contribute to defining the professional role for the Advanced Student.

A gradual move from acquiring *general knowledge* regarding how to conceptualize and act when meeting clients, toward also assessing clients in their *contexts* and focusing on *individual differences* in clients and adapting therapeutic interventions accordingly, is instrumental in seeing the therapy process as complex. However, if the shift toward focusing on individual differences is limited to see clients in diagnostic terms, and therapeutic interventions are manualized, the professional role is structured, clear, transparent, but restricted.

In the beginning of the Advanced Student phase, aspirations are typically quite high and the student therapists typically tend to think that they will be able to help all or most clients. The internalized high standards for professional functioning contribute to a tendency toward excessive and misunderstood responsibility. A female Advanced Student said, "Every single request for consultation I wanted to do. I wanted to learn things and to prove to the director of training that I could do the job." A male intern said, "I do a good job of letting myself feel responsible for everything." To refer a client to another therapist is difficult because it may signal incompetence. As one male addressing these issues at this phase said, "I thought I could and should help everybody."

As mentioned, in their striving to do things perfectly, there is little playfulness in the work of the interns. In relation to role and working style, they can be described as serious and strident and as intensely focusing on what is appropriate. Compared with therapists 20 years later, the intern is typically not relaxed, risk taking, or spontaneous. A female reflecting back said, "As an intern I had the idea of this counselor role I had to play. Later it was a revelation when I found out I could be myself."

During the advanced practicum and internship, there occurs a change in the students' view on responsibility issues and perception of what the client can accomplish through therapy. The change is partly due to the student having experienced, both personally and also vicariously through the observation of others, that all clients are not helped and that it takes longer to reach therapeutic objectives than previously thought.

Toward the end of the internship, the student therapist is developing more elaborate ways of understanding the change process in therapy and is developing more realistic expectations of what can be accomplished, at what pace, and in what amount of time. In the future, small humiliations will reduce the grandiosity of believing that one can make powerful changes in others' lives. Also, there is a movement toward no longer feeling fully responsible for the client's emotional health. The students know that they are responsible for behaving according to some, though still not fully clear, standard for professional conduct. One person described the evolution for herself as, "Intellectually I know that I am not totally responsible, but emotionally I feel that it is up to me to make the client's life better."

Increasingly, the Advanced Student is able to differentiate between more important and less important data, and consequently writes shorter case note summaries and more easily selects issues/problems to discuss in supervision. For example, a female intern found, "As I got more confident, I realized that I didn't have to remember every detail. The point of notes was not to get everything down, but to be able to connect with the client."

The intern's conceptual system is often stretched by difficult cases. Individuals at this phase mentioned the following client experiences or behavior as difficult for them: intense anger, severe pathology such as schizophrenia and personality disorders, sexual abuse, boredom and apathy, strong depression, and suicidal behavior.

Each conceptual model of therapy contains a description of, and explanation for, how client change is achieved (e.g., curative factor, effective factors, healing ingredient). Conceptual models also specify (to varying degrees of specificity) ideal characteristics of therapists and what they need to do in order to be effective helpers. We have observed that attributes of the ideal therapeutic self (as it is perceived by the therapist) often matches the explicit or implicit demands of the conceptual model chosen by the therapists. There may be a strong projective component when the student is determining what constitutes effectiveness. For example, one Advanced Student characterized himself as world traveled and world wise. Later, he cited the necessity of the counselor having varied interests and world sophistication as key elements to success. Another Advanced Student characterized herself as a good listener and as understanding. She later emphasized these elements in her "good therapist" description.

Measures of Effectiveness and Satisfaction

In the preceding phase, the students were constantly comparing their performance with peers. Effectiveness was largely assessed by the degree to which the client returned for sessions, expressed (verbally or otherwise) satisfaction with therapy and by the feedback provided by the supervisor. One female Senior Student talked of how she used to measure her success as follows, "Formerly, success was if they liked me, talked a lot, and returned. Now it is more if some kind of changes occurred." At the Advanced Student phase, the supervisor's assessment is still important as receiving good evaluations from supervisors is interpreted to mean that they have been competent and successful. As one female intern said, "I felt successful if the supervisor assessed me as doing the appropriate things, rather than just feeling successful if the client said he had improved." But as we have described earlier, feelings of ambivalence toward the supervisor, and critical evaluation of supervisor expertise may moderate supervisor impact.

Work satisfaction is directly related to therapists' sense of competence and as described earlier, it vacillates. Comparing themselves to others is still a strategy to modulate one's professional self. One male intern expressed it this way, "Since the beginning I saw PhDs who couldn't help people. So, I saw myself as no worse" and a female intern processing her lack of perfection put it this way:

I'm used to being at the top of rating scales. It was hard at first not to be defensive and take it hard. I did some reframing and said I won't be an excellent therapist yet because I am not very experienced.

Although we see some continuity in how the Beginning and the Advanced Student assesses his or her effectiveness, there is a shift away from relying heavily on client statements only, toward increasingly relying on more subtle and nuanced ways of assessing change. This is the beginning of a process that continues for many years. A post intern looked back at the Advanced Student Phase, and commented:

> When I was an intern I felt that I was to be in control and [be] powerful. That made me feel responsible. Later it was different. My anxiety went down, I gave up some of the control and I felt less responsible. That helped me see client improvement or lack of improvement as depending on more than me.

Compared with earlier phases, the intern experiences the "buffer effect" of many clients and does not need to be successful with all to feel successful. If the therapist has one client only, the aversive and potentially detrimental effects of experiencing failure with the one, in combination with a conflict with the supervisor, is highly stressful. The term *double traumatization* (Rønnestad & Orlinsky, 2005) is used for such experiences.

Notes

1. Previous versions of this chapter were published in *The Evolving Professional Self,* by T. M. Skovholt and M. H. Rønnestad (1992), pp. 42–49. Copyright is reverted to the authors. Chichester, England: Wiley, and in "The Journey of the Counselor and Therapist: Research Findings and Perspectives," by M. H. Rønnestad & T. M. Skovholt (2003), in *Journal of Career Development, 30,* 5–44, 2003. Adapted with permission from Sage. All quotes are from *The Evolving Professional Self.*
2. We share the distinction made between *generalizability of findings* from *generality of findings.* While generalizability of findings refers to knowledge claims generated from studies of representative samples, generality of findings refers to consistency in findings across studies of unknown representativeness (Orlinsky & Rønnestad, 2005).

6

THE NOVICE PROFESSIONAL PHASE[1]

I felt like it was only me going through the disillusionment with what I didn't know. Once I started talking with colleagues, I found that there were others in the same place. Then I didn't feel quite as alone.

Definition

The Novice Professional phase is defined less precisely than the two student phases, but for most therapists this phase will encompass the first 2 to 5 years after graduation. Generally, these years are experienced as highly intense and engaging; there are many challenges to master and many choices to be made.

Developmental Tasks and General Descriptions

There are four developmental tasks in this phase:

1. To develop an identification with the profession and commitment to the professional sector to which the person belongs (e.g., counseling, psychology, psychiatry, etc.).
2. To succeed in the transformation from the dependency of graduate school to the independence that is expected, both from oneself and from others, after having completed professional training.
3. To master any disillusionment with training, self, and the profession that may emerge some time after graduation.
4. To keep exploring and defining one's work role.

As will be described more fully below, the Novice Professional phase may be divided into three subphases, confirmation, disillusionment, and exploration. In the confirmation subphase, the Novice Professional invests considerable attention toward confirming the validity of the training that has been newly completed, and intensifies a process of identification with the profession. In the disillusionment subphase, the Novice Professional struggles emotionally with the disheartening experience of realizing the limitations of different aspects of self and the profession. In the exploration subphase (see pp. 90–91 for description), two active searches occur: an "inward" search toward one's professional and personal self, and an "outward" search toward the professional world (e.g., workplace, alternative work settings).

Confirmation Subphase

In the confirmation subphase, the validity and meaning of one's education is at stake. This is a serious and deeply meaningful issue for the practitioner, and one which poses particular challenges for the recent graduate. Novice Professionals want to ascertain that their newly completed education can be applied toward solving the challenges of work. They want to apply those methods and techniques that were acquired in graduate school and be assured that they are useful and meaningful in their professional practice. The emphasis is on confirmation and validation, and these processes take precedence over experimentation and innovation.

However, at this point, there is still a sense of freedom. For the first time, the Novice Professional may feel free of external constraints (e.g., practicum, internship, supervisor evaluations, oral and written exams, the cultural pressures of the training program). Typically, the recent graduate is proud to have completed training and proud to have graduated from the university or college where the training occurred. Often, the recent graduate is also pleased, and possibly even thrilled, to be considered as a professional in the eyes of the public, and perhaps be called "doctor." But, as one practitioner formulated it, "Having less guidance from professors and supervisors was scary." Another said, "People weren't protecting you from taking on too much anymore."

The developmental task of building a professional identity and cementing a commitment to the profession is crucial for work satisfaction. It is also an important building block in forming the professional self. This identification process, which, for the new professional, involves identification with commonly accepted attributes (norms, values, ethical principles, etc.) of the profession, may be enhanced if the new graduate is employed in a work setting with several colleagues of the same profession, and the profession has a good reputation and strong position within the work setting. An example may be a counselor who has trained at a reputable college of education, and who now works in a career development center that is primarily staffed by graduates from education programs. Another example may be a therapist who has received training from a clinical training program, and who is now employed in a mental health clinic with a strong clinical culture.

The identification process may be hampered, but could also be intensified, if the new graduate is employed in a work setting with a culture that does not match the new graduate's professional self and identity. Torn between identifying with the work setting or with the profession, the new graduate may experience a tension that facilitates reflections on the question: Who can I be as a professional? This question may be particularly pressing if the new graduate is employed as the only representative of a particular profession in a work setting with a culture that does not match the professional self and identity of the graduate.

The career theories of Holland (1997) and Super (1980) are particularly helpful in understanding the processes that Novice Professionals go through when their personalities encounter different work worlds. Meeting colleagues in arenas such as postgraduate training (e.g., workshops, seminars), conferences, and at professional organization gatherings are all activities that contribute to the socialization process of the Novice Professional. These activities are usually highly valued because they provide a sense of continuity with the learning process and enable contact with peers from graduate school. They may re-create the sense of companionship that perhaps was lost upon graduation.

Disillusionment Subphase

However, our empirical data suggest that, for many graduate practitioners, a surprising sense of disappointment and disillusionment is experienced after the early effort to confirm the validity and adequacy of training. Examples of difficulties that the Novice Professional may experience, and that fuel the disillusionment, are:

- Discovering that clients do not improve as much as expected.
- Finding it more difficult to establish a working alliance with clients than anticipated.
- Having clients dropping out of therapy/counseling at a greater rate than expected.
- Realizing the emotional engagement in client work is more intense than foreseen.
- Not succeeding in the emotional disengagement from difficult cases after regular working hours.
- Having intense conflicts arising during collaboration with other professionals.

Experiences such as those described in the examples above can result in a disheartening doubt arising about one's own abilities, and may also lead to questioning one's training and one's profession. Some of the specifics

85

that we have learned about disillusionment from interviews of therapists/s at the Novice Professional phase are shared below.

At the Novice Professional phase, new practitioners evaluate the theoretical foundations for their therapeutic work. An individual who had previously relied on a single conceptual system may face disappointment with that approach. A male practitioner, reflecting back to this phase, said, "I went through a stage of being depressed about work, feeling it was too much work trying to fit people to the model. I found out it didn't turn out for clients the way theory said it was supposed to."

An individual with a math and science undergraduate degree entered a graduate program with a strong, research-based, empirical approach. As he applied what he had learned, an approach with an emphasis on precision and rationality, to spinal cord injury patients, he was overwhelmed by their emotional anguish and pain. He said, "Sometimes you feel like you were trying to fight a forest fire with a glass of water." The disillusionment that he experienced, gradually led him to an industrial consulting position with which there was a better fit between his personality, the conceptual model, and the needs of the clients.

Yet another graduate, who had trained to be a therapist, found that the poor, disadvantaged clients with whom she was working benefited very little from her efforts. Clients with multiple problems seemed to be in need of much broader and more intense interventions than could be provided by the conceptual model that she had been taught as part of the clinical psychology training program. For this therapist, the uncertainty resulted in her taking a later assessment position in which she did not have to feel the impotence of her earlier work.

Disillusionment with a particular chosen theory/method seems to occur most quickly when the therapists work with a heterogeneous client population with a wide array of client concerns, or work with a client population different from the ones for which the one method was developed. As referred to in chapter 4, Maslow elegantly addressed the relationship between skills and behavior in the well-known aphorism: "If the only tool you have is a hammer, [you tend] to treat everything as if it were a nail" (Maslow, 1966, p. 15). The problem is, of course, that not everything is a nail.

Generally, the individual at the Novice Professional phase realizes that context-free theory is inadequate. There is an increasing recognition that theory alone does not provide an adequate guide, and disillusionment often relates to realizing the limits of context-free theory. A male who was in the exploration phase said, "All conceptual models blow a tire after three months. I'm always amazed by the complexity of people's minds and their unique problems. This means I need to adjust the conceptual model to the person."

Inadequate client progress can fuel a sense of inadequacy and contribute to a sense of disappointments with self. A male therapist described his reactions this way:

> I used to think that my doubts about me and my despair would go away with the degree.... Now people look at me, call me doctor, and want more and expect more. But what am I going after? It is a disorienting process because I don't know any more now, except that there are more expectations. It is great to be done, but what do I really want to be? Where did I really want to go? I didn't expect the formal training would lead to feeling adequate, until I felt inadequate, and then realized how much I expected to know by now. My professional training was over and I lacked so much.

A female subject, two years after graduate school, said:

> It was unduly optimistic to believe that graduate school fully prepared me. Instead, it provided a basic knowledge and tools for acquiring more knowledge and skill. It has taken a few years to appreciate this gradual shift in my expectations.

Feelings of anger, turmoil, uncertainty, and anxiety are common reactions to these realizations. While in graduate school, reactions such as these were normative, and, as such, also less provocative. Now, the expectations are to be competent and to master any difficulties that are encountered. Given the expectations of mastery, the unexpected hardships feel distressing. One male therapist looked back at this time and said, "There were days when everything I touched turned into horseshit. Whatever made me think I could do it or that it worked? It was a sham. People were paying me to make money off their pain."

However, the positive side of critiquing conceptual models is the Novice Professional's ability to better identify situations where general principles do not hold. In the preceding chapter, we described a gradual movement in the Advanced Student's attitude to theory, a movement away from relying on *general knowledge* toward focusing more on knowledge of individual differences. This movement is intensified at the Novice Professional phase, and accompanied with resentment toward others, such as graduate school professors or supervisors, who strongly professed a theory that now seems to be inadequate in providing a framework for the work.

As previously stated, as a student, the therapist/counselor was intensely preoccupied with learning therapeutic approaches in order to be a competent practitioner, and focused on how to use particular methods or techniques. While a Beginning Student there was little preoccupation with critiquing these approaches. But now, in the Novice Professional phase, the situation has changed. Failure is increasingly attributed to inadequacies with the training program in general, and specifically with approaches acquired earlier. This change may partly be due to the absence of the critical eyes of supervisors and professors. However, some may attribute their failures to their own inabilities, which may lead to a practitioner leaving a particular type of work, either through a major career switch, or by focusing more on administration, teaching, research, or other fields which involve less direct service commitment.

Workshops are primary arenas for finding alternative approaches for the work. At this phase of development, workshops may offer new methods, that attract attention and curiosity, and which a Novice Professional might want to apply immediately in their work. As discussed later, workshops play a less prominent role as a potent source of influence for more experienced practitioners than for students.

When the causes of perceived failure cannot be identified by the Novice Professional, then the disillusionment may intensify. This might be experienced as the "loss of old signposts and the experience of being lost and alone in a chaotic world" (Widick, Knefelkamp, & Parker, 1980, p. 94). In such a situation, the practitioners typically experience considerable emotional pain and anguish. Signs of burnout, futility, and exhaustion develop, and although some individuals will continue, waiting out the disillusionment that they hope will vanish, for others this might present as an exit point from active occupational involvement with counseling/ therapy. Disillusionment with a conceptual system might be avoided if the individual continues to work with a narrow client base for which the particular approach was originally developed (e.g., cognitive behavioral therapy for specific anxiety disorders).

Unrealistic expectations of client improvement and idealistic perceptions of therapist power and expertise may fuel the disillusionment of the Novice Professionals. One female at this phase said, "I think I become more disillusioned when I have expectations that I need to do it all; it is my responsibility or fault if this person isn't getting better." More upsetting for therapists in this phase, is a pervasive disillusionment that is experienced when they are confronted with repeated treatment failures and excessive and disabling emotionality. Our current data is insufficient to reach a conclusion as to the prevalence of pervasive disillusionment for therapists in this phase.

Positive Coping with Adversity

In examining our data, it is our view that how therapists cope with the hardships and challenges of professional work is the most important determinant for practitioner development. Given the intensity of difficulties and disillusionment of the modal Novice Professional, this phase may pose a particular challenge to the quality of the practitioner's way of coping. We will describe this in more detail in chapter 10 when we present an integrative cyclical/trajectories model of therapist development and stagnation, but will address the topic briefly here.

Practitioners' ability to continuously process and reflect on the difficulties and challenges encountered is at the core of coping. Their affective functioning, and in particular their ability to process what can be called *negative affect* (e.g., anxiety, dejection) and cognitive functioning (and specifically capacity for cognitive complexity) impact *functional closure,* the ability to process information sufficiently in order to act therapeutically.

When challenges and difficulties are encountered in their work, therapists/counselors must avoid engaging in a pre- and unconscious defensive process, which we have called *premature closure,* in order to develop optimally. This process is characterized by misattribution, distortion, or dysfunctional reduction of phenomena when difficulties are encountered. Examples of premature closure include (a) the therapist explains client dropout as being due to insufficient client motivation, although a more logical reason for dropout was lack of therapist empathy (an example of misattribution); (b) the therapist erroneously interprets client aggression toward him- or herself as a transference reaction, but it is actually a client reaction to the therapist's lack of sensitivity and skill (distortion); and (c) the therapist's work fails because the therapy plan was based on a case formulation that was too simplistic and did not consider the life context of the client (dysfunctional reduction of phenomena encountered). For optimal development, therapists/counselors need to maintain an open, exploring attitude to the challenges and difficulties that are encountered, and avoid *premature closure.*

Sources of Influence and the Learning Process

As for the previous phases, sources of influence include: professional elders, such as professors, supervisors, mentors, or therapists; clients, personal life, peers/colleagues, theories/research, and the social/cultural environment. However, in the Novice Professional phase, the individuals, for the first time since the beginning of graduate school, are less directly affected by professional elders. Although many at this phase also seek supervision, the power and control aspects of supervision have less salience. Professors and supervisors no longer have the same direct authority over the individual and can no longer control what the individual can and must do. Professors no longer instruct the individuals to "jump through this hoop and that hoop." This freedom may feel wonderful, but may also result in something else: a surprising sense of uncertainty and loneliness that have arisen from suddenly being in command of one's own work. At this phase, peers are not as consistently available as they have been before, but if they are, peer support may moderate the sense of uncertainty and loneliness. One female said, "If there weren't good peers around, the feelings would have been much harder to handle."

If the emotional pressures that arise from the experiences of adversity and disillusionment are not overwhelming or intolerable, the Novice Professionals may react by analyzing and exploring their skills, limitations, values, attitudes, and interests. This internally focused processing might be accompanied with an outward directed exploration to identify work environments and work roles that are compatible with the professional self, a process that occurs with increasing intensity as the therapist becomes more experienced.

Instead of previous attempts to be a carbon copy of a master or a composite of masters, the individual now intensifies the process toward creating a work role that is congruent with self. The practitioner may engage in shedding some aspects of what has been learned as a student, perhaps after intense effort and achievement, while simultaneously continuing to add new assumptions, theories, and techniques to the conceptual repertoire.

We have formulated the construct *anchored conceptual structures* to capture the phenomenon where the new professionals integrate their personal epistemologies and worldviews with their professional self. This process, which may be viewed as *appropriation*[2] (Wertsch, 1998) is intensified in the Novice Professional phase and is important in the development of a coherent professional self.

The verbal expressions of these structures may be similar to those formulated in earlier phases. But now, with more extensive experience and after careful reflection, these structures are experienced as being indisputably true for the individual. Examples of such structures can be as simple as: "No substantial and lasting client change can be achieved without therapist empathy," or "No substantial and lasting client change can be achieved without activation of client affect," or "Careful cognitive analysis is the basis of all client change." Although simple in their form, these structures nevertheless represent deeply based truths for the practitioner. Structures such as these also influence subsequent theoretical and conceptual choices.

Exploration increasingly involves individualized, self-directed attention to both personal and theoretical issues. The search for effective techniques and strategies is not superficial, and contrasts with the imitative modeling previously described as being characteristic of a new student. As an expression of this active search, many therapists/counselors also want to learn the theoretical foundations for concepts that have now been recognized as important. The learning process is intense and can be characterized as a learning renaissance.

The inward searching of the exploration subphase can also been expressed by many Novice Professionals seeking personal therapy and counseling. Starting personal therapy during this phase is typically done with profundity and from an explicit recognition of need. This differs from entering personal therapy as a ritual step, and in order to comply with the implicit (or explicit) demands of the therapy culture. However, seeking personal therapy can also be conceptualized as taking one of the steps to become enculturated into the profession. In the Novice Professional phase, many report greater interest in understanding their own motivation for entering and staying in the field. Also, therapists seem to increasingly believe that understanding their own motivation is important for achieving success in the field. This search is done less defensively than before because the professional is no longer under the critical eyes of professors and supervisors.

Role and Working Style

We have already described that an important aspect of the Advanced Student phase was an awareness of the complexity inherent in therapy/counseling work. Adversities and challenges experienced by the Novice Professionals add to this awareness. The therapeutic relationship is conceptualized with more nuances and sophistication, and new skills and specific interventions are added to the repertoire of the Novice Professionals.

The therapists/counselors also become able to express their understanding of the role in simple, matter-of-fact ways, like one therapist who said, "The job is to empower or unblock or enable the client." The therapist is also more clear about differentiating their own professional responsibilities from the responsibilities that clients have for their own lives including therapy/counseling. One therapist said, "I used to think I could do it for the client, but I know now that was a naive idea." Another Novice therapist expressed it this way:

> I was a pretty personal therapist with clients when I started out in the business. They would call me in a time of crisis or need. They had my home phone number. That isn't working anymore because my caseload is big and difficult. Now calls are screened and I use an answering machine. I had to change it because I was getting "fried" and mad at clients and things like that. But it is tough saying "no" to people in tremendous distress: I feel guilty when I don't respond to demands, exhausted when I do.

With increasing confidence, practitioners become more aware that their personalities can be expressed in their work, and they seem more tolerant of that happening as well. For example, their natural sense of humor, which usually disappears during the early years of training when the novice is trying to learn how to be a therapist, may reappear and can be used in ways that the practitioners see as positive.

Compared with earlier phases, the Novice Professionals are better able to absorb more of the clinical material, and are more capable of distinguishing the important from the unimportant material in clients' communications. Experience assists the practitioners in moving beyond simple rules and context-free concepts. The work of Dreyfus and Dreyfus (1986), on the impact of experience on expertise, is useful for understanding individuals at this phase. As described in the second chapter, their stages are: Novice, Advanced Beginner, Competent, Proficient, and Expert. Novice Professionals have moved beyond the advanced beginner; they have accumulated some experience to guide practice and are capable of using overall global characteristics, or aspect recognition in decision making. At this phase, it seems that a practitioner may typically function somewhere in between the competent and the proficient, as conceptualized by Dreyfus and Dreyfus in their model of skill acquisition.

In the Competent stage, the individuals are able to apply rule-guided learning in complex contexts. It seems that if the therapists have successfully mastered the disillusionment following graduation, and the reflective process of exploration has also been successfully managed, then Novice therapists are generally able to apply rule-guided learning in complex contexts. Once this has been mastered, some Novice therapists are also able to recognize situations, not only as *aspects,* but, more holistically, as *maxims,* which provide direction as to what is important. The use of maxims is an important characteristic of the Proficient stage. Similarly, Novice therapists' tales of their ability to organize and order client material hierarchically suggests that they are functioning at the Proficient stage. However, it is possible that conscious deliberate planning, which according to Dreyfus and Dreyfus is an important attribute of the Competent stage, may not be mastered as easily as other attributes of the Competent stage, such as managing complexity, and use of standardized and routine practices. Thus, our data may suggest some uncertainty on this account. Despite certain similarities between the stage model of skill acquisition, as formulated by Dreyfus and Dreyfus, and our model of phases of professional development, and although we appreciate the differentiation between modes of explicit cognitive knowledge and tacit knowledge as articulated in their model, we are nevertheless skeptical regarding the categorical nature of "stages" as described in the Dreyfus model.

Many Novice Professionals assess and critique the treatments/models they endorsed as students. In our description of the Novice Student, we presented four categories of students' attitude to theory. Here, we will suggest some possible consequences for therapeutic/counseling work that may ensue from these attitudes. The attitudes to theory are (a) laissez-faire (no conceptual model considered as being particularly important); (b) one-dominant open (priority awarded toward one model, but with openness toward other models); (c) true believer (believes in one model alone, and rejects all others); and (d) multiple attachments, also termed broad spectrum orientation (many models are endorsed as important).

It is particularly important to consider the possible consequences for the processes and outcomes of therapy for a therapist with a laissez-faire attitude toward theory. In order to address this, we will address briefly the concept of the working alliance in order to present a line of reasoning that suggests that practitioners that are not guided by theoretical framework(s) may be at a disadvantage in establishing a working alliance. The working alliance may be conceptualized as having a relational component (bond) and a task-instrumental component (consisting of task and goal), as exemplified by Bordin's (1979) formulation.[3]

A therapist's theoretical orientation influences how contracts are negotiated, including how goals are established, and also which procedures and behaviors (roles) therapists and clients are expected to perform (Bordin, 1979). Thus, therapists' theoretical orientations are instruments that therapists can use as guides for where to look, what to do, how to proceed, and what to focus on in their therapeutic work. We are concerned that therapists that have no salient theoretical orientation may also have deprived themselves of conceptual tools that may be used to improve the alliance and subsequently therapy outcome. A possible consequence of not being guided by a theoretical approach/model is that the practitioner may be more inclined to act in a conventional, that is, nonprofessional manner toward their clients.

Our interviews indicate that a curious and searching attitude toward theory is positively related to development. One Novice Professional expressed the attitude of trying out different approaches while a student as follows:

> I had an existential/humanistic teacher and so, for a while, I became an existential humanist. And then I had a behaviorist and so I became a behaviorist, and then I had a person whose orientation was sex therapy and sexual issues, and so, for a while, that became paramount in my thinking.

We are reminded of the distinctions between a developmental and non-developmental approach to mastering the complexities and challenges of therapeutic work that we presented in the description of the Novice Student phase. The laissez-faire attitude described above and also the true believer attitude are conceptualized as attitudes that place the therapists at risk of professional stagnation. However, the two other models, the one-dominant open and the multiple attachment/broad spectrum attitudes both facilitate development, and this has partly been confirmed by other research (Orlinsky & Rønnestad, 2005).

Changes in conceptual foundations for one's work may also occur without a disillusionment basis. Looking back at how her conceptual style had evolved, one therapist said:

> I've found that I was in a very cognitive behavioral style. If anyone would have asked me if I endorsed this theory while in graduate school or internship, I would have said "no" resoundingly. I didn't find an orientation via disillusionment, but rather by evolution and greater insight into what I actually do as a therapist.

At all phases of development, students or postgraduate counselors and therapists reflect continually upon their personal and professional experiences, although some clearly do so more than others. The challenges and difficulties experience by Novice Professionals stimulate reflection. In chapter 10 we will differentiate between reflection as activity, reflective stance as an attitude, and reflexivity as a capacity. Here the term *reflection* is used in the sense of reflection as activity; that is, the cognitive and affective processing of both personal and professional experiences. As such, it is the major method used by individuals who are taking responsibility for their own professional development. Reflection as activity encompasses many issues, including the meaning of the work, internal dialogues, a search for anchors, a search for techniques, and a search for theory. Reflection provides answers to questions such as: What didn't I get from graduate school? Should I deviate from the methods and ideologies that I was taught in graduate school? What do I believe in? How can I proceed? How should I proceed?

In order to develop optimally, the Novice Professional must be able to tolerate the complexities of therapeutic work, to realize and accept temporarily the personal and professional limitations experienced, and to strive continually to reconcile contradictory experiences. Disengagement, a concept described more fully in chapter 10, may occur when reflection is avoided or prematurely foreclosed.

Measures of Effectiveness and Satisfaction

In the Novice Professional Phase, the therapists are typically struggling with how to define therapist effectiveness and with issues of therapist satisfaction. As was also the case while a student, the Novice Professional measures effectiveness by the extent to which the clients verbally express satisfaction with therapy. Although the Novice Professional does not typically actively elicit client feedback to measure success, verbal expressions of appreciation are still valued. But increasingly, the Novice Professionals will use other criteria than verbal client feedback and direct expressions of satisfaction/dissatisfaction as yardsticks to assess the quality of the work done. Criteria may vary from more professionally based criteria, such as changes in client self-perception, changes in attitude towards symptoms, and changes in ability to regulate emotions, to other criteria, such as simply getting paid for services.[4]

But as most therapists lack yardsticks to measure their effectiveness, therapists find reassurance and comfort in finding out that peers are struggling with these issues as well, a version of the universality principle (Yalom, 1995) which tends to increase self-esteem. How therapists evaluate their effectiveness influences their self-esteem as professionals. Journal articles are usually poor resources for enhancing self-esteem, as they tend to focus on knowledge generation and on presenting demonstrably effective techniques, often bleaching out nonsignificant results and dispiriting ideas, and being more likely to report tales of success than of failure. Discussions with other people during moments of trust and respect, about mutual and unique struggles are keys to maintaining enthusiasm about one's work. Such discussions may happen during the break times at workshops and, more intensively, in therapist/peer supervision groups. A female at this phase commented:

> I find my colleagues to be my best resource. I tap people with similar, as well as divergent, theoretical orientations. We even have a "when therapy fails" group to help sort out what happens when we're ineffective … we think we're pretty damn good therapists and, so far at least, there's been no collective judgment to the contrary. We are quite insular in the city where I work, we feel comfortable within this group of cognitive therapists with taking risks and learning about ourselves.

The above quote illustrates what we see as important principles for increasing expertise , (a) the commitment to increase one's expertise as expressed by having created a "when therapy fails group"; (b) to have created a learning environment where both similar and divergent theoretical perspectives are represented;[5] (c) to have created a learning environment that is safe; (d) the willingness to address what is likely highly difficult (when therapy fails); (e) to dare to take risks; and (f), to have a focus "to learn about ourselves."

Applying Stoltenberg, McNeill, and Delworth's IDM model as conceptual glasses to view the above quote, it seems likely that the kind of peer-group activity described above increases the opportunity to process many of the domains they describe in their model, and in particular: intervention skills competence, interpersonal assessment, client conceptualization, individual differences, treatment goals and plans, and professional ethics.

An important characteristic of many Novice Professionals, a characteristic that will become even more pronounced for practitioners in the two later phases, is their rejection of simplistic conceptions of therapy and their recognition and appreciation for the complexity of therapeutic work. This complexity of therapeutic work is also reflected in the multifaceted definition of Evidence-Based Practice (EBP) formulated by the American Psychological Association (APA, 2006). As many will know the definition is as follows: "Evidence-based practice in psychology is the integration of the best available research with clinical *expertise in the context of patient characteristics, culture and preferences*" [emphasis added] (APA, 2006, p. 273). The formulation "*in the context of* [emphasis added] patient characteristics, culture and preferences" differs from the definition by the Institute of Medicine (Sackett, Straus, Richardson, Rosenberg, & Haynes, 2000), and specifies the need for the practitioner to have extensive knowledge about patients/clients in order to claim that their practice is evidence based (Rønnestad, 2008). In the description of EBP (APA, 2006) it is referred to Norcross (2002) who has argued that psychological services are likely to be more effective if they "are responsive to the patient's specific problems, strengths, personality, sociocultural context, and preferences" (p. 278). This perspective articulates the complexity of therapeutic work, and concurs with multiple formulations from our informants as protests and disappointment against simple methods and approaches previously endorsed.

Before we conclude this chapter, it should be mentioned that some graduates enter work roles that are well-defined and are similar to those that they were taught during graduate training. In these instances, the new formal status of these Novice Professionals, together with their familiarity with work roles, is likely to fuel confidence and satisfaction with their work, and the transition to the work situation will probably be experienced as smooth and relatively simple. However, whether a smooth transition is ideal from a developmental viewpoint has not been established. It seems possible that, in a long-term perspective, the reflective processing that follows confrontation with challenges and difficulties that are not easily mastered may actually be more favorable for optimal professional development.

The idea of an optimal discrepancy between what is mastered and what the situation demands is implicit in many theories and perspectives of learning and development. In psychoanalytic theory the "optimal frustration" as a perspective on human development has a long, although controversial, history (Bacal, 1998).[6] Vygotsky's (1978) concept of the zone of proximal development implies an optimal "discrepancy," where the developmental support contributes to increased mastery. The concepts of successive approximation and shaping within learning theory can be added to the list of concepts which imply an optimal discrepancy. Also, an underlying idea from Mueller and Kell's (1972) classic text *Coping with Conflict* is that the learner (the supervisee) needs to be sufficiently challenged and experience anxiety (and conflict) if learning is to take place. And, lastly, Csickszentmihalyi's (1990) emotion-focused inner motivation model suggests that to feel challenged is an intrinsic quality of the state of "flow." So, with this background, it seems that optimal development presupposes an ideal level of "discrepancy" between what is mastered and what the situation demands. So contrary to commonly held positions, this implies that "a smooth transition" from school to work is not necessarily beneficial for optimal growth.

Notes

1. Previous versions of this chapter were published in *The Evolving Professional Self,* by T. M. Skovholt and M. H. Rønnestad (1992), pp. 51–61. Copyright is reverted to the authors. Chichester, England: Wiley, and in "The Journey of the Counselor and Therapist: Research Findings and Perspectives," by M. H. Rønnestad & T. M. Skovholt (2003), in *Journal of Career Development, 30,* 5–44, 2003. Adapted with permission from Sage. All quotes are from *The Evolving Professional Self.*

2. Appropriation can be defined as "making it you own." Wertsch makes the distinction between mastery and appropriation. He claims that you can demonstrate mastery of a cultural tool (like, for example, use of a particular therapy/counseling technique or procedure) without appropriating it.

3. Research has shown that all aspects are associated with therapy outcome (Norcross, 2011; Orlinsky, Rønnestad, & Willutzki, 2004). A recent synthesis of the relationship between alliance and outcome showed that the overall aggregate relation between the alliance and treatment outcome was $r = .275$ (Horvath, Del Re, Flückiger, & Symonds, 2011).

4. The latter may be regarded as an expression of the cultural norm of *exchange,* which can be conceptualized within various social science disciplines such as anthropology (the study of rituals), sociology (social exchange theories).

5. Similarity in theoretical orientation provides the opportunity to receive feedback within the theoretical domain, while differences in theoretical orientation provide the opportunity for broadening the perspective on the topic discussed.

6. Bacal (1998) is critical of the concept of optimal frustration, and has suggested a refocus in psychoanalytic treatment that to a larger extent places in the forefront of theory concepts such as empathic attunement, support, self-disclosure, and validation of experiences. Many share his view.

7

THE EXPERIENCED
PROFESSIONAL PHASE[1]

I learned all the rules and so I came to a point—after lots of effort—where I knew the rules very well. Gradually I modified the rules. Then I began to use the rules to let me go where I wanted to go. Lately I haven't been talking so much in terms of rules.

Introduction

During this phase of professional development, the therapist/counselor has been practicing for a number of years. We cannot define the phase precisely because individual therapists/counselors vary in how quickly and competently they master the developmental tasks of the preceding Novice Professional phase. There seems to be a cultural norm for the definition of "being experienced" in any domain of practice that includes the individual having been exposed to varied challenges and hardships and to have successfully mastered these trials. For therapists/counselors, this entails having experience in (a) different work settings (e.g., inpatient, outpatient, school/educational settings, vocational/career settings, organizational/industrial); (b) different work-role modalities (e.g., individual and group counseling/therapy, family/couple counseling/therapy); and (c) different types of clients (with various life concerns, existential concerns, developmental arrests, disabilities, pathologies, etc.). A subjective indication for having arrived at the Experienced Professional phase is thus when both the professional her- or himself and colleagues apply this cultural norm of duration and variety as a basis for feeling that he or she is an experienced practitioner.

The overlap between therapist/counselor experience (defined as number of years of professional practice) and expertise is at least partly confirmed by the Society for Psychotherapy Research/Collaborative Research Network (SPR/CRN) research presented in chapter 14. From a cyclical/sequential model presented in that chapter, we will see that the breadth and depth of case experience (including experience with varied treatment modalities), contribute to overall career development, which is operationalized as positive skill change, overcoming limitations, and therapeutic mastery. We refer you to that chapter for a closer examination of the empirically documented relationship of duration and types of experiences on the one hand and professional development on the other. Our intention in this chapter is to argue that it is reasonable to define an experienced practitioner as one who has had many and varied experiences, and also that a precise definition is not possible for when the Experienced Professional phase begins.

Developmental Task and General Description

There are three developmental tasks during the Experienced Professional phase. They are:

1. For the therapist/counselor to maintain a sense of professional growth and resiliency while avoiding burnout and stagnation.
2. For the therapist/counselor to integrate his or her personal self into a coherent professional self.
3. For the therapist/counselor to create a work role which is experienced as highly congruent with the practitioner's coherent professional self.

The first developmental task, to maintain a sense of professional growth and to avoid burnout and stagnation, reflects what we observed as an ongoing concern by many professionals throughout their career. Professional growth includes improving one's skills and moving toward mastery. Successful completion of this task also involves having a vision for one's future. In reference to this first developmental task, in addition to our own joint findings and perspectives, we also point the reader to chapter 14 by Orlinsky and Rønnestad in this book and to chapter 13 in Skovholt and Trotter-Mathison (2010) on professional resiliency, burnout prevention, and self-care.

The second developmental task, to integrate their personal self into a coherent professional self, finds its expression when the practitioner is able to be coherent and genuine when relating to clients. The self-concept has been defined in numerous ways. The simplest definition is "a person's concept or idea of himself" (The Oxford English Dictionary, 1989). Another definition and description is formulated by Alan Ross (1992), who in his definition of self-concept, wrote that:

> the self-concept is no more than the concept a person has of himself or herself. That concept represents how one thinks and feels about oneself—how one perceives oneself. People acquire a concept of themselves as distinct individuals through their experiences with their physical and social environment. From these they learn who and what they are. (p. 2)

These definitions capture varieties of ways that the concept of the self has been understood (narrative self, multiple selves, etc.). We endorse a multidimensional perspective of the self-concept as described by Shavelson, Hubner, and Stanton (1976). They differentiate between many self-concepts, as between the academic self-concept and the nonacademic self-concept. We make a similar distinction between the personal self and the professional self. We define the personal self as how the practitioners see themselves as they relate to other people in the nonprofessional context. The professional self is defined as how practitioners see themselves in the professional context, and specifically how they see themselves when relating to clients. In addition to suggesting a multidimensional perspective of the self, Shavelson and collaborators also suggest a hierarchical perspective and an overarching general self-concept. Our data do not support a movement toward an overarching general self, but do support a movement where aspects of the personal self become integrated with a professional self. Coherence in the professional self depends on the degree to which personal characteristics have been assimilated in the professional self. Our data support the idea of differentiating between these two aspects of the self. Also, we can draw on the research within the SPR/CRN to support the conceptual validity of a two-part definition of the self. *The Development of Psychotherapists Common Core Questionnaire*, used in this survey, contains two sets of items inspired by interpersonal theory (e.g., Leary, 1957). Therapists are asked to describe their manner when relating to clients (their professional self) and how they see themselves in close personal relationships (their personal self; Orlinsky & Rønnestad, 2005). The results confirm the pragmatic validity of the distinction between personal and professional selves by demonstrated overlap but also differences between these aspects of the self.

The third developmental task involves creating a work role that is highly congruent with the practitioner's coherent professional self. Finding the right work role emerges as a highly salient concern for practitioners in the Experienced Professional phase. This searching for congruence between the self and work role during the Experienced Professional phase, a perspective that can be traced to the so-called trait-and-factor contributions by Frank Parsons (1909) and E. G. Williamson (1939), aligns well with the decades of research in career psychology on the self–job fit as central for work satisfaction (e.g., Holland, 1973, 1997). The implementation of oneself in one's career, a central idea in Donald Super's developmental theory (e.g., 1953), underscores the intrinsic relationship between the personal and professional aspects of helping practitioners' meaning construction. Although phrased in different terminology, Holland's (1997) theory of matching personalities and work environments, Roe's (1977) theory of occupational choice, and Bordin and Brooks's (1990) theory of personality and character similarly express the interrelatedness of person and work characteristics for work satisfaction.

Our findings indicate that the goal of arriving at a match between the self-concept and work characteristics become salient at an earlier phase, when the Novice Professional encounters the hardships of practice some time after graduation (for most during the Exploration subphase of the Novice Professional phase). During the Experienced Professional phase, this goal becomes of paramount concern for the practitioner.

We are reminded of the concept of anchored conceptual structures that we introduced when describing the previous phase. For the Experienced Professional, anchoring professionally based theoretical/conceptual structures to perceptions of the self continues and is a process that facilitates consistency, coherence, and ultimately integration of the personal self into a coherent professional self. This process involves assessing one's values, interests, preferences, theoretical orientations, competencies, and limitations and exploring alternative work settings and role possibilities if there is no suitable match. Modal Experienced Professionals have limited tolerance for lack of close fit between how they see themselves and the work role, with its many specific elements.

Through the years, Experienced Professionals in full-time practice will have had hundreds of clients (or more) and have learned that therapy/counseling is an effective intervention for most clients. The experience of being helpful fuels a sense of competence, which also leads practitioners to become less defensive and inhibited in their work. Some talk of being more creative. As one therapist expressed it, "The creativity I'm enjoying with my new project is delightful." Also, some will report experiences which may be described as "quiet excitement," an expression of gratitude for being a member of a profession that enables one to be engaged in deeply meaningful work.

The modal Experienced Professional continues to develop professionally. This is a central finding of our study. Professional development is clearly not limited to the years of basic training or to the years immediately following graduation. Experienced professionals continue to have a vision for their future and to turn their attention toward refinements of therapy/counseling skills, although in time they will also concentrate on doing what they do well, a process where their competence is consolidated. They are usually keenly aware of the hazards of practice, of the potential for stagnating professionally. Some also see the potential for cynicism, bitterness, and intellectual apathy, as we will describe below. Practitioners often take various measures to prevent negative development from happening and to ensure that they continue to grow.

The development of the Experienced Professional can also be conceptualized as an individuation process. The concept of individuation involves "qualities of individuality and connectedness" (Grotevant & Cooper, 1986, p. 89). By using this concept we highlight two interrelated movements that characterize the modal Experienced Professional. One is a movement toward their unique and personalized ways of relating to clients, while the other underscores a progression toward increased empathic engagement with clients. In chapter 3, where we discussed cultural discourses of helping, we contrasted sympathy and empathy with specific reference to the ability of the professional helper to be able to fluctuate between being in a participating and observing mode when relating to clients. The modal Experienced Professional feels more competent than practitioners at earlier phases. A male Experienced Professional said: "I'm more willing to test my ability in tough situations; there is more confidence." Therapists have also learned that they are not effective with all clients. Series of humiliations have contributed to a sense of realism which is also experienced as freeing. Therapists in this phase will typically say that they feel more authentic and congruent in their work, that they feel more natural, and that they are more at ease, less anxious, less threatened, and less defensive. While interviewed on television recently, a well-known Swedish actress said, "The secret with good acting is not to act." This expresses a more natural, personal, and less anxious view of acting, similar to what many Experienced Professionals will express when describing their view of therapy and counseling. Along with this natural style come a higher sense of competence, and paradoxically, a feeling of more humility about what they can accomplish.

Not all therapists are mastering the developmental tasks of the Experienced Professional phase. There may be many reasons for that. Perhaps previous developmental tasks have not been successfully completed. The Experienced Professional may not have been able to meet the expectations of the profession for more complex conceptual knowledge and the more advanced procedural competence of the preceding phase. Or, the practitioner has not been able to manage the bewilderment that many experience when meeting the variety of challenges encountered and when seeing therapy/counseling as more complex.

Studying professional development through the years has sensitized us to how important interpersonal skills are, not only for professional work, but also for professional development. This perspective is at the core of the sequential/cyclical model of the SPR/CRN network (Orlinsky & Rønnestad, 2005). Many of us would probably agree that interpersonal skills are at the heart of therapy/counseling competence and is a foundation upon which other tasks and competences are built. The paramount importance of interpersonal skills is now well documented. See, for example, *Psychotherapy Relationships That Work*, by Norcross and Lambert (2011); also, the classic text, *Handbook of Psychotherapy and Behavior Change*, by Garfield and Bergin (1971/1986), which has gone through many editions, and Lambert (2004) who has convincingly demonstrated the paramount importance of therapist interpersonal skills for therapy/counseling outcome (e.g., Orlinsky, Rønnestad & Willutzki, 2004).

If therapists do not have the interpersonal skills needed to empathically tune in to the experiential world of the client, therapists are doomed to encounter substantial difficulties in their work and will not be able to master the developmental tasks at all phases of development, including those of the Experienced Professional phase.

We have available some clinically relevant research that documents the relationship between therapist attachment styles and difficulties in relating to clients that may explain why some Experienced Professionals struggle considerably and are not able to meet the developmental tasks of this phase. In line with an interpersonal theory tradition, Horowitz et al. (2006) have suggested that therapists who are more distanced, disconnected, and indifferent in how they relate to clients establish poorer alliances with their clients. This is in accordance with the findings of Hersoug, Høglend, Havik, Lippe, and Monsen (2009). In their study the majority had many years of experience. They found that therapists who had an interpersonal style characterized by being distant, disconnected, or indifferent to clients (based on therapists' self-reports), established poorer alliances with their clients. These results were reported both by therapists and clients. Another study showed that a contrasting warm interpersonal therapist style was related to a positive client rated alliance (Nissen-Lie, Monsen, & Rønnestad, 2010). This latter study also documented the positive impact of therapists' reports of difficulties (however, not excessive) in their work for client rated alliance. These findings underscore how important it is for therapists to have the interpersonal sensitivity needed to recognize and understand the feedback clients give them. A fundamental aspect of our model is that it is the quality of the therapeutic work and specifically how difficulties and challenges are handled, that is most impactful for therapists' development and stagnation.

Practitioner Burnout

Intellectual resignation, emotional exhaustion, apathy, and disengagement from work are central characteristics of stagnation. The phenomenology of these experiences can be conceptualized by the cyclical (positive and negative) models of the SPR/CRN network (see chapter 14), by our joint cyclical/trajectories model of development and stagnation (see chapter 10), and by conceptions of burnout, which we will address below and also in chapter 13. We present our reflections on burnout in the context of the Experienced Professional phase. This in spite of the fact that burnout can be experienced during any phase of development. According to Leiter and Maslach (1988) burnout is a process evolving over time

103

with depersonalization as the end state. Although it can conceptually and empirically be argued that depersonalization may not be understood as an end state of burnout (Larsen et al., 2010), burnout nevertheless seems to peak after some years of experience, which is an argument for highlighting burnout as a risk factor for the Experienced Professional.

The burnout literature is extensive. By 2009, there were approximately 6,000 articles, books, and dissertations on the topic (Schaufeli, Leiter, & Maslach, 2009). Schaufeli and Enzman (1998), who have provided the most extensive review of the topic, present seven different definitions, five operationalizations, in addition to 19 theoretical models of burnout (Larsen, 2010). There are several ways of categorizing the models; for example, as individual models, interpersonal models, organizational, and societal models. Another way to differentiate between models is as follows: stress models, motivational models (e.g., understimulation/needs not met), negative developmental models, and burnout as depression (Larsen, 2010). The burnout concept has been criticized from many angles (e.g., theoretical inconsistency, poor construct validity, inadequate operationalizations). Many issues have not been resolved. For example, is depersonalization, which Maslach (1982/2003) regarded as the "hallmark of burnout" (p. 27) a useful concept or should it be dropped, or if maintained, what is the relationship between depersonalization (emotional withdrawal from clients) and cynicism (disengagement from work) as these concepts are operationalized in the Maslach Burnout Inventory-Human Service and the Maslach Burnout Inventory-General Survey respectively.[2]

Underlying these unresolved issues is the question whether the Maslach's burnout-syndrome consists of three or four dimensions (Salanova et al., 2005). How one resolves these questions has practical consequences for how research on the topic is carried out, and thus either limits or expands the analyses that will be done, which in turn impacts how we conceptualize the important phenomenological world of therapists' hardships. Our joint qualitative data can cast a light on this issue.

In our study, Experienced Professional therapists did not report on relating to clients in ways that can be interpreted as therapists' treating clients as objects or as therapists not really caring for some clients, which are items in the depersonalization scale of the MBI-Human Service scale. One may ask if the incidence of reporting on such experiences is low or practically nonexistent among Experienced Professionals because practitioners do not experience it. Or do they experience it, but do not express it because doing so would mean they admit to deviating from normative characteristics of the therapy/counseling culture, and to violating the ethical obligation to always act in accordance with the client's best interest? Or, have they learned how to handle such feelings? Or, have the "uncaring" burned out people dropped out of the profession by now?

According to Maslach and Leiter (1997), disengaging from clients (depersonalization) or from work (cynicism) is more likely to occur under adverse working conditions. We have numerous reports from therapists in both the Novice Professional phase and the Experienced Professional phase of adverse and nonsupportive work settings. It seems reasonable to believe that qualities of the work setting will impact how the practitioner relates to clients, in particular in the long term perspective. In a milieu-therapy setting (such as a hospital inpatient unit), this is particularly evident because the relationship among therapists/counselors constitute the treatment milieu for clients/patients.

Common sense suggests that competitive and threatening work environments are likely to influence therapists/counselors adversely and may cause the therapist/counselors to be overly cautious and defensive in their work. But, we have little data from our study to assist us in learning about these dynamics. We may ask if that is because the interviews did not sufficiently focus on these potential dynamics, or is it because therapists are more immune to such potential negative influences than we might think? It could be that therapists' strong commitment to the welfare of clients buffers such dynamics. However, research in a related area, the parallel process in clinical supervision (Doerhman, 1976), suggests that the dynamics in one relationship (supervision) could easily transfer to another relationship (therapy) and vice versa. In the Doerhman study, therapists were students, and consequently quite dependent on supervisors who are "not only admired teachers, but feared judges who have real power" (p. 11) So, we may ask if a finding suggesting subtle influences such as the one demonstrated in the study above can be transferred to practitioners at the Experienced Professional phase. In their direct client work, are these experienced practitioners able to resist being influenced by adverse organizational conditions?

In their model of burnout, Maslach and Leiter (1997) emphasize the role played by organizational factors. For example, findings from a study within a Swedish psychiatric institution suggest that Experienced Professionals were able to resist adverse organizational consequences (Bergin & Rønnestad, 2005). In this study participants were largely in the Experienced Professional phase with a median age of 48 (range 38–56 years). Median time in their profession was 18 years (range 4–25 years). In a context of a fundamental, dramatic, and adversely experienced reorganization of the institution, therapists did not abandon their identification with clients. In the turmoil of the reorganization, here is what some of the therapists were saying: "The patients are always in focus"; "You always represent the patient"; "Deep down I know it's the patient I need to somehow develop a sound cooperation and loyalty with" (p. 360).

We certainly want to support all efforts toward improving the quality of organizations within the health, social service, and education fields, and do not want our reflections on this topic to serve as an argument not to do so. However, it may be that Experienced Professionals, who have gone through a process of individuation, are, at least in the short time perspective, better able to maintain their identification with their client and resist being influenced by the adversative impact of poor working conditions that Maslach and Leiter suggest. How these Swedish therapists in this study handled this situation may demonstrate a cardinal feature of Experienced Professionals—a strong commitment to the welfare of clients.

We are skeptical of using the term *depersonalization* for therapists' disengagement from clients. However, the low frequency of reports of excessive disengagement in the form of depersonalization (such as treating clients as impersonal objects) in the results from our own joint study and the Swedish study referred to above, indicate that disengagement seems to come in other forms than the burnout literature describes. Our research suggests that the experience of *boredom* is a more common manifestation of therapist disengagement among practitioners in the Experienced Professional phase. Boredom may result from therapists performing routine tasks, from applying a limited set of conceptual lenses when interacting with clients, and from having lost the inquisitiveness and curiosity needed to maintain their vitality and enthusiasm toward their work. Boredom can also ensue from defining the work-role in a limited way. One male Experienced Professional said "Much of my work with clients involves teaching 'emotional first grade,' that is, going over basic mental health issues. It gets boring." This quote illustrates an important dynamic, the risk of disengagement when conceptualizing one's work, including the work role, in too simple ways, a strategy we described as used by many Beginning Students. If the Experienced Professionals do so, which means that they are not able to maintain "awareness of complexity," which we highlight as a prerequisite for optimal professional development at all phases of development, chances for premature closure and stagnation are substantial. We will describe these dynamics more fully in chapter 10.

Therapists' ability to regulate their involvement with clients is crucial to avoiding therapist burnout. The field of developmental psychology has convincingly demonstrated the interrelatedness of attachment styles and ability to regulate emotions (see Cassidy & Shaver, 2008).

Skovholt and Trotter-Mathison (2010) have pointed to the central role played by therapist attachment to clients in understanding therapist burnout. They suggest that therapists/counselors need to be able to successfully move through the repeated attachment–active involvement–felt separation–re-creation phases of the cycle of caring that are generic to all of the helping professions. In fact, an unsuccessful cycling through these phases may lead to erosion of morale and a style of burnout that they call "caring burnout," which they defined as "disengagement of the self from

the caring cycle of empathic attachment–active involvement felt separation–re-creation" p. 154). The idea is that over time, this process may
drain the therapist/counselor. Different metaphors can describe this: just
as the plaque in arteries builds up little by little causing the blood flow to
be choked off, or like a battery that can be energized or drained: "When
drained enough there is no spark" (p. 155). Meaning burnout is another
style of burnout: "Meaning burnout occurs when the calling of caring
for others and giving to others in an area such as emotional development,
intellectual growth, or physical wellness no longer give sufficient meaning
and purpose in one's life" (Skovholt & Trotter-Mathison, 2010, p. 152).
This style of burnout concerns the therapist/counselor's existential reflections and may typically arise when the original motivations for entering
the profession may not be sufficient to endure the challenges encountered
or fuel a continued investment in work.

In our study the Experienced Professionals report that they protect
themselves in different ways while also managing to be deeply engaged
in their work. One female Experienced Professional talked about her goal
"to continue to be present but not to be used up." Her strategy to manage this included: Less self-disclosure as a therapist, sufficient charting so
that client data was not swirling around in her head in off-hours, and also
doing a type of therapy where she felt most effective. In contrast to student
therapists and also most Novice Professionals, Experienced Professionals
typically protect themselves by having strict location and time boundaries
for their work, and regular use of vacations. As we will see in the sections
below on conceptions of the work role, realistic perceptions of what can
be accomplished in therapy/counseling and also better regulations of professional boundaries are central characteristics of the Experienced Professional phase. During this phase, versions of *boundaried generosity*, a term
derived from the study of master therapists (Skovholt, Jennings, & Mullenbach, 2004), protect the practitioner from depleting her or his morale
and vitality.

Therapist Negative Effects

One of the developmental tasks of the Experienced Professional phase is
for therapists/counselors to integrate their personal self into a coherent
professional self. An expression of this is that the practitioner is authentic
and congruent when relating to clients. However, as we have described
above, all therapists are unfortunately not therapeutic. Therefore, it is not
necessarily beneficial that all therapists become more authentic, nor that
all therapists move toward an integrating of their personal self into a professional self. One of our informants who was reacting to a draft version
that described the movement toward greater authenticity, said:

> I hope some psychologists are not themselves with clients, because their selves are not therapeutic. [For these therapists] it would be more important to learn to set limits on their personalities than to express them.

According to a literature review of therapy outcome by Lambert and Ogles (2004) between 5% and 10% of clients deteriorate during therapy. Therapists seem to contribute to these results by lacking in interpersonal skillfulness and empathy. Castonguay and collaborators (Castonguay, Boswell, Constantino, Goldfried, & Hill, 2010) have recently reviewed conceptual literature and empirical research on harmful effects in psychotherapy.[3] We interpret their review as a caution against viewing therapists striving "to be more themselves" as necessarily constructive. It need not be. They refer to a classic text by Wolberg (1967) that describes therapist traits or characteristics that "have been shown by experience to be damaging to good therapy" (p. 390). Castonguay et al. (2010) write:

> [These traits and characteristics] include, among other things, a tendency to be domineering, pompous, authoritarian, detached, passive, oversubmissive, or lacking in or not compensating for basic satisfaction in living (related to issues of sexuality, hostility, or prestige); an excessive need to be liked or admired; perfectionism; creative inhibition; a poor sense of humor; an inability to receive criticism, accept self-limitation, or tolerate blows to self-esteem (e.g., when faced with resistance); and a low level of personal integrity. (p. 43)

Do we have any empirical documentation on the relationship between therapist characteristics and negative therapist effects? Yes, we do. Castonguay referred to this research and the results are presented in Table 7.1.

Table 7.1 Some Empirically Documented Negative Therapist Characteristics Associated with Negative Client Outcome (Castonguay et al., 2010)

- Therapists' anxious attachment styles,
- Low self-esteem,
- High levels of emotional expressiveness,
- Worry,
- Impulsiveness,
- Hostile introjects,
- Negative recollection of parents,
- Disaffiliative responses

The picture painted here is troublesome, and we may ask what proportion of therapists would fit parts of the descriptions above? We do not know the answer to that question. It is unlikely that therapists who chose to participate in an interview study of therapist development and were willing to disclose their opinions on many issues, and also be audiotaped are representative of the total population of therapists/counselors.

Research within the SPR/CRN, now with data from approximately 11,000 therapists from more than 20 countries provide a better foundation to estimate the proportion of therapists who struggle extensively in their work. A few years back, when the database consisted of approximately 5,000 therapists, research had documented that approximately 10% of therapists/counselors experienced a practice pattern that was termed *distressing practice*, which consisted of low healing involvement and high stressful involvement (Orlinsky & Rønnestad, 2005). The definition of these concepts was presented in chapter 4. These therapists were also overrepresented among therapists who did not feel that they have grown much professionally during their career, which confirms the interrelation between quality of client work and development.

Our joint research has led us to formulate a process model of development and stagnation, presented in chapter 10, where we describe those processes which facilitate and hinder development and also those that are likely to contribute to professional stagnation and to practitioners leaving the field. In our model, much weight is afforded to therapists/counselors' ability to tolerate the challenges and difficulties experienced and their ability and willingness to continually reflect upon the hardships that they encounter. And it seems from the research reported above, that a clear majority of therapists are engaging constructively with their clients and are developing professionally.

Sources of Influence and Learning Processes

Major sources of influence on professional development that we have found in our study (i.e., theories/research; clients; professional elders such as professors, supervisors, mentors, or therapists; peers/colleagues; one's own personal life; and the social/cultural environment) continue to play an important role in the professional functioning and development of the Experienced Professionals. For some, these are supplemented by the influences accruing from engaging in veteran practitioner-type activities such as being a personal therapist for colleagues, being a supervisor for less experienced therapists/counselors, or a teacher/instructor of therapy/counseling. To have younger and less experienced practitioners seek their guidance and support is gratifying and appreciated. For some Senior Professionals, such activities strengthen their professional identity as experienced therapist/counselors. One practitioner in this phase said, "Hey, if they recognize me this way, I must be good at what I do." But, such transformations do not happen automatically, as expressed by one male Experienced Professional who said, "Suddenly, I was seen by others as a leader, but I didn't see it that way. I didn't feel that I belonged."

An important feature of the sources of influence of practitioners in the Experienced Professional phase is that they learn and develop from engaging themselves in more varied arenas than they did before. They increasingly report that they have increased their understanding of human behavior through professional literature in related fields such as anthropology, sociology, philosophy, or religion or through reading fiction, poetry, biographies, or through watching movies, going to the theater, and taking part in other artistic/cultural activities.

Theoretical, empirically based concepts serve an important but nonetheless secondary function as a source of learning. They are accepted only if they add in meaningful ways to how therapists understand clients. Untested ideas are only useful when the individual approaches a new area where the experience is lacking. Examples may be working with a specific client group in a new setting, working with children with cancer at a cancer hospital, or with elderly patients in a geriatric institution.

The modal practitioner in the Experienced Professional phase wants to maintain his or her skills, learn new approaches and methods, and is eager to develop professionally. However, at the same time, many report a strongly felt belief that there is not much new in the field. One said, "I've recently stopped going to workshops. They seemed to be geared to 'Freshman English' and to be old stuff. For example, assertiveness training was done long ago under a different label. I am especially not interested in new little techniques."

Even more complex approaches can be rejected because they appear as "old wine in new bottles." Contemporary comprehensive approaches that do not attract the attention by some are mentalization based therapy (e.g., Bateman & Fonagy, 2006), or mindfulness (e.g., Segal, Williams, & Teasdale, 2002) as some will claim that they are merely repackaging well-established principles of therapy/counseling. Also, some of the CBT techniques, marketed as innovative, are criticized as merely being reformulations of established clinical/counseling knowledge (Skovholt, Rønnestad, & Jennings, 1997).

To attract the attention of practitioners at the Experienced Professional phase (aside from the pragmatic need for CE credits for licensure or certification) there needs to be some special attraction, like signing up for a workshop with major theoretical leaders or an acknowledged master counselor/therapist in the field. This may involve traveling to a distant city at considerable economic cost. An Experienced Professional said, "Around this time I had my encounter with Albert Ellis."

A big shift in sources of influence relates to one's own mentors-profes-sors-supervisors. These seniors are no longer present or not as available as they were before. There is more geographic separation (e.g., the practitio-ner was trained in Los Angeles and now lives in Atlanta, and is thus no longer tied into work roles as a junior and senior practitioner in a major eating disorders clinic).

Even though seniors may not be physically present, they may neverthe-less serve an important function as internalized mentors for some practi-tioners in this phase. One expressed it this way, "I have running around in my mind words, phrases, quotes that I periodically pull back to…and sometimes I say to myself, how would John handle this situation?." The quote illustrates the intensity of previously internalized relationships and how what was learned in those relationships comes to practical use for the therapists/counselors two decades later.

Peers become more central as a valuable source of influence. As one female in this phase said, "I rely on my support network of colleagues." Another expressed it this way, "There are 50 therapists where I work. My spouse is a therapist. I get a lot from these people." Another expression of the important role of peers we see in the following quote by a female Experienced Professional. She said, "To stay alive in this field you need to talk to colleagues. For me, two long term supervision groups have been absolutely essential to continue and grow." However, the Experienced Pro-fessional may feel isolated if working as a single office practitioner. If so, workshop participation can still be a treasured activity. One of the senior members of our sample, who we interviewed three times at ages 59, 70, and 82, recalled with great fondness how he and a colleague, both in solo practice in different communities, would meet for breakfast on Saturday mornings and have peer supervision. He and she—highly competent, highly experienced—offered great professional nurturance and intense social support for each other.

Therapists/counselors in the Experienced Professional phase continue to be strongly influenced by what they learn from interacting with clients. But during this phase, practitioners learn more from reflecting upon expe-riences with the exceptional client, who may either be the client with an extraordinarily positive outcome or the client who posed a particular chal-lenge to the therapist. Examples of the latter may be clients who engage the practitioner emotionally in intense ways, which may happen when working with a highly suicidal client or a client with an interpersonal manner characterized as highly evasive/inaccessible/controlling /intensely engaging or a combination of these manners. Another example may be working with a client in long-term therapy with whom the therapist/ counselor thought she or he had a strong alliance, and then the client suddenly dropped out of therapy without an explanation. Yet another example, working with a poorly functioning client in therapy/counseling where the working alliance was assessed to be poor, then there is a sudden improvement in the therapy alliance.

Experienced Practitioners have a wealth of client experiences to draw from. One practitioner told of how memories of previous cases were activated when seeing new clients:

> With a new client I think about cases I've had. I think about how they have gone. Themes come in a case and this stimulates a memory in me. The memory is in the form of a collection of vignettes, stories, and scripts. It isn't fully conscious but new cases do kick off the memory—and the memory of how things went before provides a foundation to begin the current case. Interestingly, most of the stories come from the early days of my practice; they are the most embedded. Later cases don't stand out as much except if I was proved wrong or something dramatic happened. Then my thinking changes and my memory changes.

Specifically, these therapists report that interacting with clients and processing experiences in their personal lives have primacy as sources of learning and development. Through reflecting upon interpersonal experiences in the professional and personal life domains, the Experienced Professionals expand their horizons.

As we interviewed practitioners with more experience, we increasingly heard stories of the interrelationship between adult personal and professional life. Personal life experiences influenced their professional work and their perceptions of self and their development. The practitioners talked about experiences like being a parent, being married, being a daughter or son of an aging parent, a cross-cultural experience from living internationally, grief reactions from losing people dear to oneself, and grief reactions associated with sudden onset of physical disability. One Experienced Professional said the following:

> Certainly, my experience has been an important factor in my development as a person. My experience of being in the Peace Corps for a few years has taught me ... a sense of relativity of this culture. Raising children I think is so important. I got a chance to go back through development with my own children, and to be able to see what I felt like to them.

A female practitioner in the Experienced Professional phase commented: "I think I used to be more judgmental about marriage and parenting till I tried it myself, it's a humbling experience." Another practitioner reflecting back on the effect of her age on her work said, "I have been consistent in my work because I came into the field after 10 years in another field so I was older and more formed as a person when I started than I think many young therapists are." Another practitioner in our study said: "My father-in-law is slowly dying. There is no way to see what that is like unless you directly experience it. To go through that is a transforming experience." Another said that her divorce was the most difficult experience in her life. She found it forced her to see herself as a separate person and not a daughter or wife in relation to others. She said: "It really shocked me to the core. I had to dab in some dark places and look at things about me." The whole experience, she said, increased her connections with human pain, made her more intellectually curious, and ultimately helped her to be a better therapist. Another male Experienced Professional said that his wife's active feminism was a major influence in reorienting his approach from "cerebral to affect" and from "task to process."

Although some talked about how the fatigue from overburdening work could negatively influence family life, or how professional knowledge and competence could be transferred into one's personal life, there was more "traffic" in the other direction; that is, of how personal life was seen to influence professional functioning. One said: "You learn a lot from your kids just like you learn a lot from your clients." We heard many similar stories of the long term positive influence of adverse experiences in therapists/counselors' adult personal life on their professional functioning.

Compared to earlier phases, therapists in this phase seemed markedly more willing to share information on their personal life and also tell about how their personal life affected how they worked. Their greater self-confidence as therapists may also have contributed to these Experienced Professionals honestly disclosing some of their motives to become therapists. One therapist said:

> We are drawn to this field to fix ourselves. That is where the energy to be in the field comes from. And we tend to be controlling people without knowing it. Both of these have to be understood before the person can be really effective. In contrast to the past I now think of myself as a coach or midwife for the client who does her or his own work.

Extensive and varied experiences, generated through thousands of hours of client work and life experiences, described by an informant, as "I have lived through a lot of hell and lot of pleasures," have contributed to a contextual sensitivity in the process of abstracting or generalizing knowledge. We call this "contextually sensitive knowledge development" a central process toward the attainment of wisdom. We may express this by stating that the epistemological center for the Experienced Professional is experience based and contextually anchored.

Professional Role and Conceptual Ideas Used

Compared to earlier phases, the modal Experienced Professional reports several changes in his or her perception of the therapist/counselor role. These changes involve a movement toward (a) being convinced that the therapeutic relationship is essential for client change; (b) personalizing and individualizing the professional role; (c) changing perceptions of therapist and client power; (d) increased flexibility in role performance; (e) better regulation of emotions and involvement with clients. We will describe these changes below.

Modal practitioners in the Experienced Professional phase consider the therapeutic relationship as the most important single contributor to therapy effectiveness. However, there are nuances in perception of what role the relationship plays. All practitioners in this phase saw the relationship as important for therapy outcome. A few considered the relationship as merely providing a condition for effective therapeutic work, while others saw see the relationship as the most central arena for client assessment and as the arena where effective therapy/counseling takes place. One Experienced Professional said, "The relationship sets the tone for the rest of the work." Another in the same phase expressed, even more emphatically, the important role played by the relationship, "The relationship is the key that allows the rest to happen." As a consequence of highlighting the role played by the relationship, many therapists in this phase talk of using themselves as instruments. As one therapist said, "The therapist becomes the instrument rather than just using instrument and interviewing techniques. Skill becomes the use of self." Another said, "I am infusing my own self into therapy and relying less on techniques."

Experienced Professionals also express a more nuanced understanding, not only of the role played by the relationship, but also of how their personality and attitudes are understood and expressed in their work. One of our most experienced practitioners formulated the nuances of these dynamics as follows:

> The relationship is understood even more deeply at this point where the therapist's power, attention, expectations and own personality, including short-comings and strengths, can be seen, understood and used in a more direct and clear way than before.

We highlighted the personal and individualized quality of the work role as a cardinal characteristic of the Experienced Practitioner by choosing a quote that illustrated this for the ingress of the chapter. One practitioner at this phase said:

I learned all the rules and so I came to a point—after lots of effort—where I knew the rules very well. Gradually I modified the rules. Then I began to use the rules to let me go where I wanted to go. Lately I haven't been talking so much in terms of rules.

Compared to therapists/counselors in earlier phases, the modal Experienced Professional reports a change in perception of own (therapist/counselor) and client power. This is reflected in one of the themes (Theme 10) to be presented in chapter 9. For the practitioner there is a realignment from self as powerful to client as powerful. There seems to be a paradox here, as these Experienced Professionals are also agentic in the sense that they are more comfortable with confronting their clients. But, in spite of this development, it seems that the modal Experienced Professional does not deemphasize providing safety for the client. The safety–challenge balance is an important feature of how master therapists conceptualize their work (Sullivan, Skovholt, & Jennings, 2004).

When comparing themselves to how practitioners perceived themselves at earlier phases, Experienced Professionals describe themselves as being more flexible in the approaches and techniques they use in their professional work. One therapist used the metaphor of choosing rides in an amusement park to illustrate flexibility in the use of techniques. In contrast to how techniques were used in the past (i.e., applied in the more rigid and mechanical way typical of the Novice Student), increased flexibility was expressed by a female Experienced Professional, who said:

I am looser than I used to be in my approach to the work. Sure, everything must be done ethically and professionally. That's a given. I'm just not so frantic about answers or even questions. Now I really feel there isn't a right way to do it although there is a right way for me.

Practitioners in this phase also tell of being better able to regulate their involvement with clients, which is a consequence of the individuation process that we described earlier. Ideally, this happens as a fluctuating process both within session with one client and also between sessions across different clients. Within sessions, it means being able to be totally absorbed in the experiential world of the client at one moment while disengaging and observing what happens thereafter. Across clients, it means that within minutes after a session is ended being able to refocus and turn one's attention toward the new client.

Conceptually, regulation of involvement is closely tied to regulation of emotions. Although the modal therapists/counselors in this phase report that they are better able to regulate their involvement with clients, some practitioners clearly struggle with this. Research within the SPR-CRN can inform us about the base rate of how therapists relate to clients, and specifically of the base rate for therapists/counselors in the Experienced Professional phase (Orlinsky & Rønnestad, 2005). In this research two dimensions of work involvement were identified: healing involvement and stressful involvement. These involvement styles will also be described and placed in a larger developmental context in chapter 14. Healing involvement was defined by a sense of skillfulness, minimal difficulties in practice, use of constructive coping strategies, a sense of flow, and a sense of being invested in a genuine, affirmative, and receptive relationship. Stressful involvement was defined by therapists' experience of multiple difficulties when relating to clients, use of unconstructive coping strategies, and in-session feelings of boredom or anxiety.

On the basis of combination of high and low involvement styles, four practice patterns were identified. These were Effective Practice, Challenging Practice, Disengaged Practice, and Distressing Practice.[4] The general picture is that about one in six of these experienced therapists was involved in a Disengaged Practice, while about 1 in 15 experienced Distressing Practice. Therapists who struggle with their involvement are likely to be at risk for burnout.

Compared to practitioners in earlier phases, the modal Experienced Professional is better capable of letting go of "overresponsibility," an important aspect of boundary regulation. One therapist said, "I have a better sense of personal boundaries and blame myself less if things don't work." Being better able to regulate their involvement with clients, the therapist/counselor can end workdays more refreshed and stimulated rather than exhausted and depleted. Learning this skill, which we earlier referred to as "boundaried generosity" (Skovholt, Jennings, & Mullenbach, 2004), is very difficult, yet crucial for the long-term intimate involvement with human suffering that is central to the work of therapists. This description of boundary regulation fits some experienced informants better than others. Some reported considerable hardship and felt challenged also in the mature professional years.

Even though we have tried to describe the most general characteristics and movements that experienced therapists go through, we have not covered it all. An interesting longitudinal study of training within a psychoanalytic psychotherapy training institution (Carlsson, 2011) showed that therapists with an average of about 11 years of experience were quite vulnerable to the feedback they received from their teachers. These trainees were searching for recognition from their trainers and wanted their preconceptions about therapy (i.e., their preformed professional self) to be acknowledged by their teachers (Carlsson, Norberg, Sandell, & Schubert, 2011). So, even for experienced therapists, training experiences can lead to loss of confidence in one's abilities as a therapist. Students reacted adversely to those teachers who were authoritarian, and some of these experienced therapists handled the authoritarian teachers by conforming to their wishes. This suggests that practitioners' vulnerability is not only a function of experience, but is also influenced by the context in which learning takes place. The results of this study are an important reminder of the influence of the learning environment for the development of therapists.

Measures of Effectiveness and Satisfaction

In most phases, therapist satisfaction derives from a wide variety of experiences such as one's relationship to colleagues, the amount and quality of work setting support, degree of autonomy in work, the quality of one's personal life, self-concept, temperament, personality, perception of work role, and how one assesses therapist effectiveness and salary. Below, we address what the Experienced Professionals themselves emphasized when exploring the topics of work satisfaction and evaluation of effectiveness.

Compared to earlier phases, the modal Experienced Professional has adjusted one's view of what objectives can be reached in therapy/counseling work. The practitioner has a more nuanced perception of which clients they are most effective with, what objectives can be reached in a relatively short time period, and which clients need more longer term therapy/counseling. The "series of humiliations" experienced during a long career fuel a sense of modesty about what can accomplished during therapy/counseling. Any grandiose inclination that a therapist may have had before are gone for most in this phase.

The work setting seems important in adjusting expectations. One female Experienced Professional said, "Because I worked in a setting with very difficult patients, I was humbled early on and learned how difficult it was to change a lifetime of ingrained personality and behavior."

As modal Experienced Professionals are better able to regulate professional boundaries, have a clearer perception of the professional role, and have gone through a process of individuation, they are able to evaluate the quality of their work in ways that go beyond merely relying on clients' expressions of being satisfied or dissatisfied. One said, "Just because clients are happy doesn't mean I've done a whole lot for them." This quote also illustrates an insight that matches outcome research that has shown that the correlation between client-satisfaction measures and other outcome measures such as symptomatic distress is low. The individuation process also leads these practitioners to see more clearly their limitations as practitioners, and to change their attitude to client feedback. One Experienced Professional said, "I no longer need the client to like me as I did. Earlier I wasn't aware of my need to be liked and how I could be greatly influenced by this need."

Satisfaction with work is also related to how therapists/counselors conceptualize their work role and how they assess the quality of their work and how they react to client feedback. One said:

> I now don't work real hard at trying to change people. I'm more with them. When I first started out, my job was to make people change, now I don't get so anxious, nervous, invested in that. I'm excited for clients if they change, but don't need that for confirmation of myself. I already feel I'm good at what I do. If I find myself pushing too hard I look at issues of countertransference.

The combination of lowered expectations, increased respect of the hardships of therapy/counseling work and a clearer differentiation of responsibilities between themselves and the clients is expressed by many. One Experienced Professional summarizes this as follows:

> I am more willing to let people be and know it takes time; earlier I was too eager to bring about change ... I am more comfortable letting the problem be with the person and not take it on myself.... People have so many problems, counseling is so damn hard. I've scaled down my expectations about change and sometimes expect no changes.

Generally speaking, therapists in all phases of professional development, including the Experienced Professionals, appreciate getting positive feedback from their clients. However, at this phase, client feedback is filtered through their own evaluations of what has happened. One male practitioner said:

> When clients give me feedback about how great I am I tend not to trust it, but I do enjoy getting referrals from them. I also make good money at this. I get a lot out of it. It isn't just altruistic.

We may ask if the movement toward paying less attention to what clients are saying when assessing the quality of their work is a good movement. Certainly, extremely positive client's verbal statements may be explained by factors such as client deference, acquiescence, or reluctance to hurt or disappoint the therapist/counselor. And faced with these alternatives, assessments by other methods, such as symptom distress scales, or assessments from other observational perspectives, such as independent observers and therapists/counselors' evaluations, would add to the trustworthiness of what the client was saying.

We strongly believe that clients' negative evaluations should be taken seriously. First and foremost, it is a matter of respecting clients and their evaluation. It could very well be that no therapist/counselor, even the most highly skilled, is able to provide a treatment that would meet the needs of a client who voiced strong disappointment and dissatisfaction with a particular therapist. However, there are two sets of findings that suggest that it is unwise to disregard client negative accounts of what happens in therapy. The first set of findings concerns the rigorous studies on therapist effects that we referred to earlier (e.g., Lutz, Leon, Martinovitch, Lyons, & Stiles, 2007; Wampold & Brown, 2005), which have demonstrated substantial outcome variations among therapists/counselors. The other set concerns the troublesome finding that therapists have limited capacity to detect deterioration in client functioning (Lambert & Shimokawa, 2011). It seems likely that variations in therapists' ability to detect negative movements in therapy/counseling is due to differences in practitioners' interpersonal sensitivity.

Even though there were expressions of disillusionment and a sense of emptiness among the Experienced Professionals (as one said, "Is this all there is?") a substantial majority of practitioners in this phase voiced high work satisfaction. There were also many expressions of feeling a sense of gratitude for being able to help clients attain a better life, illustrated by one practitioner who said, "Going to sleep I say: That's my piece for humanity."

Notes

1. Previous versions of this chapter were published in *The Evolving Professional Self*, by T. M. Skovholt and M. H. Rønnestad (1992). Copyright has reverted to the authors. Chichester, England: Wiley, and in "The Journey of the Counselor and Therapist: Research Findings and Perspectives," by M. H. Rønnestad & T. M. Skovholt (2003), *Journal of Career Development, 30*, 5–44, 2003. Adapted with permission from Sage. All quotes are from *The Evolving Professional Self.*

2. The most commonly used measures of burnout are the Maslach Burnout Inventory/Human Service Survey (MBI-HSS), the MBI-Educators Survey (MBI-ES), and MBI-General Survey (MBI-GS). Other inventories are: The Burnout Measure by Pines and Aronson; the Oldenburg Bournout Inventory by Demerouti and Collaborators, the Shirom-Melamed burnout Measure by Shirom and Melamed; the Copenhagen Burnout Inventory by Kristensen and collaborators (Larsen, 2010). The content of the original MBI-HSS was based on the theoretical assumption that burnout was a special kind of stress, a distinctive phenomenon related to situations where "working with other people, particularly in a caregiving relationship, was at the heart of the burnout phenomenon" (Maslach, 1993, p. 23). The Maslach Burnout Inventory—General Survey (MBI-GS) was designed to answer the critique against the existing scale (MBI-HSS) after the burnout concept was redefined to be applicable to other than "people-oriented professions." Items were changed and the original concepts of emotional exhaustion, depersonalization, and personal accomplishment were redefined to exhaustion, cynicism, and professional efficacy respectively (Larsen, Ulleberg, & Rønnestad, 2010).

3. The first author (MHR) had the pleasure of being a discussant on a paper on this topic presented by Castonguay at the Society for Psychotherapy Research international meeting in Asilomar, CA, June 2010. One topic for discussion was: Given what we know of adverse therapy effects, and therapists' contributions to these effects, should personal therapy be mandatory in the training of psychotherapists and counsellors?

4. *Effective Practice* = High Healing Involvement+Low Stressful Involvement; *Challenging Practice* = High Healing Involvement+High Stressful Involvement; *Disengaged Practice* = Low Healing Involvement=Low Stressful Involvement; *Distressing Practice* = Low Healing Involvement+High Stressful Involvement.

8

THE SENIOR PROFESSIONAL PHASE[1]

I think about starting out on a walk. We have a very narrow path that you had to follow, and you watch your step so you don't fall off the edge. There is no edge to hold onto ... but now, at age 78, it is like walking in a wide world that has forests, deserts, rivers, oceans, and mountains, and it is like you go into it with your hiking boots and there is lots of grass, and you can sort of walk around in it without fear, and everything is more comfortable.

Introduction

Individuals in the Senior Professional phase have practiced at least 25 years as postgraduate therapists/counselors, and many have been working in the field for much longer. Some continue to practice after formal retirement ... most are between 60 and 70 years old, and in fact, one of the therapists we interviewed had a part-time practice at the age of 82 years. When we first interviewed a group of these Senior Professionals, their average age was 64 years, and when we interviewed them again, their average was 74 years. The majority of the descriptions that we provide here are based on the first round of interviews. However, we supplement these descriptions with some of the interview data that we collected 10 years later (Rønnestad & Skovholt, 2001). In a section of this chapter we present how these highly experienced therapists perceived the most important sources of influence for their professional functioning and development.

Some of these senior professionals feel that they are at the peak of their careers, and have no intention of retiring, while others are contemplating and preparing for retirement, and a few have just retired. Those who were retired gave us retrospective accounts of their experiences as practicing therapist/counselors. The span of age and experience contribute to the reports of the Senior Professionals varying in terms of active involvement in new learning and the emphasis placed on continued professional development. However, our general impression from the analyses of the transcripts, which have been confirmed by what other seniors have told us, is that the quest for new conceptual knowledge and therapeutic/counseling skills continues among practitioners during this late phase. However, a consolidation of acquired knowledge and competence also occurs. The transition from the Experienced to the Senior Professional phase is continuous, and much of what we described for the Experienced Professionals is valid for this phase as well. Nevertheless, the reality of loss of work roles and the emergence of other roles, which is common for these practitioners, is also occurring.

Developmental Task and General Description

For the preceding phase, there were three developmental tasks. The first task is valid for this phase as well. So is the third, slightly adjusted, while a new task is added. The three developmental tasks for the Senior Professional phase are:

1. For the therapist/counselor to maintain a sense of professional growth and resiliency while avoiding burnout and stagnation.
2. For the therapist/counselor to maintain a work role which is experienced as highly congruent with the therapist/counselor's coherent professional self.
3. For some therapists/counselors, to adapt to the situation of partial or full retirement approaching, adjust client load, and prepare clients for the change if necessary.

The integrated self of the modal Experienced Professional is expressed by a sense of coherence and genuineness in relating to clients, and also by a sense of consistency between his or her values, self-concepts, theoretical/conceptual models, and techniques. Some individuals in this phase must address the reduced energy that normatively occurs with aging, and must adjust their workload accordingly.

From these Senior Professionals we have heard many reports which, in fact, vary in positive and negative tone. Some are of distress, sadness, and concerns about failing health of both self and family members, of reduced energy, and of limitations in activities and accomplishments. We have also heard objections to the glamorization of old age, such as one male therapist who said, "I think the golden age is not best by any means. As far as I can tell, being old and wise is not better than being young and innocent and energetic" (Rønnestad & Skovholt, 2001, p. 183). Some expressions of regret seemed to contain elements of "too soon old and too late smart," the anticipatory grief over future losses.

There is the added challenge of staying energized and vital when facing the dynamics of been there, seen it, done it. However, generally we were impressed by the morale of this senior group. With few exceptions, they demonstrated their interest in further professional development, as well as

122

the related enthusiasm and commitment to their work that is necessary for communicating to the client the hope and encouragement that are so important for client progress, as Frank (1961) and others have taught us.

Is the generally positive picture we have obtained from these seniors, supplemented with impressions from some other sources, representative for the majority of therapists/counselors during this phase? The answer is yes because other research on the topic of professional development has demonstrated that the most highly experienced therapists, regardless of nationality, profession, theoretical orientation, or gender, state that they are currently growing as therapists (Orlinsky, Ambuehl, Rønnestad et al., 1999). So, the findings from our joint study and the Society for Psychotherapy Research/Collaborative Research Network (SPR/CRN), combine to paint a picture of continued growth throughout a therapist's entire career.

In order to obtain a sense of what is meant by "current growth" in the SPR/CRN study, we have listed the questions that constitute the scale of Currently Experienced Growth. They are (a) How much do you feel that you are changing as a therapist? (b) How much does this change feel like progress or improvement? (c) How much do you feel you are overcoming past limitations as a therapist? (d) How much do you feel you are becoming more skillful in practicing therapy? (e) How much do you feel you are deepening your understanding of therapy? (f) How much do you feel a growing sense of enthusiasm about doing therapy? On a composite scale of these items, with a response format of 0 (not at all), to 5 (very), the mean value for the most experienced cohort (between 23 and 52 years of experience) was 3.5, which was almost identical to the mean scores of less experienced cohorts. The data for these analyses are from over 3,000 therapists from many countries,[2] so it seems that senior therapists generally experience a sense of professional growth that is comparable to that of less experienced therapists/counselors.

The generally positive results from both these studies should be interpreted with caution because we do not know how many therapists have dropped out of the therapist role. It seems reasonable to assume that therapists who have not been able to find a suitable match between their personal/professional characteristics and their therapist role, or who have not integrated their personal and professional selves, are more likely to have dropped out of the profession. They may also have redefined their professional role toward teaching, research, or administration. However, in the qualitative investigation, we asked therapists/counselors the question: "What causes people to leave the field?" Few of our senior respondents knew anyone who had left the field in recent years. Our impression is that therapists/counselors seldom leave after already being in the profession for a long time. One male therapist answered the question as follows, "I have not seen that. But, by [this] time … you've seen some rather inept psychiatrists and psychologists, but they stay in the field. Unfortunately."

The modal Senior Professional expressed high work satisfaction, a general sense of being a "good enough" therapist/counselor, and also a sense of gratitude for being in the profession. During the interview, the typical Senior Professional manifested a "presence" in how they related to us as interviewers and expressed a sense of being at ease with themselves and with us. One male senior said, "I think I am more myself than I have ever been."

Modal Senior Phase Professionals express a clear acceptance of their limitations as therapists/counselors. They express more humility and see themselves as less powerful change agents. A male therapist said, "The longer I've been at it, the more I've become accepting of my limitations. That is just the way it is. Some things I do well, other things not so well." Another male therapist at this phase formulated her changing view of therapist power as follows: "Well, I think the big thing was that [when I was younger I worried that] I'd make a terrible mistake, you know and ruin somebody's life forever. And now, I feel you can't do that. I'm not that powerful." Another female Senior Professional said:

> When you start off in this there's a tremendous sense of responsibility in the sense that if …, kind of like when you start to drive a car, "Oh, my god, what am I driving here and what's going …," you know, what great damage can I do.

Even though difficulties and challenges are still experienced, these seniors expressed a positive outlook. As one said, "Hang in there, it gets better. I enjoy going to work every day, enjoy what I am doing." The sense of realism that therapists/counselors in the preceding phase expressed is maintained and refined during this phase.

Sources of Influence[3] and Learning Process

As described for the preceding phases, the sources of influence that we have found to impact professional development are: theories/research, clients, professional elders (professors, supervisors, mentors, therapists), peers/colleagues, one's own personal life, and the social/cultural environment. These resources continue to play an important role in the professional functioning and development of Senior Professionals. As with other phases, the influence of learning from interacting with clients emerged as most salient for these highly experienced therapists/counselors. There were slight shifts in reported influence for peers and younger colleagues. In the interviews of these highly experienced therapists/counselors, the relationship between personal life and professional functioning emerged more clearly than for previous phases.

With increasing experience, there seems to be a converging impression that personal characteristics have influenced the choice of becoming a therapist/counselor, and also that personal characteristics have influenced the kind of therapists that they have become. As one male Senior Professional expressed it, "I think I was destined to become the type of therapist I am today, just by my temperament." However, regarding whether personal problems have influenced career choice, opinions vary. In the preceding chapter, we quoted an Experienced Professional who stated that "We are drawn to the field to fix ourselves...." This popular notion is clearly not typical of what therapists say about their motivation to become therapists, but stimulates many to clarify for themselves whether this is so for them. We have not systematically collected data on motivation to become therapists, but know that motivations vary considerably.

A well-known male Senior Professional therapist-professor in our sample shared some of his reflections on this topic with us. He said:

> [T]here is the thought, you know, I think it used to be more widely promoted before, ... [that] a lot of people [who] go into psychology do so partly to try to resolve some of their own personal difficulties. I have never been able to establish in my mind with any sense of confidence, that personal problems had much to do with my decision to go into psychology. All that I can tell you is that I was just absolutely fascinated by the first course I had in psychology. Knew from the beginning that I had made the right choice....

This therapist went on to talk warmly about the intellectual appeal of the field, and how, throughout his career, he had pursued this intellectual interest.

Some therapists report that early in life they were affectively attuned to the needs of others and of having had a helper role early in their life. We will describe experiences in early personal life more extensively as sources of influence for professional development later in the chapter.

In the initial interviews of the Senior Professionals, and more clearly so in the interviews of 10 years later, we heard powerful, passionate, and appreciative descriptions of professional elders (Rønnestad & Skovholt, 2001). Although, the therapists/counselors were referring to interchanges with these respected seniors from many years back, the seniors continued to have a profound and direct impact many years later. Observing and interacting with respected, trusted, and competent seniors appears to us to be an essential part of being a student and a practicing professional therapist. For some, it was a mentoring relationship. When asked about mentors, one female therapist said:

I don't have them anymore, honey … I always had mentors, and wonderful mentors … and they were always there, these wonderful men…. I am sure I have internalized these mentors…. I often speak of Kurt as in the present, rather than in the past, even though it was decades ago.

It is a powerful statement on the impact of seniors that therapists/counselors with decades of experience continue to speak of strong mentoring relationships. One, looking back at a graduate school mentor, said:

I recall any number of instances in which he invited me to sit in [therapy] as a mouse in the corner during sessions, and consequently, immediately after those sessions, I could ask questions that were very pertinent and alive, and he would respond. I observed a master therapist, and sometimes he would bring me up to date on a case that he was dealing with.

We also heard of therapists/counselors being influenced by someone that they have never actually met, but whom they have adopted as a mentor, an example of a "fantasy mentor." One individual mentioned that Freud had served this role for him and said that he could think of other "older, wiser" people in this way. However, a couple of these Senior Professionals reported explicitly that they had never had anyone whom they would describe as a mentor. Both were highly reputable seniors: one was a peer-nominated master therapist (Skovholt & Jennings, 2004) and the other a highly respected male academic counselor and researcher. He said:

I don't know that I permitted myself to get close enough to any person to be genuinely calling him my mentor; good relations were there, but I would not call it a 100% bona fide mentoring relationship.

However, he clearly recognized the important influence of colleagues, and went on to list a number of senior colleagues who had influenced him greatly.

Senior colleagues can exert both a positive and negative influence. Here is a story of early disappointment told by a male senior practitioner, years after the experience. He said:

I had one supervisor at the VA whom I admired enormously. I really wanted to emulate him: but later he changed and I wouldn't have been influenced by him anymore. He changed in a very negative way. I think what he did was lose some of his humanity.

Reports such as these were rare. The general picture that emerged from the interviews was that our participants had mostly positive, influential professional elders. The impact of these people, in time, becomes what we have labeled the profound internalized influence of professional elders.

For some Senior Professionals, peers continue to be important sources of influence. One said, "They [peers] are a real strong influence. It seems to me that it is with peers along the way that I've the most prolonged and intensive conversations about what we're up to ... all the way along...." But, for many, peers seem to have faded as a powerful source of influence. At both student phases peers play a highly significant role for many reasons, including their shared position in the hierarchical power structure of the training institution. During the Beginning and Advanced Professional phases, peers represent continuity with the treasured companionship of student days, and are valuable sources of support and stimulation, as well as being resources to draw upon when encountering the hardships and challenges of practice. For the Senior Professional Phase, we ask why there are so few reports of peers being strong sources of influence on how these Seniors work. In asking this question, we are not talking about peers in their role as appreciated colleagues and friends, but as stimulating "teachers." We do not have data from our study to answer our question, but may speculate that at their age, Senior Professionals are likely to know already what their peers represent and be familiar with the ideas their peers have about effective counseling/therapy. In addition, at this phase in their professional lives, the Senior Professionals may already know the favorite ways that peers conceptualize cases and perhaps their input is already present as internalized scripts of how to deal with the issues they confront.

As described above, the modal Senior Professional is eager to learn and develop. Could it be that increasing value being placed on the influence of more junior colleagues is a substitute for the fading of peer influence? We have many reports that seem to support such a change in emphasis. Seniors who are supervising younger colleagues talk consistently about the positive consequences of relating to younger colleagues. Meeting the challenge of educating younger practitioners may assist in keeping a Senior Professional charged up and professionally alive; such experiences provide opportunities for new learning and for keeping up with new developments in the field. In describing this issue, one male Senior Professional said, "Supervising interns really did keep me going." Another said, "They get brighter all the time. I feel that I learn as much from the interns as I teach them. They have become my teachers." Another Senior Professional talked very specifically about how he was influenced by his students. He said, "From interactions and discussion from some of my grad students ..., I learned to be much more flexible and much more open and much more sensitive to client feelings in my own counseling."

Interacting with more junior colleagues also provides an avenue for expressing one's seniority and for sharing with more inexperienced colleagues some of what one has learned over the years. One said:

> I like to supervise younger ones at a volunteer agency. I like to teach them about things like handling client rejection by going for a good batting average rather than expecting perfection from oneself and also being less afraid of harming clients.

As illustrated by the quotes above, the modal Senior Professional regards younger professionals with appreciation and respect. But this is not true for all. One female Senior Professional shared her observation of many young psychologists, mostly of a behavioral orientation, as being "very rigid indeed." She formulated the movement of early rigidity (her own and others) as one of becoming less arrogant, and said about that:

> That's just the idea of being able to control or to mold or to make someone.... I sometimes hear the young therapists talk about getting the client to do XYZ and that's a role that's anathema to me. It makes me the major variable in any changes that they make.

As we will describe below, when we address the ways that Senior Professionals conceptualize how therapy/counseling works and the work role, we will see that the quote above also illustrates a movement by these Senior Therapists toward deemphasizing their power as therapists.

The Senior Professionals draw extensively from what they have experienced and learned throughout a long life. One said, "Doing a lot of living was a great help. I remember, in my 30s, I had a client in his 50s who wanted a divorce. I thought why 'bother at that age?' Then, in my 50s, I finally understood when I got a divorce." As we will describe below, life roles, such as being a parent or a spouse continue to teach the individual a great deal. Tragedies or intense stressors can have an important impact on one's work. Examples here include the death of a partner, serious physical illness, and divorce.

Early Personal Life as a Learning Arena for Professional Development[4]

In this section we will present selected sections of the results from our interviews of the most Senior Professionals. Of the 20 Senior Professionals that we interviewed the first time, we were able to locate 12 who were willing and able to participate in an interview 10 years later. This subsample had a mean age of 74 years. Their mean number of years of postdoctoral experience was 38, ranging from 25 to 56 years. Five were Board Certified by ABPP in either clinical or counseling psychology. The sample is small, so we do not know if the results are transferable to other therapists/counselors. However, these professionals are unusually experienced, so we may define the sample as being strategic. This substudy may be considered a study of possible dynamics (rather than as representative findings) between experiences in personal life and professional functioning.

All therapists expressed the view that events in their personal lives had affected them as professionals. A few gave thin descriptions, most provided rich descriptions. Eight of these 12 Senior Professionals told of how the experiences in early life (childhood, adolescence, interactions in family and with parents) had affected various aspects of their professional lives and functioning. Two of these reported explicitly about how their relationships with their parents had become models for successful therapy. Both made reference to how parents became models for them of "how therapy works." One female practitioner told us how the love of her mother became her therapy model, "therapy as love." Another female practitioner said:

I think [therapy] works first of all because a trusting relationship develops. I think it may be more important than all the other things people tend to do, but then I have always kind of thought that. I think it works when the person feels enough trust to talk about things in a way that they can hear themselves and get a little distance at the same time that they are close to it.

In her answer to our question about the origin of this, she said:

I suppose maybe it came from my parents. I never doubted ever that what they did was for my best interest. I am sure about [my understanding of] my parents and also what therapy is all about. In some ways, I never did really fit that into any of the theories and patterns that I was thrown into in professional training.

Six of the eight seniors described adverse experiences in childhood that had a negative influence on them. When interpreting these findings, we should keep in mind that these practitioners may have viewed their background with looking glasses sensitive to nuances that may escape the nonprofessional observer. Given this, we were nevertheless surprised to learn of these negative associations. We were told of feelings of abandonment, of having grown up in a demanding, achievement-oriented family, of experiencing rigid and restraining child-rearing practices, of receiving only conditional love from parents, and of growing up in a family with a rule of "no emotions." These experiences were seen as having an important influence on the professional self and functioning in various ways, such as selection of theoretical orientation, definition of work role, choice of therapeutic style and focus, attitude toward colleagues, hardships experienced, and ways of coping in practice.

As previously stated, and also expressed at the beginning of this chapter, modal Senior Professionals are confident in their abilities as therapists, and feel at ease and comfortable in interactions with clients. However, there are exceptions to this, as expressed by one Senior who conveyed that she had grown up in a very demanding and achievement-oriented environment, with exceptionally high standards of performance. She said:

> I have always had performance anxiety. I have always had it; no matter when I start or what I do, I am always concerned with how it will go … it is a damn nuisance … it is always there, and I know it …, it is a thing that keeps me careful about what I do.… I like what I do, look forward to what I do, and yet every time I am working with somebody, I am watching the clock and saying, "Only 20 more minutes of it, … am I going to be able to do the work?"

We heard stories of how early, family-related experiences sometimes found expression during adult professional years. One male Senior Professional described his quest to receive positive feedback and encouragement from professional elders and the reason for that. He said:

> From my parents, I got a lot of pretty instrumental encouragement. It was not genuine support for me as a human being. It was pressure to keep up the family reputation, so the people who became mentors for me and who really turned me on were people who were really encouraging and said "Hey, that is a good idea and come join us, be part of the team," or "Here is something that I think you will enjoy."

The above narration is one in which family experiences have had an indirect impact on choice of theoretical orientation, as was also expressed by another male practitioner. Growing up in a family with rigid child-rearing practices, one practitioner rejected therapeutic approaches that he saw as rigid. About his efforts to become a transactional analysis (TA) therapist, and his opposition to TA, he said:

> But I also saw it as being a very rigid system…and this is my personality more than my professional training. I have always been very resistant to rigid classification systems, probably growing out of my own early childhood experiences.

We also observed the dynamic of early trauma impacting on withdrawal from the profession for one retired female Senior Professional, who said:

> I think I survived those years without any ill effects on my day-to-day functioning as a professional, … but I think because of my increasing cynicism over the years, I was motivated to end my career early.… My early retirement from practice and from the profession was a function of personal experiences, but I don't think early experiences impacted me while in practice.

A Senior Professional who was very resolute about the importance of action and decision making in therapy, and who valued an intellectual, verbal, advice-giving, and rational combination that was influenced by Skinner and Ellis, told us of the trouble that he had experienced when working with clients who expressed intense emotions. He gave a detailed account of the difficulty that he had in tolerating the intense emotions expressed while working with a couple. About the couple fighting verbally, he said, "And I really could hardly stand it, when it went on and on and on." He told of his own family, in which both his parents had actively turned off difficult emotions, and described his family as being very rationally oriented. In addition to the link between early experiences and later functioning, there also seemed to be a connection between this therapist's desire for challenges on a constant basis and his perception of his mother. He expressed it this way:

> I have put myself in probably the greatest variety of situations that I could without being fearful or intimidated.… My mother was always like that; she was always adventuresome.… I keep finding things I want to get into that I don't know enough about yet. That is the way my mother was.

Surprisingly, none of the therapists that reported having a troublesome family background told us of any direct positive impact from these experiences on their professional work. However, there were reports of indirect positive consequences. For example, one Senior Professional who had grown up in a very poor family reported being driven to avoid poverty, which he did. His professional role provided much material wealth. Another stated that, because of his experiences of receiving only conditional love from his parents, he developed a sensitivity and appreciation for genuine collegial support. But generally, the reports indicated that early negative experiences continued to exert negative influences as adults, a finding that appears to be contrary to the perspective of the "wounded healer" (Henry, 1966), which suggests that "early wounds" may provide a unique potential for growth and development. Our findings from this limited sample, suggest that early wounds are not necessarily healed, and they may also find their expression in later professional years.

But again, we should emphasize caution in interpreting these results. Looking back at our methodology, we now regret that we did not inquire specifically into the potential role played by therapists/counselors' personal therapy for their professional functioning and development. We know that personal therapy ranks highly among sources of influence for professional development (Orlinsky, Botermans, & Rønnestad, 2001). The Senior Professional who experienced anxiety in her meeting with clients, even in her senior years, had not engaged in personal therapy; maybe her fate would have been different had she done so.

Research from SPR/CRN drawing from a sample of American and Norwegian therapists has provided some interesting results on the moderating impact of personal therapy on the relationship between childhood life-quality and adult functioning (Orlinsky, Norcross, Rønnestad, & Wiseman, 2005). Childhood life quality was measured by a two-item scale with a response format of 0 (not at all) to 5 (very much): "Did you experience a sense of being genuinely cared for and supported?" and "Did the family you grew up in function well, psychologically or emotionally?" First, to set the stage for the argument: The correlation between the quality of childhood experiences and adult (current) life satisfaction was r = .25 (highly significant). Therapists who reported low childhood life quality were more likely to report poor life quality as an adult. And here comes to the promising story: For therapists who reported at least one beneficial personal therapy, the correlation between childhood life quality was merely r = .07 which is not significant. In other words, personal therapy assessed to be beneficial seems to moderate (null out) the impact of early life-quality and life quality as an adult. But the good story does not end here, as "Similar differentials in correlations between childhood and adult experience were found for reliable measures of 'warmth' and 'openness' in personal self-image, and for 'healing involvement' and 'constructive coping' in therapeutic work experience" (Orlinsky, Norcross, et al., 2005, p. 218). A substantial majority of practitioners have engaged in personal therapy, and most of these report the experience as positive, so we can feel some comfort in these findings. They are a convincing argument for therapists/counselors to engage in personal therapy.

Adult Personal Life as an Arena for Professional Development

Reports on the influence of adult personal life on professional functioning and development differed from the reports of early life just presented. There were clearly more stories of being positively, rather than negatively, influenced. The quality of the relationship with one's spouse was seen as having greatest impact and these ranged from being extremely positive to negative, with the former predominating. One male Senior Professional talked about how marriage disruption had resulted in unfavorable career moves. He said:

> My personal life has probably had a lot of negative impact .... I have been divorced three times ..., the first two of those led me to make career decisions based on what was going on in my personal life, and in retrospect they were both bad decisions.

Conversely, we learned how a caring marriage could boost a practitioner's self-confidence and assurance. One female Senior Professional spoke of a rigid religious background and a similar environment in graduate school. She spoke, in an assured and confident manner, of how her husband had helped her to overcome her self-criticism in graduate school. She said:

> I used to be able to open my mouth and talk about anything under the sun, and I think that what I had to say was as worthwhile as anybody else. By the time I finished graduate school, it was like I had to look at what I was saying through about 17 pair of eyes before I could decide it was all right.... I think my husband is probably the most important influence in my life. He is extremely supportive. He really starts objecting if I start putting myself down one way or the other. It is an old bad habit of mine, and he stops it for me, and it is so positive that he does it.

The growth potential inherent in adjusting to hardships in the family was demonstrated by a male Senior Professional, who informed us as follows:

> My spouse had an emotional disorder and was hospitalized many times.... What did I learn? I learned how to be tolerant of somebody who was ill. I watched my kids learn a lot about accepting.... I learned a lot about being a good psychologist. I learned a lot about being a person. In the beginning, I was just so judgmental of my spouse.... Also, one of my children had a learning disability, ... that was hard too, ... I was an achiever and a striver in my work, so how could he have a learning disability.... I was extremely successful in my practice, and when that happens, it is easy to think you are something special. When difficult things happened in my family, it was painful, but it was good too, for perspective.

From the three therapists who were widowed, we heard of immediate distressing reactions to their spouses' deaths, but also of long-term positive consequences and increased competence in their work. In the first round of interviews, one Senior Professional said:

> I have been very happily married for 31 years and I think that has a strong stabilizing influence. I also have three children ..., I think that is a big learning situation.... We have a very close, warm family ... lots of ups and downs, ... [the family] has provided lots of support and [opportunity for] learning.

This therapist lost her husband after this interview, and in the next interview she said:

> I lost my husband not too many years ago, and I adored him. And having work was the one thing that kept me sane. I sort of felt that in this room [referring to her office], I was still the same person. Outside I wasn't anymore. And I have had a lot more widows come to me; people would send them to me and I seem to understand them.

The formulation above, and specifically *"and I seem to understand them"* reflects their own grieving and enables them to empathize better with the experiences of clients.

For one male Senior Professional, the intense grief when his wife died initiated a life transformation that dramatically changed his professional identity. In the first round of interviews, this Senior Professional talked of having been a behaviorist up to the point of the loss of his wife. He said, "Maybe I ought to preface all that by saying that at that point in my life I was a very rational, systematic, external, behaviorally oriented guy." He had said that he had previously used a lot of behavioral techniques, such as systematic desensitization. He continued by relating that "The watershed was my wife dying," which led to the opening up of other parts in him. After his wife died:

> I did a lot of spinning around and took a sabbatical.... I became much more interested in family systems and so I tended to see client problems in a family context, which was quite different. Totally different.... She had just died, and I was having a profound reanalysis, reevaluation of my life.

He mentioned going back to school, receiving supervision, and engaging in a learning experience that was similar to starting in a new internship. In the follow-up interview 10 years later, this story was retold with basically the same amount of detail, and with the same clarity of narration. He said:

> For a long time, I was very avoidant of negative feelings and did not want them expressed in the office, and when I saw them coming, I signaled that "We don't talk about that," and I think over time I have just become more accepting and better able to tolerate somebody else's negative feelings. I think I still have a tendency to try to optimize or persuade, but I am better at accepting the negative feelings.... I think one of the things that sort of shifted me out of the rational, cognitive, behavioral perspective was when my first wife passed away.... I was pretty rational and cognitive and nonemotional and a good behaviorist. And then when she died, it all fell apart and I really got in touch with a lot of feelings, ... it opened up all sorts of things that I wasn't aware of, ... feelings, emotions, vulnerabilities, strengths. And it had a tremendous impact on me and in my work.

This Senior Professional continued his story to tell of a new marriage that became another transforming event for him as a professional. In combination, these transforming events caused the largest change in therapist identity and professional self-concept in our study. He continued:

> And my second wife ... was not totally pleased to be married to a raving behaviorist, ... she has put in a lot of stuff, a lot of "affect oriented ideas" that shifted me and made it easy for me to make the kind of changes that I have done. There are a lot of influences from her.

The story of an 84-year-old therapist illustrates how traumatic experiences, when processed, can have a positive impact on outlook and functioning. We will present the story of this Senior Professional in some detail. She lost both her husband and daughter within a 2-year period, and shared the following: "Within a 2-year period, 30 years ago, I lost both my husband and my only daughter, and I went into a very tough depression after such a slug ... which was very, very difficult." This participant's narrative touched us deeply. She gave a detailed account of her recovery process after the death of her beloved husband. She said:

> Oh, I did all kinds of things to recover.... I would go back to every place that we have been together, and once I got back to the doctor's office where I had to take him every week, ... and the tears were running down my cheeks, and the nurse was saying, "Oh, ... what is happening? Can I help you?" I said, "No.... I am

just on a *pilgrimage of pain*." I found that if I went once, I could go a second time.... There were so many places where we had been, to restaurants, to the laundry ..., you see that once you face it, ... and a lot of people won't do that, ... you just have to face it.... I can talk about it now, because *I walked into the eye of the storm*, and I was determined to recover. I would go to the library every week and hunt for something to help me ..., you have to give yourself time. It took 18 months before I could feel like eating or drawing breath or anything. You have to tuck the lost person away somewhere, some place in your heart, it is really in your head, to come to a place where it no longer hurts.... that is the big recovery. When you can remember without pain, you are well.... I prayed for peace and purpose, and I eventually got the peace ..., and I sure got the purpose 'cause I had lots of clients. They came to me without advertising. I did help many, many people and eventually I had so many clients.

With intense gratitude, she spoke of the care that she received from one of her professors, "He led me through some of the toughest times after my spouse died, and I am forever in debt to him, and I learned a lot about being a psychologist by being on the other side of the table." Even though she refers to an interaction (with one of her professors) that is not framed within a therapy relationship, her report nevertheless illustrates again the learning potential of observing a "helper" from a position of needing and receiving help.

This Senior Professional, who reported that she had learned from observing a "helper," emphasized the power of modeling in therapeutic work with grieving clients. She said, "I was a living example that you can recover.... I had started a new life making progress ... and these clients who came to me who were very discouraged, could see that it could be done, that you can recover...." She continued to share her experiences:

I had one client, who wouldn't take her wedding ring off, and it had been going on for a year, and she was in such a desolate condition, and I said, "I want you to go home today and take off your wedding ring and put it in the drawer and leave it there. Start to make a break," and she called me back and said, "I did it." Sharing my experience with my clients is of great importance; I really knew what they were going through, because I had been there ... and look at me now; I am fine.... I get so disgusted sometimes when I watch TV and see people sobbing and sobbing over the fact that dear ones died 20 years ago, and I think, "Come off it; it's time you quit crying." I can talk freely about my spouse and child. I don't shed tears now.

For this Senior Professional, important components in her therapy model with grieving clients included, in addition to modeling, the following elements: the clients must face the pain; therapists must share their experiences; therapists must be caring, directive, encouraging, and convey that change takes time, and that the length the client needs varies; however, there is a limit to how much time should be taken. In addition to her own grieving being an important influence on her model of change, we also heard of the powerful impact of her mother. She said:

> I just marvel to this day of the vastness of her capacity to love, ... never did any of her children (and there were lots of them) feel that there was any partiality.... We were all so important to her, ... such stamina, strength, bravery, and courage, ... she endowed us all with her values.... From my mother, I got one very positive theory in all my work with people that I didn't change dramatically over time.... "God is love." I believed there was a bit of God in every human being.... I always treated a client with the intent of searching for the "piece of God in him."

How this therapist reacted to the death of her two most beloved persons, her husband and daughter, demonstrates a dynamic where her upbringing and image of her mother in combination with the resolution and working through of intense grief emotions, formed her conception of a professional role for therapy/counseling with grieving clients. Abstracting her experience, her story illustrates the growth potential in daring to face the situations that evoke the most painful grief emotions.

Bringing it all together, we see that the Senior Professional tells of being influenced by a large variety of sources of influence. Even though the senior type activities, such as supervision, teaching, and being a therapist for others, continue to engage the Senior Professional, clients still represent the most powerful sources of new learning for this highly experienced group of therapists/counselors. One well-known Senior Professional in an academic position, elaborated on the question of what had been most influential for him. He said:

> I will have to say clients—if you're talking strictly about what has shaped my performance as a counselor ... my clients and well, let me put it this way, an amalgam of clients and my reactions to them—how should I have done it, how do I need to change, because as a counselor I am sure that most of us do continually reflect on how we're doing and do try to make changes in our behavior and to do that we have to think about the client, so it is the clients and my having to teach courses in the field and then to interact with my graduate students—those things undoubtedly

[changed] my own perspective on the field—whether it changed it for the better or not, I don't know, but it certainly changed it.

As was the case for the Experienced Professional, the Senior Professional continues to learn in very idiosyncratic ways. At no time in one's life has the method of learning been more personally chosen. Said a male therapist, "I read more broadly than before. I really like reading psychology through literature." But, one practitioner in this phase expressed his frustration over the changing fashions that sounded new but brought nothing new. She said:

By the time a person reaches the end of one's work life, he or she has seen the wheel reinvented so many times, has seen fashions in therapy/counseling change back and forth. Old ideas emerge under new names and it can be frustrating to the senior therapist to see people make a big fuss about something he or she has known about for years. This contributes to cynicism for the person.

Another said, "Student interns one summer were talking about a new idea in a new book. To me, it was an old idea that was worth a chapter not a book." The learning now seems to be one of reinterpretation, integration, and synthesis of what is known in addition to processing the data from other sources such as one's own personal life, one's clients, and one's broad reading.

Role and Working Style

At no time during the individual's career has a person felt more of a sense of freedom to define how she or he works. Looking back at decades of professional experience, these therapists talked about all their exposure to the variety of schools of thought. Some were tried out, some rejected, and some accepted depending on what had worked for them. Some talked explicitly about having become more eclectic while others talked of maintaining a defined theoretical orientation while also drawing from other theoretical orientation. One female Senior Professional said:

Eclectic is an awfully nice word. I think all of us as we grow older, become more eclectic. Unless we are so wedded to one particular approach that we can't change ... the more experience you have had and the more thoughtful you are in looking at that experience, inevitably the more broad your viewpoint becomes.

Senior Professional therapists see themselves as having gone through a movement toward being more flexible in how they relate to clients. One therapist expressed this as follows, "I suppose at the very beginning I was considerably more rigid." She described herself as moving along a continuum from being rigid to "hanging loose." Another said:

> The change over time was one of becoming less rigid. I started with more of a psychoanalytic persuasion. I could even feel myself becoming more and more eclectic and being more and more inclusive in both my thinking about diagnosis and the process of therapy and specifically methodology. I would try new things even though I would be rather skeptical, say about Gestalt theory, and some of the practice, but I've tried things and as with most things, what works we keep and the rest, hopefully with a breath of kindness, will blow away.

This was later described in ways which suggested a continuous process of making changes as one goes along and has more experience. It shouldn't be surprising to say that a person continues to change as they go through life. But it can be. We probably as a profession have an age bias, especially in the view of younger practitioners, in that we think that a person arrives at a theory and that's it. However, this senior therapist continued to describe the changes that she felt had taken place in her way of conceptualizing therapy and her way of working. She described herself as having become much more patient in her way of working. She also said, "There's greater spontaneity ..., being OK with saying something outrageous. Humor ..., I think humor became more a part of the interchange." This therapist also talked of using cartoons in her therapy. And later, "becoming more involved, ... not be afraid that it would be seductive or ..., the boundaries simply get extended. They just are not as rigid as before." This highly respected therapist talked of increasingly realizing "that it was the interaction between me and my clients that made the difference ..." a process that she described as follows, "I think that probably coincided with my letting go of the more rigid approach I had."

Senior Professionals speak with one voice about having become more patient in their work. This coincides of course with the cultural discourse of patience as a virtue of older age. A male Senior Professional said, "I am ever so much more patient now. Things don't just have to happen and I don't insist on evidence. I'm much less intense about cure and so much less self-conscious." However, simultaneously, many of the transcript segments could also be interpreted as these experienced practitioners' sense of security and patience having stimulated a reflective awareness about the strategic element in their work. A female practitioner talked about a change she had experienced, a change that involved better timing of her interventions. She said:

> Early on I think I had the feeling that what I knew I better hurry up and tell people, and later on I had the feeling that what I knew I'd better keep to myself until I knew what they needed.

In terms of conceptions of "how therapy works," the modal Senior Professional sees the therapy/counseling relationship as the primary vehicle through which change occurs. But not all do. One male Senior Professional said:

> Well, I suppose in the past, not at a specific point in the past, but gradually, I've become aware of the limitations of what I call psychotherapy and a little more impressed with the value of environmental manipulation.... I have become more behaviorally oriented, and a more behavioral type of therapist.

How practitioners regulate professional boundaries represents an important aspect of the professional role. Finding an appropriate level of involvement with clients has been a long term career issue. The modal Senior Professional tells of having learned how to regulate the emotional involvement. A male at this stage said, "When the session is over I can leave it there." Another said, "I don't worry about it, but I do think about it." But, there are exceptions. One therapist, who described himself as having become more mellow, also said:

> I think I'm a little easier with myself, ... not too much though. I mean I want everybody to improve and while cognitively I know that they won't and cognitively also am aware that some people don't work together as well as certain other people, [I]still get very upset when something doesn't work. But less so than I used [to] I suppose that.

Measurement of Success and Satisfaction

For therapists/counselors in the preceding phase, we described a process where the practitioners were adjusting their goals and aspirations for therapy/counseling results. The Senior Professionals also report having scaled down their expectations for what can be accomplished in therapy/counseling. As one male therapist said, "My goals have become more modest with the passage of time. I don't expect to effect major personality change but rather give new options and skills." It is likely that these adjustments contribute to the practitioner feeling less threatened and experiencing more work satisfaction. One male practitioner in this phase said:

> I am more ready to say someone is doing better even if they aren't doing ideally well. Maybe that means I've discovered something about my own limits. Maybe I'm not going to make a perfectly insightful, perfectly functioning, self-fulfilled human being because I'm not that myself.

humility

Another at this phase said, "A client once told me that I don't have to help every time. That has helped me over the years." Modal Senior Professionals seemed not very concerned with assessing the effectiveness of their work. They told of receiving mostly verbal and some written reports of client satisfaction, which seemed to justify a feeling that the work they were doing was "good enough." However, the way they described their work indicated an informal assessment of the quality of the therapy/counseling process by referring to the interpersonal quality of the therapy/counseling relationship. Without reporting to use established measures of change (e.g., symptom change, employment, etc.), they felt generally confident in their ability to be effective in their work. It will be interesting to see if those who are inexperienced practitioners now will tell a different story when in the future, as senior therapists, they are asked to describe how they measure their effectiveness.

Senior Professionals generally express a deep appreciation and a sense of gratitude for having chosen to become a therapist/counselor and for being able to practice their profession late in their lives. There are few if any professions that provide such fine opportunities to practice also after formal retirement. These practitioners talk of the rewards of seeing clients resolve their problems and grow as human beings. One expressed it this way:

> [T]here are the rewards of seeing other people go on to be happier and more successful than they were before and the feeling that you had a little hand in that. For work with parents, seeing the changes that working with them can make in their children's situation is a potent motivator.

Another male Senior Professional gave this description of what was satisfying about his work:

> I would say, the chief satisfaction has come when I have been able to use a metaphor to wire my nervous system to the nervous system of the student [client] to really understand what that student [client] is trying to say—to know it—to really know it as a kind

141

of intrapsychic experience and to communicate the fact that you know it. I don't mean just communicate it by words, but somehow by the atmosphere that you created. I know that sounds a great deal like client-centered therapy in its classic form, but that is a great satisfaction in counseling. When you somehow realize that you have bridged this interpersonal gap and you are one with the individual in terms of the concern and the values of the moment. Also on those occasions when you get brownie points when you see one of your former clients or students and they either tell you that you're helpful to them or you know they are doing well, and you're arrogant enough to say that "Hey, I have a small part in the success of that individual." It is like parents seeing their children develop, seeing the success and progress in your clients is a source of satisfaction.

The Senior Professional may be savoring the moment and the work because of the realization that their work future is finite. The end is drawing near. One female Senior Professional expressed feeling a sense of ease, a sense of competence with gratitude in the following way:

With diminishing anxiety, I became less and less afraid of my clients and with that came an ease for me in using my own wide repertoire of skills and procedures. They became more available to me when I needed them. And, during those moments, it became remarkable to me that someone would have the willingness to share their private world with me, and that my work with them would bring very positive results for them. This brought a sense of intense pleasure to me.

Conceptual and empirical contributions to the understanding of the hardships and challenges of being a therapist/counselor suggest that continually having to deal with the distress, hopelessness, and adversities of clients represent a potential source of vicarious or secondary traumatization. We recommend Norcross and Guy's (2007) book, *Leaving It at the Office: A Guide to Psychotherapist Self-Care* as a practical guide on the topic. Due to the possibility of experiencing emotional depletion, and the adverse consequences of working, for example, with difficult, unmotivated, or aggressive clients, the authors strongly recommend that therapists are attentive to their self-care. Norcross and Guy rightly assert that psychotherapists and other mental health workers are ethically obligated to do so. As researchers on professional development we support that, and agree that self-care should be emphasized at all phases of professional development. Our data suggest, however, that the need for therapists to actively take care of themselves may be particularly pressing at the

Beginning and Advanced Professional phases. The reports of the Senior Professionals in our study suggest that this was not as pressing a concern, except of course for issues of physical health. It could be that these highly experienced therapists/counselors' skillfulness in managing their involvement, differentiating responsibilities, setting realistic goals, and bringing the "negative" emotions into the center of the therapeutic/counseling process, contributed to these therapists not being "victimized." Also, they had learned how necessary it was to attend to their self-care. One female practitioner said:

> Well, I think there's a knack to learning how not to carry all the problems of the day into your home life. Having a variety of other interests would be part of that. Not having all of your social contacts be with people in the same field. Associating with some well-adjusted people.

Referring to working with patients with depression, anger, and hostility, one male Senior Professional said the following:

> [W]ell …, see, that's part and parcel of what brought me to psychology and psychiatry in the beginning. I am intrigued by [it] and with abnormality and psychopathology. I see it every day. I work the psychiatric outpatient clinical here where we evaluate new patients and we see them coming in suicidal or out of control or manic or hostile and angry, and noncompliant. Those human behaviors interest and intrigue [me] and that's why I remain involved on the clinical front lines. That's why I have not retreated to my office, to the research lab, or to the classroom. I enjoy working with negative human behaviors and negative emotions.

It is not surprising that several of the Senior Professionals talked in various ways of the therapeutic potential inherent in processing "negative emotions." With the emphasis on working through the therapeutic relationship, which most of the Senior Professionals endorsed, processing emotions is at the heart of therapeutic/counseling activity. One said, "Actually, your best work comes when negative emotions begin to be expressed./…" Another put it this way:

> Well, by now, it's part of the game, part of the war, part of the battle. You've gotta accept them and you've got to deal with them. Anyway that you can … without pressing more emotions and more anger and stuff like that. Probing indirectly and subtly as to why … and if and when you succeed in getting the why of his

emotions or his anger, hatred, then begin to trace it, and develop understanding and insight on the patient's part.

The reports from the Senior Professionals seem not to support the idea that working with negative emotions impacts them adversely or reduces their level of work satisfaction. On the contrary, these aspects of the professional role are conceptualized as inherent in their professional work and according to their reports they are dealt with therapeutically and seem to fuel a sense of meaningfulness.

We will conclude this last chapter on phases of development by referring to how Baltes & Smith (1990) defined wisdom. We have previously related their wisdom model to describe knowledge development (Rønnestad & Skovholt, 2003). Their model consists of the following components: Rich procedural knowledge, rich conceptual knowledge, life-span contextualism, relativity (knowledge of individual differences), and awareness of uncertainty in ways of helping. These characteristics are expressed in the tales of therapists that we have presented. Finally, if we were to highlight what appears to us as a striking characteristic of senior therapists it is the combination of personal authority and respect, not only for clients, but for the complexities of therapeutic work.

Notes

1. Previous versions of this chapter were published in *The Evolving Professional Self,* by T. M Skovholt and M. H. Rønnestad (1992). Copyright has reverted to authors. Chichester, England: Wiley; "The Journey of the Counselor and Therapist: Research Findings and Perspectives," by M. H. Rønnestad and T. M. Skovholt (2003), in *Journal of Career Development, 30,* 5–44, and "Learning Arenas For Professional Development. Retrospective Accounts of Senior Psychotherapists," by M. H. Rønnestad and T. M. Skovholt (2001), in *Professional Psychology: Research and Practice, 32,* 181–187. Permissions provided by Sage and the American Psychological Association. All quotes are from above sources in addition to the tape recording of the original data collection.

2. The countries with the most participants in this study were: Norway N = 704–755; United States N= 580–643; Germany N = 550–562; Switzerland N = 221–227; Portugal N = 176–181. (Numbers vary due to incomplete responses.)

3. We remind the reader that the term Source of Influence is not used in a cause-effect sense, but as retrospective reports of therapist/counselors' reports of what they perceived had influenced them.

4. A full report of the substudy of the 74-year-old therapists is published in Rønnestad and Skovholt (2001).

9

THEMES OF THERAPISTS' PROFESSIONAL DEVELOPMENT[1]

In this chapter, we will present at a more abstracted level than we have done before what we have learned through the years from our inquiry into the nature of professional development. Abandoning the restraints of formulating our text within a phase format, as we did in the preceding six chapters, we will now use a different lens to describe *themes* of professional development. To do so we started by asking whether we could summarize our most important findings in one sentence? That was not possible, but we were able to formulate "summary sentences" presented initially as 20 themes of professional development (Skovholt & Rønnestad, 1992). In a reanalysis and reformulation, these were reduced to 14 (Rønnestad & Skovholt, 2003). Inspired by Goodyear's recommendation (Rodney, Goodyear, Wertheimer, Cypers, & Rosemond, 2003) to collapse and shorten the number of themes even further to reduce overlap, we have trimmed down the number of themes to 10. Here are the 10.

Theme 1: Optimal Professional Development Involves an Integration of the Personal Self into a Coherent Professional Self

In chapter 7, "The Experienced Professional Phase," we presented our conception of the self and endorsed the conception as multidimensional.

Our data has shown that with increasing experience, the changes that take place can be understood as the personal self being integrated into a coherent professional self. There are two central expressions of this integration process toward a coherent professional self. First, there is an increasing consistency between the therapist's personality and theoretical/conceptual beliefs. Second, there occurs a selection and formulation of professional roles in which the therapist/counselor can freely and naturally apply personally chosen techniques and methods in his or her work. The integration process can be understood in different ways. Intrapersonally, it includes a movement from an unarticulated, preconceptual way of functioning to a mode of functioning which is founded on the individual's experience-based generalizations or what we call Accumulated Wisdom. In its optimal expression, integration involves a process akin to Rogers's (1957) concept of congruence, where experiences are consistent with the self. It involves shedding values, beliefs, and use of methods which no longer fit the personality and the self of the therapist. Integration may also be understood in the framework of Donald Super who saw vocational development as the implementation of the self (Super, 1953/1996; Super, Savickas, & Super, 1996), or it may be seen as counselors' identity development as formulated by Loganbill, Hardy, and Delworth (1982). At the person/environment interactional level, integration may be seen as a movement toward an occupational environment that matches the personality characteristics of the person (e.g., Holland, 1997).

It is important to note that movements toward a better match between persons and environments can involve a change in self or a change in environment, or both. We have observed numerous expressions of movements toward a better match between the self and the characteristics of the environment. The most striking examples include therapists who have changed their theoretical orientation and therapeutic approach (a change in professional self) due to significant and transforming events in their personal lives.

Theme 2: The Modes of Therapist/Counselor Functioning Shifts Markedly Over Time— From Internal to External to Internal

The integration process we have described above may be differentiated into three distinct steps each characterized by a specific mode of functioning: the preprofessional training mode, the external and rigid mode of the training period; and the loosening and internal mode of the posttraining period. We will briefly describe each.

Pretraining: The "Preprofessional Training" Mode

During this period the individual operates from a culturally based commonsense conception of helping. As we presented in chapter 3, conceptions of practice within professions are not formulated independent of influence from the broader culture, and vice versa; conceptions of helping within the broader culture are not formulated independent of influence from professional conceptions of helping. We can say that the relationship between the two is reciprocal and dynamic. As we described in chapter 3, the culturally embedded or pretraining models of helping and the professional models share many characteristics, but they are also different in substantial ways. The preprofessional training mode lacks the many nuances provided by professional models of helping, and typically lacks the procedural competence that enables a skillful handling of the difficulties encountered when engaging in helping behavior. Conceptually, we may therefore differentiate professional from nonprofessional ways of conceptualizing helping and modes of helping. Behaviors and conceptions of helping reflect each individual's interpretation of effective ways of helping others, ways that are fueled by both personal dispositions and cultural discourses on helping. Some common characteristics of conventional helping in our culture possibly include: defining the problem quickly, providing strong emotional support, providing sympathy as contrasted to empathy, and for some, giving advice based on one's own experience. Prior to professional training, the individual is not socialized into the professional helping culture and is typically not guided by theory, concepts, and principles of professional helping. Sources of influence for how to help are informed by discourses provided by the general culture, and to a large extent by lived experiences (relating to, for example, friends, family, and colleagues), ways of helping are experienced as being natural and authentic.

Training: The External and Rigid Mode

There occurs a distinctive shift in focus and behavior when the lay helper enters professional training. The focus shifts toward the theoretical bodies of knowledge (e.g., developmental psychology, theories of disability and pathology, conceptions of counseling and therapy) and toward professionally based conceptions of methods and techniques. Student functioning becomes increasingly more externally driven with the student suppressing characteristic ways of functioning. Behavior becomes less natural, less loose, and more rigid. The use of humor may be seen as an index of this movement from natural and loose/flexible in pretraining to nonnatural and rigid during training, and back to natural and flexible with more professional experience. Use of humor typically disappears for the student counselor/therapist to reappear with the professional self-confidence of the experienced counselors/therapists.

Posttraining/Experienced: The Internal and Flexible Mode

After training and with more professional experience, there is a gradual shift toward a renewed internal focus. This movement is propelled by the disillusionment with training after the therapist is confronted with the hardships and challenges of practice. Disillusionment may induce exploration into assets and strengths but also weaknesses and liabilities, which eventually can lead to more confidence and flexibility in professional functioning.

The movement from "external" to "internal" can also be formulated as "the cognitive map of the practitioner is changing over time." Beginning practitioners rely on "external expertise" while more experienced practitioners increasingly rely on "internal expertise." Students' intense hunger to observe models of professionally defined expert behavior illustrates the reliance on external expertise for the beginner. So does students' appreciation for supervision which is instructive and didactic (Rønnestad & Skovholt, 1993), which is not all they want from supervision (see chapter 11). With increasing professional experience and more credentials, there occurs a marked shift toward a self-directed preference for what to learn and how to learn. Experienced practitioners vary in preferences such as seeking stimulation from traditional professional sources of knowledge, like a trusted mentor, use of peer group supervision, reading professional literature, or seeking stimulation in other knowledge domains such as studying psychological themes in movies, biographies, philosophy, or anthropology. As mentioned earlier, professional experience makes possible a shift toward contextually defined and contextually limited experienced-based generalizations.

Belenky, Clinchy, Goldberger, and Tarule (1986) have formulated a model for understanding the evolution in knowledge development that we have observed. Anchoring their model in Perry's (1981) model of cognitive meaning and development, they described seven levels of ways of knowing. Although the Belenky model was intended to describe women's ways of knowing, both Perry and our model are inclusive of both women and men. An early level, received knowledge, was described as follows: "While received knowers can be very open to take in what others have to offer, they have little confidence in their own ability to speak. Believing that truth comes from others, they still their own voices to hear the voices of others" (Belenky et al., 1986, p. 37). This seems to only partly fit the experiences of the students that we interviewed. While some students expressed themselves with confidence, others did not. There was, however, substantial convergence among students in wanting to hear and observe what seasoned practitioners had to offer.

The highest level of Belenky's model, constructed knowledge, seemed to fit many of our experienced practitioners. They define it as:

> All knowledge is constructed, and the knower is an intimate part of the known (p. 137).... To see that all knowledge is a construction and that truth is a matter of the context in which it is embedded is to greatly expand the possibilities of how to think about anything (p. 138).... Theories become not truth but models for approximate experiences. (p. 138)

Without being identical, there is some similarity between this high level of knowledge and conceptions of wisdom such as that formulated by Baltes and Smith (1990) that we referred to in the preceding chapter. In their formulation, *awareness of uncertainty* in ways of helping is one criterion of wisdom and thus similar to Belenky's recognition of the complexity of knowledge within their highest level. Belenky and Baltes and Smith reject the construct of precisely defined realities in understanding matters of human interaction.

The movements we have described above can also be interpreted in the light of the different types of learning presented in chapter 2 (see Table 2.1). The learning of the beginner may be described as type 1 (Bateson, 1972), as acquisition (Engestrøm, 2001; Sfard, 1998), as imitation (Fleming, 1953), and as the use of "rules" (Dreyfus & Dreyfus, 1988). With more experience, learning is described as type 2 (Engestrøm, 2001; Sfard, 1998), as corrective (Fleming, 1953), and as use of aspects (Dreyfus & Dreyfus, 1988). The most advanced type of learning can be described as type 3 (Bateson, 1972), as expansive/creative (Engestrøm, 2001), as creative (Fleming, 1953), and as movement from the use of maxims to tacit/intuitive (Dreyfus & Dreyfus, 1986).

Theme 3: Continuous Reflection Is a Prerequisite for Optimal Learning and Professional Development at All Levels of Experience

Reflection is understood as a continuous and focused search for a more comprehensive, nuanced, and in-depth understanding of oneself and others, and of the processes and phenomena that the practitioner meets in his or her work. As will be described in more detail later, the ability and willingness to reflect upon one's professional experiences in general, and on challenges and hardships in particular, is a prerequisite to avoid professional stagnation. A stimulating and supportive work environment, including informal dialogues among colleagues and formal supervision and consultation impact the reflective capacity and adaptive handling of the challenges encountered.

The concepts of scaffolding (Wood, Bruner & Ross, 1976) and proximal zone of development (Vygotsky, 1972, 1978) inform us of the supportive and relational conditions that stimulate reflection, learning, and development at all levels. Therapists/counselors are not only engaging in what Schon called *reflection-in-action* and *reflection-on-action,* but also *reflection-pre-action* (Rønnestad, 2009), the preparatory planning activity that precedes therapy/counseling sessions, which will be described more carefully in the next chapter.

Theme 4: Professional Development Is a Lifelong Process

Most models of development within the counseling and therapy professions emphasize student development.[2] Interviews with postgraduates informed us of major changes in many aspects of work and the professional self during the postgraduate years. One of the most important, and also startling realizations that has emerged from our analyses is how long it takes before the integration processes that we have described are completed.

We feel that that the formulation often used within our field, "to integrate theory and practice" conceals essential dynamics, in particular the important role played by therapists/counselors' perception of themselves as they grow as professionals. Our analyses suggest that choices of theory/theories, concepts, and perspectives to use as well as definition of professional roles are activities that for most practitioners engage them at a level of experienced meaning and self-definition. Formulated differently, our analyses suggest that it is only through being immersed in therapy/counsel work over time, and after having been exposed to and reflected upon difficulties and challenges, that we can expect that "theory and practice" are integrated. From our perspective, it does not make sense to expect that theory and practice "can be integrated" quickly. This process has merely begun by the end of training.

Escaping the view of those who focus on beginning therapist/counselors only, is the involvement of oneself as a professional elder in the capacity of mentor, supervisor, teacher, or consultant, roles which provide for experiences that fuel professional growth.

Theme 5: Professional Development Is Mostly a Continuous Process but can also be Intermittent and Cyclical

Professional development is generally experienced as a continual increase in a sense of competence and mastery. Reports from those we interviewed indicate that this process may at any point be barely noticeable, but appear retrospectively as substantial. Conversely, over the course of the career, some may experience development as an intense change process, perhaps initiated by a specific critical incidence (Skovholt & McCarthy, 1988), by transforming life events or epiphanies (Denzin, 1989; Miller & C'de Baca, 2001), or by defining moments (Trotter-Mathison, Koch, Sanger, & Skovholt, 2010) possibly followed by a period of slow change.

Changes may also be cyclical and conceptualized as recycling loops in which themes such as lack of confidence in one's ability may emerge repeatedly in one's career as new challenges are encountered. Our analyses confirm a previous formulation of professional development conceptualized as repeated cycles with sequences of hope (enthusiasm), experienced hardship, self-doubt, anxiety, dejection, exploration/processing (new learning), and integration (mastery; Rønnestad, 1985).

Theme 6: An Intense Commitment to Learn Propels the Developmental Process

Most of our informants, whether they were students or practitioners, impressed us with an attitude of reflective awareness and an eagerness to learn and develop. Commitment to learn and willingness within ethical boundaries to take risks and to be open to new learning are building blocks of increased professional functioning. Research on master therapists (Jennings et al. 2012; Skovholt & Jennings, 2004; chapter 12 this book) has shown this to be so also for colleague-nominated experts. As we presented in chapter 7 "The Senior Professional Phase," research within the SPR/CRN (Orlinsky, Ambühl et al., 1999) has shown that therapists' sense of currently experienced professional growth did not decline as a function of years in practice. Survey responses of therapists with two or more decades of professional experience also reported a sense of growth characterized by experiences of improving, becoming skillful, and feeling a growing sense of enthusiasm about doing therapy. The researchers' interpretation of the results was that the "therapists' sense of currently experienced growth reflects a renewal of the morale and motivation needed to practice therapy, a replenishment of the energy and refreshing of the acumen demanded by therapeutic work" (p. 212). This statement about the vitality of most experienced therapists is important because it buttresses the opinion held by some, that burnout is a pervasive risk for experienced therapists.

Theme 7: Many Beginning Practitioners Experience Much Anxiety in Their Professional Work: But Over Time, Anxiety Is Mastered by Most

The anxiety of the beginner has been discussed by many authors since Robinson's description of social work trainees in 1936 (cited by Gysbers & Rønnestad,1974; e.g., Dodge, 1982; Grater, 1985; Gray, Ladany, Walker, & Ancis, 2001; Loganbill et al., 1982; Mueller & Kell, 1972; Rønnestad & Orlinsky, 2005b; Skovholt & Rønnestad, 1992, 2003; Stoltenberg & Delworth, 1987; Strømme, 2010; see also Bernhard & Goodyear's, 2009, authoritative text, *Fundamentals of Clinical Supervision*). Generally speaking, the reports indicate moderate to high levels of anxiety when the beginning/therapists see their first clients.

However, some state that the prevalence and intensity of student anxiety is exaggerated in the developmental literature. Goodyear (2003) refers to a communication with Ellis, who refers to studies by Ellis, Krengel, and Beck (2002) and Chapin and Ellis (2002) in conjunction with constructing the Anticipatory Supervisory Anxiety scale. Ellis. stated:

[W]e come to the rather remarkable finding: anxiety just ain't there as delineated in supervision theory and the literature. It looks like less than 10 percent report even moderate anxiety even in high anxiety supervision or training situations (e.g., first video-tape review supervision in pre-practicum. (p. 78)

The discrepancy between Ellis and collaborators and our early findings (Skovholt & Rønnestad, 1992) was specifically noted. Selective memory of anxiety stemming from the vividness of specific, harmful supervision was suggested as an explanation for why we reported high levels of anxiety. We fully support the recommendation to continue to explore the prevalence and intensity of beginners' anxiety.

In our research, we were struck by the fact the reports of the intensity of student anxiety appeared more clearly when postgraduate therapists looked back at the training years than when we interviewed student thera-pists. This could of course be consistent with a selective memory explana-tion. But it could also be that the impression management and self-denial that students engage in impacts their anxiety rating.

In line with this we suggest that much is at stake when students meet their first clients. As we described in chapter 4, "Novice Student Phase," and Chapter 5, "Advanced Student Phase," many factors combine to cre-ate an evaluative focus and pervasive anxiety for many beginning stu-dents. There are, for example, high standards of performance, unrealistic expectations as to what can be achieved, the achievement orientation of academia, fear of being unsuited for counseling/therapy work, and a lack of professional knowledge and competence.

Using an anonymous self-rating procedure, many beginning therapists of various professions report that they lack professional self-confidence, feel challenged, and are anxious (Orlinsky & Rønnestad, 2005). With increasing experience and an accompanying sense of mastery and exper-tise, anxiety levels diminish markedly. One greatly respected senior infor-mant told us in the research interview: "In time you are no longer afraid of your clients." There are also indications that the prevalence and inten-sity of student anxiety is influenced by the research method used. Hanne Strømme (2010), in her doctoral dissertation, *Confronting Helplessness*, used a repeated interview design and found that students were able and willing, in a late interview but not in an early one, to report how threaten-ing the training situation had been. However, the issue of student anxiety remains unsettled.

As we presented in chapter 4, "The Novice Student Phase", a large scale substudy within the SPR/CRN that focused on beginning therapists only, suggested that already after six months of practice (typically during train-ing practicum) the mean level of stressful involvement (which includes items on anxiety) was reduced (Rønnestad & Orlinsky, 2010). It seems reasonable to believe that the characteristics and culture of the training institution, and specifically how supportive it is, impacts both frequency and intensity of threatening experiences, including novice anxiety. It seems logical to expect that in highly supportive training environments, students are less likely to experience anxiety than students in highly demanding and critical training environments.

Theme 8: Interpersonal Sources of Influence Propel Professional Development More Than "Impersonal" Sources of Influence

Our informants told us convincingly that meaningful contact with people was the catalyst for growth. People most often mentioned were clients, professional elders (i.e., supervisors, personal therapists, professors), professional peers, friends, family members, and later in one's career, younger colleagues. After a general description of this theme, we will specifically focus on two subthemes, clients and interactions in personal life.

There is striking similarity between these findings and what emerged in one of the studies within the SPR/CRN project (Orlinsky, Botermans, & Rønnestad, 2001) as well as a separate longitudinal study of a group of trainees in Sweden (Carlsson, 2011). As described earlier, therapists generally rated interacting with clients as most impactful for their professional development. Furthermore, supervision and personal therapy were rated second and third, and personal life was frequently ranked fourth. For the most experienced group of therapists, giving supervision or consultation to others was ranked fourth. Less but still moderately important as a sources of influence were: "Having informal case discussion with colleagues," "Taking courses or seminars," and "Reading books or journals relevant to your practice."

Theme 8.1: Clients are Primary Teachers

Throughout their career, clients are primary teachers for therapists/counselors. Skovholt and McCarthy (1988) first used the term *Clients as Teachers* in their early series on "Critical Incidents: Catalysts in Counselor Development." By disclosing their distress, their developmental histories, and ways of managing and coping with their problems of living, clients inform therapists/counselors about the causes and solutions to human distress. The knowledge thus attained not only supplements and expands, but also brings depth and concreteness to the theoretical knowledge obtained in formal schooling.

The counseling/therapy consulting room is a laboratory where both client and counselor/therapist engage in learning. Client reactions to counselor/therapist behaviors and attitudes continually influence the practitioner. Through the close interpersonal contact between client and counselor/therapist, the feedback provided by the client to counselor/therapist interventions adds intensity to the learning process. Negative client feedback can be a major impetus for shifts in theoretical orientation. Although clients provide valuable feedback for practitioners at all levels of experience, we had many reports indicating that inexperienced practitioners are particularly receptive and often vulnerable to client feedback. Lack of positive client feedback is typically experienced as threatening and sometimes traumatic for the student therapist, a finding which is consistent with the high level of anxiety experienced by many students.

We have previously referred to a substudy within the SPR/CRN where more than 4,000 psychotherapists from many countries assessed the importance of various sources of influence for their overall professional development. No other category matched "Experience in therapy with clients" as most important across professions (psychologists, psychiatrists, others), nationalities, and theoretical orientations. This lends support to the findings of our qualitative investigation, as illustrated by a Senior Professional who answered our question about what had been most important for his professional development in the following way, "I will have to say clients—if you're talking strictly about what has shaped my performance as a counselor … my clients and well, let me put it this way, an amalgam of clients and my reactions to them."

It is hardly surprising that clients are awarded a privileged position as "teachers" for therapists/counselors given the fact clients provide continuing feedback to the practitioner. Clients' verbal and nonverbal reactions, the degree to which they accept or reject what the therapist/counselor is saying or suggesting, the degree to which they use therapists/counselors' intervention as a stimulus for further reflections, the degree to which the goals of therapy are reached or not, provide ample opportunities for therapist/counselors to change their behavior and attitude, and thus to learn and develop. What is surprising is that, given this, why all therapists do not improve in skillfulness and mastery and grow as professionals. This is a central question in understanding the development of expertise in all the caring professions—those in which intense human interaction is central (e.g., therapy, K-12 and college teaching, health care work, such as nursing, medicine, and physical therapy, and spiritual guidance). We have suggested, and repeat it here, that variations in therapists/counselors' interpersonal sensitivity is at least part of the explanation why most but not all learn from the often subtle feedback provided by clients. Some therapists may simply not have the interpersonal sensitivity to recognize and respond to the feedback that clients are giving them.

Believing strongly in a therapeutic or counseling method can obstruct one's view of the feedback provided by clients. One of our highly experienced informants said that throughout most of his professional work, he thought that clients did not improve because they lacked motivation and made insufficient effort to change. According to him, there was nothing wrong with the method or how he "delivered" it. Only later in his career did he realize that his performance was responsible for the lack of client progress.

Another obstacle to seeing and learning from the feedback provided by clients has emerged in master therapist studies. Humility appears to be a characteristic of experts across many studies (see chapter 13) and it seems reasonable to assume that therapist humility is positively related to openness to client feedback. We are also reminded of the study by Nissen-Lie, Monsen, and Rønnestad (2010) which showed that therapists' professional self-doubt was positively related to a client rated working alliance.

Theme 8.2: Personal Life Impacts Professional Functioning and Development Throughout the Professional Life Span

In chapter 7, "The Experienced Professional Phase," we were informed of the many ways that experiences in childhood, adolescence, and adulthood impacted professional functioning and development. Family interactional patterns, sibling and peer relationships, one's own parenting experiences, disability in family members, other crises in the family, personal trauma, and so on influenced current practice and long term development in both positive and adverse ways. From the interviews with the most senior therapists we learned of experiences related to specific experiences including; psychological abandonment, a demanding achievement orientation in the family of origin, rigid and restraining child rearing practices, receiving conditional love from parents, and growing up in a family with a rule of no emotions. All of these, we concluded could influence professional life and functioning in one way or multiple ways. Examples were selection of work role and theoretical orientation, therapeutic style and focus, attitude toward colleagues, experienced hardships, and ways of coping when experiencing difficulties in sessions.

The general flavor of the reports indicated that early negative experiences continued to influence work in the adult professional years. However, low numbers in this subgroup warrant considerable caution when interpreting results. We repeat that our sample is not representative and we claim no transferability of these findings to other therapists. However, the reports of these therapists have informed us of possible dynamics mediating between personal and professional life.

Adversities and crises in adult personal life were seen to exert an immediate negative influence on professional functioning, yet, often the long term consequences were positive. This is consistent with the discourse of the interconnectedness of suffering and wisdom that we find in many cultures, which is also implied in Nietzsche's formulation that "the easy life teaches nothing." Examples of intense personal experiences that in the long run were instructive include: death of spouse and children, physical disability, or severe psychological impairment of family members. Examples of positive consequences were: increased ability to understand and relate to clients, increased tolerance and patience, heightened credibility as role model, and greater awareness of the ingredients of effective helping.

Theme 8.3: New Members of the Field View Professional Elders and Graduate Training with Strong Affective Reactions

The interpersonal orientation of the counseling and therapy professions finds its expression in students continually scrutinizing and evaluating professors, teachers, and supervisors. Students want to learn from and model themselves on seniors they see as competent. By possessing the key for entry into the profession, professors and supervisors have the power to close the gate to student continuation in, or graduation from, the training program. The power differential probably intensifies the affective engagement with which students view their seniors and contributes to the tendencies to either idealize or devalue them. Strong admiration is expressed for those more advanced in the profession whose personal characteristics or behaviors are perceived as highly positive, such as intellectual brilliance, strong therapeutic skills, outstanding supervision ability, unusual emotional support for beginners, and the modeling of professional values in personal life.

The interviewees informed us that that negative reactions to professional elders were just as common and just as intense. Devaluation seems to occur at the same intensity level as idealization. Being in a dependent and relatively low power position is the fuel that sometimes propels these strong reactions. Professional elders are devalued if they possess behaviors perceived as highly negative, such as a supervisor who is perceived as unfairly critical or a professor who teaches counseling but seems unable to practice it.

The student counselor/therapist in time, usually years later, often goes through normative transitions in the way most children regard their parents: from idealizing the parent as a child, through devaluing/criticizing parents as an adolescent, to seeing the parent as a person with all the ordinary humanness of people in general. Beyond graduate school, professional elders are idealized and devalued less and their humanness (ordinariness, strengths/weaknesses, uniqueness) is seen more clearly.

Most therapists and counselors experience some disillusionment regarding their graduate education and training. Participants report a strong expectation to be taught specifically and concretely how to do counseling and therapy, an expectation which is often not met. A common question asked by students across training programs is: "Why didn't they train us better for this?" Asking questions is often perceived as more valuable by the faculty than providing narrow answers. Good supervision seems to act as a buffer against student confusion and stress.

Even though there is a convergence in the value ascribed to interpersonal experiences in our qualitative study of 100 therapists and the SPR/CRN project, this is not an argument for deemphasizing traditional academic training such as coursework that includes reading books and journals and understanding theory and empirical research. The ratings of these activities in the SPR/CRN were moderate, not low.

How can we understand the consistent findings across studies that interpersonal experiences are consistently assessed to be highly impactful for professional work and development? We have seen it for clients, professional seniors (e.g., supervisors), and personal life. At one level of explanation, these findings simply reflect what is the nature of man. In his honorary doctoral speech at the University of Oslo, Orlinsky (2011) argues:

> Persons grow, and their lives take form, through participation in stable, intimate face-to-face relationships that occur within social and cultural communities which are relatively cohesive and coherent. From this perspective, it is not surprising to learn that *relationships* which are experienced by a distressed person as genuinely caring and securely protective are effectively therapeutic.

This line of reason can be extended to explain why the professional growth of therapists (a parallel to the personal relief of client's suffering) is impacted by interpersonal (i.e., relational) experiences.

At another level of explanation, Holland's (1997) vocational developmental therapy may assist us in understanding the reason therapists assess and articulate why interpersonal experiences are so influential for their professional development. According to his theory, therapists are social types. This means their interpersonal orientation and interests are likely expressed in a learning preference that is interpersonal. Also, the dichotomy between interpersonal sources of influence and theory/empirical research may be artificial because theory and research are often mediated by respected peers or seasoned practitioners (e.g., professors, supervisors).

Theme 9: Not All Therapists/Counselors Develop Optimally

Optimal professional development presupposes that developmental tasks are consistently well mastered. Numerous factors impact the practitioner's work and development: personal life and personal resources (e.g., values, personalities, attitudes, interests, cognitive and affective capacities, interpersonal skillfulness); the quality of training programs (e.g., basic training, practicum experiences, supervision, personal training); the quality of the work setting or milieu (opportunities for stimulation, feedback, and support); the degree of match between skills and client characteristics, etc.

In our second round of interviews, approximately 10 years after the first round, we asked the Senior Professionals the question: Who make the best counselors and therapists? Their answers may point to some personal characteristics that may help us understand why some do not develop optimally. The descriptions that were most common concerned the following two clusters of descriptions: one consisting of intelligence and brightness and the other of a capacity for empathy. All therapists who answered this question mentioned characteristics within these two clusters. So, the story is that it is intelligent and empathic persons who make the best therapists and counselors.

But other characteristics regarding who made the best therapists and counselors were also mentioned, like people who have emotional control and patience. One said: "the ability to keep your cool, not get excited, not get panicky, not get angry"; "people who have narcissism well under control, who are willing to be self-critical, who have a good balance between openness and some clear boundaries, who are generally comfortable with people." Another one said:

> Well, … bright people, nonjudgmental people, sensitive people. People who know how to listen and give another person, client, patient whatever, real attention … total attention. The empathic ability to respond, not only to the words, but also to the music of what the person is saying … the underlying content.

Few mentioned people who were well trained, which may be due to how the question was formulated. One senior therapist answered like this:

It isn't the training. I am convinced of that. [Referring to experiences with para-professionals, with only a BA level training, he stated:] … some of them are outstanding therapists … [and] the capacity to empathize with the client. Personal qualifications— ability and patience…P-A-T-I-E-N-C-E. The ability to be really patient with the client and identify and empathize with them seem to be the qualities. Some of the paraprofessionals are much better than any other PhDs, MDs, MSWs. That isn't to say that some of the latter aren't good … [and referring to the above qualities, he continues:] It's these personal qualities that they have.

When looking back at decades of training therapists and counselors, we are both struck by the great variations in natural talent possessed by students. Although training research has documented that targeted alliance training can affect client rated alliance (Crits-Christoph et al., 2006) and empathy training can improve therapist empathy (e.g., Nerdrum & Rønnestad, 2003) we are nevertheless convinced that personal characteristics as mentioned above play a major role in determining who develops optimally and who does not. The concept of interpersonal skillfulness captures many of the characteristics mentioned above. It seems that therapists with poor interpersonal skills and who lack a genuine commitment to the welfare of the client are candidates for being poorly functioning practitioners and are likely to be among those with limited professional development.

Theme 10: For the Practitioner There Is a Realignment from Self as Powerful to Client as Powerful

Increased experience with a large variety of clients, and experiences of failures and success over the years, contribute to a gradual shift in therapists/counselors' understanding of the change process. With a small risk of exaggeration, this change can be formulated as a movement from therapist/counselor as hero to client as hero. This shift in attitude parallels the emphasis of contemporary psychotherapy literature on the heroic client by Duncan and Miller (2000), for example. At the same time, as practitioners feel more confident and assured as professionals with the passing of time, they see more clearly the limitations to what they can accomplish. Fueling this process of increased realism is the "series of humiliations" which therapists experience over time. If these blows to the ego are processed and integrated into the therapists' self-experience, they may contribute to the paradox of increased sense of confidence and competence while also feeling more humble as a therapist. The master therapist characteristic of humility, mentioned previously in this chapter, is described in more detail in chapter 12.

Notes

1. The first formulation on themes of professional development was published in "Themes in Therapist and Counselor Development," by T. M. Skovholt and M. H. Rønnestad (1992, March/April), in *Journal of Counselor Development, 70,* , 505–515. The text in this chapter is in large part based on a reanalysis and reformulation of that text, published (see pp. 27–38) in "The Journey of the Counselor and Therapist," by M. H. Rønnestad and T. M. Skovholt (2003), in *Journal of Career Development, 30,* 5–44.
2. A notable exception is the SPR/CRN project on therapist/counselor development.

10

A CYCLICAL/TRAJECTORIES MODEL OF THERAPISTS' PROFESSIONAL DEVELOPMENT AND STAGNATION

Introduction

In this chapter we present a conceptual model of professional development and stagnation. Many elements of the model have been presented throughout the book, but in this chapter the elements are more fully defined, combined, and extended into an integrated cyclical-trajectory model that illustrates a movement that is initiated when therapists/counselors experience difficulties or challenges, not only in their professional practice but also in other parts of the life sphere. Our reference to the life sphere is inspired by the concept of "life space" employed by Kurt Lewin (1943/1997, 1951) and by Husserl's (1936/1970) concept of the "life world." The concept is broad and includes all experiences of the therapist in professional as well as in nonprofessional contexts.

The need for a concept like the life sphere of the therapist emerged as we analyzed the need to be continually aware of how experiences in both professional and nonprofessional life contexts influence therapist functioning and development, and are influenced in turn by them. Generally speaking, experiences at work with clients are the most impactful for therapist/counselor development, but as we have shown, experiences in other professional contexts such as supervision, personal therapy, and workplace interaction with colleagues also continually influence therapist development. These experiences are central components of the practitioner's life sphere, and how challenges and difficulties in these contexts are dealt with determines whether professional growth or stagnation will ensue. But the practitioner's life sphere is not limited to experiences in these professional contexts, and our analyses have demonstrated that experiences in personal life can also influence how practitioners perceive themselves as therapists/counselors and influence professional functioning (e.g., Rønnestad & Skovholt, 2001). Testimonies to variations in personal and professional sources of influence are found in numerous other sources (e.g., Goldfried, 2001; Guy, 1987; Trotter-Mathison, Koch, Sanger, & Skovholt, 2010).

General Principles of the Development Model

To start, here are some principles of the model, to be illustrated and defined in detail below.

1. The way that therapists/counselors handle difficulties and challenges encountered in their life sphere is decisive for whether processes of development or stagnation will ensue.
2. Optimal professional development or growth presupposes that therapists/counselors:
   (a) Are aware of the complexities of professional work and maintain a reflective stance.
   (b) Have a capacity for cognitive complexity and reflectivity that enable them to continually reflect on their experiences in the professional life sphere and engage in metacognition.
   (c) Avoid premature closure and manage to functionally close the reflection process when appropriate and needed.
3. Deficient professional development or stagnation is reflected in states of exhaustion and disengagement.
   (a) Exhaustion results from stress associated with inadequate closure in reflecting on difficulties and challenges met in therapeutic work.
   (b) Disengagement results from limited reflection and premature closure in a defensive response to difficulties and challenges experienced in therapeutic work.
4. If exhaustion predominates as a form of stagnation, development can be resumed by renewed reflection that may lead to functional closure.
5. If disengagement predominates instead of optimal development, it can be reinitiated with renewed experiences of difficulties and challenges.
6. Processes of development and stagnation are moderated by the cognitive and interpersonal characteristics of therapists/counselors. Particularly important are a capacity for cognitive complexity, including reflective capacity and tolerance for ambiguity; an attitude of openness to experience and inquisitiveness; and interpersonal skillfulness and facilitative attitudes with clients (e.g., respect, empathy, and congruence).

Cycles of Development and Stagnation

The model consists of three developmental trajectories, as shown in Figure 10.1.

Trajectory I traces the process of optimal development or growth (bottom to top on the left of Figure 10.1). Trajectory II reflects the aspect of

161

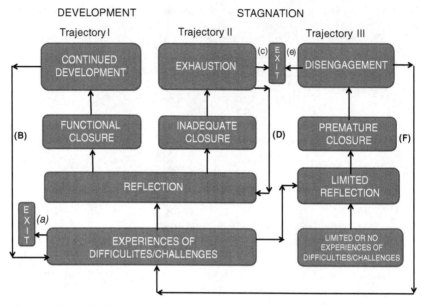

Figure 10.1 A cyclical/trajectories model of practitioner development and stagnation

developmental stagnation characterized by exhaustion (mid to top in the center of Figure 10.1). Trajectory III shows an alternative aspect of developmental stagnation characterized by disengagement (bottom to top on the right of Figure 10.1).

The positive cycle shown in Trajectory 1 is initiated by therapists' experiences of difficulties or challenges in therapeutic work. If this state is tolerated and does not lead to exit from the field or therapist role (see arrow *a* bottom left of Figure 10.1) reflection is initiated which, if successful, leads to a functional closure, which again facilitates a positive development or *growth*. The cyclical nature of this trajectory is shown by arrow (B), which implies that therapists who have met challenges and resolved difficulties through continual professional reflection in the past eventually will experience, and even seek, new difficulties and challenges to stimulate ongoing professional growth.

There are two negative cycles shown in Trajectories II and III. As for the positive cycle in Trajectory I, Trajectory II is also initiated by the experiences of difficulties/challenges in therapeutic work. But in contrast to the functional closure that characterizes a positive development, therapists in the exhaustion trajectory engage in inadequate closure. If the emotional burden is excessive, therapists may either remain permanently exhausted, exit (shown by arrow *c*), or resume an opportunity for professional growth by renewed reflection (as shown by arrow D).

Trajectory III is initiated by limited or no experiences of difficulties/challenges, which evokes limited reflection, which again leads to premature closure, and then to a state of disengagement. The lack of therapist satisfaction and meaning burnout (see chapter 13) that characterize disengagement may either be a permanent state, or lead to exiting the field (shown by arrow *e*), or to the experience of challenges (as shown by arrow F), which provide an opportunity for positive growth.

Definitions and Descriptions of Concepts in the Model

Having introduced our conceptual model of development, we proceed next to the definition and discussion of its key terms.

Professional Development

The primary characteristics of professional development are (a) a subjective experience of growth in therapeutic competence, (b) an integration of the therapist's personal traits and individual style with the theoretical and procedural aspects of work, and (c) being energized and vitalized in and by one's professional work. The concept of development as including a sense of growth and revitalization is akin to "currently experienced growth" described by Orlinsky and Rønnestad (2005).[1]

Growth in therapeutic competence includes, but is not limited to, the following interrelated elements: (a) improved mastery of client assessment procedures, which includes a more comprehensive understanding of "clients in contexts"; (b) improved mastery of therapeutic procedures; (c) improved ability to establish and maintain a therapeutic alliance, and an ability to repair alliance ruptures that may occur; (d) improved ability to regulate boundaries in professional work; (e) improved ability to understand and regulate one's own emotionality in therapeutic work; (f) improved ability to establish realistic goals for clients in therapy; (g) improved ability to assess one's own strengths and limitations as therapist; (h) improved ethical awareness and behavior; and at a higher level of abstraction, development implies (i) an increasing integration of the therapist/counselor's personal self into a coherent professional self.

Professional Stagnation

Professional stagnation is experienced as a subjective sense of arrested or discontinued improvement in therapeutic mastery. Professional stagnation also involves a felt loss of interest in and enthusiasm for therapeutic work and a corresponding absence or loss of felt energy and vitality in therapeutic work. Our interviews led us to differentiate between two trajectories of stagnation, one leading to exhaustion or sense of depletion and the other to an inner withdrawal or disengagement in one's practice.

Exhaustion. A central characteristic of therapist exhaustion is a continued experience of feeling overburdened and overworked. It is a state in which there is little time for the reflective activity needed to develop professionally. There is a sense of one's energy being drained away, and of fatigue and exhaustion at a level and frequency that causes concern and worry for the therapist. There is a sense of constant urgency in work.

The experience of exhaustion is well described by items in the Exhaustion subscale of the Maslach Burnout Inventory (MBI) (Maslach & Jackson, 1981, 1986, 1996). As operationalized by Maslach and collaborators , exhaustion is predicted by lack of therapist autonomy and organizational factors such as work setting support (Maslach & Jackson, 1981, 1986, 1996; Maslach & Leiter, 1997). See also chapter 13 for a closer examination of burnout.[2] However, a theoretical assumption is that therapists' inadequate decision-making skills (e.g., an inability to sort experiences, prioritize tasks, and make firm decisions, including the ability to say "no") increases the probability that therapists will engage in inadequate *closure* (described below), which in turn contributes to feeling exhausted.

Disengagement. Disengagement implies a sense of emotional detachment from clients or from the work setting. In our data, we observed many expressions of disengagement from clients, as when the beginning student is incapable of sharing the experiential world of the client, or when the advanced student retrospectively admits to disliking emotions and therefore learned behaviorally oriented approaches to therapy. Another example is the recent graduate who could not tolerate the emotional anguish of clients, and thereafter made changes in the professional role. As described in chapter 7, therapists can disengage from the work setting without necessarily disengaging from clients, a dynamic which may arise from therapists' maintaining their identification with clients in spite of a conflictual relationship toward the work setting (Bergin & Rønnestad, 2005).

The Importance for Development of Experiencing Difficulties or Challenges

When we give primacy to experiences of difficulty or challenge as an essential precondition for professional development, we express not only our own findings for the different phases of development, but align ourselves with cultural discourses of the potential for human growth and development that may result from experiencing and facing adversity and hardship. In this we agree with other theorists like Csikszentmihalyi (1990,

2008) who viewed challenge as the source of "flow" experience, Maddi's (2006) studies of "hardiness," and even the historian Arnold Toynbee (1965) who saw the dynamic process of challenge-and-response as central in the growth and decline of civilizations.

As noted at the end of chapter 6, "Novice Professional Phase," we question whether a smooth transition from graduate school to postgraduate work is necessarily advantageous from a developmental perspective. We referred as well to the seminal work by Mueller and Kell (1972) who convincingly argued for the need to experience conflict and anxiety if learning is to take place. We certainly do not want to idealize experiences of adversity and we want to contribute to people avoiding unnecessary suffering, but nevertheless we want to voice our concern for an uncritical norm of the benefits of the "smooth life."

Also relevant for this discussion is the relationship of therapists' experiences of a certain type of difficulty in therapeutic work to the therapy process. In a study by Nissen-Lie, Monsen, and Rønnestad (2010), student therapists who doubted their own professional skillfulness obtained higher alliance ratings by clients. This intriguing finding runs counter to viewing the confident therapist uncritically as a positive norm. In discussing this finding, the authors "suggest that therapists need not be alarmed by the experience of *some* doubt in their professional self-confidence. On the contrary, such doubt may reflect a respect for the complexity of therapeutic work" (p. 641).

Reflection

Eighty years ago, the educator and philosopher John Dewey (1933) argued for the use of reflection to assist students in becoming critical thinkers. Following in this vein, Schøn (1983, 1987) distinguished between two types of reflections: *reflection-on-action,* which refers to reflection looking back at what had been going on, and *reflection-in-action* as occurring during an "action present—a stretch of time within which it is still possible to make a difference to the outcomes of action" (Schøn, 1992, p. 58, cited in Eraut, 1994). In an earlier formulation of this conceptual model, Rønnestad (1985) considered reflection to be the sine qua non or essence of effective supervision.

Further development of the conceptual model makes it seem important to differentiate between a reflexivity, reflective stance, and reflection as activity.

Reflexivity is defined as the cognitive and affective capacity to reflect.

Reflective stance is an attitude of inquisitiveness and eagerness to explore and understand phenomena and experiences in the therapist's life sphere.

Reflective activity is a broad concept which includes thinking about all aspects of the therapist's life sphere, as well as metacognition or "thinking about how one thinks about" these aspects (as described below). A theoretical hypothesis is that the quality of reflection *as activity* is to a large degree contingent upon therapists' capacity for cognitive complexity, tolerance for ambiguity, and openness to experience, as well as therapists' ability to process unpleasant and uncomfortable "negative emotions."

Continual Reflection. By continual reflection, we mean persistent engagement in reflective activity. Having a reflective stance contributes to this persistence. It is possible that therapists' capacity for "absorption" (Tellegen & Atkinson, 1974) will influence the degree to which therapists are capable of maintaining a reflective stance over time. Those authors wrote that absorption involves "a *full commitment of available perceptual, motoric, imaginative and ideational resources to a unified representation of the attentional object* (p. 274). They also suggest that absorption is related to "openness to experience," which we have suggested as a positive condition for professional development.

The concept of *continual reflection* directs one's attention to a limitation in Schøn's (1982) model, which differentiates between "reflection-in-action" and "reflection-on-action." Our critique concerns primarily on *reflection as activity.* As noted above, reflection-on-action refers to thinking about what has happened previously, while reflection-in-action refers to thinking about what is happening concurrently. These concepts can be logically extended to include reflection-pre-action or proactive reflection, which refers to "the cognitive and emotional preparation that the professional is engaging in *before* the professional meets client(s), patients(s) and pupil(s). Examples can be a therapist reading through the journal before a therapy session, or a teacher reading through lecture notes before teaching" (Rønnestad, 2008, p. 288).

Functional Closure

In chapter 6, "The Novice Professional Phase," functional closure was contrasted with premature closure and inadequate closure. Functional closure involves a decision-making process which enables the therapist to act therapeutically. What constitutes "to act therapeutically" or "therapeutic action" can be defined in different ways, like (a) actions that lead to constructive therapy processes, such as positive "in-session impact" (Orlinsky, Rønnestad, & Willutzki, 2004); (b) a good final therapy outcome, and (c) actions which are in line with good therapeutic practice as judged by competent professionals (e.g., "adherence" to essentials in a treatment manual). Therapists' cognitive functioning (especially their capacity for cognitive complexity) and affective functioning (especially their ability to process negative affect such as anxiety or dejection) will influence the likelihood of achieving functional closure. Bandura's (1977) concept of self-efficacy is theoretically relevant as a factor that will impact functional closure because it involves a person's belief in his or her capacity to initiate some future action. It seems reasonable to assume that a moderate to strong belief in this capacity enables the therapist to "functionally close."

Premature Closure

Premature closure is a pre- or unconscious defensive process that is activated when the therapists' competencies are not sufficient to handle the challenges or difficulties they encounter.[3] This process is characterized by misattribution, distortion, or dysfunctional reduction or oversimplification of phenomena when difficulties are encountered. Examples of premature closure include: (a) the therapist explains client dropout as being due to insufficient client motivation, although a more logical reason for dropout was lack of therapist empathy (an example of misattribution); (b) the therapist erroneously interprets client aggression toward him- or herself as a transference reaction, but is actually a client reaction to the therapist's lack of sensitivity and skill (distortion) in the "real relationship" (Gelso, 2010); and (c) the therapist's work fails because the therapy plan was based on a case formulation that was too simplistic and did not consider the life context of the client (dysfunctional reduction of phenomena encountered).

Inadequate Closure

Inadequate closure refers to therapists' inability to terminate reflection resulting from an inability to integrate and synthesize their experiences sufficiently to arrive at an understanding of the client sufficient for therapeutic action. It involves a lack of capacity to differentiate essential from inessential information, and thus an inability to organize information hierarchically. Therapists engaged in this process may experience themselves as being "stuck in detail." It follows from this that therapists lacking in metacognitive ability may be more likely to engage in inadequate closures, as compared with premature closures. It also seems likely that therapists who do not believe in their capacity to organize and execute a future course of action (i.e., have low self-efficacy), will be more prone to form inadequate closure.

In order to illuminate the concepts of the cyclical trajectories model and also the cycling through trajectories, we have constructed three cases that are presented in the chapter appendix. The first case illustrates growth through developmental cycles by introducing a Novice Professional who early in therapy felt intense discomfort and anxiety in her work with an aggressive client. She decided to reenter supervision. The second case describes a movement toward disengagement for a male therapist who was trained in psychodynamically oriented therapy. He was doing reasonably well in his work with adult clients within the context of a community mental health center. After a reorganization, the institution was transformed into a treatment center for adolescents with conduct disorders, and problems arose. The third case illustrates a hypothetical case of cyclical movement—first to exhaustion, thereafter to growth. A female therapist in her late 30s was employed at a large outpatient clinic. She took on several heavy responsibilities that over time depleted her resources. A turning point for her was entering personal therapy.

Before we complete this chapter, we ask how the cyclical-trajectories model presented here relates to other models. Previously, in our description of phases of development, we have related our findings and concepts to many of the models presented in chapter 1. For the rest of this chapter we will address the relationship of our model to a model for the development of cognitive complexity (Owen & Lindley, 2010) and also briefly to the cyclical-sequential model of Orlinsky and Rønnestad (2005) presented in chapter 1. In that chapter a more comprehensive analysis and comparison of the two models will be presented.

The Relation of the Cyclical-Trajectories Model to Other Models

Throughout the book, we have referred to many of the theoretical perspectives and models presented in chapter 1. We have also frequently referred to the findings of researchers within the Society for Psychotherapy Research/Collaborative Research Network presented in *How Psychotherapists Develop: A Study of Therapeutic Work and Professional Growth* (Orlinsky & Rønnestad, 2005a). These findings have provided invaluable base rate data for many of the phenomena that we have studied, and have also assisted us in knowing which findings are transferable to other therapists.

The collaboration between researchers within the SPR/CRN has also led to the construction of models of positive and negative cycles of therapist development (Orlinsky & Rønnestad, 2005a). In chapter 14, a comparison between the cyclical/trajectories model of this chapter and Orlinsky and Rønnestad's cyclical-sequential model will be made. This comparison will encompass descriptions of similarities and differences in scientific methodology, research methods, sample characteristics, basic model characteristics, roots or origin of development, key concepts and processes of change, and also suggest steps toward modification and integration of the two models.

A Comparison of Our Findings with Owen and Lindley's (2010) Stage Model of Cognitive Complexity

Our analyses have documented that therapists vary in their ability to maintain an optimal developmental process. Central in our conception of development/stagnation is practitioners' management of the difficulties and challenges that they experience. In our descriptions, we have highlighted practitioners' skills in regulating affect and engagement in reflection as activity, practitioners' attitudes and skills in maintaining a reflective stance, attitudes to the complexities of therapeutic/counseling work, openness to experience, tolerance for ambiguity, and reflexivity as a capacity. These capacities and attitudes influence how students and postgraduate practitioners process and organize their experiences as they proceed through the developmental phases we have described.

A general finding that we have described is therapists/counselors' movement over time toward more nuanced, differentiated, hierarchically organized, and complex ways of conceptualizing and organizing knowledge. Considering the comprehensiveness and complexity of the subject matter to be comprehended and mastered in order to become accomplished professionals, it is hardly surprising that these movements take time. In a shorthand terminology, we may describe this movement as "from the simple to the complex."

The stage model of cognitive complexity suggested by Owen and Lindley (2010) that we described in chapter 1 contains many relevant parameters and also points to changes in cognitive complexity across experience levels, some of which match our findings and perspectives. We will describe some of these because we see the study of cognitive complexity as a promising area of research. According to their developmental model of cognitive complexity, therapists at Stage 1 are limited in their metacognitive ability. Their metacognitive attention is focused on knowledge identification (i.e., acquisition) and on self-monitoring. Beginners necessarily do not know as much as more experienced therapists, and consequently it is not surprising that beginners' metacognitions are more limited than among more experienced therapists. Also a focus on knowledge acquisition is well established by many theoreticians of learning as we described in chapter 1 (see Table 1.1). The intense psychologizing of the beginning student may explain the focus on self-monitoring among beginning students.

As we have described, therapists do manifest a movement toward being better able to differentiate the information they receive; they are in time better able to integrate their knowledge, which is expressed in their ability to sort relevant from irrelevant information; they do become more reflective about their therapy/counseling abilities, and the process toward a good fit between their epistemology, theoretical orientation, therapeutic method, personal value system, and personal preferences can be understood as their epistemic approach to knowledge as being more coherent and thoughtful, as Owen and Lindley suggested. However, our data do not support a stage model of the development of cognitive complexity as suggested by Owen and Lindley, with the discreteness of functioning implied by a stage model. The changes that occur seem generally to be more continuous than suggested by these authors and some changes occurred earlier than they proposed. For example, a characteristic of their Phase 3 (which we interpret to refer to functioning at the postgraduate level, given their other descriptions of functioning at this phase), is that therapists are better able to sort relevant from irrelevant information. Our findings indicate this capacity to sort information happened earlier than they proposed. About the Advanced Student we wrote: "Increasingly, the Advanced Student is able to differentiate between more important and less important data, and consequently writes shorter case note summaries and more easily selects issues/problems to discuss in supervision. For example, a female intern reported, "As I got more confident, I realized that I didn't have to remember every detail."

Our findings also confirm that, compared to inexperienced therapists, experienced therapists are more reflective about their counseling abilities. We described modal Senior Professionals as knowing what their assets as therapists were, and also knowing and accepting their limitations. They expressed more humility and saw themselves as less powerful than previously as change agents. A male therapist said; "The longer I've been at it, the more I've become accepting of my limitations. That is just the way it is. Some things I do well, other things not so well." However, it seems that the capacity to be more reflective about their counseling abilities evolves gradually, and may not be a specific quality of the third phase. Finally, we may ask if there is empirical support for Owen and Lindley's formulation that therapists rely less on idiosyncratic decisions and justifications of beliefs, and are reliant on careful analysis of their previous experiences and empirical evidence. We did find that therapists in general were continually scrutinizing their previous experiences, and certainly experienced therapists have a wide repertoire of experiences to draw from, but it is not clear if it is fair to say that therapists were engaging in careful analyses of the empirical evidence. This depends in part on what one means by empirical evidence. If it means knowledge generated through careful scientific examination, then we are not so sure. It seems that for the time being we need to leave this question open for further examination.

In summary, the cognitive complexity model of Owen and Lindley suggests some of the changes we have described in our conception of therapist development. Metacognitions of beginners are necessarily limited and increase with experience; there is an initial focus on knowledge identification among beginners, a focus which changes over time as more experienced therapists' approach to knowledge becomes more coherent and thoughtful; compared to therapists' at later phases, beginners seem to engage more in metacognitions.

However, we repeat that our results do not support a stage model of development of cognitive complexity as changes seem to occur more gradually. Our results also suggest that the tempo of change as suggested by their model may deviate from what we found in our study because advanced student therapists seem to be able to hierarchically organize knowledge, a stage 3 capacity in the model by Owen and Lindley. Finally, it remains uncertain if more experienced therapists rely more on careful analysis of their previous experiences and empirical evidence than on idiosyncratic decisions and justifications of beliefs.

We see the study of therapists' cognitive complexity as a very promising area of research. We hope to see empirical investigations that focus specifically on this topic and that future studies on the development of cognitive complexity also draw fully on the empirically informed models of therapist development and conceptions available.

Chapter Appendix

Case Illustrations of Different Developmental Trajectories

Because our interviews had a thematic rather than narrative form, we have constructed hypothetical cases to illustrate the model based on our experience as researchers, therapists, and supervisors and teachers of therapy and counseling.

Hypothetical Case of a Growth through Developmental Cycles. A Novice Professional early in therapy (third session) experienced intense discomfort and anxiety when confronted with a client's aggressive rejection of him as a therapist. The client had a long history of pushing people away. The therapist felt inclined to withdraw emotionally, become defensive, and was losing his capacity to respond empathically toward the client (*experienced challenge or difficulty*). The therapist was unsure whether the client was sufficiently motivated for therapy. The therapist felt incapable of handling the situation and felt at loss of what to do. The therapist was not at the time in supervision, but he overcame feelings of embarrassment for not being able to handle this on his own, and contacted a previous supervisor to discuss the case. Through discussing the case, and particularly by focusing on understanding the client's history, the therapist was able to see how the client's history of neglect and abuse created a sense of vulnerability that activated aggression when feeling misunderstood. After discussing the case with the supervisor (*reflection*), and after an analysis of the client's core interpersonal schemas, the therapist could see why the client reacted as he did, and the therapist's empathy for the client was reactivated. This therapist was able to critically analyze the information and come to a decision about how to deal more effectively with the client (*functional closure*). This initial insight became important in reformulating their mutual goals and designing a strategy to reach them. The therapist felt he learned something, adjusted his therapeutic approach successfully, and experienced a state of *growth* in his professional development.

In a later session, the therapist experienced an impasse with the client which again was reflected on with the supervisor. A decision was made on how to act (*functional closure*), which initiated a constructive dialogue with the client that led to resolving the impasse.

Professional development entails repeated cycles of challenge and difficulty, leading to new reflections and functional closures which, over time, lead to increased therapeutic competence, better use of therapeutic techniques, and refinement of therapeutic attitudes and skills.

Hypothetical Case of Movement Toward Disengagement. Two years after graduation, a male therapist who was trained in a university program at an institution with a predominantly psychodynamic orientation, gained employment at a community mental health center. He seemed to be doing reasonably well, the challenges he met were addressed in an acceptable fashion, and he thus seemed to be developing as expressed by cycling through the steps of the model. The treatment center lost its funding and the institution was transformed to a treatment center for adolescents with conduct disorders. He was not able to relate well to the adolescents who were dropping out of therapy at a higher rate than was usual at the institution. He did not recognize the problematic nature of the situation (*limited experiences of difficulties*), and handled the aggression of adolescent clients poorly, interpreting it as a transference reaction, but he was unable to deal with it therapeutically. He understood the high dropout rate as resulting from lack of motivation for therapy (*premature closure*). Sensing but not recognizing fully that he was not performing well contributed to his becoming defensive in relating with colleagues. He found himself withdrawing from them at work and no longer participated in social events at the institution. He became increasingly frustrated in his work, particularly with the clients whom he continued to view as poorly motivated for therapy (*premature closure*). He was not emotionally invested in his work with clients, felt no enthusiasm, and was often bored when relating to clients (*disengagement*). Lack of work satisfaction finally led him to seek other employment (*exit*), taking a job as the assistant director of small counseling center where he continued to do a little counseling but mainly did administrative work.

From another perspective, it seems more likely that the client dropouts resulted from the therapist's lacking understanding of what the adolescents needed. His focus on the family history and past of the adolescents did not correspond to their typical adolescent interest in the present and the future (Bengtson, 2011). He had a reclusive manner and lacked the directness and the forthright engagement that most adolescent clients need in order to form a working alliance. This therapist did not assume a reflective stance when encountering the difficulties that he experienced, but instead spent little time reflecting and specifically was not curious to learn whether he contributed in some way to the high dropout rate. Nor did he seek assistance from colleagues to discuss the situation. His decision to change jobs was done without reflecting much on his situation. He was not able to see *his* contribution to so many clients dropping out of therapy, did not recognize that an insufficient case formulation contributed to the problems he experienced, and failed to realize how his absence of engagement and directness pushed the adolescents away from him. His lack of emotional investment, lack of enthusiasm, and sense of boredom combined to a *subjective sense of disengagement.*

Hypothetical Case of Cyclical Movement From Exhaustion to Growth. A female therapist in her late 30s was employed at a large outpatient clinic. Client turnover was high, primarily as a consequence of high production goals both for the clinic as a whole and also for individual therapists. She was engaged in different roles at the institution. In addition to being an individual and group therapist, she was a clinical supervisor for junior colleagues. She was responsible for the postgraduate training program at the clinic, had engaged herself in a research project at the clinic in two roles, both as a researcher and also as a research supervisor. Through the years she had also been a member of different committees at the clinic. Her working capacity had always been high. She was a high achiever and was well regarded by both colleagues for her effectiveness. She got things done.

She was married and a mother of three children (ages 8, 11, and 15). The middle child had trouble in school (both academically and relationally) and was receiving professional assistance from a school psychologist. She had an aging mother living in a nursing home in a neighboring town. She had one brother who did not assume much responsibility for visiting the mother, leaving her with much of the responsibility for their mother. She visited her mother one day a week and felt guilty for not seeing her more often. She did not have much time to see her friends, and found herself saying no to invitations from them. She had for many years often worked late nights after the children were in bed in order to catch up on different work tasks. She did not need much sleep and had felt that this had worked well. However, lately people had been telling her she looked pale and tired. She basically ignored this, said the last days had been particularly stressful, but there was no need to worry about her. However, after a while, she felt increasingly tired and started to worry herself (*experienced difficulties*). Reflecting on her situation, she felt she had too many demands on her both at home and at work. She was also concerned that she was becoming more and more irritable toward her husband, at work toward her colleagues, and also more irritated and impatient with some of her clients, some of whom had started to bore her. She talked with her husband and friends about her work and home situation, but to no avail. Even though she and her husband had agreed to share equally the responsibilities at home, she clearly felt she took on more responsibility, particularly for their middle child.

Initial reflections on her situation, mostly on her own, but also some with her husband did not help. She knew it was necessary for her to cut back on her work and also adjust the responsibilities which meant that she would need to drop work tasks or reduce the amount of time she spent in different work roles. She was unable to decide what to cut. She could not reduce her client load as production goals needed to be met. She did not feel she could abandon the junior colleagues by having other supervisors take over clinical or research supervision. She knew she was assuming a motherlike role toward her supervisees, also worrying about their personal lives, but it was hard for her to do otherwise. She had taken the initiative to start the research project at the clinic, which thematically was the same as her PhD dissertation. She had the most advanced expertise in the project and it felt like a betrayal to drop out of research. Furthermore, the postgraduate training at the institution was related to her expert thematic focus on the therapeutic relationship. She felt she knew more about this topic than her colleagues, and felt it would be a shame to drop it. She could decline some of the requests to participate in committee work in the future, but this would not amount to much as committee work did not take that much time. So her situation persisted.

She felt she had no choice but to continue as she had done. She was not able to set priorities that could form a basis for deciding what to reduce (*inadequate closure*). So she felt obligated to continue as she had done, and felt increasingly tired and depleted (*exhaustion*). Incapacitating lower back pain forced her to take sick leave. During her sick leave, she entered personal therapy. Reviewing her situation in therapy (*reflection*), she was helped to see her strong need to be viewed as someone special, to be respected and to get continuous positive feedback on her accomplishments, and that these wishes expressed not only a threat to her self-concept but also fear of abandonment and isolation. She also came to realize that she was not indispensable. She was helped to resume talks with her husband and was able to enter into constructive negotiations with him. These and other insights freed her to find a better balance between the life domains of work and personal life and also to prioritize within domains. The therapy process was painful with much guilt being evoked. Her insight into what was most meaningful for her assisted her in selecting priorities. She made decisions leading to adjustments in her life that were positive for her (*functional closure*). Her husband took more responsibility for the family and she managed to get her brother to visit their mother more often. Her therapist assisted her in seeing that she actually had a choice of what to do at work. Someone else took over the responsibility for training; two of her supervisees were transferred to other colleagues, and deadlines for research were extended. Most importantly, she began to accept her limitations as a human being, reflecting a marked change in self-concept. These experiences and the change in self-concept turned out to have a positive influence in her own therapeutic work.

First, she was able to meet high achieving clients with more sensitivity and humility, and with a more profound understanding of the dynamics involved, there was an improvement in therapeutic ability. Moreover, based on her personal experience and altered self-concept, her therapeutic approach became less directive and more listening and interpretive, a modification that can be conceptualized as integrating her personal experiences into her professional work. Third, she regained her enthusiasm and vitality for therapeutic work. With these changes, the three primary characteristics of professional development that we described earlier are met: a subjective state of growth in therapeutic competence, an integration of personal characteristics with theoretical and technical aspects of work, and being energized and vitalized in professional work.

Notes

1. "*Currently experienced development* refers to the psychotherapist's present, ongoing experience or transformation—either improvement [*growth*] or impairment [*depletion*]—in contrast to a stable, basically unvarying sense of therapeutic functioning" (Orlinsky & Rønnestad, 2005, p. 108). A central feature of professional development is feeling energized and vitalized by therapeutic work. This parallels the perspective "that the therapist's sense of currently experienced growth reflects a renewal of the morale and motivation needed to practice therapy, a replenishment of the energy and refreshing of the acumen demanded by therapeutic work" (Orlinsky et al., p. 212).

2. It should be noted that the theoretical model of this chapter only relates inadequate closure and premature closure to exhaustion and the disengagement dynamics of the Maslach conceptualization respectively, and not to burnout as a syndrome, a perspective that can be questioned on empirical and conceptual grounds (Larsen, Ulleberg, & Rønnestad, 2010).

3. The theoretical assumption is that the decision making process is not at all or only partly available to consciousness, an assumption in line with a continuum view of differences between conscious and unconscious decisions (e.g. Norman, Price, Duff, & Mentzoni, 2007).

11

A DEVELOPMENTALLY SENSITIVE
APPROACH TO SUPERVISION[1]

In this chapter, we draw some implications for supervision from our findings. The chapter is divided into two parts. In the first part, we present our view of general principles of supervision that are relevant regardless of the experience level of the supervisee. These principles have a parallel to the perspective of common factors in psychotherapy. In the second part, we present ideas that are particularly relevant for the supervisor to consider in the supervision of students and therapists at different experience levels. By doing so, we hope to convey a developmentally sensitive approach to supervision. We are not advocating an approach to supervision where there are specific tasks and methods that are unique to each phase of professional development. Such an approach disregards the variations among students and practitioners at various experience levels, which we have described in the preceding chapters.

We also suggest conceptualizing the learning that takes place in supervision within the general knowledge and skill acquisition literature that we described in chapter 2, and refer specifically to the types of learning and learning expressions that we condensed in that chapter. The following contributions combine to suggest a learning sequence structure: the acquisition/participation distinction that was made by Sfard (1998), which was expanded by Engeström (2001) to include the expansive/creative dimension; the imitation-corrective-creative learning paradigm of Fleming (1953); and the rules-aspects, maxim, postmaxim sequence of Dreyfus and Dreyfus (1986).

We advocate an approach to supervision that combines some general principles of supervision with knowledge of professional development. We are aware that this is a complex task cognitively because it involves reconciling seemingly contradictory perspectives. It also requires that the reader realizes that the elements of the approach are formulated at different levels of abstraction. The general principles that we describe have priority over the phase specific recommendations. This means that in the supervision of the beginning student, for example, we recommend that the supervisor creates a reflective culture in supervision (general supervision principle) while also providing structure, direction, and a skill focus.

Having studied professional development for a large part of our professional lives, we recognize that multiple factors and conditions impact supervision within and across phases of experience. A large variety of contextual and individual conditions, such as culture, therapists' self-relatedness, quality, and characteristics of the educational (basic and postgraduate) system (including supervision and personal therapy), conditions of therapeutic practice (such as work modality and client characteristics), and qualities of therapists' personal lives, interact to impact the trajectories of change of the individual therapists. These variations find their way into the supervision room. These variations in contextual and individual conditions cannot be sufficiently controlled in experimental designs, and this is probably the reason why the impact of supervision, measured as client outcome, and studied with traditional scientific methods, has not been convincingly demonstrated.

Before we present these perspectives in more detail, we will first present our view on some common supervisory characteristics that influence the quality of supervision regardless of the level of experience.

Some General Principles of Supervision

The debate on the conceptual and pragmatic validity of different models of supervision has its parallel within the field of psychotherapy. Goldfried (1980, 2009)[2] has suggested that it is possible to reach consensus among different theoretical orientations on some common principles of psychotherapy if one focuses on midlevel abstractions; that is, abstractions above that of observable techniques, and below that of formulations specific to different theoretical orientations. Recognizing the differences between supervision and therapy and inspired by Goldfried's logic of midlevel abstractions, we have formulated some general principles of supervision that that were generated from our own qualitative research and also inspired by the converging contributions on a number of topics: positive expectations (Frank, 1961), working alliance (e.g., Bordin, 1979; Horvath and Bedi, 2002), regulation of challenge (Csikszentmihalyi, 1996; Orlinsky & Rønnestad, 2005b) and formative feedback (Bernard & Goodyear, 2009). With this background we suggest a parsimonious list of general principles for supervision (see Table 11.1).

In the section below, we will describe each principle, then proceed to present recommendations that seem particularly relevant for the beginning student, the advanced student, and the postgraduate supervisee.

Table 11.1 Supervisory Principles Relevant for Supervision at all Experience Levels

- *Supervisory Principle 1.* To lay the groundwork for the supervisees to expect that supervision will be helpful.

- *Supervisory Principle 2.* For the supervisor to give priority to establishing a supervisory alliance that provides a safe base for learning, clarity in terms of what is expected from whom, and a direction as to what should be accomplished.

- *Supervisory Principle 3.* For the supervisor to create a reflective culture in supervision.

- *Supervisory Principle 4.* For the supervisor to be attuned to regulating the level of challenge that the supervisee experiences.

- *Supervisory Principle 5.* For the supervisor to ensure that the supervisee is provided with the corrective experiences needed to develop optimally.

Supervisory Principle 1

To lay the groundwork for the supervisees to expect that supervision will be helpful.

Unfortunately, there are reasons why some students do not expect that supervision will be helpful. Even though supervision generally has a high status among members of licensing boards, training program developers, educators, supervisors, and supervisees, there is ample evidence that much supervision practice is far from optimal and that many students experience considerable conflict and dissatisfaction with supervision (e.g., Gray, Ladany, Walker, & Ancis, 2001; Ladany, Hill, Corbett, & Nutt, 1996; Nielsen et al., 2010; Reichelt et al., 2009; Rønnestad & Orlinsky, 2000; Rønnestad & Skovholt, 2001; Trotter-Mathison, Koch, Sanger, & Skovholt, 2010). Prospective supervisees know this. As we have described earlier, students are continually scrutinizing their seniors and often have accurate perceptions of differences in helpfulness between supervisors. How can we lay the groundwork for the supervisee to expect that supervision will be helpful? The answers we provide are at two levels: structural/organizational and individual/dyadic.

Structural/Organizational Level Factors. Important factors are (a) for the training institution to select training sites and supervisors with a reputation for providing training and supervision of a high quality; (b) to continually evaluate training sites and supervisors to ensure that the quality is maintained and enhanced; (c) if practice sites and the academic training institutions are separate, to create good channels of communication between them; this is an essential bridging of the gap between the cultures of practice and the cultures of academia; (d) to professionalize supervisor training; that is, to develop high quality training programs that meet the accreditation requirements of recognized professional organizations.

We will comment on the topic of training institutions' selection of supervisors, as students' perceptions of the supervisor's reputation directly impacts hope for a positive supervision experience and an expectation that supervision will be helpful. Even though in some European countries most therapists/counselors have practiced for many years before they start to supervise, there are exceptions to this as shown in the survey by Rønnestad, Orlinsky, Parks, and Davis (1997). In this survey, one in eight psychotherapy supervisors had started to supervise when they had as little as 1½ years of experience as a therapist, and one in five had begun to supervise after 3 years of practice. In the United States, it is common for advanced doctoral students to supervise master's students in beginning practicum. The first author, at that time with only 1½ years of experience, supervised master's students while in the doctoral program. This was a positive experience for the first author (MHR), an experience which sparked a lifelong interest in supervision and professional development, but it was hardly optimal for the master's students. There may be some consolation in that it may be less threatening for a beginning student to be supervised by a more advanced student. One may also argue that it may be hard for the highly experienced therapist/supervisor to communicate complex internal and personalized conceptualizations to beginning students. But these possible advantages can hardly outweigh what students miss by not being supervised by experienced therapists and supervisors. The many reports in our qualitative study by students who eagerly wanted to learn from reputable and experienced seniors underscores the argument that training programs should select their supervisors from among highly experienced and respected therapists. This increases the likelihood that the student will enter supervision with an expectation that supervision will be helpful. Some beginning students have more than one supervisor: one who runs a group and one who provides individual supervision. These supervisors may vary by experience level.

Individual/Dyadic/Group Level Factors. The supervision contract is an instrument that can be used to fuel expectations that supervision will be helpful. It is an instrument that can be used to ensure that the expectations are realistic, and the instrument to define and specify for the supervisee in *what ways* and *how* supervision will assist the trainee in developing as a professional. Underlying this is the principle of communicating hope that some positive change will take place, a principle so elegantly communicated by Frank (1961).

Supervisory Principle 2

For the supervisor to give priority to establishing a supervisory alliance that provides a safe base for learning, clarity in terms of what is expected from whom, and a direction as to what should be accomplished.

This second principle involves the application of facilitative interventions by the supervisor in establishing a mutually respectful collaboration with the supervisee which reflects his or her developmental challenges, with an agreed-upon direction and defined roles. The conceptual background for this formulation is the work by Bordin (1983) who applied the working alliance perspective to different contexts, including supervision. He wrote:

> Although I have concentrated on the therapeutic situation, I believe the model is broadly applicable to many other change situations, including the student-teacher and even the child-parent relationship. In this article I will extend the application of this model to the supervision of counselling and psychotherapy. (p. 35)

The empirical backgrounds for these recommendations are varied. First, supervisees at all levels of experience are assisted by interacting with and observing seniors who relate to them in respectful and empathic ways. Second, supervisees, regardless of experience level, benefit from engaging in learning activities that assist them in structuring their experiences so that functional closure and *not* premature closure or inadequate closure will ensue.

The Supervisory Relationship. The alliance concept is broader than the concept of the relationship because it not only includes the bond aspect (a specific definition of the relationship), but also incorporates role allocation and goal establishment aspects of the collaboration. The topic of the supervisory relationship has been subjected to extensive conceptual and empirical research. In addition to numerous journal articles on various aspects of the supervisory relationship, the field is fortunate to have available several comprehensive books that present and discuss various aspects of the topic. Classical and new books include Bernard and Goodyear (2009); Borders and Brown (2005); Carroll and Gilbert (2005); Ekstein and Wallerstein (1972); Holloway (1995); Kadushin and Harkness (2002); Kell and Mueller (1966); Ladany and Bradley (2010); Ladany, Friedlander, and Nelson (2005); and Stoltenberg and Delworth (1987).

Our experience as researchers on professional development and supervision, and our own background as supervisors convince us that the interpersonal expertise of both supervisor and supervisee is most decisive in influencing the quality of the supervision process and outcome. Interpersonal expertise is at the core of clinical expertise, one of the three components in APA's definition of Evidence Based Practice (American Psychological Association, 2006). Interpersonal expertise is, according to APA, important in *all* professional roles. We know that the quality of the therapeutic relationship is consistently associated with therapeutic/

counseling outcome (Norcross, 2011; Orlinsky, Rønnestad, & Willutzki, 2004; Wampold, 2010). As Strupp (1996) previously summarized it, "The critical feature of all successful therapy, it seems to me, is the therapist's skillful management of the patient–therapist relationship" (p. 1022). The supervisory relationship is as important for successful supervision as the quality of the therapeutic relationship is for successful therapy/counseling. We state this with an awareness that supervision differs from therapy/counseling in terms of important parameters such as the context of the activity, the objectives, the role and tasks (including the evaluative function), the quality of the relationship, and outcomes (Rønnestad, 1983).

Our research has sensitized us to the impact of the intensity of trainees' emotions as they relate to clients as well as to supervisors. A great threat to the quality of supervision is that the supervisors are not aware of the intensity of the supervisees' emotions as they relate to their supervisors. The quality of the supervisory relationship impacts what the supervisees learn. Rogers described the good supervisor in the same way as the good therapist; as empathic, respecting, congruent, and genuine. In their description of the ideal supervision, Carifio and Hess (1987) write, "In conclusion it seems that the ideal supervisor is a person who shows respect, empathy, genuineness, concreteness and self-disclosure in his or her dealings with supervisees" (p. 245). Worthen and McNeill (1996), after a phenomenological analysis of a supervisee interview transcript, describe the good supervision experience as follows:

> Supervisory relationship experienced as empathic, nonjudgmental, and validating, with encouragement to explore and experiment; struggle normalized; sense of freeing consisting of reduced self-protectiveness and receptivity to supervisory input; nondefensive analysis; reexamination of assumptions; acquisition of a metaperspective. (p. 28)

As in therapy, intense transference and countertransference reactions may occur. The power differential between supervisor and supervisee increases these reactions. Doehrman (1976) has addressed the issue of power and emotionality as follows, "Supervisors are not only admired teachers, but feared judges who have real power" (s. 11). We therefore give the following specific advice for the supervision at this beginning phase:

• The supervisor must be sensitive to the threatening character of supervision and also recognize that the supervisees' need to protect themselves.

The obvious exceptions to this recommendation are if the supervisee is excessively evasive and resists exposing any of the limitations and difficulties experienced in therapeutic work. It has long been recognized that supervisees seek to avoid negative evaluations in supervision and carefully select what they communicate to their supervisor (Ward, Friedlander, Schoen, & Klein, 1985). Empirical studies on supervisee nondisclosure represent important contributions to understanding these dynamics (e.g., Hess et al., 2008; Ladany, Hill, Corbett, & Nutt, 1996; Nielsen et al., 2009; Reichelt et al., 2009; Skjerve et al., 2009; Yourman & Farber, 1996).

The phenomenon of the supervisee not disclosing what may be threatening to the supervisor has a long history in the literature on the training and supervision of therapists and counselors. As formulated by Reichelt et al. (2009), some early contributions are the work by Ekstein and Wallerstein (1972), the work by Liddle (1986) on supervisee resistance, the work by Kadushin (1968) on supervisory games, and the work by W. F. Bauman (1972) on diversionary tactics. With reference to the need for supervisees to protect themselves, Rønnestad and Skovholt (1991) wrote: "At the same time, the supervisor must encourage student disclosure of areas of weak functioning." The works by Ladany et al. (1996) and Yourman and Farber (1996) represent turning points in research on what supervisees do not tell their supervisors, and later, what supervisors do not tell their supervisees (e.g., Skjerve, et al., 2009).

Combining this body of conceptual and empirical knowledge of nondisclosure with what we have learned from our studies of professional development, we feel strongly that the supervisory contract is potentially a powerful instrument for both supervisor and supervisees not only to agree on where to go and how to do it, but also to constructively regulate their interpersonal boundaries.

Supervision Contract. We suggest the following recommendation for the supervisor to attend to:

- Supervisors must clarify with their supervisees (a) the conditions under which supervision will take place, (b) distribution and definition of their respective roles, and (c) the goals of their collaboration; in other words structure the collaboration by establishing a supervision contract.

Supervisees' struggles with making sense of the multiple input from numerous sources of influence can be eased by interacting with a senior where the conditions and content of the interaction are well defined. Supervisees' emotional reactions to seniors can be modulated by the structure provided by a clear supervision contract. Students' search for models to emulate makes the supervision experience a teachable moment for the supervisees to learn how to structure a collaboration. This knowledge can be transferred to the therapy/counseling situation.

Our research results do not advise us on whether the supervision contract should be written. What we can say is that the supervision contract should be clear to both parties. It seems that the field is moving in a direction of recommending written supervision contracts (e.g., Ascher & Butler, 2010; Bernard & Goodyear, 2009; Osborn & Davis, 1996; Osborn, Paez, & Carrabine, 2007; Sutter, McPherson, & Geeseman, 2002; Thomas, 2007). This may be a reaction to the increased legal concerns within the fields of counseling and psychotherapy, but may also be a response to the need for clarity and explicitness as to the allocation of roles and objectives in supervision. With our findings as a context for recommendations for a supervision contract, and with input from previous formulations on the supervision contract (Reichelt & Rønnestad, 2011) we have in Table 11.2 presented our suggestions for what topics to discuss when formulating a supervision contract.

Is it an advantage or not for the supervisor and the supervisee to share a theoretical orientation? Differences in theoretical orientation can be one source of conflict in supervision. Moskovitz and Rupert (1983), for example, found that supervisory conflicts could be attributed to differences between supervisor and supervisees in personalities, preferences in supervisory styles, and differences in theoretical orientation. Hess et al. (2008) also reported that differences in supervisees' and supervisors' theoretical

---

Table 11.2 Suggestions for What to Explore When Establishing a Supervision Contract

1. Location, time (frequency and duration) and payment (if relevant).

2. Discussion of *expectations* of supervision.

3. Discussion and clarification of the supervisee's *learning needs* based on a discussion of previous experiences relevant for the present work. What are their strengths and weaknesses as therapists/counselors as the supervisees see it?

4. Discussion and *clarification of focus* for supervision based on supervisee's learning needs; e.g., relational/facilitative skills, conceptual skills, technical skills (à la Bernard & Goodyear, 2009).

5. Discussion and clarification of the *roles and responsibilites* of supervisor and supervisees. This includes reporting procedures and work form (case notes, written summaries, video-, audio-recording, one-way mirror, cotherapy etc.). Supervisors' and supervisees' preferences or requirements.

6. What are the *boundaries* of supervision? To what extent should the personal development of the supervisee be addressed?

7. *Ethical principles and safeguard procedures* for emergencies.

8. Procedures for *evaluation*.

---

orientation were one of the reasons for withholding information in problematic supervision.

An obvious advantage of a shared orientation is that the supervisee can receive feedback from someone who is competent within the tradition. The importance of accurate feedback, that is, feedback from someone competent within the theoretical tradition, was highlighted by Dawes (1994) as important for increasing competence.

However, shared theoretical orientation can limit development of competence in at least two ways, one directly and one indirectly. De la Torre and Appelbaum (1974) argued long ago that as a defense against supervisee anxiety, exchange of technical jargon could directly inhibit genuine understanding of phenomena discussed. If this happens, the supervisors need to ask themselves and their supervisees what can be done to improve the supervisory relationship and also explore with the supervisees the meaning of the terms used.

Indirectly, a shared theoretical orientation limits the variety of input for the supervisee. Some institutions use a supervision format with each supervisee supervised by two supervisors. At the University of Tromsø (in Norway), this aspect of the supervision is highly valued by the psychology students (Skjerve & Nielsen, 1999).

Supervisory Principle 3

For optimal supervision, the supervisor must create a reflective culture in supervision.

At all phases of development, the practitioners' continuous reflection is a prerequisite for optimal learning and professional development. We formulated this as one of the themes in chapter 9. Reflection is the "essence," the sine qua non of supervision (Rønnestad, 1985), and a prerequisite for successful cycling through the phases characterizing optimal professional development.

Regardless of how experienced the supervisee is, there are two primary tasks for the supervisor: To encourage the supervisee to reflect on the experiences and to assist the supervisee to organize experiences so that the supervisee can act therapeutically. We have called this *functional* closure and as previously described have differentiated this from *premature* closure and *inadequate* closure which are not conducive to optimal professional development.

A reflective culture is a safe culture. Only if the supervisees feel reasonably safe will they manage to reflect optimally on the challenges and complexities of therapy, and reflect on their own contributions to what is happening in therapy/counseling and supervision.

For us, the importance of facilitating reflection has emerged from the results of our investigation, and specifically from our finding on how difficult it may be for students and practitioners to maintain an explorative stance in the midst of the difficulties encountered. We are of course not alone in recognizing the paramount importance ascribed to reflection. Schoen (1987), in his classical work on the reflective practitioner has elaborated extensively on the topic. Other contributions are the empirical study by Neufeldt, Karno, and Nelson (1996) on reflection in supervision and an early work on adult development by Perry (1981).

We have seen and experienced how differences in preferences for action and reflection among supervisees and supervisors have contributed to supervision conflicts. If both the supervisor and the supervisee have an excessive preference for reflection, which is expressed by both parties not being particularly interested in the pragmatic aspect of supervision, that is, what the supervisee concretely should do, supervision outcome may be limited. And, if both the supervisor and the candidate for various reasons do not tolerate the discomfort associated with not immediately understanding what is happening, and "escape into" an unreflected upon action-orientation, both the supervisor and supervisee may be quite pleased with each other, but may both contribute to the other encouraging premature closure. This may be described as a folie à deux of supervision (Rønnestad, 1985).

There are many threats to maintaining an awareness of how challenging and complex professional work can be. Some of these are:

- Inadequate or erroneous assessment of one's professional competence.
- The demands within society and the profession to "know" and to be "competent."
- The wish of both the supervisee and the supervisor to appear as competent in the eyes of the other and oneself.
- A wish to reduce the client's emotional pain as quickly as possible.
- A decision-oriented and action-oriented culture, expressed by the phrase "don't just sit there, do something."

In psychodynamic language, transference and countertransference reaction represent continual challenges to maintain the reflective position. Conditions like those listed above contribute to a press to be "certain," even if the situation and complexity of the situations suggest uncertainty. Premature closure can be disguised as "to assume responsibility," to "cut through matters," and for the supervisor to overemphasize the instructional/didactic aspects of supervision.

Supervisory Principle 4

For the supervisor to be attuned to regulating the level of challenge that the supervisee experiences.

For the supervisor, this involves assisting in client selection and in establishing realistic goals for therapy/counseling as well as for supervision. There are several issues here. The supervisor is the senior who usually will have the most contact with the supervisee and knows what the supervisee's learning needs are, so he or she must assist in the decision regarding the supervisee's client load. Too few clients provide limited learning possibilities, but too many clients will prevent the supervisee from engaging in the reflective processing of experiences which we have described as crucial for optimal development. As we have described, it is positive for supervisees' development if they succeed with their first clients and do not experience a stressful involvement with their clients (Rønnestad & Orlinsky, 2005a). Premature closure and inadequate closure may result if the challenges encountered are not successfully mastered. This principle is in line with Csikszentmihalyi's (1996) model of intrinsic motivation, which basically suggests that the experience of *flow* is more likely to ensue if the individual's competence matches the challenge encountered. So, we suggest the following:

• Supervisors need to be mindful of a potentially destructive combination of therapists/counselors experiencing the supervisory relationship as conflictual or dissatisfying (e.g., not feeling supported and respected by the supervisor), in combination with experiencing stressful involvement with clients.

As described earlier, we have used the concept of "double traumatization" for the combination of the supervisee experiencing a conflict with the supervision in combination with a stressful involvement with their clients (Rønnestad & Orlinsky, 2005b).[3]

Principle 5

For the supervisor to ensure that the supervisee is provided with the corrective experiences needed to develop optimally.

In addition to organizing and regulating the supervisee's practice, this principle also involves providing feedback and evaluating supervisees in ways that increase reality-testing and thus contribute to development. This principle has a strong standing in most theories of learning. Practitioners want, expect, and actively seek feedback on their performance. Supervisors, in their capacity to observe how the student and practitioners work, have a primary responsibility to provide accurate feedback in ways that facilitate continued learning. The reader may also remember Robyn Dawes (1994) massive critique of the field of psychotherapy formulated in the book *The House of Cards*, in which he pointed to the detrimental effects of practitioners not getting accurate feedback on their work.

Bernard and Goodyear (2009) have compiled a list of suggestions for giving formative feedback that we would like to share.

- Feedback should be based on learning goals (criteria) that have been negotiated between the supervisor and the supervisee.
- Feedback should be offered regularly and as much as possible should be based on direct samples of the supervisee's work.
- Feedback should be balanced between support/reinforcement and challenge/criticism, as either extreme over time is eventually rejected by supervisees as disappointing supervision (Gross, 2005).
- Especially when feedback is corrective, it should be timely, specific, nonjudgmental, behaviorally based, and should offer the supervisee direction in how to improve.
- Feedback should address learning goals that are achievable for the trainee.
- Because communication is, in part, culturally determined, supervisors should use listening skills to conclude if feedback was received as intended.
- Feedback should be owned by the supervisor as professional perception, not fact or truth. Supervisors need to model self-critique, flexibility, and brainstorming in conjunction with formative feedback.
- Supervisors must understand that supervisees want honest feedback yet are fearful of it.
- The acceptance of feedback is integrally related to the level of trust the supervisee has for the supervisor. Supervisees must be able to trust that formative feedback has a different purpose from summative feedback.
- Feedback should be direct and clear, but never biased, hurtful, threatening, or humiliating (Bernard & Goodyear, 2009, p. 33).

Supervision within Developmental Phases

When we describe our approach to supervision as *developmentally sensitive,* we mean that knowledge of professional development should be reflected upon when establishing the supervisory alliance, and included as a conceptual background when aspects of the contract are explored. We believe that if both the supervisor and the supervisee are developmentally informed, the interaction between parties will more likely address important issues and will more likely be meaningful. A developmental approach to supervision means that the supervision reflects knowledge not only of what has emerged as particularly salient at different developmental phases, but also reflects variations within phases. This is an important point. The logic is not: if a then b, but rather if a then possibly b, but also remember c, d, e, and f. So, when we frame our perspectives and recommendations within phases, we warn that these are not considered to be rigid imperatives for a specific phase.

We are aware of objections to a developmental perspective. The main argument is that some beginners may be more advanced in skillfulness than some experienced therapists. This objection is like claiming that a developmental perspective has no validity to describe an adult man because one has observed that some bright adolescents are functioning cognitively at a more advanced level than are adults with limited cognitive capacity. We all know there are variations within phases, within ages, and within other demarcations of temporality. Variations in talent and possibly interpersonal skillfulness probably play an important role. But such findings are not in themselves arguments against the validity of a developmental perspective, they are merely statements for variations within phases.

Supervision of the Beginning Student

We remind the reader that we consider the general principles described earlier as relevant for supervision at *all* phases of development. They are (a) *Supervisory Principle 1*: To lay the groundwork for the supervisees to expect that supervision will be helpful. (b) *Supervisory Principle 2*: For the supervisor to give priority to establishing a supervisory alliance that provides a safe base for learning, clarity in terms of what is expected from whom, and a direction as to what should be accomplished. (c) *Supervisory Principle 3*: For the supervisor to create a reflective culture in supervision. (d) *Supervisory Principle 4*: For the supervisor to be attuned to regulating the level of challenge that the supervisee experiences. (e) *Supervisory Principle 5*: For the supervisor to ensure that the supervisee is provided with the corrective experiences needed for optimal development.

The above principles constitute the core components of supervision. If these core components are not successfully mastered, it is likely that the specific recommendations will be of limited help.

The specific recommendations are based on the descriptions of the Novice Student we presented in chapter 4. We may recall that the developmental tasks of the Novice Professional are (a) to make preliminary sense of an extensive amount of new information which the individual is primarily acquiring from graduate classes and professional literature; this means to meet the criteria for conceptual knowledge set by the educational system; (b) to demonstrate in practicum sufficient procedural competence; that is, sufficient mastery of assessment and therapy/counseling skills; (c) to handle the intense emotional reactions that ensue from seeing their first clients in practicum; and (d) to maintain an openness to information and theory at the metalevel, while also engaging in the "closing off" process of selecting therapy/theories and techniques to use.

These tasks reflect the varied and intense experiences that the Novice Student experiences. There is much self-awareness which is expressed by an intense psychologizing that adds to a sense of vulnerability. Compared to the quality of client involvement at later phases, it is more likely that the Novice Student experiences a stressful involvement with their clients (Orlinsky & Rønnestad, 2005). This is at least partly due to the Novice Student's limited knowledge of the therapy/counseling role. The search for a way to conceptually organize the complexity experienced, and the search for procedures (techniques and strategies), prompt many to overly simplify the challenge, thus closing off and restricting their learning. An attitude to theory that we called "the true believer" was one expression of this closing off process. The potentially threatening character of therapy/counseling and supervision suggest the following recommendation:

- *Specific recommendation 1*: Supervisors must do all they can to create a "holding" environment for their supervisees.

Communication of a respectful attitude on the part of the supervisor and an understanding and recognition of what the supervisee is struggling with—in combination with facilitative supervisory interventions —are the building blocks of such a safe environment. But, there is a paradox here. It is likely most difficult for the supervisor to provide a "holding" environment for the student when it is most difficult for the supervisor to do so. This has to do with the ethical obligation of the supervisor to oversee and ensure that the therapy/counseling that the supervisee is conducting meet the norms for professional conduct. As a rule, Novice Students are less competent than they are at later phases, and, as stated above, they are more likely to experience a stressful involvement with their clients. The Novice Student may be struggling with competency issues, experiencing multiple difficulties in practice, experiencing anxiety in sessions, and coping nonconstructively, so supervisors need to consider carefully what to give priority to in their efforts to assist the supervisee. The contract in general, and specifically the specification of the supervisee's learning needs, is a guiding principle for the supervisor.

Much is at stake when the Novice Students meet their first clients and many raise the question if they are suited for this kind of work. The response they get from their peers and supervisors on their work is important for how this question is answered. Negative feedback and nonsupportive supervision are likely to increase novice anxiety, can be detrimental to perception of self, and can seriously inhibit professional development. Adelson (1995)[4] has described how frightening the learning experiences of the trainee can be. She points to supervisees not only being taught psychotherapy by their supervisors but also being evaluated by them. She furthermore points to the subjective and ambiguous character of the skills assessed to be complex, intensely personal, and difficult to assess. In addition to providing a holding environment for the supervisee, we suggest also the following recommendation for the Novice Student:

- *Specific recommendation 2*: In the supervision of Novice Students, supervisors may assume more of an instruction/teaching role than they do in the supervision of more experienced supervisees; but this must be done with attention to the general principles of supervision and to the supervision contract.

It is important that this is not all that supervisors do. With reference to Bernard's (1997) discrimination model that describes the supervisory roles of teacher, counselor, and consultant, we fully endorse Bernard and Goodyear's (2009) admonition: "There are many reasons to choose a role, but the worst reason is habit or personal preference independent of the supervisee's needs" (p. 102).

As the two first developmental tasks involve conceptual knowledge and mastery of therapeutic/counseling skills, Novice Students will generally benefit from the supervisor focusing at least part and probably much of supervision toward those pressing issues, an implication of which is that the beginning supervisees will prefer that the supervisor is more task focused, instructional, and directive and provides more structure in supervision than at other phases of development. This recommendation is controversial. Ladany, Walker, and Melincoff (2001) in their critique of developmental models stated that the theoretical assumption that beginning supervisees need more structure is based on clinical lore and not on research.

We do not see that this critique is warranted; first, because it rejects both the validity of conceptual research and the value of clinical expertise. To discard the validity of extensive, experientially based expertise by prominent contributors within the field of supervision on the basis of limited research is not warranted. Second, there is much empirical research that runs counter to the critique. A specific focus in supervision on "how to" is implicit in many models of supervision that describe one of the supervisor roles of the supervision of the novice as that of the teacher (e.g., Carroll, 1996; Hess, 1980). In an early study (Rønnestad & Winje, 1984), inexperienced and experienced practitioners agreed that the supervisory methods of demonstration, didactic instruction, and support were important when supervising beginners, but were diminished in importance in the supervision of more experienced supervisees. This study will be described in more detail in the next section, which addresses the supervision of the advanced student.

Bernard and Goodyear (2009), in their thoughtful review of conceptual and empirical studies on the supervision environment, presented some evidence that the literature tends toward a general view differentiating supervisees' preferences along the lines suggested by the developmental models, and particularly so for the novice supervisees, but that the supervision of more advanced trainees may be more idiosyncratic. These authors have focused on the matching of supervisory conditions (or supervisory environments) with developmental conditions. The importance of structure, direction, and support is typically mentioned as important in the initial stages of supervision. However, they write:

> As supervisees gain some experience, expertise, and confidence, they are ready to have some of the structure diminished, to be challenged with alternative conceptualizations of the cases that they have been assigned, to be given technical guidance as needed, and to begin to look at personal issues that affect their work. In short, to accommodate the different developmental needs of supervisees, supervisors alter their interventions of the supervision environment. (p. 122)

With reference to the early developmental models, and referring to 23 published scientific contributions, they write: "By and large, research has supported, or partially supported, the supervision environment premises of counselor developmental models ..." (p. 122). However, they also suggest that some of the finer distinctions suggested by the developmental literature are not yet supported, a reservation we endorse.

There are some specific studies that we would like to mention that specifically address the issues of a didactic focus and with results that we cannot see as having been refuted. Goin and Kline (1974) after analyzing videotapes of outstanding and moderately good supervisors, concluded that:

> [T]he content of the hours of the outstanding supervisor-teachers showed that they made more didactic comments about patients and technique than did their moderately good counterparts. These supervisors were also neither extremely passive nor authoritatively directive, but seemed to find a middle ground of activity. Their residents also heard them as making more helpful, information-giving comments about the techniques and the principles of psychotherapy. (p. 208)

In a study of events which weakened and then repaired the supervisory alliance, Burke, Goodyear, & Guzzardo (1998) found that supervisees with various levels of experience raised different issues. All counselors had completed a master's degree, but the researchers found experience effects. For example, counselors with less than one year of postgraduate experience, raised issues in supervision that concerned development of professional skills (e.g., definition of diagnostic terms). Lazar and Eisikovits (1997) found that undergraduate BSW students (i.e., beginning supervisees) preferred supervision with a structured and directive style. They wrote, "Findings indicated that students preferred a structured and directive style with clear and unambiguous directives, focus on tasks rather than on processes and clear setting of boundaries ..." (p. 25). They go on to conclude, "The findings of this study demonstrate well that a clear preference for directives and focus on tasks can coexist with balancing other crucial dimensions of human interchange (in this study control and autonomy), and also creative discussion of dilemmas." This conclusion converges with our supervision approach of combining general principles (e.g., creative discussion of dilemmas as an expression of a reflective culture) with tasks that are more likely to be beneficial for supervisees at specific phases (a structured and directive style for beginning supervisees).

We may also note Worthington and Roehlke's (1979) study, in which they demonstrated an interesting discrepancy in supervisors' and supervisees' assessment of what was vital to good supervision, a study that underscores so well the decisive role of the perspective of the observer. One of their conclusions of how *supervisors* were thinking was stated as follows:

> Supervisors did not perceive some of the more didactic-instructional aspects of supervision as being vital to good supervision. For example, supervisors did not think it was very important to allow supervisees to observe them counseling clients (40), to role play during supervision sessions (37), to give appropriate literature about assessment and intervention techniques (34), and to provide structure during early supervisory sessions (35). (p. 65)

This conclusion that supervisors did not think that it was important for supervisees to observe them, stands in sharp contrast to the intensity with which the Novice Students in our qualitative study wanted to observe how respected seniors work. So, how one views the issue of a preference for structure, directiveness, and structure in the supervision of beginning supervisees may also be a function of *who* makes the assessment. And that is exactly what Worthington and Roehlke (1979) found. Focusing on the perspective of the beginning student (and not the supervisor), they wrote:

> Beginning counselors rated their supervision as good, however, if (a) a personal and pleasant supervisor-supervisee relationship existed; (b) supervisors provided relatively structured supervi-

sion sessions, especially during early sessions; and (c) supervisors directly taught beginning counselors how to counsel (by example, by using literature, and by didactic instruction) and then encouraged the new counselors to try out their new skills. (p. 64)

We have a hypothesis that the few results in the literature that claim that inexperienced supervisees do not prefer supervision to be more structured/instructive and technique oriented, may be attributed to limitations of the research method, to the local training culture, or to the fact that in the supervision studied, the basic principles of supervision (hope, alliance, reflection, challenge, and corrective experiences) did not receive sufficient attention. Clearly, if a beginning student supervisee experiences the supervision as negative—a poor alliance, little reflection, no balance between challenge and competence, and no corrective experiences, the student will likely not want more structure, more instruction, and more focus on technique. On the contrary, the student will probably want less of it. But, if these basic conditions are met, we think that research will generate a supervisee preference for a supervisory "task or methods structure." Such a perspective can coexist with awareness of many moderators that may impact supervisees' preferences. See, for example, Bernard and Goodyear (2009) who described supervisees' cognitive complexity, ego development, and personality profile as moderators. We would like to add to this list: tolerance for ambiguity, openness to experience, and tolerance for and ability to process negative affect, which can all be conceptualized as aspects of ego functioning.

Limitations with an Instructional and Skill-Focused Supervision.   Are there any limitations associated with supervision where the supervision role is primarily instructional and skill-focused? As we have shown, our own research and the bulk of the supervision research tell us that students generally appreciate that supervision has such a focus. In spite of this, it is our opinion that there are serious limitations to such an approach if the basic principles of supervision are not observed. It is especially important that sufficient time is set aside for the reflective processing of the experiences of the supervisee. More importantly, if a supervisor's instruction and skill focus conveys an attitude of the supervisor as a true believer, which implies that there is one proper way to do things, supervision is seriously restricted as an arena for professional development. For supervision to be optimal, supervision needs to be based on the learning needs of the supervisee and must be conducted in accordance with the supervision contract. This may imply that a supervision focus of the novice may certainly also be on the interface between the supervisee's personal and professional selves and parallel process issues if such a focus is based on the learning needs of the supervisee and in accordance with the role-definitions reflected in the contract.

An excessive instructional and skill-focus in the supervision of the beginning student may jeopardize the opportunity for the beginning supervisee to reflect continuously on the experiences activated in professional work. Continuous reflection was highlighted as so essential for the professional development of therapists/counselors (see Theme 3 in chapter 9). It seems that at no phase in professional development, is there a greater risk for the supervisee not to reflect on experiences activated in professional work. Considering this, we suggest the following recommendation, a variant of the general principle to create a reflective culture:

- *Specific recommendation 3*: In the supervision of the beginning student, the supervisor must pay particular attention to providing the opportunity for the supervisee to reflect on the experiences activated in therapy/counseling work.

Without reflection, the beginning student is not provided with the opportunity to begin to integrate conceptual knowledge and procedural skills. Also, optimal supervision of the beginning student seems to mean that the supervisees focus their attention toward both "knowing" and "doubting." We have called this the *certainty-uncertainty principle of supervision*. At a metalevel, the supervisor must ideally encourage supervisees to maintain an awareness and respect for the complexity of therapy/counseling work, so that the supervisees are encouraged to search for a deeper and more comprehensive understanding of therapy/counseling work, while simultaneously at a microlevel relate to the supervisee in ways that assist the supervisee in acquiring comprehensible, specific, and concrete competence.[5]

Lastly, are there some positive aspects of student therapists/counselors' doubts about their mastery of professional skills, of doubting their ability to be of help to the client that have implications for supervision? Yes there are. In the study by Nissen-Lie, Monsen, and Rønnestad (2010) student therapists who doubted their professional skillfulness, obtained higher client rated alliances. On this background the authors wrote, "We suggest that therapists need not be alarmed by the experience of *some* doubt in their professional self-confidence. On the contrary, such doubt may reflect a respect for the complexity of therapeutic work" (p. 641).

Considering this, we suggest the following recommendation:

- *Specific recommendation 4*. For the supervisor to communicate to the supervisee that doubting their skillfulness as beginning students may be conducive to establishing a constructive therapeutic relationship.

Supervision of the Advanced Student

We may recall that there are five developmental tasks at this phase. The first three are similar to the developmental tasks of the beginning student:

1. To continue to learn more complex conceptual knowledge that meets the criteria set by the training institution.
2. To demonstrate procedural competence; that is, sufficient mastery of assessment and therapeutic skills as assessed by supervisors in particular.
3. To maintain an openness to information and theory at a metalevel, while also engaging in the "closing off" process of selecting therapy/counseling theories and techniques to use.

In addition to these three, the advanced student will increasingly alter unrealistic and perfectionistic images of psychotherapy and counseling and of the role of the practitioner, and also manage the bewilderment that comes from seeing psychotherapy/counseling as increasingly complex.

Some of the key characteristics of the Advanced Student were: Fluctuation between a sense of competence and failure; experiencing conditional autonomy; feeling vulnerable; being more critical toward the educational system; intense investment in supervision experience (conflict in supervision may be at its peak); wanting feedback from multiple sources, and more direct feedback from supervisors; perceives therapy/counseling as more complex; basic skills generally mastered and a search for learning the specifics with a focus on individual differences; high standards of performance; not risk taking. Adding to this is the increased vulnerability ensuing from the innocence of the beginning student; that is, diminished freedom to fail. Getting close to graduation, expectations to perform competently are naturally higher than was the case as a beginning student.

With the demanding developmental tasks and varied key characteristics of the Advanced student phase, the supervisor needs to carefully attend to the general principles of supervision relevant for supervision at *all* phases of development. Key concepts in the general principles were: expectation of supervision to be helpful, creation of a supervisory alliance, creation of a reflective culture, and regulation of level of challenge, and provision of corrective experiences.

Given the many tasks that the advanced student needs to master, and the diversity of the dynamics of the advanced student, the supervisor needs to exercise sensitivity to the needs of the particular student. We are in agreement with Bernard and Goodyear's (2009) recommendation that the supervision of the advanced trainee may be more idiosyncratic. However, tailoring the supervision to the needs and preferences of the individual advanced student can likely be done with more skillfulness if the supervisor is also aware of the research on the professional development of therapists/counselors and the rich, clinically embedded knowledge on supervisory methods across experience levels.

Our qualitative research documented the high intensity in the advanced students' continued quest to master therapeutic skills, and in particular to develop skillfulness with meeting the demands of the particular client, this as a consequence of seeing therapy/counseling as increasingly complex.

A study that underscores the salience of different supervisory methods for supervisees at various experience levels (including change in preferences from the beginning to the advanced student) was conducted by Rønnestad and Winje (1984). This study addressed many of the methods/technique issues discussed in the literature. We present it here because it informs us of changes in supervisory methods across supervisee experience levels. We cannot see that the conclusions in this study are refuted by more recent research. Furthermore, the findings are in general agreement with the findings in our qualitative study.

In this study, we assessed how inexperienced and experienced psychologists assessed the importance of different supervisory methods for supervisees at different levels of experience. By asking the opinions of both inexperienced psychologists (with less than 5 years of experience—the average number of years was 3.4) and experienced psychologists and supervisors (the average number of years of experience as supervisor was 7), we hoped to identify a possible common supervisory "methods-structure" for supervisees at different experience levels. The experienced group were all specialists (comparable to a Diplomate certification in the United States) in clinical psychology. We defined three "prototypes" of supervisee experience levels. The category of supervisees with "little experience" was defined as true beginners with no prior supervision (probably comparable to beginning practicum, i.e., beginning students); supervisees with "some experience" had 2 or 3 years of client experience and at least 1 year of supervision (probably comparable to advanced practicum; i.e., advanced students); supervisees with "much experience" had at least 3 years of experience (which is not really a whole lot) with at least 2 years of supervision (probably comparable to internship or postgraduate supervision). Many of the findings in this study, which are presented in Figure11.1, are in agreement with some important findings in our qualitative study, and specifically students' preference for structured didactic learning experiences early in supervision (which has potential drawbacks), the need for concrete and specific feedback, and the paramount importance of continual reflection on the experiences for optimal professional development.

As we see from Figure 11.1, for four of the supervisory methods, there is a change in their importance as assessed by both specialists and nonspecialists across supervisee experience levels (all significant, $p < .05$) for both specialists and nonspecialists.

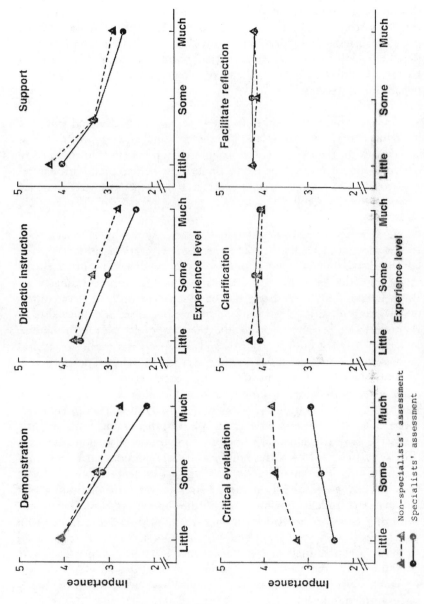

Figure 11.1 Specialists and non-specialists rating of importance in the supervision of supervisees with little, some and much therapy exprience.

For three of the methods, the specialists and nonspecialists have quite similar ratings. Demonstration and Didactic instruction and Support received high ratings in the supervision of supervisees with little experience, and progressive lower ratings for supervisees with some and much experience. Demonstration and Didactic instruction may be regarded as the "how to-method" of supervision. So, with careful attention to the general principles of supervision, and with the limitations of an instructional and skill-focused supervision that we addressed for the beginning student, we provide the following recommendation for the supervision of the advanced student:

- *Specific recommendation 1*: In the supervision of advanced students, supervisors may assume less of an instructional and teaching role than they do in the supervision of beginning supervisees. However, these roles should not be abandoned, and must be executed with careful attention to the supervision contract and to the advanced students' need for autonomy.

We described the advanced students as actively seeking feedback from their seniors; and feedback from supervisors is particularly valued. The advanced students want more honest and clear feedback from their supervisors than they feel they get. This is in line with other findings (e.g., Reichelt et al., 2009), and can also be interpreted in light of the differential rating of "critical evaluation" of nonspecialists and specialists in the supervision of supervisees at all experience levels. We see an increase in mean scores of both specialists' and nonspecialists' rating of critical evaluation across supervisee experience levels. However, and possibly more importantly, there was a substantial difference between how specialists and nonspecialists rated the importance of critical evaluation. A Cohen'd for the difference in rating of critical evaluation by specialists and nonspecialists, was .87; that is, a large effect size. In other words, nonspecialists assess the critical evaluation to be more important than nonspecialists. This converges well with the findings of the Scandinavian research on nondisclosure (Nielsen et al., 2009); advanced students did not feel that they got enough feedback on their work. "It was a major finding that although the students obviously sensed the supervisors' typical cautiousness, they expressed a wish for more direct and directive comments on their clinical work, and also more specific suggestions [emphasis added] for how to master their new professional role" (p. 51). Supervisors were communicating that they were adjusting their feedback and for pedagogical reasons were not as critical as they could have been, which the supervisees seemed to know.

On the basis of the results above we suggest the following recommendation

- *Specific recommendation 2*: In the supervision of the advanced student, for the supervisor to give feedback to the supervisee that is more direct and honest than the supervisor is inclined to believe is positive.

Given the evidence, we feel it is timely to give this recommendation; however, we give it apprehensively as we do not want to reinforce the harsh supervision practice of the supervisor who is not capable of providing a supervision environment that is in agreement with the general principles that we have outlined. However, we think that if the feedback provided is perceived as being relevant in light of the supervision contract (e.g., based on learning needs and mutually shared objectives) and is provided according to the guidelines presented above (Bernard & Goodyear, 2009), and especially is "timely, specific, nonjudgmental, behavioral based" that honest and clear feedback will strengthen the supervisory alliance and further the acquisition of therapy/counseling skills and the professional development of the advanced student.

As described earlier, we formulated Theme 3 in our study as follows: Continuous Reflection is a Prerequisite for Optimal Learning and Professional Development at All Levels of Experience. We see from Figure 11.1 that Clarification and Facilitate Reflection consistently receive high ratings by both specialists and nonspecialists in the supervision at all supervisee experience levels (ranging from a low of 4.0 to a high of 4.3; for the Advanced student, ratings are slightly above 4.0. We see Clarification and Facilitate Reflection as task expressions of the sine qua non of supervision. On this basis we recommend:

- *Specific recommendation 3*: In the supervision of the advanced student, the supervisor should encourage the supervisee to continually reflect on the experiences in therapy/counseling, in supervision, and in personal life that are interpreted to be relevant for professional functioning and development.

As we have described, advanced students are more likely than beginning students to want to explore how personal issues are expressed in their therapeutic work. As the basic therapy/counseling skills are better mastered, attention is freed for the advanced student to increasingly explore how personal issues are expressed in therapy/counseling and also to explore the related issue of using their own emotional reactions as a means for diagnostic assessment and therapeutic intervention. For therapists/counselors "to use themselves as an instrument" has a strong standing in both dynamic and experiential therapies. The usefulness of this perspective rests on at least two assumptions: one has to do with the quality of how therapists relate to their clients, the other concerns the assumption that therapist/counselors have insight into their emotionality. There are two studies that are relevant for supervisors and supervisees that bear directly on these assumptions.

Nissen-Lie et al. (2010) found that therapists' use of advanced relational skills was positively associated with client rated alliance only if the therapist had a warm interpersonal style. This means that therapists/counselors' uncritical use of their own emotional reaction to the client, can be detrimental to the alliance. The condition of feeling warmth and empathy for the client must be present. We present this as a warning against the uncritical use of the perspective "to use oneself as an instrument" and specifically the uncritical and unreflected use of one's own countertransference reactions in therapy.

The results of a study on countertransference reactions deserve mention. Holmquist (1995), in his study on countertransference feelings in milieu therapy in Sweden, found that therapists' emotionality in their meeting with clients was not necessarily a reaction to the interaction with the client. In fact, what explained most of the variance in therapists' emotionality, was therapists' habitual personal emotions. This finding is quite important. If the findings can be generalized, it is in other words more likely that therapists' feelings of, for example, anxiety, apprehension, worry, dejection, or depressiveness are an expression of their habitual emotionality and not a reaction to the individual clients. If so, the idea of "using oneself as an instrument," which implies a fine tuned reactivity to what the client is communicating may be seriously questioned. It follows from the argument above that self-insight is a likely prerequisite for successful use of one's own emotionality as a valuable source of information about the client and also as an instrument for therapeutic action. Fortunately, the great majority of therapists/counselors value personal therapy as a means for personal and professional development and engage themselves in personal therapy at least once in their lives. We also know that this activity can constructively impact how therapists relate to their clients (Orlinsky, Norcross, Rønnestad, & Wiseman, 2005). Supervisors and supervisees should be aware of the findings presented above, and should not assume that therapists' own emotionality is an accurate indicator of what goes on in therapy/counseling. Given these ideas, we provide the following two recommendations:

- *Specific recommendation 4*. If a goal of supervision is to increase supervisees' mastery of "using themselves as an instrument," this should be done with the knowledge of, and with respect for, how demanding it is to do this in an optimal way.
- *Specific recommendation 5*. For supervisors to argue for personal therapy as a constructive activity to enhance personal and professional development, and to encourage supervisees to start personal therapy if the timing and conditions to do so are right.

We are aware that there are some issues that the supervisor needs to be aware of when making such a suggestion. It is important that this recommendation is made not as a reaction to some shortcoming in the supervisee, but as a general recommendation (i.e., to all trainees). Recommending personal therapy should be done in a way that communicates a respect for the demanding nature of therapy/counseling work. In this context, the supervisor may want to disclose how personal therapy has assisted her or him in their professional work because making such a recommendation may otherwise reinforce the hierarchical and power-differential nature of the supervisory relationship.

Parallel Process. The parallel process perspective (Doehrman, 1975) is one conceptual tool that may be used to analyze the personal reactivity of the therapist/counselor as this is expressed both in the therapy/counseling and supervision. "Parallel process" originally termed the *reflection process* by Searles (1955), is comprehensively described by Ekstein and Wallerstein (1972) and empirically studied by many, of which Doehrman (1976) and Friedlander, Siegel, and Brenock (1989) were early empirical contributions to its study. The perspective is at the heart of modern psychoanalytic supervision. Adelson (1995) wrote: "The most effective supervision depends on active insight into the interplay of forces in the parallel processes of psychotherapy and supervision" (s. 51). According to Searles (1955), the therapist's identification with the patient will be reflected in supervision. Doehrman (1976) has documented that students develop intense transference reactions toward their supervisors, and that the direction of the parallel process dynamics are not only *from* therapy *to* supervision (as originally thought) but also *from* supervision *to* therapy. All four therapists in her study identified with their supervisor and "played supervisor" with their patients. The mechanism of transfer of processes was either identification or counteridentification (p. 37).

Bernard and Goodyear (2009) have recently summarized research on parallel process. They refer to several works that documented the relationship between what happens in the client/therapist dyad and what happens in the supervisee/supervisor dyad. M. J. Patton and Kivlighan (1997), for example, found weekly variations in the supervisory alliance which predicted variations in therapy alliance. Williams (2000, in Bernard & Goodyear, 2009), in a comprehensive study of 44 supervisory dyads, showed that the more facilitative the supervisor's interpersonal style, the less domineering and controlling the therapist was in how they related to their clients.

The parallel process perspective provides an opportunity to teach the analytic attitude and to apply the supervisory relationship to better understand client dynamics and therapy process. By applying the parallel process perspective in supervision, the supervisee is provided with an opportunity to engage in experientially learning the interplay between intra- and inter-personal processes and between conscious and unconscious processes.

A survey by Raichelson, Herron, Primavera, and Ramirez (1997) showed that participants in psychoanalytic supervision believed more strongly than nonpsychoanalytic representatives that focusing on parallel process issues had several positive consequences. Some of these were:

> [S]upervisees become more comfortable inviting negative trans-ference feelings into the therapy; supervisees gain a deeper aware-ness of countertransferences issues and subjective emotional responses to the patient; supervisees gain an appreciation of the value of nonverbal, behavioral enactments; supervisors gain a better awareness of the patient's dynamics; supervisees' ability to learn from supervision increases; supervisees feel freer to act spon-taneously, warmly and interpersonally in the therapeutic process. (p. 44)

Jacobsen (2007) has described how the parallel process perspective can assist trainees in increasing their awareness of both the subtle and the complex interpersonal processes of psychotherapy. Even though this per-spective seems particularly relevant for the supervision of the advanced student and postgraduate supervisee, it can, as we stated earlier, also be a valuable tool in the supervision of the beginning student if the learning needs favor it and if it is reflected in the supervisory contract. A critical point for us is that effective application of this perspective rests on the assumption that supervisor and supervisee have a realistic picture of the sources of the emotions experienced and expressed in supervision.

Supervision during the First Years After Graduation

Again, we remind the reader of the general principles for supervision at *all* phases of development. They are (a) *Supervisory Principle 1*: To lay the groundwork for the supervisees to expect that supervision will be help-ful; (b) *Supervisory Principle 2*: For the supervisor and supervisee both to be successful in working toward establishing a supervisory alliance that provides a safe base for learning, clarity in terms of what is expected from whom, and a direction as to what should be accomplished; (c) *Supervisory Principle 3*: For the supervisor to create a reflective culture in supervision; (d) *Supervisory Principle 4*: For the supervisor to be attuned to regulating the level of challenge that the supervisee experiences; (e) *Supervisory Prin-ciple 5*: For the supervisor to ensure that the supervisee is provided with the corrective experiences needed to develop optimally.

Optimal supervision at this phase presupposes that the supervisor is aware of the recent graduate's developmental tasks. As described in chapter 6, they are (a) to develop a sense of identity with the profession and commitment to the professional sector to which the person belongs (e.g., counseling, psychology, psychiatry, etc.); (b) to succeed in the transformation from the dependency of graduate school to the independence that is expected, both from oneself and from others, after having completed professional training; (c) to master any disillusionment with training, self, and the profession that may emerge some time after graduation; and (d) to keep exploring and defining one's work role.

We divided the Novice Professional phase into three subphases; Confirmation, Disillusionment, and Exploration. We may recall that in the Confirmation subphase, the Novice Professional invested much attention toward confirming the usefulness and validity of training. In the Disillusionment subphase, the Novice Professional was struggling with the disheartening experience of being disappointed with self, training, and the profession. In the Exploration subphase, an "inward" and "outward" search took place; "inward" toward one's professional and personal selves and "outward" toward the professional world (e.g., workplace, alternative work settings, etc.). Successful completion of the Exploration phase entailed that the Novice Professional was able to maintain a reflective stance when encountering difficulties in her or his professional work, and not engage in the processes we called *premature closure* and *inadequate closure*.

The supervisor plays a major role in assisting the recent graduate in coping with the challenges encountered and in mastering the developmental tasks of this phase. The conditions of supervision vary considerably. For some, supervision may be sought to meet the requirements for licensure; for others supervision may be an obligatory part of psychotherapy training, while for others supervision is sought, not for external reasons, but in order to hone one's skills, to learn a new therapy/counseling approach, to develop professionally, or for other reasons.

Power Dynamics and Intersectionality.   Compared to the supervision that takes place during basic professional training, the power dynamics in the supervision of the postgraduate professional may be less, but not necessarily absent. In fact, the power dynamics can be exaggerated, as is the case if the therapist/counselor is temporarily employed and is supervised by the head psychologist at the institution. Under such conditions, the scene may be set for the supervisee to make a good impression and conceal mistakes. Novice Professionals are keenly attentive to the power dynamics of the institution, dynamics than may find their way into supervision. The supervisee may ask if the supervisor's relationship to the organization is characterized by solidarity, loyalty, or conflict? For example, we have observed negative consequences for a supervisee who became a delegate for the supervisor's critical attitude toward the dominant treatment model of an institution. After voicing his critique at a staff meeting, the supervisee was not sufficiently supported by his supervisor, leaving the supervisee feeling betrayed.

Understanding how context can impact supervision is, of course, relevant for supervision at all phases of therapist/counselor development. However, while a student, much attention is directed toward the immediate mastery of therapy/counseling techniques and client conceptualization. Therefore, we think that an in-depth discussion of the impact of context or supervisee learning can be made with more depth and sophistication at the Novice Professional phase.

Given this background, we make the following recommendation:

> *Specific recommendation 1*: For the supervisor to ensure that in the initial phase of supervision the context of therapy/counseling and supervision is discussed; particular reference should be made to possible power dynamics and tension within the institution.

Let us make the picture more complex. Imagine two scenarios: First; a CBT-oriented older male European American supervisor is supervising a young dynamically oriented American Indian female graduate working in an institution with a psychodynamic orientation. A second scenario: an older CBT-oriented female Hispanic supervisor is supervising a young European American therapist/counselor working in an institution with a dynamic orientation. To understand the diversity expressed in the two examples above is vital to the high level of professional conduct. In fact, individual and cultural diversity is one of the core competencies as formulated by Rodolfa et al. (2005) which was also adopted as a core competency in a formulation by The Assessment of Competency Benchmarks Work Group[6] (Fouad et al., 2009). We have few theoretical concepts to assist us in understanding diversity and which can serve as pragmatic tools to use to recognize and deal with diversity. The concept of intersectionality is such a tool.

The concept was originally formulated by Crenshaw (1989). It has been applied in the analyses of supervision (e.g., Gray & Smith, 2009; Hernandez & McDowell, 2010; Porter, 2010; referred to in Ulvik, 2011) and offers a perspective that can assist the supervisor in addressing issues not only relating to social categories such as gender, social class, and ethnicity, but in a more abstracted sense also to the analyses of social institutions in which supervision takes place. The perspective of intersectionality in combination with the technique of "Reflective conversation and questions"(RCQ; Gray & Smith, 2009) provides the supervisor with a conceptually sound and pragmatic tool that can assist supervisees in maintaining an open, reflective, and solution-focused approach in supervision as well as in therapy/counseling. RCQ, which builds on the principles and techniques of solution-focused and narrative therapies, converges well with our emphasis on continuous reflection, respect for the complexity of therapy/counseling work, the paramount importance of an open, exploring attitude when confronting difficulties in therapy/counseling, and the detrimental consequences of not tolerating the discomfort of temporarily not understanding what is going on and consequently engaging in premature closure.

The perspective of intersectionality is relevant for all phases of therapist/counselor development. However, as suggested above, the student therapist/counselors are likely to focus much of their attention on immediate mastery of therapy/counseling techniques and client conceptualization. Although not considering issues such as power, gender, ethnicity, and social class may adversely influence the quality of therapy/counseling techniques and certainly also influence how one conceptualizes clients, it seems that these issues can be explored with more depth and sophistication after basic skills have been mastered.

On this background, we make the following recommendation:

- *Specific recommendation 1*: Supervisors should encourage their supervisees to reflect upon how the concept of intersectionality may assist the supervisee to better understand cultural diversity and stimulate a greater awareness of the interpersonal aspects of supervision as well as of therapy/counseling.

Dealing with Supervisee Disillusionment. It is disheartening for the Novice Professional to experience disillusionment with self, training, and the profession that many experience some time after graduation. Client drop out, an inability to establish good working alliances, and poor treatment outcome are some of the adversities experienced, not only by clients but by therapists/counselors as well. If the work environment stimulates discussion of such experiences, the burden is lessened. The supervisor plays a major role in assisting the supervisees dealing with this in constructive ways.

Recent research has sensitized us to the disconcerting fact that there are large variations in the results that therapists/counselors obtain (Wampold, 2010). The research by Lambert and associates (Okiishi et al., 2006) has shown us that some therapists obtain higher client deterioration rates than other therapists. Although some clients are clearly more challenging and difficult to help, poor results by therapists across different clients, also after repeated feedback to the therapist/client is provided, is an indication that these practitioners may be engaging in unethical practice (as competency is an integral part of professional ethics), and may be unsuited to be therapists. If the supervisor suspects that the supervisee is not performing up to some minimal standard for professional conduct, it is paramount that the supervisor discusses the situation with respected colleagues before deciding how to proceed.

However, for most Novice Professionals who experience disillusionment with self, training, and the profession, the issue raised is *not* one of suitability as a therapist/counselor. Rather, such experiences are a common and normative part of professional development and should be dealt with as such. Disillusionment is a reaction to doubting one's ability and not feeling competent as a therapist/counselor. If the disillusionment and self-doubt are not extreme, we understand such a reaction as constructive for professional development because they convey a respect for the complexity of therapy/counseling work. In addition to referring to the results of our qualitative study, which has demonstrated such feelings as common for the Novice Professional, supervisors can also draw on the findings of two other research studies to ease the concern of the new professional.

First, Najavits and Strupp (1994) reported that effective therapists were reported to be more self-critical and to have made more mistakes in therapy than less effective therapists. Second, as reported earlier, Nissen-Lie et al. (2010) found that therapists' reports of experiencing difficulties in their work, and in particular the type of difficulties called personal self-doubt (PSD), was positively associated with a client rated working alliance. In other words, the more personal self-doubt, the higher client rated working alliance. It should be noted that the values reported were all moderate. This latter finding is intriguing. The authors suggested that PSD may reveal an attitude of therapist humbleness and caution that the client may experience as respectfulness, and that may strengthen the alliance. The authors also wrote:

> PSD may also entail what Rønnestad and Skovholt (2003) termed "awareness of complexity" as a central characteristic of psychotherapist development. Higher levels of PSD surely express an open and more permissive attitude towards admitting one's shortcomings as a therapist. It may well be that this openness can be linked to the beneficial effect of therapists' ability and willingness to address inevitable and relatively frequently occurring alliance breaches, admitting to their responsibility as part of the interaction (e.g., Safran et al., 2002), as was previously mentioned. (p. 14)

So, we view admitting to failures and shortcomings as therapists/counselors as generally positive. We are more concerned and worried about practitioners who see themselves as highly competent because such an attitude communicates a lack of respect for, and awareness of, the challenging and infinitely complex nature of therapy/counseling work. Given these points, we make the following recommendation:

- *Specific recommendation 2.* When the supervisee experiences disillusionment with self, training, and the profession, for the supervisor to assist the supervisee in exploring these feelings, but also communicate the normative character of such feelings and point to the potentially constructive consequences of doubting one's ability as a therapist/counselor for the working alliance as well as for professional development.

Throughout our book we have pointed to how important it is for therapists/counselors at all phases to maintain a reflective stance. During the Novice Professional phase, the disillusionment poses a particular challenge to abandon the reflective stance. If so, the practitioner will not engage in the Exploration subphase, the "inward" search toward one's professional and personal selves, and the "outward" search toward the professional world (e.g., workplace, alternative work settings, etc.). This search, which is a step toward creating an integrated and personally based work role, is a prerequisite for what in chapter 6 we called Anchored Conceptual Structures. The consequences for the Novice Professional *not* to continually reflect on the challenges and difficulties experienced are so negative that we suggest the following specific recommendation:

- *Specific recommendation 3*: For the supervisor to be particularly mindful of encouraging and facilitating the supervisees at the Novice Professional phase to continually reflect on the difficulties and challenges experienced.

Some Novice Professionals do not experience disillusionment as described above. If the transition from training to postgraduate work is smooth, which typically means that during training the student was exposed to a limited and clearly defined work role, which is continued in a postgraduate setting (e.g., manualized individual therapy for patients with phobic disorders), the supervisor may facilitate the professional development of the supervisee by encouraging work with other clients and other work modalities. Breadth and depth of case experience facilitates professional development (Orlinsky & Rønnestad, 2005).

Supervision of the Experienced Therapist

As we have describe earlier, therapists/counselors at all experience levels express a wish to develop professionally. From our qualitative inquiry, we have many reports of experienced therapists who learn from engaging in peer supervision. The proportion of experienced therapists who are currently in supervision varies greatly across nationalities due to differences in requirements for licensure, accreditation, and professional cultures. In

Denmark, for example, as many as 75% of psychotherapists with between 20 and 30 years of experience report being currently in regular supervision (Jacobsen & Nielsen, 2011), a likely testimony to the meaningfulness of supervision at all experience levels. Analyses of data from 5,000 therapists from more than 15 countries show that psychotherapists with between 15 and 45 years of experience gave getting formal supervision or consultation high ratings as sources of influence for their overall career development (Orlinsky, Botermans, & Rønnestad, 2001).

Given the popularity of supervision among experienced therapists, it is surprising that we know so little about how this professional activity is carried out, how it is experienced, and what consequences it has. From an analysis of supervisors from many countries, we know that as therapists get more experience, many (approximately 50%) will have supervised other therapists (Rønnestad, Orlinsky, Parks, & Davis, 1997), that this activity is valued highly, but we have little direct knowledge of what actually goes on in the supervision of experienced therapists.

However, based on what we know about professional development of the experienced therapist/counselor, we may make some assumptions about the supervision of the experienced practitioner. The experienced therapists are highly selective in choosing their learning arenas; for example, reading professional literature, nonprofessional literature (e.g., prose/poetry), attending plays, visiting art exhibitions, participating in workshops or professional conferences, taking part in collegial discussion, supervision, etc.). We can be reasonably certain that if the experienced therapists chose to engage themselves in individual or group supervision, it was done with the intention and agency that characterize experienced therapists/counselors. This means that the experienced therapists/counselors choose their supervisors. Knowing the professional community and the reputation of therapists/counselors and supervisors, they can seek a supervisor who fits their professional needs.

The experienced supervisees are likely to know what their developmental needs are, a knowledge that is reflected in their choice of supervisor. The process of discussing the supervision contract, which we see as one of the general supervision principles, will likely take less time in the supervision of the experienced supervisee.

Both the supervisor and supervisee are experienced therapists and in general feel professionally competent, and the supervisor is typically an established and respected supervisor, so the supervision scenario is typically not a threatening one for either party. Less time is likely used to develop a supervisory relationship. If transference and countertransference reactions are less prominent (i.e., the interaction between the two is more matter of fact), the parallel process perspective may be less useful in the supervision at this phase. An exception may be when an experienced therapist/counselor with little knowledge of psychodynamic therapy seeks supervision to develop competence in this therapeutic approach.

If the experienced supervisee seeks supervision to learn a specific therapy approach, the supervision, seen from the outside, may appear much like supervision of the beginner in that the supervisor maybe assume the role of a teacher; the supervision may be instructional, technique oriented, and the learning that takes place may have a modeling character. However, from an inside perspective, the situation and processes are different because the interaction is framed as symmetrical and collegial as seen from the perspective of both the supervisor and supervisee.

Much of the supervision of experienced therapists may be conceptualized as a learning process akin to a qualitative research process where both participants create a new, extended, and more in depth understanding of therapy/counseling. This form of supervision, where the interaction can be understood from the perspective of the hermeneutic circle (Gadamer, 1975; Lesche & Madsen, 1976), can be an enriching for both the supervisor and the supervisee. The supervisees, many of whom may be supervisors themselves, can through their participation in both roles and immersion in perspectives, deepen their understanding of both supervision and therapy/counseling.

From the supervisor's perspective, to supervise others provides an opportunity to clarify and articulate how they conceptualize client dynamics, therapeutic attitude, technique, and therapy/counseling processes. Also, supervisees may provide a "holding" and confirming environment for supervisors. Supervising others also provides an opportunity for generativity (Erikson, 1968), so that supervision can be experienced as deeply meaningful also for the supervisor.

Notes

1. This chapter is an extension of "Om terapeuters profesjonelle utvikling og psykoterapiveiledning i et utviklingsperspektiv" [Professional development and psychotherapy supervision from a developmental perspective], by M. H. Rønnestad and T. M. Skovholt (2011), in *Veiledning iv psykoterapeutisk arbeid* [The supervision of psychotherapeutic work], M. H. Rønnestad & S. Reichelt (Eds.). Oslo: Univeritetsforlaget. Permission granted by Univeritetsforlaget.

2. Goldfried (2009) suggested the following therapy change principles: (a) initial expectations that therapy can be helpful, as well as the presence of some level of motivation to work with the therapist; (b) the therapeutic alliance; (c) having clients become aware of those factors that contribute to their current life problems; (d) clients' engagement in numerous corrective experiences; (e) ongoing reality testing.

3. Stressful involvement is a dimension consisting of a combination of frequently experienced *difficult, non-constructive coping, and feelings of anxiety and/or boredom in sessions* (Orlinsky & Rønnestad, 2005).

4. Adelson is the same person as Doehrman.
5. The certainty-uncertainty principle is similar to Perry's (1981) highest stage of intellectual development, "committed relativism, where the focus is to make choices within the boundaries of a deep understanding of the multidimensionality of human reality. The principle is also similar to the "uncertainty" aspect of wisdom as conceptualized by Baltes and Smith (1990).
6. The work group was initiated after a proposal from the Council of Chairs of Training Councils (CCTC) to the APA. The CCTC consist of the "chairs of the major professional psychology education and training councils in the United States and Canada" (Fouad et al., 2009, p. 6).

Part III

EXPANDING VIEWS

12

MASTER THERAPISTS

Explorations of Expertise

Len Jennings, Thomas M. Skovholt, Michael Goh, and Fengqin Lian

Introduction

The search for the master therapist has taken many twists and turns over the past half-century. We will describe three different paths that have been taken in this search to understand mastery in therapeutic and counseling work.

The first path involves a practitioner who uses the epistemology of active practice to learn about the complexity of human nature and how specific therapy methods can help people. He or she then tells others—through publications and presentations—about these psychological insights. This work captures still others and they become followers of a leader who is considered a master. This is how the terms *Freudian, Jungian* or *Adlerian* evolved. A mental health practitioner became a Freudian, Jungian, or an Adlerian. For the follower, the hope is that by emulating the master one too becomes a master. Taking this path is still very popular as a way to achieve mastery. Often these method creators were very clear writers (e.g., *On Becoming a Person*; Rogers, 1961), very active presenters like Albert Ellis, or charismatic presenters like Michael White, a founder of narrative therapy (White & Epston, 1990). The famous Gloria tapes with Carl Rogers, Fritz Perls, and Albert Ellis communicated a similar type of expertise, although it is important to add that Rogers used empirical research of his own methods too as an epistemological source.

There are many other examples such as *Existential Therapy* by Irwin Yalom (1980) and the creation of eye movement desensitization and reprocessing (EMDR) by Francine Shapiro (1995). Many of the most revered ideas in practice have come from practice and private life. This is the history of much of psychotherapy and counseling. A more detailed view is told in *History of Psychotherapy: Continuity and Change* (Norcross, Vandenbos, & Freedheim, 2011).

There are problems with becoming a follower of a famous practitioner and his or her method. There is no systematic evidence that following a famous method developer actually produces better outcomes. Fame through publications or presentations does not mean one produces better outcomes. Second, is the issue of research on method equivalence. Two different methods most often produce equally positive results (i.e., Wampold, 2010; Wampold & Weinberger, 2010). For example, the Frank chapter in *Bringing Psychotherapy Research to Life* (Castonguay, Muran, Hayes, Ladany, & Anserson, 2010) is filled with this assertion. To devoted followers of a method, the research result of method equivalence is deeply frustrating.

The second way that the search for expertise has occurred is through empirical-based research. This is the most prestigious and widely accepted method used to certify legitimate therapist expertise. Broad names for this expertise go under the terms *empirically supported treatments* and *evidence-based practice*. The epistemology here is the research lab and legitimate knowledge comes from the person who conducts research studies and then publishes these in high status journals and books. Having extensive experience as a practitioner is not considered necessary to arrive at this knowledge. Two highly valued books are *The Handbook of Psychotherapy and Behavior Change*, now in its latest edition titled *Bergin and Garfield's Handbook of Psychotherapy and Behavior Change* (Lambert, 2004) and *Bringing Psychotherapy Research to Life: Understanding Change Through the Work of Leading Clinical Researchers* (Castonguay, Muran et al., 2010). The editors and authors of this last book have sought to bridge the research–practice gap because of the realization that the practice suggestions coming from the gold standard research methods of empirical research are often rejected by practitioners as not usable in everyday practice with real clients. Angus et al. (2010) noted that "critics have questioned the utility, generalizability, and validity of randomized controlled trials (RCT)-based research findings for clinicians who practice in real world settings" (p. 355). An analogy is that research professors seldom turn to the empirical research on college teaching to guide their own teaching. They more often trust their own teaching experience and their own practice-based evidence. This route of using research to get to mastery has been handicapped by the limitations, as we have said here, of the controlled scientific lab as a breeding ground for the swamp of ambiguity that is the reality of day-to-day clinical practice where the full range of human variability is evident.

A third way to search for expertise is to find individuals who excel at the skill being researched. The epistemology here is very different from the other two. It is like the way individuals in general search for a physician, car mechanic, or attorney. We often ask others if they know of an expert. The criterion for expertise is mastery in the domain. However, the expert may not be well known to others, he or she may toil relatively unknown to the broad community. Here is an example of this method of finding experts: In an attempt to find excellent conflict resolution methods for inner city school children, Skovholt, Cognett et al. (1997) turned, not to academic experts, but to children who then nominated peers who were talented at resolving conflicts. The methods of these inner-city experts were then studied. This same approach has been used with this third method of finding therapy expertise and has been shown to be an effective sampling strategy.

Studying Master Therapists

A group of researchers in Minnesota conducted six studies on master therapists, including four dissertation studies conducted by Thomas Skovholt's doctoral advisees (Harrington, 1988; Jennings, 1996; Mullenbach, 2000; Sullivan, 2001). In the fifth study Jennings, Sovereign Bottorff, Mussell, and Vye (2005) reanalyzed the transcripts from the Jennings (1996) study to examine the ethical values of master therapists. In the sixth study, Skovholt, Jennings, and Mullenbach (2004) conducted a qualitative meta-analysis of four of the five studies just mentioned. The Harrington study was not included in the qualitative meta-analysis because it was a quantitative study. In addition, Goh, Starkey, Skovholt, and Jennings (2007) studied culturally competent master therapists. Finally, five international master therapist studies were conducted with two studies (Hirai, 2010; Jennings, D'Rozario et al., 2008) making comparisons to the original Minnesota master therapist studies. In the remainder of the chapter we will: (a) describe the methodology used to identify these master therapists; (b) provide an overview of the characteristics of master therapists based on studies conducted in the United States; (c) summarize and compare U.S. and non-U.S. studies for universal and culture/country specific themes; (d) address the juxtaposition of cultural competence and master therapist studies; (e) provide an update of the current master therapist cognitive, emotional, and relational (CER) model; (f) describe a prototypical developmental pathway of the master therapist; and (g) conclude the chapter with a discussion of possible future research directions.

The Validity of the Peer Nomination Sampling Method: Identifying Master Therapists

A key element in studying master therapists is how to identify them. We, therefore, felt that it was important to explain to readers the rationale and justification for the peer nomination method employed in most of the studies mentioned in this chapter.

Chi (2006) suggested three ways of identifying someone who is truly an expert. One method is to look at the outcome retrospectively. Another method is to use a kind of concurrent measure, such as a rating system or exam. The third method is to use an independent index, such as the Knight's Tour in chess. Chi, Glaser, and Farr (1988) illustrate how the Knight's Tour can be used to assess a person's chess skill level:

In chess, for example, there exists a task called the Knight's Tour that requires a player to move a Knight Piece across the rows of a chessboard, using legal Knight Moves. The time it takes to complete the moves is an indication of one's chess skill. Although this task is probably not sensitive enough to discriminate among the exceptional experts, a task such as this can be adapted as an index of expertise. In short, to identify a truly exceptional expert, one often resorts to some kind of measure of performance. The assessment of exceptional experts needs to be accurate since the goal is to understand their superior performance. Thus, this approach studies the remarkable few to understand how they are distinguished from the masses. (p. 21)

The first two methods are not very feasible when it comes to identifying master therapists. First, there is no clear agreement in the counseling psychotherapy and counseling field about treatment outcome. In addition, due to client confidentiality, psychotherapists usually do not collect outcome data systematically. It is more common that therapists observe the outcome through sessions. The third method, an independent index to test a therapist's competency level, does exist through the 13 different boards of the American Board of Professional Psychology (ABPP). The ABPP exam requires work samples (e.g., session videotape, oral exams, etc.) and therefore ABPP psychologists are certified to have advanced competencies in their specialty areas. The second author has been an examiner for 50 oral exams for ABPP and is therefore familiar with this method of assessing advanced competence. Although the initial master therapist study (Harrington, 1988) used the ABPP as its sampling criterion, we found that the use of ABPPs was limited because we wanted to reach a broader, local sample that included other professionals in addition to psychologists. We believed that the use of peer nomination had the potential to identify relatively "unknown gems" or expert practitioners in the mental health field and expert psychologists who did not necessarily seek ABPP status.

This section will discuss the use of peer nominations methods for selecting master therapists. For example, one strategy for identifying master therapists is to use the combination of peer nomination, snowball sampling, and extreme case sampling. In this method, local, well-situated, information-rich key informants (e.g., training directors, well-regarded senior therapists, etc.) are asked to nominate master therapists. Nomination criteria of master therapists are given to nominators. Individuals who are repeatedly named by a variety of informants constitute the core participant pool. The nomination process concludes when certain individuals are repeatedly nominated and few new names emerge (Patton, 2002). Those nominees who have received more than a certain number or the highest percentage of nominations are considered "master therapists." Most of the existing master therapist studies used this sampling method (Goh et al., 2007; Hirai, 2010; Jennings, D'Rozario et al., 2008; Jennings, Gulden et al. 2012; Jennings & Skovholt, 1999; Jennings, Sovereign, Bottorff, Mussell, & Vye,, 2005; Kwon & Kim, 2007; Mullenbach, 2000; A. G. Smith, 2008; Skovholt, Jennings, & Mullenbach, 2004; Sullivan, 2001).

Peer nomination has been widely used, and has been demonstrated to be an effective way to identify excellence and competency in different professional areas. In a meta-analysis, Norton (1992) analyzed 32 studies on the correlations between peer assessments and criterion measures and reported a mean correlation of .69. In the 32 studies, there were a wide range of ability/performance dimensions (e.g., performance test, promotion, supervisor ratings) and professionals (e.g., military services, insurance, medical students, management, secretary, factory workers). In the medical field, student peer evaluation has long been suggested as a better predictor of performance during residency training than medical school grades or faculty evaluations (Korman & Stubblefield, 1971; Kubany, 1957; Lurie, Nofziger, Meldrum, Mooney, & Epstein, 2006). Cole and White (1993) asked 1,249 elementary school students to assess their peers' competencies in five areas (scholastic competence, social acceptance, athletic competence, physical attractiveness, and behavioral conduct). The results revealed that students' ratings were significantly correlated with teachers' ratings and their peers' self-reports. Research also has shown that peer nomination outcomes may not be reduced to likeability and that peer nominations can be regarded as one suitable method for identifying high performers within expertise research (Sonnentag, 1998). Sonnentag analyzed performance and likeability ratings provided by 123 software professionals for high and average performing coworkers. Differences in performance ratings remained stable when taking likeability into account as a covariate.

Psychotherapy researcher Lester Luborsky and colleagues (Luborsky, McLellan, Woody, O'Brien, & Auerbach, 1985) found peer nomination of value in selecting expert therapists when they wrote: "therapists are able to identify other potential effective therapists and to discriminate them from those who were less effective" (p. 609). In addition, former APA President and measurement expert Anne Anastasi endorsed peer nomination: "when checked against a variety of practical criteria dependent on interpersonal relations, such ratings usually have been found to have good concurrent and predictive validity" (Anastasi & Urbina, 1997, p. 468). In addition, research has shown that snowball sampling does not necessarily lead to unrepresentative samples. Welch (1975) compared snowball sampling and screening to select samples. The two groups obtained through snowball sampling and screening showed no differences in sex, age, occupation, citizenship, number in household, religion, per capita income, and political opinion.

In most of the existing master therapist studies, only nominees receiving a certain number of nominations based on a few criteria were selected to be participants and considered as master therapists. This means that the participant's competency is agreed upon among other therapists. This selection is consistent with Chi's (2006) definition of masters which states that "a master can be that expert who is regarded by the other experts as being 'the' expert, or the 'real' expert, especially with regard to sub-domain knowledge" (p. 22). One example of using the above method (i.e., combination of peer nomination, snowball sampling, and extreme case sampling) to identify excellence is the classic Peters and Waterman (1982) study, in which the authors used this method to identify the most innovative and excellent companies.

Master Therapist Studies in the United States

Although not a peer nomination study, Harrington (1988) was the first to directly examine characteristics of master therapists. In his study, American Board of Professional Psychology (ABPP) Diplomates, psychologists rigorously assessed by ABPP to have expert competency, were selected as master therapists. (Note: At that time the ABPP exam was set at the expert stage, now it is set at the competent stage.) Harrington surveyed 507 ABPP Diplomates out of the 2,000 Diplomates in counseling and clinical psychology in the United States. Participants completed the Adjective Check List (ACL; Gough & Heilbrun, 1983) and a personal qualities inventory developed by Harrington. The results of ACL scores indicated that the respondents consistently scored high on "ideal self" (having a strong sense of personal worth), "achievement" (to strive to be outstanding), "endurance" (to persist in any task undertaken), and "mature adult" (attitudes of independence, objectivity, and industriousness). Respondents consistently scored low on "unfavorable" (socially undesirable), "succorance" (to solicit sympathy, affection, or emotional support from others), and "adaptive child" (deference, conformity, and self-discipline associated with the concept of a very dutiful child). Results of the personality qualities questionnaire revealed master therapists' central personality characteristics as: (a) sensitive, empathic, kind; (b) intelligent and competent; (c) consistent, reliable, and loyal; (d) honest; (e) driven to grow and succeed; and (f) emotionally stable. Concerning the master therapists' personality characteristics that contributed to making their psychotherapy effective, a few themes also emerged: (a) relationship skills (warm, empathy, kind, caring, and compassionate); (b) therapy skills (competent, theoretical knowledge, technical skills, and intelligence); (c) a strong sense of self (being able to tolerate strong emotions, being able to maintain ego boundaries and personal stability).

Although Harrington's study began the exploration of master therapists, it was apparent that quantitative methods alone were not able to capture the complexity of the phenomena of master therapists. Therefore, qualitative methods became the method of choice for the master therapist studies that followed.

In the first qualitative study on master therapists, Jennings and Skovholt (1999) interviewed 10 master therapists to identify their personal characteristics. Master therapists were identified using peer nomination and a snowball sampling method. Three well-regarded practicing psychologists were chosen as key informants. Each key informant was asked to nominate three master therapists. The following criteria for nomination of master therapists were given to key informants: "(a) this person is considered to be a master therapist; (b) this person is most frequently thought of when referring a close family member or a dear friend to a therapist because the person is considered to be the 'best of the best'; and (c) one would have full confidence in seeing this therapist for one's own personal therapy, as this therapist is considered a 'therapist's therapist'" (p. 4). The nominated person was then contacted and asked to nominate others who might fit the three-part selection criteria.

A total of 213 peer nominations, of 103 different practitioners, were obtained from 65 practitioners who were themselves considered, by at least one person, to be master therapists. This sample group was chosen through the combination of peer nomination, snowball sampling, and extreme case sampling. Of the 103 nominated, those with at least four nominations were chosen for the final sample. This resulted in a sample of 10 therapists. It is important to note here that this qualitative study was not a study of one person—it is a composite portrait of 10, thereby increasing both dependability and trustworthiness of the results. Two in-depth interviews were conducted with each research participant and a total of 1,043 concepts were used as part of the inductive analysis which is described in more detail in Jennings and Skovholt (1999).

Inductive analysis was used to examine the interview transcripts. Based on the results, Jennings constructed a cognitive, emotional, and relational (CER) model, published in Jennings and Skovholt (1999), to describe master therapists' personal characteristics. For the cognitive domain, master therapists are voracious learners; they draw upon accumulated experiences; they value cognitive complexity; and they embrace the ambiguity of the human condition. For the emotional domain, master therapists appear to have emotional receptivity defined as being self-aware, reflective, nondefensive, and open to feedback; they also seem to be mentally healthy and mature individuals who attend to their own emotional well-being; and they are keenly aware of how their emotional health affects the quality of their work. For the relational domain, master therapists possess strong relationship skills; they believe that the foundation for therapeutic change is a strong working alliance; and they appear to be experts at using their exceptional relationship skills in therapy.

A series of four qualitative research studies followed utilizing the same 10 master therapists from the Jennings and Skovholt (1999) study. In the first study of this series, Mullenbach (2000) explored master therapists' professional resiliency and emotional wellness. Ten master therapists were invited, and nine consented to be interviewed again. Using qualitative analysis methods similar to the Jennings and Skovholt (1999) study, Mullenbach identified 23 themes within 5 categories as being integral to the emotional functioning of these master therapists. She concluded that (a) master therapists have sought out supportive experiences throughout training and their professional careers; (b) master therapists have developed effective coping skills and are experts in their ability to create a positive work environment, manage professional stressors, and nurture the self through a balance of solitude and relationships; and (c) protective factors for these master therapists included proactive problem solving, ongoing learning, and maintenance of a diversified practice.

In the next study of this series, Sullivan (2001), using the same participant sample from the Jennings and Skovholt (1999) study, examined master therapists' construction of the therapy relationship. All 10 master therapists were invited and all agreed to participate. Sullivan (2001) found that master therapists' construction of therapy relationships could be summarized in two domains: safe relationship domain and challenging relationship domain. For the safe relationship domain, master therapists have a heightened responsiveness to clients. They actively collaborate with clients, and they seek a strong and deep therapy relationship with clients. For the challenging relationship domain, master therapists use "self" well in the therapy relationship; they intensely engage the clients, and they maintain an objective stance in the therapy relationship. The composite description of these master therapists was of functioning at a very high level in these two domains—the two classic domains of being and doing.

Jennings, Sovereign and associates (2005) conducted the next study in this series by exploring the ethical values inherent in the practice of master therapists. They qualitatively reanalyzed the transcripts from the Jennings (1996) study. They grouped the nine most salient ethical values of master therapists into two categories. The first category was building and maintaining personal attachments. Master therapists' strive to build and maintain personal attachments and held the ethical values of promoting beneficence, honoring clients' autonomy, maintaining nonmaleficence, and building and maintaining positive relationships with clients. The second category was building and maintaining expertise. Specifically, these master therapists' displayed the ethical values of competency, professional growth, knowing limitations, being open to complexity and ambiguity, and self-awareness.

Table 12.1   Portrait of Master Therapist Paradox Characteristics

Drive to mastery	**AND**	Never a sense of having fully arrived
Able to deeply enter another's world	**AND**	Often prefers solitude
Can create a very safe client environment	**AND**	Can create a very challenging client environment
Highly skilled at harnessing the power of therapy	**AND**	Quite humble about self
Integration of the professional/ personal self	**AND**	Clear boundaries between the professional/personal self
Voracious broad learner	**AND**	Focused, narrow student
Excellent at giving of self	**AND**	Great at nurturing self
Very open to feedback about self	**AND**	Not destabilized by feedback about self

In the next study of the series, Skovholt, Jennings, and Mullenbach (2004) combined the results of studies by Jennings and Skovholt (1999), Jennings, Sovereign et al. (2005), Mullenbach (2000), and Sullivan (2001) to develop a portrait of master therapists. The portrait that evolved from these studies included paradox characteristics, identifying characteristics, word characteristics, and central cognitive, emotional, and relational (CER) characteristics. The paradoxical characteristics (see Table 12.1) in particular illustrate the complex, highly sophisticated ways that these master therapists perform their craft as well as live their lives.

Master Therapist Studies Outside the United States

Five master therapist studies have been conducted outside the United States. Four of those studies will be discussed in this section. The fifth will be discussed later in the section on cultural competence. In 2007, Kwon and Kim used peer nomination and snowball sampling to select five expert or "master group therapists" in South Korea. The researchers used grounded theory methodology to analyze the interview transcripts. Based on the results, the researchers suggested a paradigm model of master group therapists' characteristics. This paradigm described causal conditions, textual factors, and moderating conditions that led to the phenomenology of master group therapists' involvement in group therapy. This involvement then led to function/interaction strategies that master group therapists used, illustrating their expertise in group counseling. The authors also summarized master group therapists' development: reasons to choose group therapy, being absorbed in group therapy, having a mentor, dealing with challenges in group therapy, impact of early life pain, contextual factors to achievement in group therapy, strategies used for growth, personality characteristics, and expert characteristics (see Table 12.2).

Table 12.2   Themes from Kwon and Kim (2007) South Korean Master Group Therapists

Personality Characteristics	*Expert Characteristics*
-not afraid of self-disclosure	- sensitive to group dynamics
- favors and seeks diversity	- able to create the desired group dynamic
- takes high risks	- able to handle difficult group dynamics
- patient	- leadership that emphasizes a relationship with
- has deep trust in people	whole group
- accepting of others	- comfortable facilitating a group, has realistic
- high level of empathy	expectations about group members
- authenticity	- flexibly manages group goals and individual goals
- flexibility	- extends group counseling to issues of
- has sense of humor that helps	organizational, social, and racial issues
counteract heaviness and	- respects resistance
pain	- understands each member quickly and accurately
- less fearful of experiencing	- cognitive competency/effectiveness: a lot of
strong diverse emotions	information, integration of information, distinctive
	application, excellent memory
	- has realistic expectation of one's own capability
	- has individualized and specialized skills
	- creates one's own theory

Jennings, D'Rozario et al. (2008) explored the characteristics of master therapists in Singapore and compared the results with the original peer nomination Minnesota study (Jennings & Skovholt, 1999). In Singapore, peer nomination and snowball sampling yielded a total of 47 nominated master therapists. The top nine nominees were interviewed with the same questions used in the Jennings and Skovholt (1999) study. The authors used grounded theory as the overall framework and consensual qualitative research (CQR) methodology (Hill, Thompson, & Williams, 1997) to code each transcript, achieve consensus on coding, and organize codes into themes. The authors then conducted a cross-case analysis to identify the themes that were broadly represented among the participants, and finally arranged the themes into categories. The authors identified 16 themes in 4 categories: personal characteristics, developmental influences, approach to practice, and ongoing professional growth. Personal characteristics of the Singapore master therapists were: empathic, nonjudgmental, and respectful. Developmental influences for Singapore master therapists included a view of experience as an important factor that leads to expertise, a high self-awareness, humility, and self-doubt. In the approach to practice theme, Singapore master therapists maintained a balance between support and challenge, had a flexible therapeutic stance, used an empowerment/strength-based approach, valued the primacy of therapeutic alliance, were comfortable addressing spirituality, and embraced working within a multicultural context. In the theme of ongoing professional growth, Singapore master therapists valued professional development practices, viewed teaching/training as an opportunity to hone their own skills, and acknowledged challenges to professional development in Singapore.

As part of this same study, Jennings, D'Rozario et al. (2008) conducted a qualitative meta-analysis (Timulak, 2007) to compare the Singapore data with the Minnesota data from the Jennings and Skovholt (1999) study. Briefly, a qualitative meta-analysis involves in-depth comparisons of categories and themes of conceptually related studies in an effort to identify similarities and differences of findings across studies. Comparing the Singapore and Minnesota studies, Jennings and his colleagues found several commonalities regarding the personal characteristics, developmental influences, and therapy practices of psychotherapy experts. For example:

1. Therapists in both the Singapore and Minnesota master therapists' groups engage with their clients in an empathic and nonjudgmental way. They also use relational skills to guide their sense of timing, pacing, and dosage of interventions. This ultimately serves to create a safe and secure therapeutic atmosphere.
2. Singapore and Minnesota master therapists support their client's growth through the use of the therapeutic alliance.
3. Singapore and Minnesota master therapists draw on life and work experience to inform and advance their skills.
4. Singapore and Minnesota master therapists value ongoing learning within and outside their area of practice, and they benefit from articulating their work when teaching students.
5. Singapore and Minnesota master therapists have a healthy perspective on their own sense of importance and recognize their limits of competence.
6. Singapore and Minnesota master therapists are open to reflection and feedback from many sources to help them recognize their limitations and areas of growth.

Jennings and his colleagues (Jennings, Rozario et al., 2008) also found themes that are different between Singapore and Minnesota master therapists. For instance:

1. Most Singapore master therapists reported challenges to professional development in Singapore, although not necessarily for their own development since most of them received training abroad.
2. Most Singapore master therapists also expressed that they embraced working within a multicultural context, they were comfortable addressing spirituality, and they still experienced self-doubt in their work.
3. One unique theme of Minnesota master therapists was that they value cognitive complexity and the ambiguity of the human condition.

A third international study investigated therapists in Canada (Smith, 2008) using peer nomination and snowball sampling procedure to select master couples therapists. One criterion in the peer nomination process for this master couples therapist study was different from previous studies: "the nominating therapist has made a referral and heard positive feedback about the work of this therapist or has consulted with this person on a case and is, therefore, familiar with this therapist's work" (p. 55). Therapists who were nominated a minimum of five times by colleagues were invited to participate in the study. Following the process, nine therapists participated in the study. Prior to the interview, the nine master therapists were asked to write a narrative about their experience of becoming a master couples' therapist and what it means to them to be in that role. Later, the nine master therapists were interviewed about their master therapist characteristics. Following the interviews of the nine primary participants, therapists who nominated them were randomly chosen and contacted by phone for a brief 15-minute interview to expand on their decision to nominate these particular practitioners. The findings gleaned from these brief interviews were included when the authors acknowledged unique information not identified by the primary participants. Therefore, the data in Smith's study include the nine master therapists' written narratives, as well as the transcript of the interview with master therapists and the nominators. Smith (2008) used a basic interpretive and descriptive analysis to analyze the data. A thematic analysis and category construction of the data was performed. The themes and categories were constructed using the constant comparison method as described by Merriam (2002) and originally developed in grounded theory research by Glaser and Strauss (1967).

Smith found that the participants described a remarkable level of commitment in three main areas: personal development and self, professional development, and relationships. In terms of the master therapists' commitment to personal development and self, they were committed to maintaining their emotional health (e.g., being emotionally grounded) and took active steps to pursue this goal (e.g., personal therapy, doing other productive activities, monitoring self when doing therapy). Therapists were also dedicated to developing their own personal self-awareness and growth as a therapist (e.g., including a wide range of knowledge and experience, being aware of one's own professional limitations, and obtaining consultation/help). Participants described the role of a couples' therapist as a natural one for them to adopt (e.g., being naturally inquisitive, intuitive, and interested in relationships; being drawn back to therapy after trying other professions) and described themselves as passionate about the profession. Participants also displayed a combination of confidence in their abilities and modesty. In terms of commitment to professional development, many participants enhanced learning by teaching. They appeared to display a curiosity for the human condition and a commitment to ongoing learning in the field of psychotherapy. Participants had developed a remarkable ability to conceptualize client issues, and each participant showed commitment to their own style of developing a model of therapy (e.g., fits the couple they are working with, fits the therapist's personality, validated by empirical research, etc.). In terms of commitment to relationships, each participant endorsed a belief in the importance of a strong therapeutic relationship (e.g., consider both clients' positions and have a balanced relationship with both). Each participant also appeared to have personal qualities that would facilitate the development of strong relationships (e.g., authenticity, genuineness, empathy, warmth, unconditional positive regard, trustworthiness, honesty, a good sense of humor, willingness to join the client, and conveying honor and respect) evidenced in therapy and in their lives in general. Participants generally placed importance on their personal peer relationships. Participants adhered to the approach of trusting clients to lead in therapy, and the participants effectively managed conflict in couples therapy (e.g., stop the conflict before it becomes abusive).

The fourth international study of master therapists was conducted in Japan (Hirai, 2010). Peer nomination was used to identify master therapists. Eleven Japanese therapists were chosen to be the participants in the study and 10 agreed to participate. The master therapists were interviewed in Japanese. Similar to Jennings, Rozario et al.'s (2008) study in Singapore, Hirai used grounded theory and CQR (Hill et al. 1997) to analyze the data. As Table 12.3 illustrates, Hirai (2010) identified 18 themes within 5 categories.

Hirai (2010) also compared results from the Japan study with the Jennings and Skovholt (1999) original study. Overall, the characteristics of Japanese master therapists appear to have several commonalities with the master therapists in Minnesota (Skovholt & Jennings, 2004). Examples of similar themes are: (a) strong interests in new learning, (b) importance of self-awareness and reflection, (c) acceptance of ambiguity, and (d) exceptional ability to form trustful relationships.

Additionally, mentor's guidance and therapist humility were emphasized. Differences in Japan-U.S. characteristics were:

1. Japanese master therapists placed more value on understanding the client without depending on the verbal interaction between the client and the therapist.
2. Boundaries between the Japanese therapists and the Japanese clients are more ambiguous.
3. The Japanese therapeutic relationship is described as a shared psychological space where all persons in the therapeutic process (i.e.,

Table 12.3 Themes from Hirai (2010) Japanese Master Therapists

Category A: Cultivates Abundant Learning	1. Proactive learning style
	2. Abounds in ingenuity
	3. Diligently manage massive learning
	4. Learned from great mentors
	5. Existence of supportive environment
Category B: Perceptive Understanding of Self and Others	6. In-depth self-reflection
	7. Finely tuned understanding of the client
	8. Able to take a comprehensive view of the client
	9. Capacity to embrace different aspects that seem contradictory to each other, and find a balance between them
Category C: Effective Intervention	10. Performs at a high level of therapeutic effectiveness (interest in pursuing effective and efficient treatment)
	11. Multidimensional therapeutic approach (mind–body holistic approach)
	12. Precise yet flexible intervention
Category D: Relationship Building with the Client	13. Deep respect for the client
	14. Openness toward the client
	15. Active engagement in the mutually therapeutic relationship
Category E: Therapist's Humanity	16. Therapist's personality (modesty, absence of self-centeredness and dominance, sincerity, and stability)
	17. High level of resilience
	18. Respect for the profundity of human beings

clinician and client) journey together in reflection and action often without explicit goals or stated outcomes.

Exploring Universal and Culturally Specific Themes across Studies

The above studies suggest a number of master therapist characteristics that appear to be shared across the countries involved in the studies thus far. Table 12.4 compares themes from each study. The Skovholt and Jennings (2004) book, *Master Therapists: Exploring Expertise in Therapy and Counseling*, described and summarized five studies with the same master therapist participants, including Jennings and Skovholt (1999), Mullenbach (2000), Sullivan (2001), Skovholt, Jennings, and Mullenbach (2004), and Jennings, Sovereign et al. (2005). For the sake of simplicity, Skovholt and

Table 12.4 Comparison of Master Therapist Characteristics from Studies around the World

		Themes				Potential new domains
Minnesota studies (5) (Skovholt, & Jennings, 2004)	Korean Study (Kuon & Kim, 2007)	Singapore study (Jennings et al., 2008)	Canada study (Smith, 2008)	Japan study (Hirai, 2010)		
• High self-awareness,	• Not afraid of self-disclosure • Knowing one's limitations	• Self-awareness • Self-doubt	• Dedicated to developing self-awareness and growth	• In-depth self-reflection		• High self-awareness
• Able to intensively engage others • Have acute interpersonal perception • Relational acumen	• Patient • Acceptability • Empathic • Authentic • Fearless of strong emotions	• Empathic • Nonjudgmental • Respectful • Primacy of the therapeutic alliance	• Relationship qualities(e.g., authenticity, genuineness, empathy, warmth, unconditional positive regard, trustworthiness, honesty, a good sense of humor, willingness to join the client, conveying honor and respect) • Belief in the importance of a strong therapeutic relationship	• Therapist personality (sincerity) • Deep respect for the client • Being open toward the client • Active engagement in the mutually therapeutic relationship		• Therapeutic alliance and the required relational qualities/ abilities

Similarity

(continued)

Table 12.4 Continued

	Themes					Potential new domains
	Minnesota studies (5) (Skovholt, & Jennings, 2004)	Korean Study (Kwon & Kim, 2007)	Singapore study (Jennings et al., 2008)	Canada study (Smith, 2008)	Japan study (Hirai, 2010)	
	• Profound understanding of the human condition • Embrace complex ambiguity	• Cognitive competency and effectiveness	• Embracing working within a multicultural context	• Remarkable ability to conceptualize client issues	• Finely tuned understanding of the client • Comprehensive view of the client • Embrace antinomy • Respect for the profundity of human being	• Conceptualization/ understanding of the client and complex human condition
	• Guided by accumulated wisdom (reflected data, book learning, synthesized life experience) • Voracious learners		• Learning by teaching/training others • Professional development practices • Learn from experiences	• Enhance learning by teaching • Deep commitment to ongoing learning in the field of psychotherapy	• Proactive learning style • Diligently manage massive learning • Learning from great mentors	• Voracious Learning
Similarity	• Genuinely humble		• Humility	• A lovely combination of confidence in their abilities and modesty	• Therapist Personality (modesty, absence of self-centeredness and dominance)	• Humility and confidence

• Intense will and behaviors to grow • Deep acceptance of self • Quietly strong Vibrantly alive	• Use humor to handle heaviness and pain		• Maintain emotional health and take active steps to pursue this goal • Place importance on their personal peer relationships	• Existence of supportive environment • Therapist personality (Stability) • High level of resilience	• Emotional health
	• Flexible • Creating one's own theory • Taking risks	• Flexible therapeutic stance	• Commitment to one's own style of therapy that fits for them and their clients	• Precise yet flexible intervention • Abound in ingenuity	• Flexible intervention
	• Trust in people	• Empowerment/strength-based approach	• Trust their clients to lead in therapy		• Trust in clients
• Insatiably curious			• Curiosity for the human condition		• Curiosity
• Passionately enjoy life			• Passionate about the profession		• Passion
• Welcomed openness to life feedback • Have nuanced ethical compass	• Unique skill sets of group counseling (e.g., seeking diverse clients in the group, recognizing and handling group dynamics)	• Comfortable addressing spirituality • Challenges to professional development in Singapore (for trainees)	• The role of a couple therapist as a natural one for them to adopt • Effectively managed conflict in couple therapy	• High level of effectiveness (interest in pursuing effective and efficient treatment) • Multi-dimensional therapeutic approach (mind-body holistic approach)	

Differences

Jennings (2004) is used to refer to all five Minnesota studies in the comparison. As the comparisons in Table 12.3 indicate, the category arrangement between Skovholt and Jennings (2004) and A. G. Smith (2008) has the highest correspondence. Although the category arrangement of Hirai (2010) seems different from the other three, based on the detailed description of each theme, several of the themes from Hirai correspond to the themes from the other studies. Our comparisons of the above studies show that three domains were shared by master therapists from all five countries (Minnesota (USA), Korea, Canada, Singapore, and Japan):

1. High self-awareness.
2. Remarkable ability to conceptualize the client and complex human condition.
3. Ability to build a strong therapeutic relationship with clients, and possession of the required relational qualities.

Four domains of characteristics were shared by four out of the five countries:

1. Voracious learning using all kinds of resources (by Minnesota (USA), Singapore, Canada, and Japan).
2. A combination of humility and confidence (by Minnesota (USA), Singapore, Canada, and Japan).
3. Being emotional healthy and working hard to maintain emotional health (by Minnesota (USA), Korea, Canada, and Japan).
4. Being flexible and inventive with clinical intervention (by Korea, Singapore, Canada, and Japan).

The characteristic of *trusting and being optimistic about human nature* was shared by three countries (Korea, Singapore, and Canada). The characteristics of *curious about human conditions* and *passionate about life and profession* were shared by two countries (Minnesota (USA) and Canada).

Each of the studies showed culturally specific themes as well. In the Korean study, Kwon and Kim (2007) reported several characteristics specific to group therapy (e.g., seeking diverse clients in group, recognizing and handling group dynamics, etc.). A. G. Smith (2008) showed that Canadian master couples therapists adapt the role of couples therapist naturally and manage the conflict in couples therapy effectively. The unique characteristics from the above two studies seem intuitive and reasonable given that the participants were group therapists or couples therapists.

On the other hand, the unique characteristics from the other three studies might be just unique to the group of therapists or the culture in which they are embedded. Skovholt and Jennings (2004) revealed that Minnesota master therapists have welcomed-openness to life feedback, and have a nuanced ethical compass (meaning that the moral compass is internal and deeply embedded in higher moral principles or virtue ethics). Jennings, D'Rozario et al. (2008) showed that Singapore master therapists are comfortable addressing spirituality, and concerned with the challenges to the practitioner's professional development in Singapore. Hirai (2010) showed that Japanese master therapists emphasize the efficiency of treatment effectiveness and value the multidimensional or holistic mind–body approach.

In Search of Cultural Competence in Master Therapist Research

Research has shown that a positive relationship exists between therapists' multicultural competence and therapy outcomes (Kim & Lyons, 2003). Further, multicultural competence has been shown to play a significant role in effective mental health treatment for all populations (Sue & Sue, 2008).

The saliency of culture competence is further illustrated by two significant milestones of the American Psychological Association. The first involves the introduction of the set of guidelines for working with multicultural populations in clinical, education, and research situations (American Psychological Association, 2003). Second, in 2006, the American Psychological Association Task Force on Evidence-Based Practice (EBP) redefined EBP to include an understanding of the influence of individual and cultural differences on treatment. The following excerpt from the report emphasized the increasing role that culture plays in therapeutic effectiveness:

> Clinical expertise requires an awareness of the individual, social, and cultural context of the patient, including but not limited to age and development, ethnicity, culture, race, gender, sexual orientation, religious commitments, and socioeconomic status. Clinical expertise allows psychologists to adapt interventions and construct a therapeutic milieu that respects the patient's worldview, values, preferences, capacities, and other characteristics. APA has adopted practice guidelines on multicultural practice, sexual orientation, and older adults to assist psychologists in tailoring their practices to patient differences. (p. 277)

Norcross and Wampold (2011) cite culture as an important patient characteristic through which adaptations are made to make therapy effective. Similarly, T. B. Smith, Rodríguez, and Bernal (2011) illustrated in their meta-analyses of 65 experimental and quasi-experimental studies with over 8,000 subjects that treatments were most effective when cultural adaptations were generously applied.

Therefore, it has intrigued the authors of this chapter how studies of cultural competence and studies of master therapists to date have had parallel but separate agendas and yet achieve findings that echo each other. This interesting element led us to ask three questions:

1. Should cultural competence and master therapist research programs be linked?
2. If so, why was cultural competence not more evident in earlier master therapist studies?
3. Do we know anything more now than we did before about the link between cultural competence and master therapists?

To answer the first question, Goh (2005) argued that cultural competence and mastery are inextricably linked. Goh reasoned that if mastery in therapy now occurs within increasingly diverse communities in the United States, then mastery cannot be studied apart from cultural competence.

Goh (2005) presented ways in which cultural competence and expertise research share common characteristics:

1. Capturing the essence of cultural competence and expertise is elusive.
2. Cultural competence and mastery in therapy are complex and multifaceted.
3. Both concepts are described as developmental processes.
4. Both concepts are portrayed as developmental characteristics, and these characteristics can be taught or trained.
5. There is a positive goal orientation for both concepts in the sense that developing each set of characteristics is highly desirable.
6. Multiple diagrams of all shapes, forms, and dimensions—such as cubes, circles, layers, and radial diagrams—have been attempted to portray each concept.
7. Both concepts represent ideal or exemplary role models for maximizing effectiveness in mental health counseling.
8. Both concepts are difficult to operationalize and translate into training goals. (p. 74)

Goh further outlined ways to enhance cooperation in the two areas of research on the grounds of their conceptual relatedness, the mental health needs of diverse individuals and their communities, the interrelatedness of the two research agendas, the ethical requirements of our field, and, in order to reduce bias, how research is conducted.

Which leads us to the second question: so why was cultural competence not more present in the earlier master therapists studies? The best response is likely zeitgeist. Consequently, the master therapist researchers were not necessarily seeking answers about the role of cultural competence and neither were the researchers intentionally ignoring cultural factors. When one reviews the chronology of master therapist research, studies prior to the APA Multicultural Guideline publication (APA, 2003) did not focus much on the concept of cultural competence. Even though a qualitative approach encourages any given phenomenon to evolve without being limited by any preconceived boundaries, it was not necessary for the zeitgeist at the time to be in search of cultural variables in expertise research. Interview questions that framed the qualitative investigation may also limit the type of narrative data that emerged. So, what does it mean about the approach of master therapists nominated in earlier studies (e.g., Harrington, 1988; Jennings & Skovholt, 1999)? Although these therapists may be highly skilled at the individual and cultural differences of multicultural counseling, the role of culture and clinical work with culturally diverse clientele was simply not a focus of the phenomenon being explored. Hence, the interview questions did not probe for answers to the role of culture. Furthermore, can we ever find out if cultural competence and master therapists have any relationship? Yes, the easiest way to find out obviously is to reinterview the nominated master therapists from the Jennings and Skovholt (1999) study or to conduct further studies. Absent the reinterviews, do we have any new knowledge about the link between cultural competence and master therapists?

To answer this question, Goh and Starkey joined Jennings and Skovholt to replicate the 1999 study but with criteria that were adapted to include multicultural competence. In this study by Goh et al. (2007) the peer nomination criteria to nominate expert multicultural therapists was modified as such: (a) considered to be a "master multicultural counselor/therapist"; (b) most frequently thought of when referring a close family member or a dear friend to a counselor/therapist because the person is considered to be the "best of the best" when it comes to working with culturally diverse clients; and (c) one would have full confidence in seeing this counselor for one's own personal counseling. Seven therapists who received three or more nominations were invited to participate in the study and six agreed. The six therapists were interviewed. Modified CQR and inductive analysis were used to analyze data. The results indicated that nominated multicultural master therapists:

- Possess a strong sense of cultural identity
- Are avid cultural learners
- Possess specific attributes that contribute to cultural competence
- Possess a finely tuned self-awareness
- Are relational experts
- Evidence cross-cultural strategizing
- Believe training in culturally specific knowledge is important

In another study, Jennings, Gulden et al. (2012) builds on two previous qualitative studies, which examined characteristics of those considered to be master therapists and aimed to explicate the cultural competence of master therapists. As described earlier, Jennings and Skovholt (1999) examined cognitive, emotional, and relational characteristics in master therapists in the United States. In the other study, Jennings et al. (2008) examined personal characteristics, developmental influences, therapy practices, and ongoing professional growth experiences in Singaporean master therapists. Also noted earlier, there were many similarities found between the two groups of master therapists.

In the Jennings, Gulden et al. (2012) study, six of the nine Singaporean master therapists, already identified by earlier research (Jennings, D'Rozario et al., 2008), were reinterviewed. Unfortunately, two of the original participants had moved away from Singapore and another participant had died. In the earlier study, Singaporean master therapists were nominated by colleagues and were considered to be master therapists. Utilizing CQR methodology, the researchers identified eight themes strongly related to cultural competence:

1. Self-awareness
2. Cultural immersion
3. Cultural knowledge
4. Knowledge of systemic/historic oppression
5. Respect
6. Multicultural misunderstandings lead to humility and cultural competence
7. Ask, don't assume
8. Suspend judgment/avoid imposing values

Two other studies that did not apply peer nomination the same way as the master therapist studies are worth mentioning here because they both studied expertise by sampling exemplary therapists. The first study by Goh and Yang (2011) arose from trying to adapt a popular cultural competence measure of intercultural communication to counseling. The Intercultural Development Inventory (IDI; Bennett, 1993). Out of approximately 400 counselors who took the IDI as part of cultural competence training, less than 20 participants, or less than 5%, had an IDI profile that reflected a culturally sensitive worldview. This 5% appeared to have "mastered" cultural competence in a manner that made them stand out. They were exemplary. Therefore, the authors decided to investigate what distinguished this exclusive, small group of students and clinicians who reflected an *ethnorelative* profile. Sixteen out of the 20 agreed to be interviewed. Participants were mental health providers at a Midwestern, urban, community-based mental health agency and graduate students in counseling. The semistructured interview asked such questions as, "Given two equally experienced counselors, why does one become more culturally competent and sensitive whereas the other remains less culturally competent and sensitive?" "How do you develop intercultural competence as a counselor?" Analysis of the data was based on inductive analysis (M. Q. Patton, 2002) as well as a modified Consensual Qualitative Research (CQR) approach described by McCarthy, Veach, Bartels, and LeRoy (2001), similar to previous master therapist studies. A total of 43 concepts were generated from 232 pages of data from the 16 interviews. The final CQR process resulted in 18 themes being identified under four domains. The counselors in this sample seem to possess a strong desire to actively participate and engage in other cultures. They view cultural differences as learning opportunities and find exposure to other cultures as energizing and as a source of excitement and enrichment to their lives. These counselors appear to be emotional observers of their cultural environments. They seem to have a deep sense of empathy for those afflicted with discrimination at an individual, group, and world level; they are aware of oppression of groups from certain backgrounds; recognize their privilege statuses (e.g., race, ethnicity, SES, education, etc.); and retain a belief in social justice. There is fluidity to this sample's conceptualization of intercultural competence that parallels their comfort with ambiguity. Their conceptualization of intercultural competence is not scripted but instead is an evolution of personal experiences, theories, possession of certain characteristics, and their understanding of humans and human needs. These counselors appear to be suspended in a "wait and see mode" and seem to be comfortable with second guessing their conceptualizations in their work with clients; and hold a stance that they may "never really know." Participants in this study also voraciously sought opportunities for diverse experiences and are tolerant of complexity and the discomforts that may come with being in culturally different situations. These counselors are insightful and self-aware and use these attributes continuously in their work and personal lives. The deliberateness of their acquisition for cultural competence sets these counselors apart. They are humble in recognizing competence they may possess as cultural communicators and believe that intercultural counseling competence is a process in which they continue to develop.

In the second study by Goh, Sumner, Hetler, and the Cultural Providers Network (2010), participants were 18 mental health service providers and administrators who are members of the Cultural Providers Network (CPN). Participants were nominated by the CPN and chosen by consensus. All providers work with children and families from diverse communities. Membership in the CPN is fluid with more than 85 providers in the Twin Cities engaged to a varying degree. The study was conducted in the spirit of community based participatory action research, defined as a collaborative effort between equal partners to meet community-defined needs (Calleson, Jordan, & Seifer, 2005). This study sought to develop an understanding of how committed, experienced clinicians go about working with clients from diverse communities. The results represent a consensus about facets of mental health service that hold true across therapists who work with culturally diverse communities. The results suggest a framework for delivering a culturally sensitive mental health service that requires cultural knowledge, skills, flexibility, and sophistication. The participants in this study actively balance their professional training with the values and traditions of culturally diverse communities. The model generated by this study can best be considered as foundational and transtheoretical. The providers use their cultural knowledge and awareness, conceptual framework, understanding of barriers, and investment in culturally relevant outcomes to generate appropriate roles and to select effective practices. Providers actively seek out practices, roles, and theoretical frameworks that meet the needs of the communities they serve.

So what do these studies tell us about the juxtaposition of cultural competence and master therapists? While exploratory in nature, these four studies support the growing literature that emphasizes the role of culture and cultural competence in the therapy process (La Roche & Christopher, 2008; Smith, Rodriguez, & Bernal, 2011; Whaley & Davis, 2007). In particular, these studies provide rich anecdotal evidence about how master therapists and exemplary therapists provide services to culturally diverse populations. Interventions ranging from acknowledging the cultural identity of the therapist and client to cultural-specific practices all reveal the valuable nuance that is provided by the master therapists.

This research genre allows researchers to mine for rich narratives that illuminate the nature of cultural competence and mastery in therapy. In fact, the therapist characteristics described in these studies closely resemble factors of cultural intelligence—an emerging and leading theory of cultural competence (Goh, Koch, & Sanger, 2008). Therefore, these exploratory and initial studies lend support to the attendant nature of cultural competence and master therapists' attributes and the promise that future studies hold.

An Update to the Cognitive-Emotional-Relational (CER) Master Therapist Model

Upon review of the accrued master therapist studies, we see the need to update the CER model of the master therapist. Many of the themes noted in the earlier model have been supported by the more recent research efforts. Two new themes have emerged as important characteristics of master therapists. The first is "Trust in Clients" which is the newest addition to the relational domain. Several studies (Jennings, D'Rozario et al.,

2008; Kwon & Kim, 2007; A. G. Smith, 2008) found that master therapists implicitly trust that their clients have the internal resources necessary to make positive changes. This positive view of human nature is not surprising considering some of the companion themes that emphasize the importance of the relationship, deep acceptance of self, and intense will to grow.

"Cultural Knowledge and Competence" is the newest addition to the cognitive domain. Recent master therapist studies (Goh, Starkey et al., 2007; Goh, Sumner et al., 2010; Goh & Yang, 2011; Jennings, Gulden et al., 2012; Jennings, D'Rozario et al., 2008) clearly illustrate the importance of knowing the client's cultural background and having built multicultural counseling skills in order to understand the client, and help them. Our updated CER model now contains the same core attributes that Sue, Arredondo, and McDavis (1992) theorized as necessary for the culturally competent counselor: (a) knowing self, (b) knowing others, and (c) possessing multicultural skills.

As you examines the revised CER model, keep in mind that this updated model (Figure 12.1) represents a prototype of an ideal therapist. No one therapist embodies all of these desirable characteristics. Each therapist possesses his or her own unique constellation of gifts, characteristics, and skills that need to be cultivated and leveraged in order for that individual to become the best therapist possible. The master therapist studies do suggest, however, that those considered to be master therapists possess many of these characteristics across three broad domains: cognitive, emotional, and relational. We hope that our model serves as a guidepost for developing therapists (i.e., all of us) to consider as we reflect upon our developmental journey toward psychotherapy and counseling mastery.

The Developmental Path to Becoming a Master Therapist

Beginning students and novice practitioners are especially interested in the path to mastery. They ask: How does one become a master therapist? Can I follow that path? What are the markers along the way? As we have in two other places (Skovholt, Jennings, & Mullenbach, 2004; Skovholt, Vaughn, & Jennings, 2012), here we will outline our view of the path to mastery, based on the master therapist studies and the counselor development studies outlined in other chapters of this volume.

Here are three preconditions for the novice before setting out on the mastery path.

Being Relationship Oriented. Since the work is so relationship oriented, a vocational orientation toward people vs. objects is fundamental. For example, one of the master therapists said: "I have always maintained ... that the primary tool that I use is the

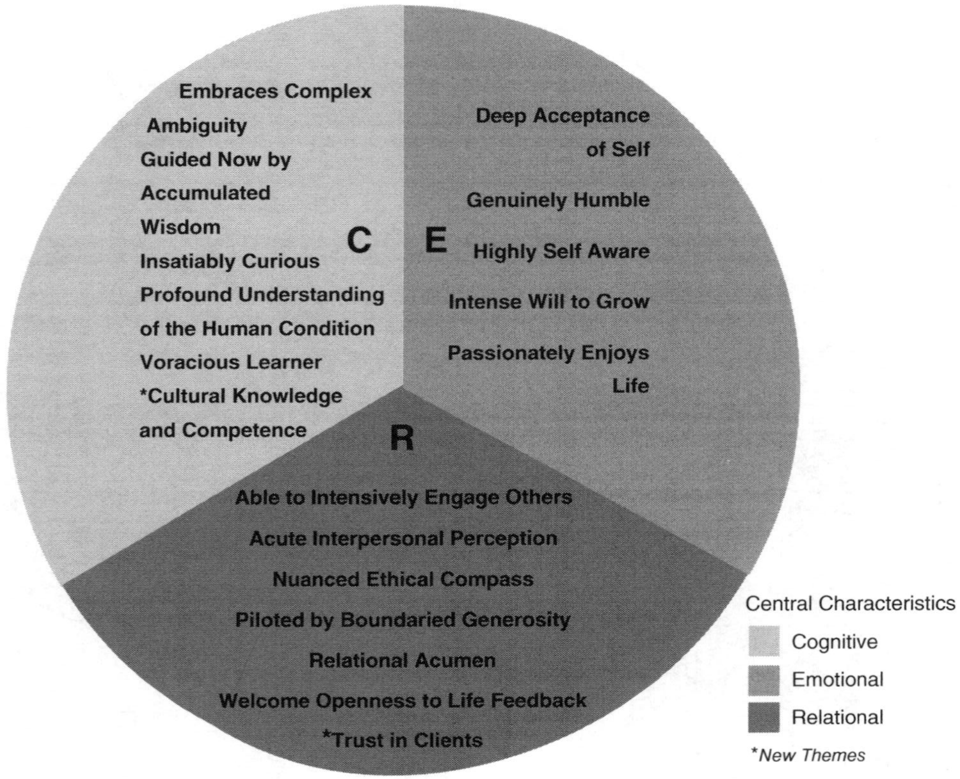

Central Characteristics

Cognitive
Emotional
Relational

*New Themes

Cognitive (C):
Embraces Complex Ambiguity
Guided Now by Accumulated Wisdom
Insatiably Curious
Profound Understanding of the Human Condition
Voracious Learner
*Cultural Knowledge and Competence

Emotional (E):
Deep Acceptance of Self
Genuinely Humble
Highly Self Aware
Intense Will to Grow
Passionately Enjoys Life

Relational (R):
Able to Intensively Engage Others
Acute Interpersonal Perception
Nuanced Ethical Compass
Piloted by Boundaried Generosity
Relational Acumen
Welcome Openness to Life Feedback
*Trust in Clients

Figure 12.1 Updated Portrait of Master Therapists

relationship. I have a lot of knowledge, I have a lot of skills, but they're wasted if the relationship isn't there" (Sullivan, 2001, p. 97). Attachment bonds are of importance in these individuals' lives. Perhaps they were inspired by a teacher or parent. They are drawn to people and the themes in people's lives.

Drawn to Uncertainty. Some people are drawn intellectually to topics that are mastered through logical, linear, sequential thinking patterns. In contrast, counseling is filled with ill-defined problems that can forever seem murky and are often not solved through sequential rational problem solving. Those who thrive in the career world of therapy are comfortable in the seemingly paradoxical reality of searching for clarity while enjoying the ambiguity and confusion of the human condition.

Being Affectively Attuned to the Needs of Others. In a workshop setting on professional development with a group of 70 therapists with an average 20 years of experience, the second author recently heard the audience members agree that this third attribute is the essential quality for a successful career as a therapist or counselor. Often, learning to be empathetic starts early in one's life when the person, within early attachments bonds, becomes oriented to the needs of others. In that early environment, one's own welfare seems tied to one's emerging capacity to care for others—and early "practicum" begins. Learning how to care for others and develop finely tuned affective sensitivity then grows so, over many years, affective expertise develops.

These are preconditions as one begins on the master therapy track: Now for the markers along the path.

Marker 1: Rage to Master

Certain people put themselves through years or decades of punishing, intensive daily work that eventually makes them world-class great.

(Colvin, 2010, p. 204)

Mastery in a complex domain takes a lot of effort over a long period of time. "A lot of time" is a consistent finding from the expertise research, as we will discuss in Marker 2. Here, we are discussing the motivation to master. In the Minnesota master therapist studies we called this the "Intense Will to Develop." How to manage the many periods of discouragement and failure that are part of trying to master complex tasks? What keeps the new practitioner pressing ahead? What keeps the new practitioner being reminded of the famous Thomas Edison quote about genius being 1% inspiration and 99% perspiration? One ingredient is the rage to master. This term comes from Winner (2000). When writing about gifted individuals, Winner (2000) says, "Gifted children have a deep intrinsic motivation to master the domain in which they have high ability and are almost manic in their energy level...This 'rage to master' characterizes children we have traditionally labeled gifted..."(p. 163).

Marker 2: Deliberate Practice Over Many Years

Expertise in a complex professional domain takes many, many hours of deliberate practice for expertise to emerge. This is one of the conclusions of the expertise research (Chi, Glaser & Farr, 1988; Ericsson, Charness, Hoffman, & Feltovich, 2006; Gladwell, 2008). Much study and exposure yields complex cognitive representations within a domain which is often thought of as specialized knowledge. Lots of experience is necessary. It is logical, therefore, that "The most salient positive influence on career development reported by therapists was direct clinical 'experience in therapy with patients'" (Orlinsky, Botermans, & Ronnestad, 2001, p. 4).

Deliberate practice often includes increasingly difficult steps as part of learning new skills and rigorous, time-consuming focus. Setbacks and frustration are necessary parts of this process of increasing expertise as expressed in the saying, "no pain, no gain" Many successes and many failures get mixed together. The value of sports training is connected to this capacity to keep trying in such a competitive situation where one team wins and one team loses each time. Imagine if half the high school teachers every day were publicly told they had either succeeded or failed. It is this environment that give sports training an advantage in learning how to fail and keep trying. Persistence is important. Learning through failure is often very unpleasant yet it seems to be a staple on the path to mastery of difficult domains.

Marker 3: Open to Feedback but Not Derailed by It

> The journey to truly superior performance is neither for the faint of heart nor the impatient. The development of genuine expertise requires struggle, sacrifice, and honest, often painful self-assessment. There are no shortcuts.
>
> (Ericsson, Prietula, & Cokely, 2007, p. 115)

Like Marker 6, "Boundaried Generosity," this one of "Open to Feedback but Not Derailed by It" comes from the Minnesota master therapist studies (Skovholt, Jennings, & Mullenbach, 2004). In addition, both of these are paradoxical terms with qualities pulling in both directions at the same time.

About this Marker 3, being open to life feedback is an essential quality for effective living. In fact, the second author, reflecting on his many years as a therapist, clinical supervisor, and teacher, believes that it is not problems that produce so much human misery as much as it is the inability for people to address their problems productively. Getting accurate feedback is essential for that task. Avoiding feedback, or distorting feedback, negates growth. This same principle operates in the professional world.

And it is the fine tuned version of useful feedback that increases performance: Openness to it while not being derailed by it. Derailing means two things. One of these is being so discouraged by the feedback that the individual wants to give up. Giving up is, of course, a very attractive option on the road to mastery in any complex domain because failure is normative as one learns more and more complex skills. Think of Olympic divers and how they must continue to get accurate feedback about failed attempts and then keep at it.

Another kind of derailing relates to the fact that some feedback is not accurate or helpful. Inaccurate feedback, taken in by the person, can cause serious derailing. Part of the reason we need to be cautious in accepting feedback is because it is, as Yalom says, "extraordinarily difficult to know really what the other feels; far too often we project our own feelings onto the other" (Yalom, 2002, p. 21). Projected feeling from the other can easily produce feedback that is not sophisticated in its accuracy or helpfulness. For example, another practitioner giving feedback has her or his own filters that guide the feedback. These filters shape the person's own perceptual reality and the feedback given to another about performance. Clinical supervision is an extremely important part of therapist development in part because supervisors are taught to give feedback that is not part of their own projections but rather valid in its own right. Another kind of feedback involves self-monitoring and reflection on one's own work. Practitioners naturally do this.

Being open to feedback is part of deliberate practice. Another part of turning experience into expertise is the use of reflection (Neufeldt, Karno, & Nelson, 1996). There must be a feedback loop so that the individual can learn from the practice. When therapists are fully licensed and working alone, they can fall victim to not learning from their own practitioner experience if there is no deliberate practice feedback system that includes self-reflection and self-monitoring of oneself as a practitioner.

Marker 4: Humility

All of us, and especially experts, are prone to an exaggerated sense of how well we understand the world.

(Holt, 2011, p. 16)

Jim Holt made the statement above in the course of a book review regarding the complexity of cognition. Our research on experts suggests an opposite conclusion. Repeatedly, in the studies of master therapists, the characteristic of humility rises to the top of the list (see Table 12.4). An example is a statement from the Minnesota master therapist studies related to the person's view of himself and the importance of a vacation. The exact quote is: "the trick is to be gone long enough...so you recognize your entire replaceability. That you are absolutely replaceable" (Mullenbach, 2000, p. 100). In our view, humility is an important marker on the way to being a master therapist because it continually opens up the person to keep learning. It is hard to face the "series of humiliations" that the novice therapist faces when trying theories and methods (global macrotheories) when working with a new client (a specific microtheory environment). As human beings—as fragile creatures—we often yearn to turn away from the humiliations. To not rest on one's laurels, to not let one's credentials—advanced degrees, professional licensure—be enough. These are important qualities it seems for professional improvement. Colvin (2010) says: "great performers never allow themselves to reach the automatic, arrested-development stage in their chosen field" (p. 83).

In a study of expert college teachers, Bain (2004) used the word *humility* to describe those he interviewed. One of his participants attributed his own success as a teacher to "how slow I am" (p. 142). Parker Palmer, the author of the influential book, *The Courage to Teach* (1998) illuminates the humility factor in expertise when he writes:

> [Sometimes] the classroom is so lifeless or painful or confused—and I am so powerless to do anything about it—that my claim to be a teacher seems a transparent sham.... What a fool I was to imagine that I had mastered this occult art—harder to divine than tea leaves and impossible for mortals to do even passably well! (p. 1)

Another example is from the Dlugos and Friedlander (2001) sample of "passionately committed" therapists. They studied 12 therapists who received at least three peer nominations as "passionately committed." One of the major categories describing their sample was "Transcendence/Humility."

We can also gauge the value of humility by considering its polar opposite of narcissism. With narcissism, there is a rigidity about being right with things just the way there are, now in this way, at this time. Why be open to feedback when there is no need? Freeman (2003) describes the danger of narcissism. He says the top three indicators of therapist narcissism are: "We think we are smarter than we are. We think we are more skilled than we really are. We think that charisma is an adequate substitute for skill" (p. 129). From the Freeman list, we can sense how humility can be like a personality characteristic that continually helps the therapist learn and learn, improve and improve while developing the rich cognitive schema of expertise.

Marker 5: Deep Coaching Attachments

> Mentors and apprentices are partners in an ancient human dance....It is the dance of the spiraling generations, in which the old empower the young with their experience and the young empower the old with new life, reweaving the fabric of the human community as they touch and turn.

(Palmer, 1998, p. 25)

Multicultural counseling expert Patricia Arredondo has this to say:

> My ninth grade and high school counselors took me under their wing and involved me as their aide. They encouraged and praised my performance and became important role models in my career development. (Arredondo, 2005, p. 35)

In a series of intense qualitative research interviews, Levinson and colleagues (1978) unearthed the importance of mentoring in successful career development. From that early study has now come a gushing flow of research, theory, and programs on the importance of mentoring in career success.

In parallel measure, Garmezy and his students (Masten, Best, & Garmezy, 1990) discovered children that were thriving although living in adversity. The authors called these children resilient children. One characteristic of these children was that they had the capacity, even under stress, to attach positively to caring adults. As with mentoring, the term resilience has grown in popularity, as has the accompanying research, theory, and programs.

Both of these terms, mentoring and resilient children, are tied to the more basic concept of human attachment. The term attachment was described in depth by the English psychiatrist John Bowlby in his three book series of *Attachment* (1969), *Separation* (1973), and *Loss* (1980).

All of these research ideas relate to our Marker 5 of being able to make deep coaching attachments. We are using the term coach here to cover professional caring-instructional relationships. The coach can be in a variety of roles such as clinical supervisor, director, teacher, mentor, parent, older sibling or other prized relative, guide, counselor, advisor, or consultant. Deep coaching attachments are usually sought after by the novice toward those who show both professional skill and a caring for them as a person. In one study of best teachers, we found that the word *caring* was used most often to describe these teachers (Skovholt & D'Rozario, 2000).

The best kind of coach for the person usually changes as the person moves along the developmental path. Often the coach is more demanding as the novice moves along on skill and confidence variables. Development is increased best when support and challenge are in balance. We need the classic kindergarten teacher—very encouraging, supportive, and instructional—early. This description also fits with the request of beginning students in counseling practicum who really want a supportive clinical supervisor. In time, the best coach for moving the person along the path changes so that highly sought coaches for experts are often much more demanding and exacting in their coaching.

Being able to develop deep attachments with our coaches is important. The learning from the relationship comes in many forms. Here is one of many versions: "By watching the master and emulating his efforts in the presence of his example, the apprentice unconsciously picks up the rules of the art" (Polanyi, 2002, p. 51).

Marker 6: Boundaried Generosity

The term *boundaried generosity* came from our analysis of the three dissertation studies, involving over 100 hours of interviewing, of the N = 10 Minnesota master therapists sample group. The composite portrait description included this concept (Skovholt, Jennings, & Mullenbach, 2004). Like Marker 3, "Open to Feedback but Not Derailed by It," this concept of boundaried generosity, is paradoxical, like the word *bittersweet*. It captures more complexity that a straightforward concept. Here, the path to mastery indicated a marker of both constraint, as in *boundaried*, and deep giving of oneself, as in *generosity*. The balance beam of professional vitality requires a balance of other-care and self-care. The optimal route often involves a person who is by nature, training, and background focused on the needs of the other, the crucial "affective attunement to the needs of the other." In time, engulfed in human need and becoming exhausted, the person needs to learn more expertise-level self-care skills. Learning how to do this and do it well is a marker on the way to mastery. See chapter 13 of this book devoted to "Therapist Professional Resiliency" for more on this marker.

Marker 7: Cultural Competence

Being skillful in accurately constructing and understanding the client's worldview has long been an aspirational aspect of therapist mastery. Being really understood by the other is enormously encouraging and is central for the engagement of the client's self-healing capacity (Bohart & Tallman,

2010). Socioeconomic status, age, gender, ethnicity, religious perspective, sexual orientation, and nationality are variables that together weave a pattern of individual differences. Decades ago, Wrenn (1962) warned of the culturally encapsulated counselor. Commitment to understanding worldwide in its complexity means awareness and skill in cultural competence. Here is another signpost on the way to therapist mastery.

In this section of the chapter, we have highlighted seven signposts on the path to mastery. These seven may be especially instructive for the beginner therapist or counselor who, although brimming with excitement about a professional career as a therapist, is also asking for direction and guidance. Here is some direction for that path.

Future Research

One direction for future research relates to actual in-session behavior. For example, research that uses video or audio recordings of master therapists (those selected on actual practice competence such as peer nominations) conducting therapy could be objectively analyzed through qualitative and quantitative methods to identify outstanding skills and qualities of master therapists. Also, what are the distinguishing characteristics of master therapists who are generalists versus specialists? These types of contrasting explorations will continue to build our understanding of the various ways mastery is demonstrated.

We encourage more studies both domestically and internationally on the topic of master therapists. When more studies become available, our ability to glean both universal and culturally specific characteristics of master therapists from these studies will contribute greatly to our current knowledge base.

Concluding Remarks

A note about the power of epistemology: At the beginning of this chapter we noted how the source of legitimate knowledge about therapy mastery has had three different sources. First, there has been the practitioner who learns through practice and tells others about his or her method through publication and workshops. Scores of methods have been developed this way. Giants in the field like Freud and Ellis have been given the title of master therapist through this method to mastery.

The second method to mastery comes from the research lab where academic clinical researchers have claimed mastery through research. The scientific to the applied route is used for the distribution of mastery ideas. Practitioners are often instructed to use manualized treatments based on empirical-based treatments and evidence-based practice if they desire to be master therapists. Many well established and respected ways to help people in distress have come from this epistemological source.

The third source of mastery ideas in therapy have come from active practitioners. For the chapters of this book thousands of practitioners have been interviewed or surveyed. Some have been nominated as master therapists by those around them who know of their actual clinical work in helping people in need. These nominated therapists usually have thousands of hours of professional experience (a reflection of the expertise literature and the claim that expertise in a domain requires extensive experience in the domain so that complex pattern recognition can occur; Ericsson et al., 2006). These active practitioners often labor unknown to the larger world because their work is guarded by confidentiality requirements of therapy and they often do not publish or present their methods. It is this third group that we have researched and discussed in this present chapter. They can be a version of unknown gems in our midst.

The search for professional expertise, to address and heal human pain, is ongoing. Together, these three epistemological sources can form a gestalt of therapy mastery.

13

THERAPIST PROFESSIONAL
RESILIENCE

Thomas M. Skovholt and Michelle Trotter-Mathison

This chapter focuses on preventing professional burnout and developing practitioner resilience. As we begin to discuss the topic, we invite you to assess your own resiliency and self-care through the *Skovholt Practitioner Professional Resiliency and Self-Care Inventory* found in the appendix of this chapter. You may use the inventory to consider areas of relative strength and growth as a means for self-reflection as you read through the chapter.

Before We Turn to the Difficulties

As we consider the topic of practitioner resiliency, we first turn our attention to the potential emotional difficulties of practicing as a therapist. However, before we begin an examination of hazards of the work, we want to note that burnout and related afflictions do not affect all therapists. There is variability between therapists and for individual therapists over the career life span. Many therapists report less stress and more satisfaction than one may think. In one study, a sample of marriage and family therapists reported low to moderate levels of burnout (Rosenberg & Pace, 2006). In an in-depth examination of hospital nurses, and especially their capacity for empathy, Bradham (2008) discussed "episodic burnout" within this group over the course of decades. One could use the term *tipping point* when reading her account for how personal life stressors, for example, exhausted these nurses' capacity for professional caring. Overall though, she found that most of the hospital nurses in her sample did not currently score high on burnout. The largest quantitative survey study of therapists (Orlinsky & Rønnestad, 2005a) and the largest qualitative interview study of therapists (Rønnestad & Skovholt, 2003; Skovholt & Rønnestad, 1992/1995), as well as the research on master therapists (chapter 12 of this book), were used as joint data to map professional development here and in other chapters of this book. What is an overall view regarding therapists and burnout-type reactions? Are senior therapists ground down, burned out, and bitter? Not necessarily. In chapter 7, a summary sentence is as follows: "Senior Professionals generally express a deep appreciation and a sense of gratitude for having chosen to become a therapist and for being able to practice their profession late in their lives." So although we will now present the dangers of the work here in this chapter on therapist resilience, we do not want to oversell the vicissitudes of the work.

Establishing the Need for Assertive Professional Self-Care

Therapists and others in related caring professions—counselors, teachers, health professionals, clergy, and other people careers—are in "high touch" fields and have work that can be very meaningful but also very difficult and demanding in a deeply personal sense. Therapists and counselors interact with clients and provide services which rely heavily on the ability of the clinician's self as an instrument in his or her work. Therapists are often on the frontlines as they witness and care for people's emotional fallout, which in turn can take an emotional and physical toll on practitioners. Overtime, work overload, emotional demands, and lack of time for self-care can make an impact and potentially manifest themselves in a difficult form for those in the caring professions, such as emotional depletion, compassion fatigue, vicarious traumatization, or professional burnout. The demands on the self of the therapist make it especially important to practice assertive professional self-care. The goal is to work toward being what we call *the resilient practitioner* (Skovholt &Trotter-Mathison, 2011).

As therapists and counselors, one of the primary tools in practice is to continually engage in the use of the self. This means there are great demands on one's time and one's emotional and cognitive selves. Use of self is crucial in relationship building, which is a core curative common therapeutic factor (Duncan, Miller, Wampold, & Hubble, 2010). Real life challenges exist in our work in the caring professions. A therapist has clients scheduled back to back, and paperwork time at the end of each hour dissolves into attending to case management issues and returning phone calls from clients. Suddenly, there goes the paperwork time! Yet the paperwork demands are still there at the end of an emotionally demanding day. Here are just a few examples of daily practitioner demands: A counselor works to attend to the incongruent needs of members of a therapy group. A social worker strives to connect her client to dwindling housing and food assistance resources. A psychiatrist tries to keep up with the schedule when clients have only brief appointment times.

Situations arise in which there is no clear answer as to the "right" path. As a part of the caring professions, the demands on a practitioner's time and personal resources often create a tension between the whole spheres of other-care and self-care. The image of a see-saw, also called a teeter-totter, communicates the delicate balance between feeding the other and feeding oneself. Memories of being on a see-saw as a child bring back the experience of the wild swing between being down with feet on the ground and way up in the air. It was fun! But now thinking about the see-saw analogy, there can be such a delicate balance between pouring one's energy into the other person, the one in need, and the practitioner's own needs, hopes, and dreams. Of course, the optimal solution for long-term vitality is a balance between the two. The idea of balance doesn't mean a steady state at every moment, that isn't how a see-saw works—it is more of a back and forth, up and down reality. Those in the caring professions must maintain the self in order to be able to continually draw on the self in practice; this is an instrument in our work.

The need for self-care, what we call "assertive professional self-care" means focusing on cultivating practitioner resiliency. Key to the vitality of the resilient practitioner is being able to find sources of energy for the work. For sustainability and longevity, the therapist must be able to devote enormous energy to the work, and have renewable sources of this energy. How and where do therapists find this energy? Here, in this chapter, we will explore this question. Researchers have developed terms such as burnout, compassion fatigue, secondary trauma, and vicarious trauma to help us to more fully understand the potential pitfalls of work that is out of balance. In studying and understanding these terms, we also seek to understand the importance of assertive self-care over the career life span.

Burnout

Maslach (1982) defines burnout as "a syndrome of emotional exhaustion, depersonalization, and reduced personal accomplishment that occurs among individuals who do 'people work'" (p. 3). The definition of burnout has evolved to include what Maslach, Schaufeli, and Leiter (2001) define as a "prolonged response to chronic emotional and interpersonal stressors on the job, and is defined by the three dimensions of exhaustion, cynicism and inefficacy" (p. 397). Pines and Aronson (1988) describe burnout as "a state of physical, emotional, and mental exhaustion caused by long term involvement in emotionally demanding situations" (p. 9).

Reflecting on 25 years of research on burnout, Maslach, Schaufeli, and Leiter (2001) outline the impact of burnout on job performance and health. Burnout has been correlated with employee absenteeism, desire to leave the job, and high turnover rates. When people continue to work within a job where they feel burned out, the effects can include lower productivity, effectiveness, job satisfaction, commitment to the job, and caring about the larger organization. Burnout also impacts health, particularly mental health. Employees experiencing burnout may react by creating an emotional and cognitive distance between themselves and their work, conceivably a way to create a boundary to cope with exhaustion, cynicism, and inefficacy.

Burnout can manifest itself in a number of physical and emotional symptoms. Figley (2002) outlines the symptoms of burnout which include: physical exhaustion, sleeping difficulties, somatic problems, irritability, anxiety, depression, guilt, and a sense of helplessness (p. 1436). In terms of behavioral responses to burnout, a person may become aggressive, callous, pessimistic, defensive, cynical, and may avoid clients or develop problems with substance abuse. Interpersonally, an individual may be less able to concentrate and communicate effectively, withdraw socially, lack a sense of humor, or have poor patient interactions.

Maslach and Leiter (2008) mention a key theme related to organizational risk factors for burnout job–person incongruity. This theme relates to the person–environment fit concept in the career development literature. Namely, that a better fit between personal qualities and preferences and work environment predicts greater job satisfaction and adjustment. When a person is incongruent with their work environment, burnout can follow. Maslach and Leiter (2008) identify the following six occupational risk factors: workload, control, reward, community, fairness, and values. For example, a counselor who is overworked, has a low level of control over his or her environment, views the job as having insufficient rewards, does not feel connected to colleagues and supervisors, and feels as though decisions made within the work environment are unfair would be a prime candidate for burnout.

Researchers have studied the effects of burnout on professional and personal well-being and have also looked at its impact on patient care. Soderfeldt, Soderfeldt, and Warg (1995) reviewed 18 studies that relate to burnout of social workers and identified work related factors associated with burnout: low work autonomy, lack of challenge on the job, low degrees of support, role ambiguity, low professional self-esteem, low salary, dissatisfaction with agency goals, difficulties providing services, and high degree of work pressure. There were also factors related to how therapists interact with their clients including personal involvement with clients, negative impressions of clients, and the level of the practitioner's empathy. Through an anonymous self-report questionnaire, Mahoney (1997) discovered that psychotherapy practitioners report emotional exhaustion and fatigue as their most common personal problems.

In a qualitative and quantitative longitudinal study, Collins and Long (2003) examined the effects on the practitioner of providing care to victims of a serious bombing in Ireland. The research participants were 13 people who were members of a trauma and recovery team and were from disciplines ranging from mental health practitioners to occupational therapists. Results indicated that participants had increased levels of burnout in the first year. They also experienced symptoms such as fatigue and disturbed sleep. Participants reported using self-care strategies such as exercise and reading, but indicated that they did not engage in these activities often enough.

Lee, Lim, Yang, and Lee (2011) completed a meta-analysis of 17 studies related to the antecedents and consequences of burnout for psychotherapists. Three primary dimensions of burnout (i.e., emotional exhaustion, depersonalization, and lack of personal accomplishment) and the antecedents to burnout (i.e., job stress, overinvolvement, control, job support, and professional identity) were investigated. Among other findings, the analysis showed a significant positive correlation between overinvolvement and emotional exhaustion. From this study, we learn that when a therapist becomes overinvolved in work and helping, emotional exhaustion can follow.

Meaning/Caring Burnout

As was also referred to in chapter 6, "Experienced Professional Phase" we highlight two types of burnout in the caring professions: meaning burnout and caring burnout (Skovholt, 2008). Meaning burnout occurs when the rewards of caring for others no longer provide adequate meaning and purpose for the practitioner. The joy of helping another through emotional difficulties no longer carries with it a deep sense of calling. Meaning burnout may be present for a range of reasons including a reduced sense of challenge stemming from the work, a feeling that one's work is no longer helpful to clients, or a decreased connection to the original reasons a person chose a career in the caring professions.

Caring burnout, the second type, corresponds with a concept that we refer to as the Cycle of Caring (described in more detail later in the chapter), the continual cycle of attachment, involvement, separation, and re-creation that practitioners move through over and over again in their life span as therapists. Engaging in the cycle of caring and the ability to attach, engage, separate, and re-create with vitality is essential to being an effective therapist. When one begins to find it difficult to repeatedly move through these phases, to attach and then let go, caring burnout can creep in.

Compassion Fatigue and Secondary Traumatic Stress

In addition to burnout, another concept related to practice in the caring professions is compassion fatigue, defined by Figley as "the natural consequent behaviors and emotions resulting from knowing about a traumatizing event experienced by a significant other—the stress resulting from helping or wanting to help a traumatized or suffering person" (Figley, 1995, p.7). In Figley's later work, he adds to the definition: "a state of tension and preoccupation with the traumatized patients by re-experiencing the traumatic events, avoidance/numbing of bearing witness to the suffering of others" (Figley, 2002, p.1435). The term *inadequate closure*, as described in chapter 9, may capture the process leading to the state of tension characterizing compassion fatigue. The term *secondary traumatic stress disorder* (STSD) is often used synonymously with compassion fatigue, although the latter term is used more often in recent years than STSD. Compassion fatigue can mimic symptoms of PTSD and lead a practitioner to struggle emotionally and feel disconnected from his or her support network and experience higher degrees of helplessness.

Vicarious Traumatization

The term *vicarious traumatization* was first identified by McCann and Pearlman (1990) who indicate that practitioners who work with victims of trauma may experience "profound psychological effects, effects that can be disruptive and painful for the helper and can persist for months or years after work with traumatized person" (p. 133). They especially identified as a core of vicarious traumatization changes in the cognitive scripts of the practitioner. For example, the person may feel more fearful and less safe after listening to stories of sexual assault. McCann and Pearlman (1990) found that novice practitioners, especially those with a personal trauma history, a background that could aid in understanding the client, had increased vulnerability to vicariously experiencing the trauma. In a qualitative interview study, Froman-Reid (2011) found notable levels of vicarious traumatization among practicum counselors at a community clinic serving a low income population.

Summary of the Practitioner Vulnerability Concepts

There is a significant amount of research that tracks the dangers of professional burnout, compassion fatigue, and vicarious trauma. This research creates a compelling case for thoughtful attention to developing and sustaining energy sources that allow one to engage and reengage in the essential work of the therapist. The task is to become a resilient practitioner. Our view is that it is important to attend carefully and mindfully to potential streams of energy which function as protective factors for continuing to enjoy the work and continue to be effective in assisting clients. A resilient practitioner is also better able to master the developmental tasks described for therapists at different phases of development, and will thus be more likely to develop optimally.

Cycle of Caring

In the past, it was thought that the practitioner was the vessel delivering the treatment in the form of a theory, method, or school. More recently, it is thought that the theory, method, or school is the vessel delivering the practitioner. This puts more emphasis on fundamental concepts like the working alliance and the practitioner's ability to form warm, caring, hopeful relationships with clients. This focus on the practitioner's ability to connect fits well with the concept of the cycle of caring.

A fundamental task of an effective practitioner is to attach, form relationships, say goodbye, and engage in the process of renewal, preparing to reengage in the caring process again and then again. This essential work of the therapist involves this series of attachments and separations, what we call the Cycle of Caring (Skovholt, 2005; Skovholt & Trotter-Mathison, 2011). Born out of Bowlby's attachment work presented in his books, *Attachment* (1969), *Separation* (1973), and *Loss* (1980), the cycle of caring encompasses the following four discrete phases: Empathic Attachment Phase → Active Involvement Phase → Felt Separation Phase → Re-creation Phase.

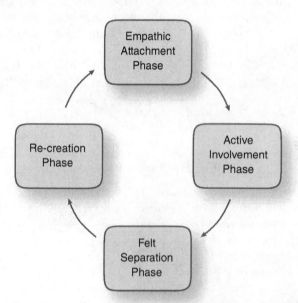

Figure 13.1 From Skovholt & Trotter-Mathison. *The Resilient Practitioner: Burnout Prevention and Self-Care Strategies for Counselors, Therapists, Teachers, and Health Professionals,* Second Edition (Routledge, 2011). Reprinted with permission.

Empathic Attachment Phase

Research on the working alliance emphasizes the value of the relationship between counselor and client (Sexton & Whiston, 1994). The empathic attachment phase deals with actively developing this working alliance, or attachment with the client. The extent to which a therapist is able to engage in this attachment phase is thought of as central to therapeutic outcome. Optimal attachment occurs when the therapist finds a balance between becoming overinvolved in the world of the other and having difficulty attaching. Between these two extremes, of too much and not enough, lies optimal attachment, in which a therapist is able to understand and empathize with the client, without becoming overwhelmed by the client's world and his or her difficulties.

Active Involvement Phase

The active involvement phase emphasizes the continual and consistent attachment to the client. Engaging in the active part of the counseling process, the therapist and client set out to work on the presenting problems. In the active involvement phase, the sustained commitment to working with the other is central. The therapist enlists his or her areas of competence—knowledge, skills, techniques, methods, experiences with previous clients, and insights from supervision and consultation—to help clients work through their struggles. Throughout this phase and the others too, the internal schemas, the product of hundreds of hours (thousands for some) of clinical work of the experienced practitioner, are activated and used to guide the work. (Rønnestad & Skovholt, chapter 8 of this book; Skovholt, Vaughan, & Jennings, 2012)

Felt Separation Phase

Separating well, an often overlooked part of the rhythm of the therapeutic process, involves parting with the client. Terminations happen in a number of ways that include planned terminations after long-term therapy, consultations that end after one session, and unplanned terminations. Unplanned terminations are an example of what we call ambiguous professional loss, a stressful process for the engaged therapist. Often without warning, the client ends the therapy, perhaps by just not returning. The therapist is unaware of the outcome for the client and left to wonder about the therapeutic alliance and the client's well-being. The therapist must consolidate the therapeutic experience and move on. A classic example of saying good-bye in the caring professions occurs every May in the United States, when elementary teachers and the students that they often call "my children" (an indicator of their attachment level), go through a ritual of ending the school year. Like the school teacher saying goodbye to students at the end of a school year, the therapist says goodbye to the client. However, the therapist–client good-bye occurs more frequently and in private. There is no group ending ceremony and no closing of the building until the fall.

Re-Creation Phase

The re-creation phase represents the pause before entering, once again, into a therapeutic relationship with another. Here, the therapist works to recharge his or her batteries so as to be able to future engage with clients, to have energy (or battery life) for the journey.

This phase is the summer break time for the school teacher. Within the context of the Cycle of Caring, *break* does not mean sloth or laziness. This is a critically important time for the teacher because it makes possible an intense emotional reinvestment in new children in the fall.

The work of the brain during sleep serves as an analogy for the re-creation phase. In the past, sleep was not considered as important as it is now. During sleep, the brain is actively consolidating itself and getting ready for life as it emerges in the morning; so too with the therapist. For therapists, this phase lasts until the practitioner begins the cycle of caring once again with a next client.

Hazards of Practice

There are many obstacles that impede the therapist's ability to effectively engage in the Cycle of Caring. We use the term *hazards* in discussing this topic here because the process of helping our clients involves obstacles such as client motivational conflicts, elusive measures of success, and multilayered complex problems that at times exceed resources. The space between the therapist and the client can be punctuated by these *hazards of practice*. Similarly, a practitioner's development of resiliency can be disrupted by these types of roadblocks. Here, we discuss two types of hazards of practice, those that are internally generated by the therapist as a reaction to the work and those that are externally generated by the nature and demands of the work and the helping environment.

As we begin our exploration of the hazards of practice, we look to a list of hazards generated by Regelson (1989), who asserts a number of problems, within the parallel field of medicine, that lead health care providers to burn out. His list includes (a) economics; (b) jealousy, professional competition, and power struggles among providers; (c) importance of public image; (d) technological displacement and rotational responsibility; (e) lack of recognition; and (f) difficulty in maintaining a balance between professional and personal life. In previous work, we have identified and discussed 20 hazards of practice (Skovholt, 2001; Skovholt & Trotter-Mathison, 2011). Here, we will highlight 11 significant hazards of practice. These hazards can make a feeling of success, so important for career satisfaction, elusive for the therapist.

1. Clients often have an unsolvable problem that must be solved. For example, a client may desperately want to be both very thin and very healthy. It can take a lot of therapy to work through the significant losses with either choice.
2. They have motivational conflicts such as being an involuntary client—as in, sent by the legal system, one's wife, one's parents.
3. There is often a readiness gap in getting at the core issues between the client and therapist.
4. Sometimes they project negative feelings onto us.
5. Sometimes we cannot help because we are not good enough.
6. They have needs greater than the social service, educational, or health system can meet.
7. The therapist often must live in an ocean of stress emotions.
8. The therapist experiences ambiguous professional loss—ending before the ending.
9. The covert nature of the work makes it difficult for us to share our work life with others, like most people do.
10. Doing good work demands constant empathetic engagement and one-way caring relationships.
11. There are elusive measures of success. What is success?

Joys of Practice

While the hazards of practice are important to acknowledge and manage, we cannot neglect an exploration and recognition of the significant joys and rewards of therapy practice. Therapists are engaged in work that is a direct response to human need and suffering. Individuals pursuing careers in the caring professions often do not pursue such a career with financial gains as the primary motivator, rather in response to the desire to help others and take on work that fills a need and is inherently meaningful. As Norcross and Guy (2007) express in their book, *Leaving it at the Office*, "There is no greater pleasure than knowing that you made a real, lasting difference in the life of another human being—a common experience for effective psychotherapists, one that never loses its special meaning" (p. 21). They go on to cite some of the key rewards of helping: satisfaction of helping, permanent membership in the client's world, freedom and independence, variety of experiences, intellectual stimulation, emotional growth, reinforcement for personal qualities, and life meaning.

There are many joys in therapy work. As mental health practitioners, we are invited into the world of our clients. We are deeply privileged to be invited into this inner world, when at times no one else has been welcomed. Just as therapists can experience vicarious traumatization, we can also experience *vicarious growth*. As we walk alongside clients who are working on self-development, we learn along with them. As a byproduct of engaging in work as a therapist, many practitioners learn valuable interpersonal and attachment skills that are assets in the broader world of the counselor.

In addition to these emotional rewards, there are also cognitive rewards. As a therapist, part of the work is continually engaging in opportunities to further develop skills and competencies. Lifelong learning is not only a requirement for licensure, it is also a significant opportunity for those that practice in the caring professions. Work as a therapist is always changing. Never will you meet two clients who are exactly the same; or the same client who, years later, is the same as before. There are always opportunities to work with clients who present challenges to our existing competencies and invite us to challenge ourselves to grow.

Strategies to Promote Resilience and Self-Care

Foundational ideas expressed in this chapter are (a) the importance of the self in the therapy relationship and (b) the core expertise of engaging in the Cycle of Caring. Through the phases, Empathic Attachment Phase → Active Involvement Phase → Felt Separation Phase → Re-creation Phase, practitioners continually offer the healing power of the therapy relationship. In order to do this well, the practitioner often has positive energy streams for the work. There are so many examples of energy sources told us by therapists at the workshops we have offered (e.g., joy of nature, joy of intimate love, joy of hobbies). We recognize the importance of attending to resiliency development both in and out of the office, in the professional and personal life.

To counter the significant problem of burnout, positive psychology looks to promoting resiliency factors. Seligman and Csikszentmihalyi (2000) indicate that there are human strengths, including courage, future-mindedness, optimism, interpersonal skill, faith, work ethic, hope, honesty, perseverance, the capacity for flow, and insight that can serve as protective factors or buffers against mental illness. We can add this information to our toolkit for developing practitioner resiliency, the personal characteristics and strengths we can harness or further develop to deepen our reserves for the work of the caring professions.

In a parallel field, Meier, Back, and Morrison (2001), in their conceptual piece, propose self-awareness and self-care steps for physicians who care for seriously ill patients. They assert that physicians who have difficulty dealing with emotions can find that this affects their patient care and well-being. They propose a model for physician self-awareness that includes the use of boundaries to facilitate emotional engagement that is "not too close and not too distant" (p. 3008). Meier et al. utilize a medical model for effectively managing emotions: (a) identifying risk factors that predispose clinicians to either identify too closely with their patients or disengage; (b) noticing signs and symptoms of emotions that may affect patient care (including anger, contempt, sense of failure, or self-guilt); and (c) identifying a differential diagnosis for possible causes of the physician's emotions. In the final step, the authors encourage physicians to "respond constructively to the presence of the emotion" (p. 3012); they offer the following strategies: name the feeling, accept the normalcy of the feeling, reflect on the emotion and its possible consequences, and consult a trusted colleague.

Stevanovic and Rupert (2004) studied professional psychologists and their key career-sustaining behaviors. The top 10 most highly selected behaviors included: spend time with partner/family, maintain balance between professional and personal lives, maintain a sense of humor, maintain self-awareness, maintain professional identity, engage in quiet leisure activities, maintain a sense of control over work responsibilities, engage in physical activities, take regular vacations, and spend time with friends. Mullenbach (2000) offered a similar list after researching expert therapists.

Specific Strategies for Increasing Practitioner Resiliency

Strategy 1: Focusing of Professional Development and Work Mastery Creates Its Own Energy

Our studies of master therapists found that these practitioners got energized by being continually like engaged students who had to use a term from the gifted and talented literature, a *rage to master* (see chapter 12; Skovholt, Vaughan, & Jennings 2012 for more on this topic).

Strategy 2: The Cycle of Caring

The Cycle of Caring offers the therapist a process model of success that increases his or her sense of control, and as a natural consequence, increases work satisfaction. Although we as therapists wish so much for positive client outcome, we control only a part of that equation. We cannot control client reaction to us or how supervisors or colleagues react to our work. We can control two activities; expert knowledge about the client issue and being competent in engaging in the four-phase Cycle of Caring.

Strategy 3: Boundaried Generosity

Boundaried generosity is a concept that emerged from the master therapist studies, and it is a useful paradoxical term for a stance regarding our work long-term. Giving and sharing oneself for the welfare of others is a core therapist attitude. Yet, the terms of emotional depletion, compassion fatigue, vicarious traumatization, and the classic one, burnout, serve as warning lights. The takeaway message here is to pace oneself and have boundaries so that giving is still possible as the future, of many more opportunities to be helpful with clients, unfolds.

Strategy 4: Embracing the Ambiguity of the Work

So much is unclear when working in therapy and counseling. Here is a short list: What is the nature of human nature? How do we really understand another person, or even oneself? What is success in therapy? What are the core elements when trying to help person A or person B? In therapy work, so much is unknown. Often we can feel as if we are swimming in a sea of ambiguity. And we are. Even as we learn theory after theory as a way to be more clear, the confusion keeps surfacing. It can be less stressful as a therapist to view the ambiguity of human nature as a positive, and a way to keep oneself curious and engaged in the great adventure of trying to understand and help another person.

Strategy 5: Enjoy the Small Victories

Small victories are everywhere but we often neglect them as we go from big task to big task. Working with people does not yield new skyscrapers or big, ripe fields of grain. Rather, it consists of the sudden client realization of an important truth, the appreciation expressed by a colleague, or our own pleasure after spontaneously responding in a therapeutic way. The small victories help sustain us and give us energy for the hard work of therapy and counseling … if we cherish them and find joy in them before rusing off the the next challenge.

Strategy 6: Useful and Honorable Work

Therapy and counseling is one of the great inventions of the last half of the 20th century and practitioners can find joy, pride, and meaning in doing such honorable work. We *now* have a language about changeable human conditions—for example, chemical dependency, learning disabilities, anger management, marital intimacy, depression treatment, desensitization for anxiety. What was once thought of as unchangeable human fate, that a person was labeled as stupid, drunk, or evil, is now conceptualized in more hopeful and changeable language. The therapy, counseling, and helping professions are part of this more hopeful way of viewing human nature. How exciting to be part of it!

Strategy 7: Our Own Personal Attempts toward Growth and Maturity

Our own personal attempts toward growth and maturity can give us energy for the work. A long-term focus on personal maturity, using terms like *depth, integrity,* and *spiritual growth* is important, not for narcissistic reasons, but for a more complete giving of the self. Clients want to know how to handle loss, pain, and disappointment. Learning from our own suffering is a primary epistemology for our work.

Strategy 8: Therapist Enthusiasm For the Work

Being well loved and well fed, experiencing happiness, and feeling joyful, gives the therapist enthusiasm for the work. This is essential because of the important therapist attribute of being hopeful for clients, who often come to therapy with little hope. Having really good personal relationships is fuel for the work. Being a helper of others as the only role one has in personal life can be draining and problematic.

Strategy 9: Intense Physical Exercise

Intense physical exercise serves as a buffer against the physiological stress of the work, which is often very hard. It can be very stressful and exhausting. Vicarious traumatization and compassion fatigue lie around the corner. A common saying is that if exercise came in pill form, it would be the number 1 prescription because of its benefits.

Strategy 10: Having Fun and Being Playful

Having fun and being playful occupies the life of resilient practitioners. Playfulness, pleasure, and fun serve as antidotes to the serious work of the therapist. It comes in many forms.

> The world of play favors exuberance, license, abandon. Shenanigans are allowed, strategies can be tried, selves can be revisited. In the self-enclosed world of play, there is no hunger. It is its own goal which it reaches in a richly satisfying way. (Ackerman, 1999, p. 6)

Summary

It is wonderful that we now have words like *burnout* and *compassion fatigue* to describe the corrosive effects of exhaustion, despair, and discouragement in the lives of caring professionals, such as therapists and counselors. Thanks go to Herbert Freudenburger (1974) who made a great contribution when he first used the term *burnout* to describe negative effects of the work in mental health practice. We can now focus on prevention as a way to enhance the pleasures of being a therapist. We can now prepare ourselves to become resilient therapists as we work in practice to help people feel less distress and more joy in their lives.

Appendix: Skovholt Practitioner Professional Resiliency and Self-Care Inventory[1]

The purpose of the inventory is to provide self-reflection for practitioners and students in the caring professions. The term *practitioner* here refers to individuals in the caring professions—such as the helping professions, teaching, and health care. Examples are psychologist, counselor, social worker, academic advisor, K-12 teacher, college professor, clergy, human resources specialist, physician, registered nurse, dentist, and family law attorney.

Questions are addressed to both active practitioners and also students in training programs. There is no total number that is considered best. In fact, some of the questions are not relevant to some professionals or students who fill out this inventory. The inventory is intended to help decrease stress, not increase it!

The checklist consists of four subscales: Professional Vitality, Personal Vitality, Professional Stress and Personal Stress.

1 = Strongly Disagree, 2 = Disagree, 3 = Undecided, 4 = Agree, 5 = Strongly Agree

Professional Vitality   *Circle your Response*

1. I find my work as a practitioner or as a student to be meaningful.   1 2 3 4 5

2. I view self-care as an ongoing part of my professional work/student life.   1 2 3 4 5

3. I am interested in making positive attachments with my clients/students/patients.   1 2 3 4 5

4. I have the energy to make these positive attachments with my clients /students/patients.   1 2 3 4 5

5. The director/chair at my site/school is dedicated to practitioner welfare.   1 2 3 4 5

6. On the dimension of control of my work/schooling, I am closer to high control than low control.   1 2 3 4 5

7. On the dimension of demands at my work/ schooling, I have reasonable demands rather than excessive demands from others   1 2 3 4 5

8. My work environment is like a greenhouse--where everything grows—because the conditions are such that I feel supported in my professional work   1 2 3 4 5

Subscale Score for Professional Vitality (Possible score is 8–40)   _____

Personal Vitality

9. I have plenty of humor and laughter in my life   1 2 3 4 5

10. I have a strong code of values / ethics that gives me a sense of direction and integrity   1 2 3 4 5

11. I feel loved by intimate others   1 2 3 4 5

12. I have positive /close friendships   1 2 3 4 5

13. I am physically active and receive the benefits of exercise   1 2 3 4 5

14. My financial life (expenses, savings and spending) is in balance   1 2 3 4 5

15. I have lots of fun in my life   1 2 3 4 5

16. I have one or more abundant sources of high energy for my life. (examples—other people, pleasurable hobby, enjoyable pets, the natural world, a favorite activity)   1 2 3 4 5

17. To balance work ambiguity in the caring professions, I have some concrete activities in my life that I enjoy where results are clear cut (e.g,. a rock collection, painting walls, growing tomatoes, washing the car)   1 2 3 4 5

18. My eating habits are good for my body   1 2 3 4 5

19. My sleep pattern is restorative   1 2 3 4 5

Subscale Score for Personal Vitality (Possible score is 10–55)   _____

Professional Stress

20. There are many contradictory messages about both practicing self-care *and* meeting expectations of being a highly competent practitioner/student. I am working to find a way through these contradictory messages   1 2 3 4 5

21. Overall, I have been able to find a satisfactory level of "boundaried generosity" (defined as having both limits and giving of oneself) in my work with clients/students/patients   1 2 3 4 5

22. Witnessing human suffering is central in the caring professions (e.g., client grief, student failure, patient physical pain.). I am able to be very present to this suffering, but not be overwhelmed by it or experience too much of what is called "sadness of the soul."   1 2 3 4 5

23. I have found a way to have high standards for my work yet avoid unreachable perfectionism.   1 2 3 4 5

24. My work is intrinsically pleasurable most of the time   1 2 3 4 5

25. Although judging success in the caring professions is often confusing, I have been able to find useful ways to judge my own professional success   1 2 3 4 5

26. I have at least one very positive relationship with a clinical supervisor/mentor/teacher   1 2 3 4 5

27. I am excited to learn new ideas—methods—theories—techniques in my field   1 2 3 4 5

28. The level of conflict between staff/faculty at my organization is low   1 2 3 4 5

Subscale Score for Professional Stress (Possible score is 8–40)   _____

Personal Stress

29. There are different ways that I can get away from stress and relax (examples—TV, meditating, reading for fun, watching sports)   1 2 3 4 5

30. My personal life does not have an excessive number of one-way caring relationships where I am the caring one   1 2 3 4 5

31. My level of physical pain/disability is tolerable   1 2 3 4 5

32. My family relations are satisfying   1 2 3 4 5

33. I derive strength from my religious/spiritual practices and beliefs   1 2 3 4 5

34. I am not facing major betrayal in my personal life   1 2 3 4 5

35. I have a supportive community where I feel connected   1 2 3 4 5

36. I am able to cope with significant losses in my life   1 2 3 4 5

37. I have time for reflective activities such as journaling-expressive writing or solitude   1 2 3 4 5

38. When I feel the need, I am able to get help for myself   1 2 3 4 5

Subscale Score for Personal Stress (Possible score is 10–50）   _____

Total Score for the Four Subscales (Possible score is 38–195)   _____

There are a total of 38 questions in the Skovholt Professional Resiliency and Self-Care Inventory. All are scored in a positive direction with 0 low and 5 high. As stated earlier, the scoring system is a method for self-reflection by practitioners and students in the caring professions. There is no total number that is considered best. In fact, some of the questions are not relevant to some professionals or students who fill out this inventory. We suggest that you use the inventory in any way that can be helfpful for your own professional development.

Note

1. Copyright © 2010 by Thomas Skovholt

14

POSITIVE AND NEGATIVE CYCLES OF PRACTITIONER DEVELOPMENT

Evidence, Concepts, and Implications from a Collaborative Quantitative Study of Psychotherapists

David E. Orlinsky and Michael Helge Rønnestad

The findings and concepts presented in the preceding chapters of this book are based primarily on *qualitative* studies of counselor and therapist development. In this chapter, by contrast, we summarize some major findings, theoretical formulations, and practical implications of a *quantitative* study of the same subject. In addition to presenting further research findings, we hope to show how quantitative and qualitative research approaches to a common topic can be complementary, providing both breadth and depth of perspective.

The origin of this quantitative study dates back to 1989, when a group of colleagues met at an international conference of the Society for Psychotherapy Research (SPR) held in Bern, Switzerland. Finding among themselves a shared vital interest in the topic of therapist development, this group of clinical researchers organized the SPR Collaborative Research Network (CRN) and decided to combine resources in order to conduct a large-scale study of the topic. As researchers who were also practicing therapists, teachers, and supervisors with extensive clinical experience, the SPR/CRN has become a self-supporting, self-directed organization that has been able to work productively without restraints imposed by the research grant system (deadlines, progress-reports, concluding reports, etc.), and has grown in scope and international coverage as new collaborators generated more extensive data, novel research questions, and fresh perspectives. A main feature of the SPR/CRN project is that it has focused on the studying of how therapist *experience* their work and development, although recently this has broadened as members of the network participating in other projects have explored the relationship of therapists' experiences to processes and outcomes of therapy cases assessed from other observational perspectives, including client-rated working alliance (Nissen-Lie, Monsen, & Rønnestad, 2010). Presently, research is also being conducted to study the relationship between therapists' experiences and client-rated psychotherapy outcome.

For more than two decades, the SPR/CRN has produced a series of conference presentations, journal articles (e.g., Lorentzen, Orlinsky, & Rønnestad, 2011; Lorentzen, Orlinsky, & Rønnestad, 2010; Orlinsky et al., 1999; Orlinsky, Botermans, & Rønnestad, 1998; Rønnestad & Orlinsky, 2005a; Schroder, Wiseman, & Orlinsky, 2009; Smith & Orlinsky, 2004; Wiseman & Egozi, 2006), book chapters (e.g., Ambühl & Orlinsky, 1998; Orlinsky, Rønnestad & Willutzki, 2010), and a book titled *How Psychotherapists Develop: A Study of Therapeutic Work and Professional Growth* (Orlinsky & Rønnestad, 2005) based on extensive reports from approximately 5,000 therapists and counselor of varied professions, theoretical orientations, and career levels. The present chapter summarizes the main findings of the SPR/CRN about professional development and discussed the theoretical and practical implications of those findings.

Research Questions and Methods

The initial core questions of the SPR/CRN study were: In what ways do practitioners experience their development as psychotherapists or counselors? How do they experience their therapeutic work with patients? In what ways do the therapists' experiences in clinical work influence their professional development? How do phases and states of a therapist's development, in turn, influence his or her therapeutic practice? In the autumn of 1989, an international group of SPR colleagues decided to undertake a collaborative study in order to explore these questions, and others that eventually arose in their wake.

To pursue these questions, the initial members of the group designed a survey instrument called the Development of Psychotherapists Common Core Questionnaire (DPCCQ), which inquired about a broad range of therapists professional and personal experiences (Orlinsky, Ambühl, et al., 1999). The DPCCQ was conceived as the analogue of an interview between colleagues seeking to elucidate these varied topics from the psychotherapist's perspective. To date, information has been gathered from approximately 11,000 therapists of diverse professions, theoretical orientations, and career levels, in more than two dozen countries. (The results reported in our book were based on the first 5,000 of the therapists and counselors who were studied). Statistical analysis of the data was conducted primarily through multi-level factor analyses of DPCCQ items, focusing initially on specific item sets and then on the reliable multi-item scales representing the dimensions of variance in those sets. Through this procedure, general dimensions of therapists' work experience and professional development could be empirically determined, and studied in relation to one another and to varied therapist characteristics.

Experiences of Therapeutic Work

Two broad dimensions of practitioners' experience of therapeutic work were identified in this way, by focusing first on specific facets of work surveyed in the DPCCQ (e.g., therapists' skills, difficulties in practice, coping strategies, modes of relating with patients, and in-session feelings), and then more broadly by factor analyzing the reliable dimensions found in those facets. The most general dimensions that underlie all therapists' experiences of therapeutic work were found to be *Healing Involvement* and *Stressful Involvement*. All therapists concurrently experience some level or degree of *Healing Involvement* as well as some level or degree of *Stressful Involvement*.

The dimension of *Healing Involvement* was defined by a sense of current skillfulness in work; minimal difficulties in practice; reliance on constructive coping strategies when difficulties occur; a sense of being personally invested in genuine, affirmative, and receptive relationships with patients; experiencing feelings of "flow" in sessions (Csikszentmihalyi, 1996), and an overall sense of therapeutic efficacy. Quantitative assessments of therapist difficulties and coping strategies utilized scales based on prior qualitative research by Davis and colleagues (Davis et al., 1987; Davis, Francis, Davis, & Schroder, 1987).

The therapist characteristics that most strongly predicted therapists' *Healing Involvement* were breadth of theoretical orientation, implying flexibility of approach; feelings of support and satisfaction in the work setting; breadth and depth of case experience in several treatment modalities (couple, family, and group as well as individual therapy); and positive work morale. The independent, contrasting dimension of *Stressful Involvement* was defined by the therapist's experience of multiple difficulties in practice, together with therapeutically unconstructive coping strategies (e.g., avoidance or blaming when in difficulty), and in-session feelings of anxiety and boredom. Relatively few therapist characteristics were predictors of *Stressful Involvement*, suggesting that this dimension of work experience instead reflects situational factors (e.g., the therapist's current caseload). *Stressful Involvement* was greater for therapists who felt little support or satisfaction in their main work setting, who had no private practice, and who seemed to be trapped in a cycle of demoralization.

Practice Patterns

Because *Healing Involvement* and *Stressful Involvement* are statistically independent, we were able to characterize therapists' overall experience in therapeutic practice by cross-tabulating high and low scorers on each dimension. One the one hand, some therapists experienced "much" while other therapists experienced "not much" *Healing Involvement*. On the other hand, some therapists experience "little" while other therapists experienced "more than a little" *Stressful Involvement*. (Statistically and clinically meaningful cutoff points were established for each dimension.) In this way, four broad patterns of current therapeutic work experience were defined: about 50% of the nearly 5,000 therapists we had studied experienced much *Healing Involvement* and little *Stressful Involvement*, a practice pattern that we designated *Effective Practice*. Another 23% showed a practice pattern that could be called *Challenging Practice*, in which much *Healing Involvement* was combined with more than a little *Stressful Involvement*. Overall, nearly three-fourths of the therapists were experiencing much *Healing Involvement* in their therapeutic work.

By contrast, 17% of the therapists showed an apparently unproductive but (for them) non-distressing practice pattern of *Disengaged Practice*, in which they experienced little *Stressful Involvement* but not much *Healing Involvement*. Finally, and of even greater concern, about 10% of therapists caught in a pattern of *Distressing Practice*, where they experienced not much *Healing Involvement* and "more than a little" *Stressful Involvement* in their therapeutic work. From their own perspective, these therapists were suffering in their work and were not being of help to their patients.

As one might expect, the incidence of *Effective Practice* increased from 40% among novice therapists (those with less than 1.5 years in practice) to 60% among seniors (those with more than 25 years in practice), and the total of all therapists experiencing much *Healing Involvement* rose from 60% among novices to 80% among seniors. Similarly, there was a decline in the *Distressing Practice* pattern, which was experienced by 20% of the novices but only about 6% of established therapists (7 to 15 years in practice), seasoned therapists (15 to 25 years in practice), and senior therapists.

Some of this variation may be due to attrition among those therapists who experienced distress in clinical work and altered their professional focus, but it is also likely that much of the variation is due to improvement in therapeutic skill over time. Whatever the circumstances, our findings show rather dramatically the comparative vulnerability of novice therapists, and their need for supervisory and collegial support. These findings on the vulnerability of inexperienced therapist are consistent with the description of the Novice Student Phase, the Advanced Student Phase, and the Novice Professional Phase as described in chapters 4, 5, and 6 in this book.

Experiences of Professional Development

A conceptual analysis of the term *development* suggested that four distinct aspects of professional development can be studied (Orlinsky & Rønnestad, 2005, chapter 7). From the therapist's perspective, one aspect of development is the experience of current growth, and a second is the retrospected experience of "improvement" over time. From an external or objective perspective, a third aspect of development can be studied by investigating positive changes or "advances" in skill levels displayed in successive career cohorts, and a fourth aspect of development might be observed by following the "progress" made by the same set of therapists assessed longitudinally over time. The design of the DPCCQ included scales for assessing the first three aspects of therapists' professional development that could also be used in research designed to study development longitudinally.

Currently Experienced Development

Analysis of scales created to reflect therapists' experiences of ongoing development yielded two dimensions, one showing *Currently Experienced Growth* and the other indicating a sense of *Currently Experienced Depletion*. The experience of *Currently Experienced Growth* included an awareness of dynamic change and improvement, deepening understanding of therapeutic process, enhanced skillfulness, enthusiasm for practice, and overcoming past limitations as a therapist. Growth in this sense was interpreted partly as the continuing renewal of the therapists' work morale (necessitated by the stresses associated with therapeutic work), and partly as the gradual accumulation of lessons learned from experience (Orlinsky et al., 1999).

Currently Experienced Depletion, by contrast, involves a sense of deteriorating skills, loss of empathic responsiveness to patients, routinization of practice, and doubt concerning the effectiveness of therapy. This was interpreted as a process of therapist demoralization resulting from the experience of *Stressful Involvement* with patients—a demoralization that further impairs the therapist's positive investment in clinical work and, if unchecked, may lead to therapist burnout. The model suggests that if the difficulties with the patients are not handled constructively, they engender a reaction that Rønnestad and Skovholt (1991) called "premature closure—defined as a pre- or unconscious defensive process (characterized by misattribution, distortion, or dysfunctional reduction of complexity) that occurs if practitioners are unable to master the challenges encountered in therapeutic work" (Rønnestad & Skovholt, 2003, p. 39).

When *Currently Experienced Growth* predominates, the therapist's experience of development reflects a sense of *Progress*; but, when *Currently Experienced Depletion* is stronger, this negatively inflected change shows a contrasting sense of *Regress*. In some cases, both *Currently Experienced Growth* and *Currently Experienced Depletion* were observed, with the total experience being one of *Flux*. Therapists who experienced little depletion but also not much growth were described as in *Stasis*, which, depending on the circumstances, can be construed positively as stability or negatively as stagnation.

269

Cumulative Career Development

Analysis of DPCCQ scales created to reflect therapists' experiences of cumulative development yielded a single second-order dimension that was called *Cumulative Career Development*. This combined (a) a reliable, multi-item scale of Retrospectively Perceived Development, (b) a computed index of directional change in skill levels rated for the beginning and current stages of clinical work, and (c) a scale reflecting the therapist's self-rated level of attained Therapeutic Mastery expertise. Surprisingly, the dimension of *Cumulative Career Development* was only modestly correlated with years in clinical practice, and in fact was more strongly related to the breadth and depth of the therapist's case experience across diverse treatment modalities than to mere length of service.

In our study, higher levels of *Cumulative Career Development* were positively related to *Currently Experienced Growth*, as expected, and were inversely related to *Currently Experienced Depletion*. This suggests that the negative effects of *Stressful Involvement* in clinical work are experienced less intensely by therapists at advanced levels of development, and that relatively inexperienced practitioners (e.g., trainees) are most vulnerable.

Comparative Cohort Development

To study therapists' development by comparing successive career cohorts, we distinguished six levels based on clinical and statistical considerations. These are broadly comparable to the phases of practitioner development presented in chapters 4 to 8. Chronologically demarcated, *novice therapists* were those who had as little as one or two month up to less than 18 months of clinical practice doing therapy with real patients (i.e., not in role-play situations). *Apprentice therapists* were defined as having done from 1.5 years up to 3.5 years of clinical work. In most professional disciplines, both groups would consist of trainees and generally would be supervised by more experienced therapists, and corresponding more or less to the Beginning and Advanced Student phases discussed in chapters 4 and 5.

Therapists with from 3.5 to 7 years of therapeutic work were classified as *graduate therapists*, since in most professions they would have already completed their basic training and qualified for independent practice. This would approximate the Novice Professional phase described in chapter 6. Therapists who had continued in practice from 7 to 15 years were termed *established* therapists, and those with 15 to 25 years in practice were called *seasoned* therapists (borrowing the term from Goldberg, 1992). Most of these would likely correspond to those in the Experienced Professional phase discussed in chapter 6. Finally, therapists with 25 to 50 years of clinical practice were designated *senior therapists*, like many of those in the Senior Professional phase discussed in chapter 8.

Comparison of therapists in successive career cohorts revealed both differences and continuities in their experiences of therapeutic work and professional development. Although the number of years a therapist had been in practice was not, in itself, the strongest predictor of *Cumulative Career Development*, it nevertheless formed a meaningful basis for descriptive cross-sectional analysis. For example, *novice* therapists felt more anxiety during therapy sessions than *apprentice* therapists, and (as would be expected) both cohorts experienced significantly more anxiety than *senior* therapists.

The most telling marker of *Comparative Cohort Development* probably was the scale reflecting the practitioner's Sense of Therapeutic Mastery. Indications of a *high* therapeutic mastery (i.e., self-ratings of 4 or 5 on a 0–5 scale) were only found among 2.5% of *novice* therapists and 4% of *apprentice* therapists, and increased gradually to 10% of *graduate* therapists, 23% of *established* therapists, 37% of *seasoned* therapists, and to 50% of *senior* therapists. On the other hand, the frequency of really *low* levels of therapeutic mastery (ratings of 0 or 1 on the 0–5 scale) declined noticeably from 61% among the *novice* therapists to 34% among *apprentice* therapists, 17% of *graduate* therapists, 7% of *established* therapists, and only 5% of *seasoned* and *senior* therapists.

There were also striking similarities between therapists in all career cohorts. For example, most were strongly invested and affirming in relating to patients, and experienced consistently high level of rapt interest or "Flow" (Csikszentmihalyi, 1996) during therapy sessions. Also, high level of *Currently Experienced Growth* were observed for therapists at all career levels, even among those who had been in practice for many years. The fact that no diminution was found in *Currently Experienced Growth* suggests that this aspect of development reflects a process of continually renewal of the therapist's work morale that compensates for *Stressful Involvement* in therapeutic work.

Regarding influences on their development, therapists at all career levels emphasized the importance of learning directly from their work with patients, receiving supervision, and having their own personal therapy. *Novice* therapists rated formal supervision as the most important influence, whereas learning from experience in personal life was more salient as a source of influence for *senior* therapists.

The results described above, together with additional findings, led to the formulation the following theoretical model of development.

The Cyclical/Sequential Model of Psychotherapeutic Development

A distinctive feature of our Cyclical/Sequential Model is a recognition of positive as well as negative aspects and trends in development. The *positive* aspect leads to a progressive enhancement of clinical motivation, understanding and skill across an expanded range of clients, treatment modalities and problematic situations. Operating concurrently, the *negative* aspect of development leads to deterioration and a decline in motivation, understanding and skill with clients, which may lead to practitioner burnout and a virtual (or actual) withdrawal from therapeutic work. Each aspect reflects the operation of a particular cycle of influence that links the quality of the therapist's therapeutic work (*Healing Involvement* vs. *Stressful Involvement*), the therapist's currently experienced development (*growth* vs. *depletion*), and the level of his or her cumulative career development—as the effects of each variable are promoted or mitigated by ancillary conditions. As a result, the course of development attained and experienced by each therapist will depend on the balance between these positive and negative cycles in practice over time.

Positive Cycle

The potential for positive, progressive development rests on the fact that constructive, intrinsically rewarding engagement in therapeutic work (i.e., *Healing Involvement*) engenders a sense of *Currently Experienced Growth* in the therapist, which feeds back into work with patients in the form of enthusiasm and dedication (positive work morale) and feeds forward through the accumulation of lessons learned in clinical work to the gradual enhancement of the practitioner's therapeutic abilities (i.e., *Cumulative Career Development*)—and this, in turn, elevates the level and positively enhances of the practitioner's adeptness, resourcefulness and flexibility in clinical work (i.e., increases the likelihood of experiencing *Healing Involvement*).

This positive cycle is represented in Figure 14.1 as a pattern of interlocking loops—a short interior loop and a long exterior loop—each with some independent (external) influences. The *short interior* loop (in the lower left quadrant of the diagram) reflects the reciprocal influence of *Healing Involvement* and *Currently Experienced Growth*, both directly and indirectly through the effect of each on the therapists' work satisfaction. The *long exterior* loop (extending from lower left to upper right quadrant and back) reflects the less immediate but cumulative connection between *Healing Involvement* and *Cumulative Career Development*.

Our findings indicate that therapists' experiences of *Healing Involvement* occur more often among therapists with greater theoretical breadth, presumably because this enables them to meet a wider variety of therapeutic challenges, and enriches the process of "continual professional reflection" (Rønnestad & Skovholt, 1991; Skovholt & Rønnestad, 1995) through which therapists are able to learn from their clinical experience. Similarly, the therapist's level of *Cumulative Career Development* is

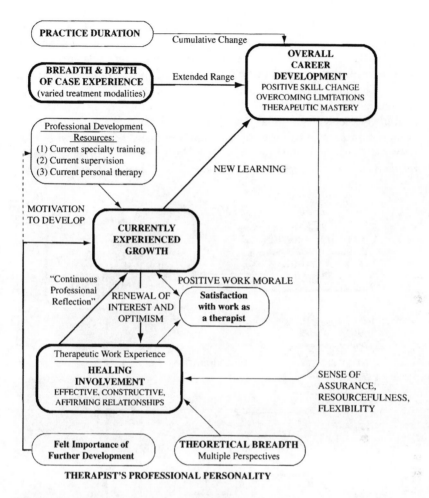

Figure 14.1 Positive developmental cycle linking therapeutic work to professional development

positively (and independently) influenced by the extent of case experience across varied treatment modalities, and by the length of time the therapist has been in practice.

Negative Cycle

In the same way but with opposite effect, the likelihood for negative, deteriorative development stems from the fact that obstructed, frustrating, emotionally disturbing practice experience (i.e., *Stressful Involvement*) engenders *Currently Experienced Depletion*. The latter feeds back into work with patients in the form of pessimism, avoidance and disinclination to engage personally (occupational demoralization), and feeds forward to erode the practitioner's level of *Cumulative Career Development*—and this, in turn, restricts and undermines the therapist's ability to confront the variety of challenges that patients may present.

Figure 14.2 represents the negative cycle of influence between therapeutic work and professional development, which resembles the positive cycle but includes a number of different variables. The *short inner* loop (lower left quadrant) illustrates the reciprocal relation of *Stressful Involvement* and *Currently Experienced Depletion*. The *long outer* loop (extending

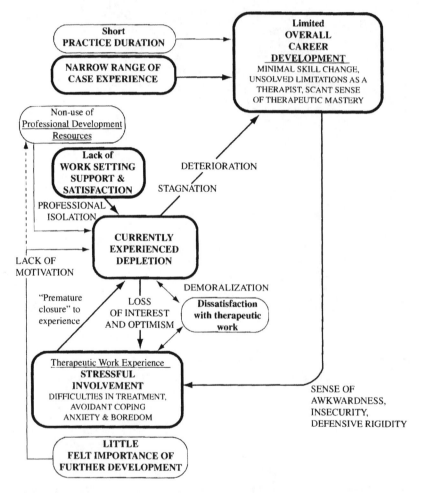

Figure 14.2 Negative developmental cycle linking therapeutic work to professional development

from lower left to upper right quadrant and back) includes the therapists' *Cumulative Career Development*, although the emphasis in this context is on the relative lack of career development.

Stressful Involvement has two main sources. Therapists with a low level of *Cumulative Career Development*—either because they are beginners, or have deteriorated from a higher level—would more likely be relatively awkward, insecure, and rigid in their approach to patients, and elicit negative reactions from patients. Another contributor to *Stressful Involvement* is demoralization and dissatisfaction with therapeutic work, which can affect therapists at all career levels. Therapists who are disillusioned are likely to impart a sense of pessimism and ambivalence to patients that can produce harmful results (e.g., Henry, Schacht, & Strupp, 1990).

Lack of motivation for further professional development and, independently, a lack of support in one's main work setting, are also sources of *Currently Experienced Depletion*. The character of these influences imply that therapists who are motivated to continue their development, and who feel well supported at work, are less prone to *Currently Experienced Depletion*—even when their practice becomes a *Stressful Involvement*. *Currently Experienced Depletion* can be further diminished by the use of resources such as supervision, continuing education, and personal therapy.

In the longer term, *Currently Experienced Depletion* has a negative impact on *Cumulative Career Development*. Minimally, it may promote a state of stagnation, and at worst, a protracted period of *Currently Experienced Depletion* can induce a process of deterioration. In turn, limited or diminished career development increases the probability that therapeutic work will be a *Stressful Involvement* rather than a *Healing Involvement* for the therapist since, all things being equal, lack of adequate career development will be reflected in a sense of awkwardness and insecurity in the therapist's approach and a tendency to defensive rigidity under pressure. On the other hand, a high level of *Cumulative Career Development* moderates the effect of the negative developmental cycle by minimizing the long-term impact of *Currently Experienced Depletion*. This mitigating effect, unfortunately, is not available to therapists at an early stage in their careers, for whom large doses of support through supervision, training, personal therapy, and in their main work setting, are essential in limiting the negative effect of *Stressful Involvement*.

Temporal Sequence

When viewed as temporally extended, stretched out through time, these apparently circular cycles are seen as spirals of influence that operate concurrently, one promoting positive development and the other instigating a process of decline. Every therapist's experience of practice reflects some level of *Healing Involvement* and some degree of *Stressful Involvement*, and

275

hence some positive and some negative developmental pressure. The actual course of a therapist's development is determined by the balance between these two interrelated and partially interpenetrating cycles as they operate *concurrently.*

The balance between *Healing Involvement* and *Stressful Involvement* tends to shift over time as the levels of each change in response to varying conditions, such as the addition or departure of difficult patients from the therapists' caseloads, the acquisition or loss of a supportive supervisor, or a gradual increase in therapeutic mastery as the therapist matures. The balance between *Currently Experienced Growth* and *Currently Experienced Depletion* may also shift over time as the levels of each change, largely but not solely as a response to variations in the quality of the therapist's work experience.

Sequential Development

The *sequential* aspect of the Cyclical/Sequential Model reflects the unfolding course of change over time in individual practitioners. This is represented schematically in Figure 14.3, which traces the ongoing interplay of positive and negative developmental cycles from Time 1 (on the left) to Time 3 (on the right).

The levels of *Healing Involvement* and *Stressful Involvement* existing at Time 1 jointly determine the levels of current growth and depletion experienced by the therapist, These, in turn, have a strong impact on the therapist's experience of *Healing Involvement* and *Stressful Involvement* at Time 2. At the same time, the levels of current growth and depletion at Time 1 contribute to the therapist's overall experience of *Cumulative Career Development,* which also (but more indirectly) affects the therapist's experience of *Healing Involvement* and *Stressful Involvement* at Time 2. With the further passage of time, changing or stable levels of *Healing Involvement* and *Stressful Involvement* at Time 2 influence the extent of current growth and depletion experienced by the therapist, which contribute to shaping the therapist's practice experience, and level of overall development, at Time 3.

As this sequential unfolding proceeds—from Time 3 to Time 4, and so forth—the therapist's practice experience may fluctuate from an effective pattern to a distressing one (or vice versa), and, correspondingly, the therapist's experience of current development may alter from progress to flux to regress (or vice versa, as dictated by actual circumstances).

Through these circumstantial variations, the passage of time typically brings an increasing level of *Cumulative Career Development* for most therapists—that is, a noticeable improvement in therapeutic skills, a gradual surpassing of past limitations, and a progressive rise in current level of therapeutic mastery. This steady upward trend also must be reckoned

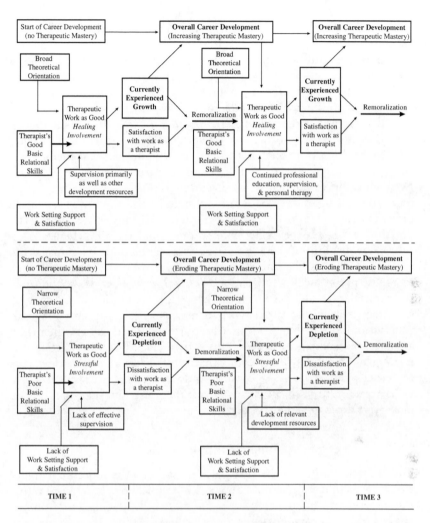

Figure 14.3 Temporal sequence of therapeutic work and positive and negative developmental cycles

as an important factor as the complex linkages between therapeutic work and professional development evolve.

An interesting question arises from the foregoing model about *novice* therapists at the point when they are about to begin to practice (Time 0). In theory, neither positive and negative states of currently experienced development, nor an accumulated level of overall career development, can exist. How, then, does the development process begin? How is a therapist who has no prior clinical experience able to engage patients in a way that generates an experience of *Healing Involvement*? By the same token, how can a beginning therapist prevent or limit how much therapeutic work becomes a *Stressful Involvement*? How can the developmental cycles get started as a rewarding rather than a depleting experience for the *novice* therapist?

To answer this question, we point to a key aspect of *Healing Involvement* (shown in Figure 14.3): a factor that was identified in analyses of the DPCCQ as the therapist's *Basic Relational Skills*. These include the ability to engage with others in a helping alliance, to empathize with others who differ from oneself, to be natural in interpersonal encounters, and to communicate understanding and concern to persons in distress. Even when our respondents "first began ... training as a therapist," they report possessing of these basic skills at high levels, which we have interpreted as the "natural therapeutic talent" (Orlinsky et al., 1998) that practitioners have when they enter professional training. Figure 14.3 shows how beginning therapists who possess good basic relational skills will infuse these skills into their therapeutic work, and thus will tend to experience clinical practice as a *Healing Involvement*. If, in addition, their initial training has provided a theoretical orientation broad enough to guide them with a variety of patients, *and* if they receive adequate supervision, *and* if they work in a supportive clinical milieu, then they are likely to experience a sense of investment and efficacy in practice and feelings of "Flow" during sessions that typify *Healing Involvement*. On the other hand, when these conditions do not occur, the result is likely to be *Stressful Involvement* for the novice therapist, and the beginning of a negative developmental cycle.

Practical Implications

The research findings of the SPR/CRN project and the conceptual model based on them have a number of practical implications for clinical training, supervision, and practice. These are more fully described in Rønnestad & Orlinsky's *How Psychotherapists Develop* (2005).

Training

Beginning therapists need to have good basic relational skills, and this should be one of the main concerns in selecting candidates for training. However, once selected and given initial training, the overriding implication of our findings is to urge that practicum settings ensure, as far as possible, that *novice* and *apprentice* therapists experience *Healing Involvement* with patients, and minimize detrimental experiences of *Stressful Involvement*. This requires that training cases are carefully selected to match the skill level of beginning therapists, and that trainees have been provided

278

with the skills they will need to treat these cases. The provision of supervisory and peer support is also essential. With appropriate training and supervision—but only with these—we also recommend a relatively early exposure to clinical work. This is based on reports by therapists at all career levels that working directly with patients is the leading positive influence on their development. Moreover, to optimize learning, this early practice should include participation in a range of treatment modalities— couple, family, and group therapy (as co-therapists with more experienced clinicians)—as well as individual therapy.

Supervision

The importance of clinical supervision is reflected in its consistent ranking, by practitioners at all career levels, as one of the three main positive influences on their development. In fact, supervision was ranked as the *most* important influence by *novice* therapists. The value of supervision is indicated by surprising fact that more than half of *established* therapists and more than a third of *seasoned* therapists reported they were still seeking supervision for some cases. The use that therapists make of supervision clearly extends beyond what their initial training may require.

However, our study also highlights a negative potential of supervision, which is linked to the fact it often functions as a means for evaluating of the trainee's competence and suitability to become a professional practitioner. This creates a power differential between supervisor and supervisee that can easily undermine the supportive aspect of the supervisory relationship. Recent research on non-optimal supervision has highlighted conflicts in supervision (Moskowitz & Rupert, 1983), distorted and restricted communication (Yourman & Farber, 1996), non-disclosure of relevant material (Ladany, Hill, Corbett, & Nutt, 1996), counter-productive events (Gray, Ladany, Walker, & Ancis, 2001), impasses (Nigam, Cameron, & Leverette (1997), and other factors that make supervision unhelpful and potentially harmful (Reichelt & Skjerve, 2002). Negative experiences in supervision tend to erode the trainees' self-confidence, and inspire self-doubt about their ability to become effective practitioners. Negative supervisory experiences tend to evoke self-criticism in the trainee, as well as negative personal reactions to the supervisor and negative counter-transferences to clients. When combined with *Stressful Involvement* in therapeutic work, negative experiences in supervision can induce a state of *double traumatization*, a painful and potentially destructive experience to which *novice* and *apprentice* therapists are especially vulnerable. Supervisors need to be constantly aware of the potential for *double traumatization* when supervisees are experiencing *Stressful Involvement* in their work, and remain sensitive to the quality of the supervisory alliance and the need to confront and repair alliance ruptures when they occur.

Practice

The most important implication of our study for practicing therapists stems from the reciprocal influence of the practitioner's positive or negative work morale (growth vs. depletion) and their experience of therapeutic work. Positive morale is both a consequence of and a contributor to *Healing Involvement*, just as demoralization is a consequence of and contributor to *Stressful Involvement*. In effect, therapists' experiences of current growth or depletion can be viewed as indicators of the quality of their work with patients. To assist in monitoring both therapeutic involvement and currently experienced development, we formed two brief self-assessment forms from the most relevant items from the DPCCQ to make a Therapeutic Work Involvement Scales and Current and Career Development Scales, which are reproduced here as Tables 14.1 and 14.2. Any persistent rise in levels of *Stressful Involvement* and/or *Currently Experienced Depletion* should serve as a warning to therapists that corrective measures are indicated.

To therapists who are currently experiencing little or no growth, we recommend considering diversification in their therapeutic practice (e.g., by doing couple, family, or group therapy as well as individual therapy), and encourage broadening their theoretical perspective by learning about other therapeutic approaches. Breadth and depth of experience in diverse treatment modalities facilitate *Cumulative Career Development* more than additional practice in one modality. Theoretical breadth facilitates the experience of therapeutic work as *Healing Involvement*. Another good source of stimulation to consider is supportive individual or peer supervision.

To those currently experiencing more than a little depletion, we urge that they seek ways to protect themselves as well as their patients from potential harm. This can take the form of a change in caseload, where that is possible, to find a better match between their current skills and the challenges presented by patients. Having supportive supervisory or personal therapy relationships also help to buffer the impact of current depletion and *Stressful Involvement* in therapeutic work.

We found that a disproportionate number of practitioners who work *only* in institutional (and especially inpatient) settings were vulnerable to experiencing little growth and more than a little depletion. According to therapists' reports, this is a consequence of the institutional conditions in which they work rather than the challenge presented by treating severely disturbed patients. It is worth noting that the addition of some private practice to the therapist's work load seemed to protect clinicians from this negative effect.

Finally, to indicate the convergent implications of the SPR/CRN study and the qualitative study of practitioners presented elsewhere in this book, we note that two leading sources of professional growth for all therapists are found in supervision (Orlinsky et al., 2001) and in personal psychotherapy (Geller, Norcross, & Orlinsky, 2005). These sources of support and stimulation facilitate the process of "continuous professional reflection" that Rønnestad and Skovholt have found to be an essential factor in therapist development.

Reflections on the Two Models of Therapist Development

Inclusion in this book of a chapter describing the SPR/CRN international study of the development of psychotherapists provides a special opportunity for us to comment on the similarities and differences we see between the conceptual model that emerged from the SPR/CRN study and the one that was presented here in chapter 10. Similarities between the two models are apparent in their names: the SPR/CRN "cyclical/sequential" model and the Minnesota "cyclical/trajectory" model (not surprising, given the overlap in authorship). Another similarity is that both models are based on data collected from therapists at all phases of their professional careers, draw on the unique observational perspective of therapists, and thus reflect subjective experiences that are both directly and indirectly relevant for understanding their professional development.[1]

Additionally, both studies used an inductive (bottom-up) discovery-oriented strategy of data analysis. The SPR/CRN study proceeded from analysis of single items to factor-analysis of thematically related subsets of items, from which meaningful and reliable multi-item dimensional scales were formed, that were, in turn, factor analyzed across subsets to determine an overall set of higher order constructs reflecting therapists' experiences of their professional work and development. The Minnesota study proceeded in a similar way from the initial step of identifying specific themes or meaning units that were subsequently organized into successively more general categories.

The most significant difference at the root of the two models is that the SPR/CRN study was a extensive survey using quantitative research methodology, whereas the Minnesota study was an intensive interview study that used qualitative research methods. The data of the SPR/CRN study consisted of responses, from several thousand therapists in many countries, to structured- response items in a wide-ranging but predesigned questionnaire that presented limited opportunity for follow-up questions to explore the meaning of a therapist's response in greater detail. By contrast, that data of the Minnesota study consisted of audio-recordings and transcriptions of live interviews with 100 therapist/counselors in one

Table 14.1   SPR Collaborative Research Network — Development of Psychotherapists

THERAPIST WORK INVOLVEMENT SCALES[†]

Therapist Identification Code: _____   Date: _____

0 = None ...... 5 = Total

1.   How much <u>satisfaction</u> do you currently find in your work as   0 1 2 3 4 5
      a therapist?

2.   How much <u>dissatisfaction</u> do you currently feel in your work   0 1 2 3 4 5
      as a therapist?

Overall, at the <u>present</u> time...   0 = Not at all.... 5 = Very

3.   How effective are you at engaging patients in a working   0 1 2 3 4 5
      alliance?

4.   How 'natural' (authentically personal) do you feel while   0 1 2 3 4 5
      working with patients?

5.   How empathic are you in relating to patients with whom you   0 1 2 3 4 5
      had relatively little in common?

6.   How effective are you in communicating your understanding   0 1 2 3 4 5
      and concern to your patients?

Currently, how would you describe yourself as a therapist—your actual style or manner
with patients?

0 = Not at all, **1** = Some, **2** = Much, **3** = Very much   **0** = Not at all, **1** = Some, **2** = Much, **3** = Very much

7.	Accepting.	0 1 2 3	14.	Involved.	0 1 2 3
8.	Committed.	0 1 2 3	15.	Organized.	0 1 2 3
9.	Detached.	0 1 2 3	16.	Reserved.	0 1 2 3
10.	Effective.	0 1 2 3	17.	Skillful.	0 1 2 3
11.	Friendly.	0 1 2 3	18.	Subtle.	0 1 2 3
12.	Guarded.	0 1 2 3	19.	Tolerant.	0 1 2 3
13.	Intuitive.	0 1 2 3	20.	Warm.	0 1 2 3

Currently, how often do you feel ...?

0 = Never, **1** = Rarely, **2** = Occasionally, **3** = Moderately, **4** = Often, **5** = Very often

21.   Unsure how best to deal effectively with a patient.   0 1 2 3 4 5

22.   Lacking in confidence that you can have a beneficial effect on   0 1 2 3 4 5
      a patient.

23.   Unable to have much real empathy for a patient's   0 1 2 3 4 5
      experiences.

24.   Demoralized by your inability to find ways to help a patient.   0 1 2 3 4 5

Currently, how often do you feel ...?

0=Never, 1=Rarely, 2=Occasionally, 3=Moderately, 4=Often, 5=Very often

25. Unable to withstand a patient's emotional neediness. 0 1 2 3 4 5

26. Distressed by your powerlessness to affect a patient's tragic life situation. 0 1 2 3 4 5

27. Unable to generate sufficient momentum to move therapy with a patient in a constructive direction. 0 1 2 3 4 5

28. Conflicted about how to reconcile obligations to a patient and equivalent obligations to others. 0 1 2 3 4 5

When in difficulty, how often do you...?

0=Never, 1=Rarely, 2=Occasionally, 3=Moderately, 4=Often, 5=Very often

29. Review privately with yourself how the problem has arisen. 0 1 2 3 4 5

30. Seek some form of alternative satisfaction away from therapy. 0 1 2 3 4 5

31. Try to see the problem from a different perspective. 0 1 2 3 4 5

32. Simply hope that things will improve eventually. 0 1 2 3 4 5

33. Consult about the case with a more experienced therapist. 0 1 2 3 4 5

34. Discuss the problem with a colleague. 0 1 2 3 4 5

35. See whether you and your patient can together deal with the difficulty. 0 1 2 3 4 5

36. Seriously consider terminating therapy. 0 1 2 3 4 5

37. Avoid dealing with the problem for the present. 0 1 2 3 4 5

38. Show your frustration to the patient. 0 1 2 3 4 5

39. Criticize a patient for causing you trouble. 0 1 2 3 4 5

40. Just give yourself permission to experience difficult or disturbing feelings. 0 1 2 3 4 5

Recently in sessions with patients, how often have you found yourself feeling...

0 = Not at all, 1=Some, 2=Much, 3 = Very much   0 = Not at all, 1=Some, 2=Much, 3 = Very much

41.	Absent	0 1 2 3	47.	Inattentive	0 1 2 3
42.	Anxious	0 1 2 3	48.	Inspired	0 1 2 3
43.	Bored	0 1 2 3	49.	Overwhelmed	0 1 2 3
44.	Challenged	0 1 2 3	50.	Pressured	0 1 2 3
45.	Drowsy	0 1 2 3	51.	Stimulated	0 1 2 3
46.	Engrossed	0 1 2 3	52.	Trapped	0 1 2 3

(continued)

Table 14.1   Continued

Scoring:

Healing Involvement =

[(7 + 8 + 10 + 11 + 13 + 14 + 15 + 17 + 18 + 19 + 20 + 44 + 46 + 48 + 51) x 5] + [(3 + 4 + 5 + 6 + 29 + 31 + 33 + 34 + 35 + 40) x 3] / 25.

Stressful Involvement =

[(41 + 42 + 43 + 45 + 47 + 49 + 50 + 52) x 5] + [(21 + 22 + 23 + 24 + 25 + 26 + 27 + 28 + 30 + 32 + 36 + 37 + 38 + 39) x 3] / 22.

---

†Orlinsky, D. E., & Rønnestad, M. H. (2005). *How psychotherapists develop: A study of therapeutic work and professional growth.* Washington, D. C.: American Psychological Association.

geographic area, but often with one or more follow-up sessions both initially and, for some, looking back and reconsidering after many years had passed. Accordingly, somewhat different aspects of therapists' personal and professional experience were accessible in each study, and different elements were emphasized in the models of development that emerged from them.

One basic difference between the two models is the emphasis in the Minnesota cyclical/trajectory model on the therapist's experience of challenge or difficulty and work overload, as a main source or stimulus towards professional development, whereas the data supporting the SPR/CRN cyclical/sequential model highlight the importance of positive work experience (specifically, *Healing Involvement*) as the root of therapist development. In the Minnesota model, difficulties or challenges serve as irritants that initiate development (like sand grains in a pearl oyster) by producing an experience of work overload. This stressful experience provokes the therapist to reflect on the factors that caused the work overload, and the outcome of this reflective process determines whether the therapist's development will progress or stagnate. As illustrated in Figure 10.1, when effective or functional closure is attained, a progressive developmental trajectory ensues. Alternatively, if the reflective process is too limited, a trajectory leading to disengagement tends to follow; and when the reflective process continues but fails to attain an adequate closure, the result for the therapist is exhaustion. By contrast, the SPR/CRN model of development is rooted in the experience of therapeutic work as a healing involvement. This has its roots in the therapist's basic interpersonal skills, which are exercised, tested, and stretched to a new level of refinement. Thus, experiences of adversity are viewed in the Minnesota model as the origin of trajectories that lead alternatively to positive development or one of the two forms of professional stagnation (i.e., to exhaustion or disengagement). Experiences of success rather than difficulty in helping clients are depicted as the main source of development in the SPR/CRN model.

Table 14.2   SPR Collaborative Research Network — Development of Psychotherapists

THERAPIST PROFESSIONAL DEVELOPMENT SCALES[†]

Therapist Identification Code: _____   Date: _____

Overall ...   Years   Months

1. **How long is it since you first began to practice psychotherapy?**
   [Count practice during and after training but exclude periods when you did not practice.]   ____   ____

<u>Since</u> <u>you</u> <u>began</u> working as a therapist...

0=Not at all **1**=Slightly **2**=Somewhat **3**=Moderately **4**=Much **5** =Very much

2. How much have you <u>changed</u> overall as a therapist?   0 1 2 3 4 5

3. How much do you regard this overall change as progress or <u>improvement</u>?   0 1 2 3 4 5

4. How much have you succeeded in <u>overcoming</u> past limitations as a therapist?   0 1 2 3 4 5

5. How much have you realized your full <u>potential</u> as a therapist?   0 1 2 3 4 5

Overall, at the <u>present</u> time...

0=Not at all **1**=Slightly **2**=Somewhat **3**=Moderately **4**=Much **5**=Very much

6. How much mastery do you have of the techniques and strategies involved in practicing therapy?   0 1 2 3 4 5

7. How well do you understand what happens moment-by-moment during therapy sessions?   0 1 2 3 4 5

8. How well are you able to detect and deal with your patients' emotional reactions to you?   0 1 2 3 4 5

9. How good are you at making constructive use of your personal reactions to patients?   0 1 2 3 4 5

10. How much precision, subtlety and finesse have you attained in your therapeutic work?   0 1 2 3 4 5

11. How capable do you feel to guide the development of other therapists?   0 1 2 3 4 5

In your <u>recent</u> psychotherapeutic work, how much ...

0=Not at all **1**=Slightly **2**=Somewhat **3**=Moderately **4**=Much **5** =Very much

12. Do you feel you are changing as a therapist?   0 1 2 3 4 5

13. Does this change feel like progress or improvement?   0 1 2 3 4 5

14. Does this change feel like decline or impairment?   0 1 2 3 4 5

15. Do you feel you are overcoming past limitations as a therapist?   0 1 2 3 4 5

16. Do you feel you are becoming more skillful in practicing therapy?   0 1 2 3 4 5

17. Do you feel you are deepening your understanding of therapy?   0 1 2 3 4 5

18. Do you feel a growing sense of enthusiasm about doing therapy?   0 1 2 3 4 5

19. Do you feel you are becoming disillusioned about therapy?   0 1 2 3 4 5

20. Do you feel you are losing your capacity to respond empathically?   0 1 2 3 4 5

21. Do you feel your performance is becoming mainly routine?   0 1 2 3 4 5

22. How important to you is your further development as a therapist?   0 1 2 3 4 5

Scoring:

Overall Career Development $= (2 + 3 + 4 + 5 + 6 + 7 + 8 + 9 + 10 + 11) / 10$

Currently Experienced Growth $= (12 + 13 + 15 + 16 + 17 + 18) / 6$
Currently Experienced Depletion $= (14 + 19 + 20 + 21) / 4$

---

†Orlinsky, D. E., & Rønnestad, M. H. (2005). *How psychotherapists develop: A study of therapeutic work and professional growth.* Washington, D. C.: American Psychological Association.

Another difference is that the Minnesota model presents one trajectory of continuing professional development and two trajectories whose outcomes reflect different modes of professional stagnation, whereas the SPR/CRN model distinguishes one positive and one negative cycle of development that can shift over time in relative salience without defining a specific trajectory. On the other hand, the SPR/CRN model distinguishes between short-term developmental effects (currently experienced growth or depletion) and long-term results (cumulative career development or decline), whereas the Minnesota model does not discriminate between short-term and long-term phases of development and instead presents its three trajectories as a more or less continuous processes of transformation.

Finally, the Minnesota model focuses on continuous professional reflection as the central strategic consideration in determining whether the therapist's professional (and personal) experiences lead to positive development or one of the forms of stagnation. Insufficient or limited self-reflection by therapists leads to premature closure, which, in turn, leads to disengagement. Inadequacy or lack of closure in the therapist's reflective process results in exhaustion due to work overload. Alternatively, attainment of functional closure or problem resolution in the therapist's reflective process results in the continued professional development. There is nothing in the SPR/CRN model that resembles "continuous professional reflection" as a key determinant of development, although it was recognized as a likely mediator linking *Healing Involvement* to *Currently Experienced Growth* (see Figure 14.1).

The question that confronts us is, can the two conceptual models can be integrated? Can sufficient convergence or complementarity between them be found to serve as a basis for more comprehensive model? We believe that they can and turn next to consider the changes that might make this possible.

First among these changes has to be clarification of what is meant by 'difficulties' in the two models, and a proposal to consistently use the term *challenges* in its place. In the SPR/CRN model, frequently experienced difficulty is a core component of therapists' *Stressful Involvement*, the leading predictor of the negative developmental outcome known as *Currently Experienced Depletion*. It is important to note that while experiences of difficulty were not part of the therapist's complementary experience of *Healing Involvement* with clients, there was no indication that difficulty was incompatible with *Healing Involvement*; and, in fact, there was a clear hint in this pattern of therapist experience that difficulties do arise occasionally but are met with constructive coping strategies. It is also important to recall that SPR/CRN study found a variable level of *Stressful Involvement*—and thus some amount of difficulty—characterized the experience of therapeutic work for all therapists.

Based on these considerations, it seems worthwhile to distinguish more clearly between difficulties met with constructive coping (as in *Healing Involvement*), and difficulties that are met with unhelpful coping strategies (as in *Stressful Involvement*), by calling the former challenges and reserving the term *difficulties* for the latter case. The difference is one of shades or nuances of meaning, and should not be overemphasized. We could reasonably say that difficulties reflect therapeutic challenges that were not successfully met, whereas challenges are difficulties that have been effectively mastered.

Looking at the Minnesota model of developmental trajectories (shown in Figure 14.1), one way that the distinction just made between challenges and difficulties might be depicted would be to start the cycle from a box in the diagram representing experiences that test the therapist's clinical skill. Then, if the therapist coped with the test situation successfully, an arrow would lead to the box labeled challenge representing the start a positive or growthful developmental trajectory. Alternately, if the therapist did not meet the test, an arrow would lead to a box labeled difficulty (work overload), initiating a negative developmental trajectory ending in one or the other form of stagnation. In support of this, we would argue that every new client that therapists see constitutes a test of their clinical skills, and indeed every session with a client to some degree also constitutes—or should constitute—a test of a therapist's clinical skill. When therapists succeed in meeting the challenges and/or coping constructively with clinical situations that test their skill, they experience the deep interest and intrinsic reward that Csikszentmihalyi (1990, 1996) described as "flow" (identified as an element in *Healing Involvement*). The likelihood of therapists responding successfully to a test is greater if they command a broad array of theoretical perspectives (found in the SPR/CRN study) and possesses the cognitive complexity and flexibility (found in the Minnesota study) to deploy those as resources for perceiving and meeting the client's needs.

The Minnesota study found that therapists' openness to experience, awareness of complexity (and absence of dogmatism), tolerance for ambiguity, meta-cognition, and an attitude of inquisitiveness are important parameters that facilitate optimal professional development. These characteristics may be seen as aspects of the capacity for cognitive complexity, expressed for example in therapists' ability to integrate different theoretical perspectives. In this volume, Rønnestad and Skovholt wrote:

> In our view the *one dominant "open"* and the *multiple attachment* attitudes are expressions of an inquisitive, curious and exploring stance, which we interpreted to be conducive to optimal professional development. The *laissez-faire* and *true believer* attitudes, however, may be restricted in their learning and developmental potential and may be candidates for later stagnation.

The capacity for cognitive complexity represents a bridge between the Minnesota study and the SPR/CRN study. The capacity for cognitive complexity enables therapists to engage in professional reflection and attain the effective closure that leads to continued development—similar to the SPR/CRN observation that theoretical breadth contributed significantly to likelihood of the therapists' experiencing *Healing Involvement.*

A second modification that might lead to a combined model of therapist development centers on the Minnesota model's proposal of "continuous professional reflection" as the key factor differentiating between the trajectories that lead to continued development, exhaustion, and disengagement—but which is only minimally represented in the SPR/CRN model (Figures 14.1 to 14.3). Limited or insufficient professional reflection about the difficulties that lead to work overload produces premature closure in which the therapist opts for an overly simple and often self-serving view of problems (e.g., the client is unmotivated or not suitable for treatment), which results in a state of therapist disengagement. Engagement in professional reflection that fails to achieve adequate closure or problem-resolution with respect to difficulties experienced with clients results in a state of therapist exhaustion. By contrast, engagement in professional reflection that leads to effective closure or problem-resolution in coping with the challenges involved in treating clients results in continued development for the therapist.

Where might this key factor of in professional reflection be found or fit into the SPR/CRN model of development? Our answer is that professional reflection can be identified, not only as a potential mediating variable between *Healing Involvement* and *Currently Experienced Development* (as shown in Figure 14.1), but also as the process that results in new learning along the path leading from *Currently Experienced Development* to *Overall Career Development*. In other words, reaching effective closure in continuous professional reflection is the process through which ongoing, short-term experiences of current growth are transformed into cumulative, long-term (i.e., "continued") professional development. The diagram in Figure 14.1 could easily be amended by inserting the phrases "effective closure" and "continuing professional reflection" (with "new learning") to explain more clearly the condition that allows current growth to become career development. To support this interpretation, we cite the SPR/CRN study's finding that cumulative development is facilitated most strongly by breadth and depth of case experience in different treatment modalities—more so even than the number of years in practice (Orlinsky & Rønnestad, 2005). This breadth and depth of case experience provides fertile ground for stimulating the therapist's reflections about the contrasting and convergent facets of therapy and about the aspects of clients that are most effectively revealed and treated in different modalities (e.g., relationship problems treated in individual vs. couples therapy).

Similarly, the interruptions and failures of "professional reflection" represented in the Minnesota model by trajectories leading (respectively) to "disengagement" and "exhaustion" as forms of stagnation can be located in the SPR/CRN model (Figure 14.2) along the path leading from currently experienced depletion to stagnation or deterioration resulting in limited career development. This would be made more likely if the therapist's case experience was narrower or more superficial range (e.g., only in individual therapy, and mainly with fairly similar clients), and if the therapist had been practicing a relatively short time—which highlights the vulnerability of novice and apprentice therapists and their need for supervisory and peer support, as emphasized elsewhere (e.g., chapter 10, this volume; Rønnestad & Orlinsky, 2000, 2005). As the negative effect of currently experienced depletion is tempered by practice duration, we would hypothesize that (other things being equal) stagnation would more likely take the form of disengagement among highly experienced therapists and would more likely result in "exhaustion" among relatively inexperienced therapists.

The Minnesota model could likewise be modified to better reflect the fact that currently experienced growth also serves to regenerate and renew the therapist's work morale, reducing or eliminating the stresses involved in therapeutic work, improving the therapist's resilience and increasing the likelihood that 'tests' provided by clients will continue to be well met.

For example, Figure 14.2 might be modified to do this by adding a feed-back loop from "challenges met" to "tests of clinical skills."

Thus, with relatively minor modifications and extensions, both to the SPR/CRN model and the Minnesota study model, a new conception can emerge from our quantitative and qualitative research data that is both more comprehensive and more detailed in its representation of the development of psychotherapists.

Note

1. Extensions to other observational perspectives have been made by members of the SPR/CRN to examine the relationship between key aspects of therapists' self-perception and client-rated assessments of therapeutic process and outcome (e.g., Heinonen et al., 2009, 2010; Nissen-Lie et al., 2010; Willutzki, 1997).]

Part IV

APPENDICES

APPENDIX A

RESEARCH METHODOLOGY AND SAMPLE FOR SKOVHOLT AND RØNNESTAD (1992/1995) THE EVOLVING PROFESSIONAL SELF

Stages and Themes in Therapist and Counselor Development.

Introduction

When beginning this study, we wanted to construct a model of development with a methodology that had the following characteristics:

1. the inquiry covered the entire professional life span;
2. the analysis took into account both personal and professional sources of influence;
3. the model was research based;
4. the method was qualitative with the use of semi structured interviews and follow up feedback from informants;
5. the inquiry generated knowledge pertaining to broad band parameters (e.g., challenges, emotional reactions, attitudes toward work, influential factors in development, learning method, perceptions of role and working style, conceptual ideas used, and measures of success and satisfaction).

These parameters would then serve as points of entry for data gathering and data analysis.

Methodology

Our methodology was qualitative, a mode of inquiry receiving both commentary and support within the therapy and counselling professions in the United States (Brown, 1989; Goldman, 1982, 1989; Hoshmand, 1989; Howard, 1986; Neimeyer & Resnikoff, 1982; Patton, 1991; Shontz, 1982).

One of the great advantages of this methodology is that it taps into the natural interviewing skills possessed by individuals with training in counseling work. For example, in a qualitative methodology text, Patton (1990) devotes 83 pages to describing interviewing methods in qualitative research. For individuals with intensive counselor training, this chapter, although of high quality, seems to be a summary for beginners. Also, the qualitative research skills of Theoretical Sensitivity (Strauss & Corbin, 1990) parallel what professional therapists and counselors call therapeutic sensitivity. All of the research interviewers in the present study had received this extensive graduate counselor training before beginning the qualitative research work.

Goldman (1989) describes the link between therapy/ counseling practitioner skills and the qualitative research approach.

> Most practitioners never do any formal research after the dissertation, and those who ever read published research find it seldom relates in any meaningful way to their work ... [qualitative methods] invite us to *search*, to *discover*, to come in with lots of blank paper and an incomplete, and loose, conceptual structure, and to try very hard to develop and continually modify the structure over the entire period of the study ... the research has a continuous task of puzzling, developing, and crystallizing ideas all the way through the process. No, these new methods are not for the faint of heart. They demand imagination, courage to face the unknown, flexibility, some creativeness, and a good deal of personal skill in observation, interviewing and self-examination some of the same skills, in fact, required for effective counseling. (pp. 81–83)

Qualitative methodology fits very well with the approach (i.e., understand the person holistically vs. a small reductionistic part), skill development (i.e., depth interviewing vs. a quantitative score), and way of understanding (i.e., textured script pieces woven together to form an individual's life story versus comparison of dependent scores after manipulating an independent variable) of individuals who are practicing therapists and counselors. Their way of understanding the human world through intense interactions with suffering people their clients is very different than the most rigorous scientific methods that the human service fields have borrowed from the natural sciences. We chose this method in part because it fits so well with the way our informants understand their human world while doing their investigative work as practitioners.

Regarding methodology, we have been influenced by Sprinthall (1975), who provided an early invitation to think about methodology in a different way. Also, impactful has been the emerging methodologies within feminist work. Most notable here is *Women's ways of knowing* (Belenky, Clinchy, Goldberger, & Tarule, 1986). The qualitative methodology tradition in Europe has also been influential. For example, see Kvale (1986a, 1987) for a review of dialectical and hermeneutical psychology and methods in Scandinavian countries.

During recent decades, qualitative research methodology has increasingly been applied in different investigation domains. Recently, the use of qualitative research methodology has partly emerged from a critique of the positivist research tradition, the philosophy of science on which this tradition is based, its perspective on validity and reliability, and its methodology. Phenomenology is a primary philosophical foundation for qualitative research methodology. For reviews of the "logical positivist phenomenology inquiry" paradigm debate, see Hoshmand (1989), Lincoln and Guba (1985) and Patton (1991). The arguments for alternate models to the positivist science can be summarized under three groupings (Hoshmand, 1989): (a) epistemological, (b) conceptual empirical, and (c) ideological.

The epistemological arguments against reductive positivist science concern the nature of knowledge, how we know what we know. As Hoshmand (1989) pointed out, meaning context impacts interpretations of observation. There are numerous contributors to this perspective. Constructivists have argued for the impact of language on descriptions of social realities. For example, subject object dualism in inquiry has been severely criticized. As Polkinghorne (1986) pointed out:

> Humans are conceived as meaning givers who compose a conceptual scheme of interpretation through which they determine what counts as objects, while at the same time remaining objects themselves very much like other objects in the world. Each side of the doublet is supposed to yield a complete description without reference to the other. (pp. 144)

Polkinghorne (1986) argues that the fullness of humanness cannot be captured by either position and that the contextual instability of human concepts makes it impossible for the human sciences to become theoretical sciences. Human sciences can at best produce empirical generalizations. Furthermore, the contextual meaning of human concepts not only varies across individuals, but "changes individually as experiences accumulate and as situations change" (p. 144), and furthermore:

> There is enough cross contextual stability in interpretations to produce probability expectations, but not enough to fit into explanatory schemes producing deductive laws. (p. 145)

In the study of professional development, it makes intuitive sense that the continual processing of complex interchanges that the therapist/counselor engages in and observes, leads to changes in contextual meaning of concepts. For our inquiry, it, therefore, seems essential to choose a method of investigation which takes this into account.

The conceptual empirical arguments against reductive experimental methodology concern limitations of its conceptual base. Hoshmand (1989) has formulated the idea that standards of precision by measurement and objectification by operationalism has inappropriately reduced human phenomena to behavioral and biological laws which do not fit with recent conceptual formulations from the study of cognition, physics, and biology. The perspective of active cognition and concepts such as feed forward capacity of the mind, violates reductionistic formulations and are examples of necessary conceptual empirical revisions.

The *ideological arguments* against the reductive experimental methodology concern how one perceives human nature. The reductionistic conceptions of human behavior and the deterministic perception of humans portray a different image than that of humanity characterized by self-determination. Hoshmand (1989) also points to the value aspect of inquiry: "How we map social realities may transform the future that we envision" (p. 9).

Abandoning or supplementing the quantitative methodology with a qualitative methodology, with its accompanying shifts in epistemology and conceptual base, necessitates discussion of standards of reliability and validity of this other method.

Qualitative research presupposes a conception of truth that goes beyond the classical positivist empiricist conceptions of truth. Kvale (1987) refers to the three classical criteria of truth within philosophy: *correspondence, coherence, and pragmatic utility.* The positivist empiricist conception adheres to the correspondence criterion, i.e., degree to which a statement corresponds to some real nature of the world. This conception presupposes subject/object dualism in inquiry and an objective world with unequivocal facts. The coherence criterion, central in rationalist philosophy and in hermeneutical philosophy, "... involves whether a statement is logically coherent, is there an internal logic in the results, do they form good *Gestalt*" (Kvale, 1987, p. 42). One may add here that the search for logical consistency, for example within psychoanalytic concepts, may lead to greater validity on the coherence criterion, without increasing validity on the correspondence criterion. The pragmatic criterion of truth concerns the degree to which a statement has practical consequences, a utility aspect which is so central in pragmatic philosophy.

> Validity of a text interpretation takes place in a dialogue, it is an argumentative discipline, involving a logic of uncertainty and of qualitative probability. It is then illogical to apply a logic of certainty developed for the observation of unequivocal behavioral

facts to the interpretation of ambiguous meanings of texts. (Kvale, 1987, pp. 47–48)

In our investigation, we have strongly emphasized the perspective of *validity through dialogue* which will be accounted for in the description of how we collected our data.

Kvale (1983) has outlined aspects of the phenomenological and hermeneutical mode for understanding the qualitative research interview. It centers on the interviewee's life world; it seeks to understand the meaning of phenomena in her/his life world; it is qualitative, descriptive, and specific, presuppositionless; it focuses on certain themes, is open to ambiguities, it changes, is dependent upon the sensitivity of the interviewer, takes place in an interpersonal interaction, and may be a positive experience.

These aspects are similar to the major themes of the qualitative inquiry of Patton (1990): qualitative designs are naturalistic, i.e., there is no manipulation of the research setting; the designs are inductive; one uses a holistic perspective; one uses qualitative data, i.e., detailed, in depth inquiry, thick descriptions; the inquiry is characterized by personal contact and depends on insight of researcher; there is an attention to dynamic systems, i.e., to process and change; there is a unique case orientation; there is a sensitivity to context, as, for example, social, historical, temporal; the attitude is one of empathic neutrality; and there is design flexibility.

According to Kvale (1983, 1987), one can interpret the interview text at three different levels: the self-understanding level, the common sense level, and the theoretical level. At the first level, the researcher aims at clarifying how the interviewee understands the meaning of what is communicated. The validation of statements at this level is simply agreement or disagreement by the interviewee. At the second level, interpretations go beyond the interviewee's own understanding. A broader, common sense aspect is added. The validity of statements at this level is contingent upon logical coherence and upon general consensus of common sense interpretations among readers. At the third level, interpretation is made from relevant theory. The validation process entails assessing if interpretations follow logically from theory. Specific theoretical competence is required both to generate theoretical interpretations and to assess validity of interpretations.

Kvale (1983) has pointed to the continuum between description and interpretation and has outlined six possible phases of interpretation. During the first phase, the interviewee describes spontaneously his/her life world, i.e., what he/she does, feels, and thinks about a theme. Here, and in the subsequent phase, there is no interpretation. During the second phase, the interviewee discovers new relations spontaneously, on the basis of own description. In the third phase, the interviewer condenses and interprets the meaning of the interviewee's descriptions. This, occurring during the

297

interview, enables the interviewee to provide verification or correction of interpretations. At this stage, the interview has the form of a dialogue.

The fourth phase represents a shift, in that at this point the interviewer or another person interprets a completed and transcribed interview. At this phase, the interpretation can be made at the level of self-understanding, at the common sense level or at the theoretical level. The fifth phase is called a reinterview because the initial interview is analyzed and reinterpreted and forms a base for a new interchange. A possible sixth phase is also suggested; here new insight leads to action.

The hermeneutical circle is a concept used to tap the process of arriving at better interpretations of meaning. The essence of this concept is that both the meaning of parts of the text and global meaning of the text are continually modified through an analysis of both. One arrives at a better understanding of the parts through analysis of the global meaning, and one arrives at a better analysis of the global meaning through analysis of parts. This is a continuous and, in principle, finite back and forth process where one reworks the data shifting emphasis on parts and wholes. The process ends when one has arrived at a coherent, part whole unity, free of contradictions (Kvale, 1983).

Our Specific Method

Inductive analysis (Patton, 1990) served as our overall focus. Our specific method of inquiry was a modified version of what has been labeled the "constant comparative method of analysis" (Glaser & Strauss, 1967, pp. 101–116) or Grounded Theory Methodology (Strauss & Corbin, 1990). This involves a continual reexamination and modification of the data. Grounded Theory is inductively derived from studying the phenomenon it represents which is discovered, developed, and refined. This research study was conducted over five years (1986–1990) and consisted of five phases.

Phase 1

We began with our own written work with a background of work on the topic of supervision (Rønnestad, 1977, 1982, 1983), professional development (Rønnestad, 1985; Skovholt, 1985), our own work as supervisors and teachers in graduate programs, our own work as practitioners, and the literature on professional development, e.g., literature on stages of development, supervision, occupational burnout. From this base, we developed a 23-item questionnaire (included in this appendix) that was refined through a series of pilot interviews. We also used this base to create eight categories for structuring the flow of data. They are Definition of the Stage, Central Task, Predominant Affect, Sources of Influence, Role and

Working Style, Conceptual Ideas Used, Learning Process, and Measure of Effectiveness and Satisfaction.

Phase 2

This was the initial data gathering phase in the study. One to one-and-a-half hour individual interviews with therapists/counselors as informants served as the first data gathering method. Here we were guided by Kvale (1983, 1986a, 1986b, 1987), the Norwegian methodologist, and Patton (1990), regarding use and validity in the interview method of data collection.

We interviewed a group of 100 therapists/counselors who were divided by education and experience into five groups from the first year of graduate school to 40 years beyond graduate school. This use of education and experience in therapy/counseling as the developmental level variables is similar to the conceptualizations of Dreyfus and Dreyfus (1986) in their work on expertise.

In studying professional development, this kind of cross sectional design contains both strengths and limitations. There is the possibility of cohort differences confounding stage differences. However, according to a leading developmental researcher (James Rest, personal communication, March 28, 1991), there is a legitimate place for cross sectional design in studies of development. Most criticisms of cross sectional designs have occurred within the framework of quantitative methods (e.g., Ellis, 1991). Our methodology was quantitative and contained two elements that made it a modified cross sectional design: (a) 60 of our 100 informants were again interviewed 2 years after the first interview; (b) informants provided information regarding their own development at earlier education and experience points. Despite these qualifications, a longitudinal study over 30 years would have been advantageous as compared with the current design.

The total sample consisted of 50 females and 50 males, 96 Whites and four minorities with a mean age of 42.4, standard deviation of 12.4, and a range in age from 24 to 71. (Although the ethnic diversity may reflect the professional population in Minnesota, it does limit the transferability of the results.) These individuals had graduate training in 34 different universities and had been in 47 different programs in these universities. The sample group had received Master's degrees from 29 different universities and within these 29 universities had been in 37 different graduate programs. At the doctoral level, this sample group had received doctorates from 26 different universities and been in 37 different graduate programs in these 26 universities. Since the sample group was interviewed within the Twin Cities area of Minneapolis and St Paul, the large university in that area, the University of Minnesota, was the modal university for training at both the Master's and doctoral levels. Individuals in the sample received training within different graduate programs at this university.

The sample group consisted of 23 individuals who had a doctorate in counseling psychology or a very closely related field, 21 individuals who had a doctorate in clinical psychology and 17 who had a doctorate in a closely related field such as school psychology and human development. Fifty-six of the hundred person sample were licensed at the doctoral level and this included almost all of those individuals who were eligible, that is the postdoctoral psychologists. Ten individuals were Diplomates of the American Board of Professional Psychology, the highest credential in the field. Five were in clinical psychology, three in counseling, and two in school. These 100 individuals had had practicum, internship, and current work experience in a wide variety of settings such as agencies, hospitals, academics, industrial settings in a variety of states and cities in the United States.

The five groups in the sample can be described as follows: Group A consists of 20 individuals who were interviewed during the first year of their graduate program in either counseling or clinical psychology at one of four different graduate programs, at two different universities. Reflecting the general gender and racial composition of members in these programs, there were 16 females and 4 males. Eighteen of these individuals were Caucasian, two were minorities. Seventeen were U.S. citizens and three were non-U.S. citizens. The average age was 32 with a standard deviation of 7 and a range of 24 to 47. Individuals at the lower end of the age range often were coming to graduate school immediately after a bachelor's degree whereas people at the upper range often had had extensive employment in one or more occupations. These individuals had a wide variety of experience in human services, often as volunteers or paraprofessionals in a human service capacity of some kind.

Group B consisted of 20 advanced doctoral students who had had at least 4 years of graduate school. Some of these individuals were in their doctoral internship at the time of the interview; some had already finished the internship and were working on the dissertation. All of these individuals were doctoral students at the University of Minnesota in one of two different departments and one of three separate programs in these departments. All of these individuals were in counseling or clinical psychology. There were 13 females and seven males. Nineteen were White; one was a minority. All were American citizens and the average age was 33 with a standard deviation of 4.2 and ranged from age 26 to 44. These individuals had had a wide variety of pre professional experiences and, in addition, had also had a variety of practicum and internship experiences.

Group C, as with Groups D and E, were chosen from the membership of the Minnesota Psychological Association. Members of this group of individuals had received the doctorate and had had approximately 5 years of post-doctoral experience. The group was chosen based on a number of factors such as being active as a practitioner, being accessible for the interviews, i.e., living within the greater Twin Cities metropolitan area, willingness to conduct the interview, accessibility in terms of being able to be contacted. Also, there was a general attempt, as in Groups D and E, to find some balance across the group in terms of degrees, training program, and work setting. This group consisted of eleven females and nine males. All these individuals were Caucasian and all were US citizens. The average age was 37 with a standard deviation of 6.1 ranging from 31 to 61. This group of 20 had received Master's degrees from 11 different universities and doctorates from one of eight universities, with the University of Minnesota being the predominant graduate university. Nine of these individuals identified themselves as counseling psychologists, eight as clinical psychologists, and three as other. Their current work setting was varied across the group and included settings such as hospitals, public and private agencies, colleges and universities, and private practice.

Group D consists of 20 individuals who had their doctorate and approximately 15 years of post-doctoral experience. They were chosen from membership in the Minnesota Psychological Association and lived in the greater Minneapolis St Paul area. Group D reflects a changed gender balance in the sample with a predominance of males. This seems to be true generally in the field, that is, in the entering group of people within the therapy/counseling field in recent years there are many more females than males, whereas in the most senior levels, especially at the higher levels of education, there are more males than females. In Group D, there were 14 males and four females. Nineteen were Caucasian and one was a minority. All these individuals were U.S. citizens. This group was chosen like Group C through trying to find balance between factors cited above. The average age was 47 with a standard deviation of 8.8 and a range of 38 71. These individuals had received Master's degrees from ten different universities and doctorates from 12 different universities with the University of Minnesota being the predominant university. Eight of these individuals identified themselves as counseling psychologists, seven as clinical, five as other. Eighteen were licensed at the doctoral level and one was a Diplomate in counseling. They currently work in the greater Minneapolis St Paul area. These settings included private and public agencies, private practice (which was more predominant than with Group C), and colleges and universities. In their previous experiences, these individuals had worked in a variety of settings.

Group E numbered 20, were chosen from membership in the Minnesota Psychological Association, and lived in the greater Minneapolis St Paul area. All of these individuals had the doctoral degree and approximately 25 years of post-doctoral experience. There were six females and 14 males. All 20 were White. All were U.S. citizens. Average age was 62, standard deviation was 6.4, and the range was 50 to 70. They, as a group, received a Master's degree from eight different universities, and doctorates from one of 10 different universities with the University of Minnesota being the predominant university. Six of these individuals identified themselves as clinical psychologists, five as counseling psychologists, and nine as other. All 20 were licensed at the doctoral level in the state of Minnesota, and nine of them had received the Diplomate from the American Board of Professional Psychology, five in clinical, two in counseling, and two in school. As with Groups C and D, they represented a wide variety of current work settings: private practice, agency, hospital, and academic. They tended to be more in private practice than other groups, although some had recently retired and were involved in part time employment. They had, as a group, a wide variety of post-doctoral experience as well as internships and practicums in many settings.

In addition to the sample of 100, we also interviewed 20 other individuals. Some of whom were interviewed at the beginning pilot phase when we were working on the questionnaire. Others were interviewed to help us derive at the characteristics of people at the Conventional Stage. For this purpose, we interviewed lay helpers. Others were people that we interviewed because they seemed to be knowledgeable informants.

The initial interviews were conducted by a research team of the first author and four doctoral students in counseling psychology at the University of Minnesota (two White males, one White female, and one minority male). Each of the individuals completed one or more pilot interviews. Each interview was audiotaped, lasted one-and one-half hours and was guided by the semi-structured, 23-item questionnaire. (The questionnaire is included at the end of the appendix.) After the 20 interviews in each group were completed, the research team met to discuss the interviews. Using the interview outline as a discussion guide, each debriefing meeting served as an intense cross case analysis (Patton, 1990). At each debriefing, the focus was on capturing essential concepts, subcategories, and categories for the group interviewed (Strauss & Corbin, 1990). These included what Patton (1990) calls sensitizing concepts and indigenous concepts for the group interviewed. The thematic content was then put into the eight categories developed earlier by the two authors in Phase 1. After each debriefing meeting, the first author prepared a written description using these eight categories. Members of the interviewing team and informants were asked to read and assess these preliminary descriptions. Each member of the research team and approximately 25% of the informants (5 of 20 in each group and 25 of 100) read and reacted to these descriptions. Based on this feedback, the preliminary descriptions were revised. This was an essential aspect of our modified "constant comparative" and modified Grounded Theory Methodology research process that was used throughout the study (Strauss & Corbin, 1990).

The lay helper Stage 1: Conventional was constructed differently than the others. Here the insights of the total sample group, a review of the literature on nonprofessional helping, and a sample of lay helpers were used to construct this stage.

Phase 3

As a next step, the senior research assistant listened to 75 of the 100 taped interviews. At least half of the interviews in each group were included in this critique. The research assistant listened for congruity between the revised preliminary written descriptions and the content on the tapes. The research assistant also chose quotes that would illuminate theoretical concepts. As a next step, again using modified "constant comparative" and Grounded Theory Methodology, the authors met and completely reviewed and revised the manuscript on the basis of the 30-page critique of the research assistant and by listening to selected interviews.

Phase 4

Next, 60 of the 100 member sample group were individually re-interviewed. Approximately 12 of the 20 in each of the five sample groups were interviewed for a one-and-one-half-hour period by members of a second research group of the first author, a university staff psychologist (a White female), and three graduate students in counseling psychology (two White females, one White male). Each subject in the second interview responded to the accuracy of one or two of the written stage descriptions and was asked via a short form, "How accurately does this describe you when you were at this stage in terms of education and experience?" (The form used for this interview is included at the end of the appendix). After the second interview, the first author met with each research interviewer individually for those interviews that the first author did not conduct. This use of informants to help the research process is very much in keeping with "constant comparative" Grounded Theory Methodology (GTM) (Strauss & Corbin, 1990).

Using several interviewers and the continual collaboration of the two authors may be perceived of as investigator triangulation as formulated by Denzin (1978) and elaborated by Patton (1990). Checking back with our informants may also be understood as triangulation. Patton (1990) suggested:

> Another approach to analytical triangulation is to have those who were studied review the findings. Evaluators can learn a great deal about the accuracy, fairness, and validity of their data analysis by having the people described in that data analysis react to what is described. (p. 468)

Throughout this process, the authors often met, listened to tapes, discussed and revised the descriptions. Strauss and Corbin (1990) suggest that as researchers "you should be asking questions all along the course of your research project" (p. 59). We attempted to be maximally open to the data presented to us so that we could let concepts, subcategories, and categories emerge or decline. For example, the original differentiation on five levels did not sufficiently account for the variations we observed and we finally ended up with eight stages of therapist/ counselor development.

Phase 5

The process of generating the themes started after we had completed the stage model and was initiated by trying to distill the essence of our findings. First, from a 120-page summary of the narrative, we jointly extracted the strongest themes within each of the eight categories (Definition of the Stage, Central Task, Predominant Affect, Source of Influence, Role and Working Style, Conceptual Ideas Used, Learning Process and Measures of Effectiveness and Satisfaction). Themes were not extracted unless we jointly agreed that the data provided clear and consistent evidence for such a decision. After this initial extraction, the themes were ordered according to strength of the support in the 120-page narrative. Again, this decision was based on a joint decision by us as researchers. At this point, some themes were dropped. Last, the themes, 20 in number, were arranged within the following categories: Primary Characteristic Themes, Process Descriptor Themes, Source of Influence Themes, and Secondary Characteristic Themes. In line with the strength of qualitative research, we believe that the themes, like the earlier stage descriptions, best serve as hypotheses to be proved or disproved by more precise empirical studies.

Phase 6

An initial model of professional development and stagnation was constructed based on data from different data sources (Rønnestad & Skovholt, 1991):

1. The investigation method described above in Phases 1 to 5.
2. Data generated through supervision seminars and supervisory experiences in Norway. For many years, the first author (MHR) conducted a series of workshops on supervision for Norwegian psychologists, psychiatrists and social workers. Theoretical presentations on development and stagnation, and systematic feedback from participants and dialogues with supervisors led to a preliminary presentation on the topic (Ronnestad, 1985). This rotation between presentation and feedback has continued during the last years as well.

3. The methodology of the initial analysis may be conceptualized as source triangulation and as methods triangulation, processes which integrate data from several sources and apply different methods of inquiry (Patton, 1990).

ORIGINAL QUESTIONNAIRE

Introduction

We are aware that there are many issues we could cover when interviewing counselors and therapists. There are issues of public versus private practice, working with groups versus individuals, questions regarding licensure, referrals, ethics, etc. But what we are exclusively interested in is what goes on in the counseling or therapy session. We are hoping to discover if there are common patterns or phases that counselors and therapists go through over the course of their careers. In answering these questions, please use the way you conceptualize counseling and therapy and the methods you use as a frame of reference.

Structured Questions

How does counseling/ therapy work? Has your view of it changed over time?

What characteristics describe you now in relation to your counseling or therapy that might not have applied in the past?

Are you or have you ever been strongly invested in a particular model of counseling/ therapy? Have you ever become disenchanted with that model? How did you come to that conclusion and what did you do as a result?

Transitions

Can you recall and describe any major changes that have occurred along the way? What precipitated them? When did they occur?

Sources of Influence

Theories can be a major source of influence. Which have strongly influenced you? Has this changed over time?

Experience with clients can be a strong influence. Has this been true for you? Can you elaborate?

Do you think of other specific people or groups as playing an important role in your approach? If so, can you describe how they affected you?

Events in your personal life, either positive or negative, can also be a source of influence. Is this true for you? Can you elaborate?

Considering these three separate areas of possible influence theories and research, experience with clients, events in your personal life can you rank them in order of importance in affecting your work?

Personal Theories of Counselor Development

Do you see counseling or therapy becoming more complex or simple for you as you have gained in experience? Can you explain?

Do you see yourself progressing along a continuum (or perhaps more than one)? Can you identify it/them?

Have you ever felt disillusioned with the process of counseling or therapy? What caused this and how did you deal with it?

What kinds of people make the best counselors and therapists? Why?

What causes people to leave the field?

What exactly are the satisfactions you get from your work? Have these changed over time?

Miscellaneous

What effect does working with negative emotions much of the time have on you? How do you relate to these emotions and manage them?

Has comparing your ability to help others versus other counselor/therapists' ability to be helpful been an issue for you? If so, when?

Has your knowledge of counseling or therapy been helpful in resolving your own problems?

What issues do you find difficult or threatening to deal with in the counseling or therapy that you do? Have these changed since you began?

How do you measure your success? Has this always been so?

How do you measure the success of your clients? Has this always been so?

What primarily concerns you in your counseling or therapy thought, emotion, or behavior? How did you come to this view?

Do you find yourself being fairly structured and organized, or having a less structured and more ambiguous approach in your work? Is this different from the past?

Reinterview Form

Stages of Therapist/Counselor Development
Participant's Feedback Form

Participant's Research No. _____

A. How accurate does the content in the *Definition of Stage* Section describe your development when you were at the _____ Stage?

Circle one below.

1	2	3	4	5
It is a very inaccurate description	Part of the description is accurate but most of it is not	The description is about divided between being accurate and inaccurate	Most of the description is accurate but part of it is not	It is a very accurate description

What comments do you have concerning the *Definition of the Stage* **description we have written?**

B. How accurate does the content in the *Central Task Section* describe your development when you were at the _____ Stage?

Circle one below.

1	2	3	4	5
It is a very inaccurate description	Part of the description is accurate but most of it is not	The description is about divided between being accurate and inaccurate	Most of the description is accurate but part of it is not	It is a very accurate description

What comments do you have concerning the *Central Task description* **we have written?**

C. How accurate does the content in the *Predominant Affect* Section describe your development when you were at the _____ Stage?

Circle one below

1	2	3	4	5
It is a very inaccurate description	Part of the description is accurate but most of it is not	The description is about divided between being accurate and inaccurate	Most of the description is accurate but part of it is not	It is a very accurate description

What comments do you have concerning the *Predominant Affect* **description we have written?**

D. How accurate does the content in the Sources of Influence Section describe your development when you were at the _____ _____ Stage?

Circle one below.

1	2	3	4	5
It is a very inaccurate description	Part of the description is accurate but most of it is not	The description is about divided between being accurate and inaccurate	Most of the description is accurate but part of it is not	It is a very accurate description

What comments do you have concerning the *Sources of Influence* **description we have written?**

E. How accurate does the content in the *Role of Working Style* Section describe your development when you were at the _____ _____ Stage?

Circle one below.

1	2	3	4	5
It is a very inaccurate description	Part of the description is accurate but most of it is not	The description is about divided between being accurate and inaccurate	Most of the description is accurate but part of it is not	It is a very accurate description

What comments do you have concerning the *Role of Working Style* **description we have written?**

F. How accurate does the content in the *Conceptual System Used* Section describe your development when you were at the _____ _____ Stage?

Circle one below.

1	2	3	4	5
It is a very inaccurate description	Part of the description is accurate but most of it is not	The description is about divided between being accurate and inaccurate	Most of the description is accurate but part of it is not	It is a very accurate description

What comments do you have concerning the Conceptual System Used description we have written?

G. How accurate does the content in the *Learning Process* Section describe your development when you were at the _____ Stage?

Circle one below.

1	2	3	4	5
It is a very inaccurate description	Part of the description is accurate but most of it is not	The description is about divided between being accurate and inaccurate	Most of the description is accurate but part of it is not	It is a very accurate description

What comments do you have concerning the *Learning Process* description we have written?

H. How accurate does the content in the *Measure of Effectiveness and Satisfaction* Section describe your development when you were at the _____ Stage?

Circle one below.

1	2	3	4	5
It is a very inaccurate description	Part of the description is accurate but most of it is not	The description is about divided between being accurate and inaccurate	Most of the description is accurate but part of it is not	It is a very accurate description

What comments do you have concerning the *Measures of Effectiveness and Satisfaction* description we have written?

APPENDIX B

THEMES IN INTERVIEWS WITH THREE SENIOR INFORMANTS

Introduction

The content in this appendix consists of interviews with three senior informants in our study. All three have 20 to 30 years of experience beyond their graduate training. All three are considered master practitioners in the local Minneapolis St. Paul community and are sought out by younger practitioners for supervision and therapy/counseling.

The interview with Dr. S., a clinical psychologist, was conducted by the first author as part of the original 100 interview sample. The interview with Dr. M., a counseling psychologist, was an extra interview. It was conducted jointly by the two authors. The interview with Dr. A., a clinical psychologist, done jointly by the two authors, was conducted as an extra interview.

Interview with Dr. S.

Dr. S. is a senior clinical psychologist. She is recognized as a master clinician and a very wise practitioner.

I.   How does counseling/ therapy work? Has your view of it changed over time?

Dr. S.   My persuasion is that therapy works because we are creatures of symbols, and we need to understand reality before we can handle it effectively. So, we need accurate labels for things, and that is a form of insight. Then, the process is one of recognizing alternatives and options and going through the process of selecting and testing. The change over time for me was one of becoming less rigid. I started with more of the psychoanalytic persuasion but I could feel myself become more and more eclectic and being more and more inclusive in thinking about diagnosis, the process of therapy and the method of therapy. I would try new things even though I would be rather skeptical. But I increasingly have tried things and, like with most things, what works we keep and the rest, hopefully with a breath of kindness, we blow away.

I.   How does a person know if something works?

Dr. S.   I label it useful if it furthers a process of those things I said were important to the client. Having some knowledge of origins is useful although I got further and further from the historical perspective of psychoanalysis. So I modified the dredging operations of my earlier days.

I.   You have been talking here about becoming less rigid, more and more eclectic and more inclusive. When did that process happen to you?

Dr. S.   It has been a continuing process for me.

I.   What characteristics describe you now in relationship to your therapy that might not have applied in the past?

Dr S.   Well, I am ever so much more patient. Things just don't have to happen. They can be very gradual indeed. In some sense I suppose I don't insist on evidence. I am more willing to make the assumption that as the client encounters various aspects of her/his content, this process makes a difference.

I.   Do you think this says something about a therapist's own increased sense of professional security? Is this the meaning of being ever so much more patient, of realizing that things don't have to happen quickly and insisting less on evidence? In other words, with professional self-confidence, you know it makes you know that one does not need those external markers.

Dr. S.   I think that is a very good way of describing it. As a neophyte therapist, I was much too intense about cure and ever so much more self-conscious about what I was up to until I realized it was the interaction between me and my clients that made the difference, not the ideas I was promulgating.

I.   When did you discover that?

Dr. S.   Oh, I think that came out of my letting go of a more rigid approach. I notice this is also true of the beginning therapists I have supervised at a volunteer counseling center. They are terribly rigid. I think it relates to the extent to which a person feels comfortable with being a therapeutic instrument. You don't have to have 10 rules, you don't have to say certain things, you don't have to get the client to say certain things in order to feel that you're achieving certain things.

I.   In time, you didn't have to be the expert and "on" all the time?

Dr. S.   No, the ease I developed and felt in time was very useful. Formerly, I felt that if I missed something the process would bog down and evaporate in time. Making, controlling, moulding, getting the client to do X, Y, Z—this is the mindset of newer therapists. It is real arrogance, but it also contributes to the therapist's worry that one can be harmful. One is concerned about being harmful when one also has a view of oneself as so important to the client's life.

I.   With this view, one has to be careful of everything he/she does?

Dr. S.   Yes. Weight the phrases, measure the words. That brings me to another change, this is being more free in form.

I.   Have you ever been strongly invested in a particular model of therapy/counseling? Have you ever become disenchanted with this model? If so, how did this change occur?

Dr. S.   Yes, very strongly psychoanalytically oriented. Gradually, the rigidity of this style has left me. The psychoanalytic model was effective but only in limited situations. Psychoanalysis still appeals to me. Periodically through the years, when with a client, I would say to myself—"Freud was right. There it is!" Two factors stand out: (1) The demands of the practice—where short-term approaches are useful. (2) The distancing demands of the Freudian tradition, which are at odds with my personality. In time, it got easier to add my own thinking and my own way of doing things.

I.   Gradually with time, your own personality came through more and more?

Dr. S.   Yes, absolutely.

I.   Theories and research can be a source of influence. Has this been true for you?

Dr. S.   Yes, but not the statistical studies as much as work studies from areas such as philosophy.

I.   More textured work?

Dr. S.   Yes, not the laboratory studies. That always seemed so far away from me.

I.   How about experience with clients as a source of influence?

Dr. S.   That has been a big influence. I am a firm believer that clients teach us a great deal.

I.   How do they do that?

Dr. S.   It occurs through the way they reinforce the therapist. They will say "yes" or "I hadn't thought of that before." They are so reinforcing! They train us. They also taught me a lot about the whole matter of living and struggles that are probably, in many ways, common to all of us. They taught me about their felt needs and what they wanted. Sometimes this was not always what was best for them. When I wasn't as structured with clients, which I did in time, the client could more easily use the therapy to work out relationship problems. Perhaps, for example, I would end up being "Mother" and, in this context, good work could occur.

I.   Why didn't you do this earlier?

Dr. S.   Because I was taught to have a very structured role.

I.   The theoretical approach dictated your role as what?

Dr. S.   Don't get involved, don't encourage people to see you in anything but this blank role.

315

I. How did this change?

Dr. S. Gradually, I just changed through client experiences.

I. Were individuals such as professors, supervisors, mentors a big influence for you?

Dr. S. Not very much. I had one supervisor at the VA who I admired so much and who I wanted to emulate. Later, he changed in a negative way and became more self-absorbed. He disappointed me! He fell from grace!

I. In the mentoring literature, there is discussion of painful endings to mentoring relationship. Was that true for you?

Dr. S. Yes. It was so disappointing! I respected him so much.

I. And that was the best relationship you had with a senior person in the field?

Dr. S. I learned things from other supervisors but I don't think they influenced me in my new found roles.

I. How about the process of being a supervisor/teacher for younger practitioners? Has that been a source of influence for you?

Dr. S. That is hard to answer. Some of the things taught in the training programs now seem to be counterproductive to developing good practitioners. All of that gets in the way.

I. Often they want to go into private practice right away. Is that bad?

Dr. S. Yes, they are raw. Early on you need constant colleague contact and supervision. Early on it is easy to get caught up in a fad and to rigidly apply procedures to everyone coming in.

I. Events in one's personal life can also be a source of influence. Is this true for you?

Dr. S. Yes, I think it is true, perhaps more in later years and specifically to do with my health problems. The health problems raised many new questions regarding what my clients could expect of me.

I. Has the experience made you better?

Dr. S. Yes, in that I have worked considerably more with individuals who have physical illnesses. And it certainly was a strong motivation to learn about hypnosis and use it in therapy. I probably have been especially good at helping individuals who have become depressed because of physical illness. These individuals don't really get listened to because people don't want to hear things. They are prone to minimize and "buck you up" and insist upon your strengths and optimism. People demand that the physically ill abandon all of their negative thought. I, on the other hand, encourage it. My physical illness has made me very much more sensitive.

I. The power of your own illness has taught you this?

Dr. S. Yes, but one of my professors taught me long ago that it was not necessary to have the experience to help people with it, i.e., one does not need to be a parent to help parents in child rearing. But, I did find myself being more effective including a willingness to be openly sympathetic I would say, "I feel really bad for you," "That makes me really sad."

I.   Of all the sources of influence we have discussed, what have been the most impactful?

Dr. S.   There is another—peers. It is with peers that I have had the most prolonged and intensive conversations.

I.   All the way along?

Dr. S.   Yes, but perhaps more after I developed a sense of confidence in the world of practice. It was peers who validated things for me. They come to you with their problems or send their kids to you. Those add, in my opinion, great increments of esteem to a therapist. In the same way, clients do the same thing by their referrals of friends and family. They also tell you about what there is about you that makes them feel positive about you.

I.   Does positive feedback like this give one a sense of security that the beginner can never have?

Dr. S.   Oh, yes, that's true. That is one of the reasons experience is such an important aspect in the development of the therapist. For me, this kind of feedback from experience was so much more validating than the minimal feedback from supervisors I received! The best I ever got from one supervisor and, remember, this was years ago was "You have a good therapy voice." I did not even take it as much of a compliment, but that is the most he gave.

I.   Now adding peers as a source of influence, how would you rank these?

Dr. S   Peers, clients, personal life, and the literature, but not much the empirical literature. Then professional elders, some but not much being a supervisor. I have enjoyed supervising but don't know that I have learned much from it.

I.   Do you see counseling/therapy more complex or simple for you as you have gained experience?

Dr. S.   Both! I don't have to be as self-conscious and, therefore, it is simpler. I also appreciate the complexities more than I have in the past. You see and you hear and you incorporate much more as you go along. One also has less of a necessity to emphasize content and more ability to understand meaning. And, in that way, it becomes complex because what people say and also how they say it suddenly matters.

I.   Is there any continuum along which you have progressed?

Dr. S.   Age has an impact. One becomes a "wise old owl," and it defines you in a certain way.

I.   What kind of people make the best counselors and therapists?

Dr. S.   Lovers of people. Individuals who really like people and who feel a personal commitment to justice and equality.

I.   What causes people to leave the field?

Dr. S. They can cut it academically but are not good at it. They are cold fish and really don't like people in the way it is necessary for a practitioner. They are miserable, fearful, uncomfortable.

I. What exactly are the satisfactions you get from the work? Have these changed over time?

Dr. S. The satisfaction of entering another's private world and helping that person has increased over time because my anxiety about performance has greatly diminished.

I. Do you measure success much differently than before?

Dr. S. Yes, in a less narrow way. There is less pressure on me.

Interview with Dr. M.

Dr. M. is a well-respected counseling psychologist who works as a psychotherapist and an organizational consultant.

I. If you were going to now look at your career and look at critical incidents in your development, what would pop out to you?

Dr. M. There seems to be a life full of crises (laughs). Probably I would say my father's alcoholism was one of the issues that was a critical one. So was codependency stuff. That was probably pretty important and underlying for me to get into this line of work, I would imagine. Because all along the way I don't think I really made a clear career choice until I was 30, and at that point I had been into a number of different things. My father lost the business in a poker game when I was in high school, so in a pique I joined the Air Force, and that was just to get away, that was the geographical cure. And I wound up being selected, as a result of all the testing, for the Russian language school. And I felt if that's what they want me to do, I compliantly went and then I got a nomination for an appointment to the Naval Academy at Annapolis, and it was kind of the same way. My great aunt had told me that they were offering this state- wide examination for an appointment to the Naval Academy, and I thought, well, why not. So I took it, and I was in Japan as an airman and I got a notification that I had been accepted for the nomination.

I. How did you react to that at the time?

Dr. M. Well, I completely forgot I had done that, and so I didn't know what they were talking about.

I. You're supposed to be excited and glad.

Dr. M. Well, they had a program whereby people who were coming out of the enlisted ranks could go through a prep school. So, I came back in early January to attend this prep school. I talk about these things, I guess, because I was kind of just drifting along in life; that's kind of a theme for a long time, going to the Naval Academy and even going

318

into the submarines. Well, I did take a class for the submarines. But many of those things kind of just happened to me and I responded to them. It wasn't a sense of clear direction. I was an engineer which is clearly not what my heart's desire was all about. (laughs) When I was in submarines and I was on a nuclear submarine in the latter stages of my career, I saw this tremendous waste of talent and people who were so so bright and who were still enlisted men or they were mismatched. They were not properly placed, and it struck me as such a misuse of talent.

I. You were really in close quarters there, too. I wonder if that's how you got to know others.

Dr. M. Yes, but the new submarines are quite large; they're 425 feet long and 30 feet wide including carpeting. Pretty plush stuff compared to the old diesel electrics which were very cramped. But that was one of the things that got me thinking about it, and, when I left the Navy, I went into a monastery, and the person I worked with there at this monastery in Kentucky said: "You really ought to work with people and not be in this cloistered order." And that was one of the things that got me thinking, and then I saw, after I left the monastery, on my way back to North Dakota, I stopped in Detroit, and there I saw a counseling psychologist and went through a battery of tests looking at what I would be good at because I was thinking about medical school and other things and at that point one of the careers that came to the fore for me was counseling psychology and not clinical. We had some people who had some pretty severe disabilities even in the Navy. Alcoholism, of course, and the last patrol I was on, someone had a psychotic break. It was clear to me at that point that I wanted to work with people who had some things going for them, that their functioning was relatively good. That was a key. So I applied to only one graduate program in counseling psychology.

I. It seems like you were just drifting along, but also several people saw some resources that you had and kind of pulled you into something.

Dr. M. That's true. I think even when I was in the Navy a captain said, "We need people like you in the Navy who can talk to people, who can understand." There was a little period of time there when I really wrestled with that whole notion of a religious vocation, whether I was actually going to do that, and I actually submitted my resignation in February of 1963, but because I was assigned to a nuclear submarine at the time, they didn't let me out until February of 1965. So, I tell people I lived my first 2 years of monastic life in the Navy on a submarine (laughs). Even before that when I was at Syracuse University studying Russian one of the things I found was being in the library and reading Karl Menninger's Man Against Himself. It first got me interested in the psychodynamic aspects. I remember thinking then how powerful this was, and I was really impressed with the effect people could have in their lives by virtue of their emotions and their thinking. That was probably the first inkling of a move in that direction, and it was then a little bit later when I was just finishing my first year at the Academy when I got into the more existential stuff and started looking at the ultimate meanings of life. And that search started.

I. You seem to have a real active curiosity, and that you find things, like you find existential literature at the Naval Academy. I wonder if there's an inquiring mind or curiosity, what's the dimension here?

Dr. M. Well, one thing I would say is just that there was an existential void. Although I was going off in this direction and becoming a career Naval officer, there was something that didn't quite fit with what I thought was really important in my life, and so I started looking around for things that would help me make sense of what could fit, and that's when I first got into reading Thomas Merton and reading some theology, especially monastic works and some philosophy. On my first cruise, I was on a destroyer and one of the people who was on the destroyer with me was a professor of philosophy from Notre Dame. He was a reserve officer, and when I got back from that cruise that fall and school started again, I found a whole set of books on the history of philosophy that this guy sent to me. I really appreciated that!

I. I was wondering if the geographic cure, as you put it, was active here in the Navy far away. I was wondering if the impact of your father's alcoholism was at work here.

Dr. M. Oh, yes, because to me it seems like he was somehow not looking at that, like life is precious. He was anesthetizing himself. It was amazing to me that he could not see what he was doing to himself and his life and to our family. Yes, these issues couldn't be dealt with geographically. There had to be kind of a self-exploration. I will say, even when I was in the Navy, I found myself affiliating with people who were also what I would call searchers. One of the most remarkable people I ever met in my life was the doctor aboard this nuclear submarine. He was truly remarkable, and while we were in the shipyard, we started talking about these kinds of things. Very talented guy, he was in his thirties at that time, and he was starting to explore some of the same issues I was about the meaning of life. We wound up having this group of people, and we met once or twice a month. I always thought of Jim as being kind of a big brother, but in a sense, he was someone who in some ways was more naive than I was. But that was a powerful group for me. I think it was being attracted to people who I could talk about those things with, inquiring people.

I. How about the transition to graduate school in psychology?

Dr. M.   When I started graduate school, it was a fluke; I mean I applied to graduate school in July. And somebody had just dropped out. I was absolutely at the beginning in counseling.

I.   Did you begin graduate school without any undergraduate psychology?

Dr. M.   None at all. I was taking Psych 1 and graduate psychology at the same time (laughs).

I.   Obviously it worked out well, but how was it at the time?

Dr. M.   I was terrified at the time in some ways; in other ways, I was so interested in it, and I got a 4.0 average. I was just so intensely involved in it. It really was extremely intense. I was so fascinated, I just couldn't quite find enough about it. The first year, I was on a fellowship and felt kind of isolated; and then they brought me back and I was a T.A. in the Psych department, and that's when I met some other students, people like Linda Smith. Wonderful, wonderful woman. And Ellen Johnson. We had a lot of interesting discussions. I think very early on I got exposed to leaders in the field. Exciting, yes, but sometimes I felt just terror that someone was going to find out I really didn't know …

I.   How did you deal with the terror? What was your kind of internal strategy?

Dr. M.   I think at that point it was trying to make sure by reading and reading, but also connecting with people who I felt really knew their stuff, and there was a real connection with what I saw as the clear authority figures, the people I saw who were the best folks around. There was a group of people that were kind of there that I saw as mentors and competent senior people.

I.   Were they supervisors and professors who you respected and could identify with as a way to handle the anxiety?

Dr. M.   That was right. I would talk about my concerns when I didn't know what to do. A lot of times they helped me see that I really did have a lot more insight into something. I had been reading quite a bit and it was very different.

I.   So it was reading and connecting with people?

Dr. M.   That's right. I forgot about something. It really even was kind of a revolt. A group of graduate students got together, and we got a group going of graduate students talking about our concerns. I forgot about that.

I.   It was enlisting the support of peers.

Dr. M.   Yes, it really was. There were some people who were there who seemed like they were above it all. But there was a real core group who you felt like you could really talk to and share these things with. They were very important.

I.   Important in terms of ….

Dr. M.   Of bouncing ideas off, talking about things you'd read, or talking about your concerns. I remember, I had a suicidal client and I think I probably got more what I call real solid support from my peers, my fellow graduate students, than I could possibly have gotten from people who were supervising me at the time. In that respect, there were clearly no boundaries. I mean I was so … I had this savior complex.

I. No boundaries in terms of what? Just kind of leaping in to help, doing anything?

Dr. M. That's right, yes, that was true.

I. I was wondering, you mentioned extra workshops you took. Was that part of the searching process?

Dr. M. Yes, it was. In many ways it was; I think of it now as being defiant against the way things were supposed to be in the department. In some ways I think it was a way of coping with fear. I think first of all was the feeling of being the complete novice and really not knowing anything. That was one, but when I started working with some clients I saw that the approach I was taught just wasn't sufficient.

I. How did you find out that the approach didn't work?

Dr. M. It just wasn't sufficient. There were a lot of times that family of origin issues were so pervasive and so important in causing the problem, but not helped by the model I was taught.

I. OK. Going back to an earlier point, is it correct to say that in the beginning there was this tendency to connect with people you admire and then there's a point where you were searching, but more autonomous? Does that make sense?

Dr. M. Absolutely.

I. You finished everything except the dissertation in 1969 and took a full time job and then finished your dissertation in 1972 so there was that period where you were …

Dr. M. I was an instructor and I was an administrator and I was supervising people in student advising, but I still wound up getting involved in some counseling at that point. And I think that the advising job was really a delaying factor. It was something that probably gave me an excuse to delay finishing my dissertation. But also it was secure. We had just had a child at that time. I always knew there would be a next step. There were several possible routes.

I. Was it an extended moratorium?

Dr. M. Right, that's what I did. Absolutely. And so actually what happened, I have to laugh at the way things worked out. I was supposed to have a day off to work on my dissertation study, and of course, there never seemed like there was time. I didn't have time to do it. The summer of 1972 my wife said, "Listen, I'm going to take the kids and I'm going to your folks. Call me when you're done." And I did it, I finished it in seven days. laughs)

I. If you think about the moratorium again, what were your motivations for that?

Dr. M. It was … first of all, I saw what possibilities there were, and I wasn't sure which direction to really pursue.

I. Was there any sense of not feeling quite ready to have the doctorate?

Dr. M. Oh, absolutely. I used to say that as a result of going to the Naval Academy, I felt that I was trained and not educated; and in a sense, having gone through graduate school, I still felt like I had been trained but not necessarily educated in a real grounded formation process to help launch me into being a full-fledged psychologist. There were missing parts in the graduate program, and I started to find some of those things. But in the spring of 1973, after 4 years of budget cuts for my advising program every year they cut me 10% I was preparing to teach a course, and I'd just gotten through with the budget and gotten cut again, and I got an ulcer. And I said, This is crazy. I got a call from a medical center, and the director said he needed someone to head the counseling unit. And I did that for 5 years. It was an opportunity to get some experience, and I started being an internal consultant.

I. Within the medical center?

Dr. M. Yes. It was probably the seeds of my destruction of a career in the medical center. I found myself being cast in the role of a change agent in an organization that was dedicated to maintaining the status quo. You know they were not about to change. It took a year to change a form. And trying to get people to shift out of their roles to try something new was difficult. So that's when I started looking around and started working at an industrial consulting firm part time.

I. How did you get into the internal change agent role at the medical center? I mean, that was not part of your job.

Dr. M. There was a highly respected clinical psychologist there. She had some credibility with the powers that be because of her longstanding clinical experience. They were getting letters, complaints from people who felt like they were being treated like numbers, very impersonal. So, the medical center developed a program called TIGER, which stood for Training in Individual Group Effectiveness and Resourcefulness. And what we did was to get into an interdisciplinary team building process. There was about a four week training period on being a consultant. Part of that was an intensive T group experience. This was a very constructive experience. It was an intensive and emotional experience for me. Some of those training people were from Houston. There was a lot of emphasis on choices and responsibility, and that's when I started doing some things in Gestalt.

I.   T group and Gestalt training. What came in what order?

Dr. M.   First T group and then Gestalt. A Gestalt trainer would come to town once a week, and I joined the training.

I.   It seems like there was a shift occurring at this time in your orientation, more like an inward orientation.

Dr. M.   Oh, yes, very much so.

I.   Can you recall some of the things you were dealing with?

Dr. M.   At this point I was doing a lot of super vision. I was working with about a dozen graduate students at the time and two or three other psychologists and one guy who was a vocational counselor; he did job search. And I think some of it was interaction with those graduate students from a different perspective. It was a whole new area for terror (laughs) and feelings of uncertainty. It's one thing to be a colleague and talking about this and another thing to be a supervisor and to be in charge.

I.   Like a challenge to you.

Dr. M.   Oh, it was that! The thing that was really important was that these doctoral interns were from different training programs around the country.

I.   Do you remember at times feeling like you wanted to confirm the value of your training, that you wanted to feel like this really was important or useful.

Dr. M.   It was trying to convince, especially some of these people who had not been brought up in my tradition, the real value of our approach to assessment and testing. Yes, I think there was a little bit of proselytizing.

I.   Changing the topic, I am wondering if you can talk about starting graduate school after some life experience versus right after college.

Dr. M.   It was 1965. I was 30 years old, and I remember a classmate. She was sitting next to me in class, and she was about 21, and there was a guy who was also 21. They were such babes in the woods when it came to looking at some of these things. They could talk about theory, but they didn't have a sense of what life experience was about. And in some ways, I always felt like I didn't have either, mine was so biased by 12 years in the military; it's not really real life either. There were a number of young people like that, and they were just incorporating the material.

I.   Is that one of the things that's different about having experience?

Dr. M.   Well, I don't know, but that was for me, I think; probably I was a little bit more skeptical about that, things being that simple. But there were differences between some of these people too.

I.   It sounds like there were some similarities between people without experience, a vulnerability, a dependency; and then there are some individual differences too between them. So, you were searching and being challenged and stimulated by other students. That kind of started a new phase.

I.   Did you get involved in any other activities at the medical center?

Dr. M.   I got into lots of things such as a program in chemical dependency counseling. I started getting into that, and I started getting into things like the cardiac rehab program, the psychological medicine program, working with people in that program. Also biofeedback. Those were some of the things that I was interested in; I wanted to find out about them. There was some overlap with some of the things I was doing in Gestalt.

I.   Any other impactful people for you at this time?

Dr. M.   There was another person when I was still a graduate student who was very helpful to me. She had a Master's degree in theology; she was just about a year or so younger than I was. She was so bright! She converted to Catholicism, and she really got into the yoga stuff. She met a guy, brilliant young guy. They were married in a Hindu wedding, and he really got into looking at yoga at that point. He got into doing some meditation. They were important in that sense that they got me interested in methods of body relaxation.

I.   It seems that other people have been very important to you in terms of your own development. You keep talking about these other people.

Dr. M.   Yes. They're usually people I find fascinating or interesting or something about them. It is like their version of what it takes to make life good.

I.   How did you get from the medical center to industrial consulting?

Dr. M.   The last 2 years I knew I wasn't going to be able to stay in the medical center because of my experiences there. I was doing fine, but the more I ran into that bureaucracy, the more I thought, this is crazy. It just does not fit for me. So I started working at a mental health clinic. I worked there for a half day per week, and then someone at the industrial consulting firm asked me to go over and do some work for them. This was in 1977, and I worked at the industrial consulting firm for two or three days per month for a year. At the medical center I began working with in patients who had little incentive to get better. It was really kind of impossible. There were 120 patients! You couldn't believe it. That's when I said, I do not want to work in just strict clinical psychology with psychopathology. That helped me make my decision. I could have worked at a big local clinic in administration.

I.   What made that attractive to you?

Dr. M.   The thing that made it attractive was the variety of people that you'd see there. You saw just such a broad variety of things, like young people who were facing marital/vocational/ adjustment problems; but they weren't psychotic. You saw one once in a while, but psychotic patients were very rare. I was interested in that. And then when the decision came whether to work for a mental health clinic or industrial consulting firm, that was a tough one for me. I thought my internal consulting interests could be developed more in industrial consulting. So I did.

I. How was the transition?

Dr. M I worked through Sunday to finish things at the medical center, and during that last week I got, a call from the president of the industrial firm. He said, "We had somebody get sick. Could you please come to work tomorrow?" So, I went off on a five-day stretch. I didn't have 24 hours off. Five days in a row, each day probably 12 hours; and then as a result of that I wound up having like three major reports to write. And that's what I did starting at that firm. I kept getting overextended. No matter what I was doing, there were always these other things; you could do assessment and you had outplacement counseling and the key part was billable time, billable time. Sometimes we went home after midnight, and we were back at 6:00 in the morning. And I felt like I was caught between doing what people wanted me to do, but I didn't want to do, and disappointing people I didn't want to disappoint.

I. It seems like this was really a very strenuous situation.

Dr. M. That wasn't all the time, but it was pretty consistent. And if you were to go there right now, matter of fact, I think you'd find most people are working probably 60 hours a week.

I. But if we were to look at this, you had the medical center where there was the administrative bureaucracy, very severe pathology, the rules of the administration, all the constraints that did seem to facilitate progress. It seemed that it produced almost a loss of meaning; it just was not meaningful in a very basic sense.

Dr. M. That's right.

I. And then the next phase where you were trying out working with a varied client population in the mental health clinic. That seemed like it was a good time.

Dr. M. It was.

I. But that had a time limit on it.

Dr. M. That's right.

I. And then it sounded like the industrial consulting firm was a place to use some resources that you hadn't used before.

Dr. M. That's right. Or hadn't developed the level of competency that I really felt that I wanted to have. Yes, and I was going through the Gestalt program the last year at the medical center and the first year at the industrial firm. Of course, that program was very helpful for doing lots of groups and looking at oneself, a time for reflection, a time for being clear about my own values.

I.   What I hear is a theme of trying to find optimal environments for development and each environment provided things, but then there are liabilities that forced you then to search for people and places and move on. And that's been a consistent kind of theme. Does that sound right?

Dr. M.   Right.

I.   And now, how does this environment, the private practice and consulting firm that you created here, fit for you?

Dr. M.   I started 4 years ago. It was a scary thing at first, but I was confident that I had some of the skills to survive. I survived, I set up shop here, started doing some individual work and corporate consulting, and gradually I started doing work with school systems, health organizations, hospitals, and clinics. A lot of my clients now tend to be in health care education. There's still quite a bit of variety; some of it is more the individual coaching. When you ask what I do, it's hard for me to say sometimes what I'm doing.

I   Conceptually, you mean?

Dr. M.   Oh, yes. It is all so combined in so many ways.

I.   It seemed when listening to your background that this setting is excellent for utilizing all of your experiences in an integrated way—the medical center, the academic, the research, the mental health clinic, the industrial consulting, the military background that you can pull from in a setting like this.

Dr. M.   Yes, I think that's true. The other thing I found myself doing though is molding different things I do with my personal way of doing it. I do not use much of a formula any more.

I.   Does that just gradually go away?

Dr. M.   Yes, I use some models but I've done some other things that other people would think are wacky, like the technology for creativity program or the empowerment workshop I recently did or the leadership and mastery program.

I.   You seem to have come to a point where your experiences are so rich and you've done so much, that your theoretical structure is unique, almost like it is you.

Dr. M.   More and more.

I.   Perhaps because it's your unique version that you don't need to put labels on it so much because you're not having to present it quite that way.

Dr. M.   Except with clients and client companies.

I.   Is part of your development process that you have to have new things?

Dr. M.   New things are important. I don't think it's just the newness. It's things that seem to be more consistent with my style, with my values. I have also along the way been in and out of my own therapy. That's been very important to me. And I have been with a very good older therapist who has given me a lot.

I. If you look ahead, what are your thoughts for the future?

Dr. M. Sometimes I think I should go drive a cab or something like that (laughs). I see myself doing more and more the things I want rather than what other people want me to do, and I seem to be getting more and more clear about what those things are and doing things that are exciting and interesting to do or that I think have value to other people as well. And I am getting very much involved with alcoholism in families and the way it affects the members of a family adult children of alcoholics and codependency. It is really interesting. But now it comes out of more who I am, the early experiences with alcoholism and all the things professional and personal since then. The more I do that, the more I feel excited about that process, and I don't think I'll ever retire in that sense.

I. Thank you so much for everything. This has been very exciting.

Interview with Dr. A.

Dr. A is a senior professional psychologist. He is recognized as a therapist for therapists and is widely respected by his colleagues.

I. What are key parts of professional development?

Dr. A. The people. There was not another psychologist on the staff in my first job after graduate school. I was the psychologist, there were three social workers, we hired an occupational therapist, and then we had the psychiatrist part time. I got to respect those people and respect their knowledge and tried to find out what they could teach me. I found out that psychologists weren't the only people in the mental health field, the only ones who knew anything. I developed a tremendous amount of respect for other mental health professionals, especially in the social work field, the ones who knew something about treatment.

I. How competent did you feel after graduating and going out into your first job?

Dr. A. Oh, I was scared. You had to be scared. That's an experience.

I. That state of being scared, what happens to that over the years? Is there a way of talking about that?

Dr. A. You see, that's why I think it's so important to have that experience as a member of a team; you get a kind of group therapy, you get the experience that you're not alone and that other people are having the same kind of problems, and also get the support for what you're doing and an opportunity to talk about it. The people I worked with were good clinicians who were thinking about people the same way I was, and so we were able to share our successes and our failures and really support each other and, of course, at that clinic we also had a terrible population to deal with. These were chronically ill patients, most of them, a majority of them with very little ego strength.

I. So defining success really gets to be an issue because these aren't the people who are going to get much better no matter what you do?

Dr. A. That's right, so your idea of success changes. You go for little gains, you know, the primary goal is to keep people out of the hospital, not to get them well, but to keep them from regressing, keep them in the community somehow and keep them functioning.

I. We have the idea that people when they finish a graduate program have a real desire to show that the training was worthwhile and that what you learned in school and maybe on internship was valuable. It is confirming the value of your training. Does that ring any bells for you?

Dr. A. I think you are right. The area in which I got the most confirmation was in my diagnostic skills. I think that's what happens to most clinical psychologists who go into clinics in their first jobs, if they are well trained. They are well trained in diagnostic skills; that's where they get their major confirmation.

I. That term sounds right to you, the idea of confirmation of your training, that's something important?

Dr. A. Absolutely. If nothing else, confirmation to the extent that the person feels that the skills he/she was trained in are needed. Now that's another problem area for many psychologists. For example, if you're only trained in one therapeutic modality, that's pretty narrow. When you go into a clinic and they say, we need you to see this kind of patient and do this and do that, and you're not trained to do that ...

I. Then what happens to the new professional?

Dr. A. I think they get pretty frantic.

I. And you were saying that you really felt scared?

Dr. A. Yes, sure. We felt like frauds, you know, and we got really angry at the graduate school.

I. Yes, we've noticed this same anger in some of the interviews with people.

Dr. A. Yes, absolutely. Graduate school faculty have too little contact with the outside world in that sense. I think there is a tremendous parallel between development in the medical field and in the psychology field. The development in medicine went through the same phases. Medicine went through a phase when medical training was separate from practice; they had very little relationship to each other and there were the same kinds of problems.

I. What's the big problem right now?

Dr. A. What happened, of course, was that practice took over the medical schools. So medical school and practice are almost the same thing in many ways. I bet that's what will happen in psychology and clinical psychology also. Then the split is going to be between the practice field, the professional practice field of psychology and the research field; that split is already building.

I. How did you get through those early years?

Dr. A. I talked about it and asked for a lot of support and leaned on my wife a lot. Support is really important. As much as possible you should be encouraged to develop new skills and expand yourself and how you understand things.

I. One of the reasons we're asking you is because you have a reputation of being a therapist for therapists and that's a very eminent position. When we talk about your development, we're talking about some important things, and maybe how people deal with being scared would be an example of something important to understand and to describe.

Dr. A. Yes, I think so.

I. What about clients, what kind of impact do they have for you?

Dr. A. Early, as I said, the client population was pretty strange and so you learn to set limited goals, and you're not going to get a lot of support from your clients as such. Clients taught me a lot about dealing with pathology and about dealing with emergencies. I learned a lot but was scared a lot, too. I think an important thing you learn over time as a clinician with experience is to be able to deal with any kind of thing that comes before you.

I. How does that happen?

Dr. A. Just purely experience.

I. What happens with the experience, do you rely more on your experience, previous experience?

Dr. A. Sure.

I. How long does it take to really feel comfort able as a clinician? How long before a person really feels that he/she knows what is going on.

Dr. A. Well, I'd say it is a gradual process. We used to say that it took 5 years of full time therapy work to really feel that you know what you're doing. By then you've dealt with most of the things with which you're going to be confronted. There are still things, of course, people are unlimited.... But, you've dealt with most everything, you feel that you can handle it one way or another, and you also build up your resources. You've dealt with all the major kinds of threats to your feeling of worth and confidence, suicide issues, you've hospitalized people and you've diagnosed people in terms of medication and drugs. With all of the problems you've looked at and confronted, you've hopefully worked with most of the ethical issues, like how, why, and when to see patients and what to do and what not to do with them.

I. I was thinking about the Dreyfus and Dreyfus (1986) work. These are people who have looked at the impact of experience in different fields, like chess players and taxi cab drivers. They suggest that at the beginning people use theoretical ideas but they don't know about the exceptions or they don't have any experience so they just apply things dogmatically and, of course, it doesn't always work very well. With lots of experience, they don't use other people's theories, they use their own experience. They become more atheoretical in the sense that it isn't atheoretical, it's much more personalized, and their own experience provides the paradigms for what they do in certain situations. I wonder if that's true for you.

Dr. A. Yes, I think you agree with me as a trainer of clinicians that one of the differences between the good clinicians and the bad clinicians is how much they can give up their rigidity. The ones who can't get beyond their training, their system, and try to fit all the patients to their system rather than fit the system to the patients are the ones who are not the good therapists. That is a big difference. Does that make sense?

I. Yes. Why can't they?

Dr. A. They're stupid, they weren't ever given permission to, they were too rigidly trained, or their personalities are so rigid that they can't get beyond themselves and their system. Those are the usual explanations.

I. We are trying to find out what therapists are doing when they are confronted with difficulties which they are not adequately prepared to handle. What do therapists do there how do therapists handle that? These issues are pretty important in terms of how a person develops.

Dr. A. That's why I don't like the idea of people going into private practice right after they graduate; they're too alone. If you go into a private practice clinic setting where there's supervision available, that's different. Too many people just go out and hang up their shingle by themselves or with another person who doesn't know any more than they do. In that situation, there is just not enough support and not enough information available. In our system in the USA, the graduates of most of the schools that I know about need supervision after they graduate. They can go out and do some therapy, but they need continued supervision.

I. If a person would go into the private practice by oneself or with somebody else, would the person become more rigid then in the way he/she categorizes or be just too anxious perhaps to be able to open up and expand and think different ways?

Dr. A. They would certainly be anxious and then it depends on how they handle the anxiety, some of them will handle it quite rigidly

331

and some of them will handle it by just getting out of the field.... It (anxiety) chases people away. Then, for the wrong reasons, they try teaching, research, or administration; it really hurts them. They often end up in therapy since it is a breakdown of their system.

I.   That may be the time when therapists make niches for themselves where they are not exposed to so many threatening experiences.

Dr. A.   Oh, yes, sure. That's the rigidity. If they can find it, sure. A safe way to solve their problem, but it's not necessarily a good way to solve their problem because you can't rely on the niche staying the same for you over time.

I.   It could be a conceptual rigidity or it could be a niche in terms of only working with certain kinds of people.

Dr. A.   Sure. You may open up an anxiety clinic following rigid ways of treating anxiety such as behavioral techniques and that's all you do. Of course, then you're in a really dangerous position because a narrow population supports you, you just treat one diagnosis.

I.   Is there a tendency to make everybody into that diagnosis?

Dr. A.   Yes, that too easily becomes a problem.

I.   So support is really important. Is it important to be able to say I don't know what I'm doing?

Dr. A.   Sure.

I.   We use the term Pseudodevelopment for when someone is selecting a niche and may be engaged in a lot of activity, may be engaged in a search but it is kind of a repetition, and confirming what one knows already instead of attempting to discover something new. How do you react to this idea?

Dr. A.   That's part of the reason for the fads that we go through. People are looking for something that will give them structure and support. People jump on a new theory bandwagon because they are scared and don't know what they are doing or don't know enough about what they are doing and feel unsure. A system comes along and it looks attractive, it says some of the things that you've learned, and it gives you some new ideas about putting things together so you get yourself retrained as a "such and such" therapist, then you're stuck in another theory that isn't broad enough.

I.   To handle everything?

Dr. A.   To handle everything that's going to come through your door.

I.   When do you think people are most susceptible to looking and finding and jumping in their career to a tight conceptual system?

Dr. A.   I don't know. I see a lot of young professionals who aren't adequately trained, and I also see a lot of the 40 year olds who are beginning to question: Where am I? What am I doing? Is this really worthwhile? There are also some who have gone through some kind of trauma.

I. Personal trauma maybe?

Dr. A. Or they're going through a treatment trauma - somebody committed suicide or they're being sued for something. That kind of trauma.

I. Does it happen at one time in a person's career?

Dr. A. It doesn't. There are always internal and external threats.

I. Is openness to experiences and an active searching attitude essential?

Dr. A. Yes, essential all the time.

I. Is the sect movement in therapy really contrary to development?

Dr. A. Yes, in many ways I think it is.

I. Is it possible that if you take a small therapy group that has its own journals, own membership, and then you just go around that small circle, feeling like you're doing something, you may in fact never really be asking questions to find answers, but rather asking questions to feel better about the fact that you already know it. Is that right?

Dr. A. In all the systems, the extremes, people are the same. You can get too self-contained in any system.

I. We're trying to speculate on the difference between that and development. When you get self-contained, is that when you get stagnation? And the openness to continue to grow, changing produces development? We are just trying to really work on how to conceptualize the difference between development and stagnation.

Dr. A. Yes. But, of course, the term that you are trying to define is development. I think some of the people in, say, orthodox analysis, would say as long as they keep questioning within their system, they develop; they rarely step out of the system.

I. Perhaps a working answer is that it is development if the question is really being asked to find the answer, which may disagree with what you already thought was true, versus you are asking the question in a way that can't come up with an answer that's different than what you already believe is true. If you are staying within the conceptual framework, and the problem that you are confronted with really should have forced you to look other places and you are still staying within that system, then that would be pseudodevelopment. So in a way it's the extent that you fit the patients to the system or the system to the patients.

Dr. A. That's the struggle that goes on with us all the time, all of us, I think. That's part of the struggle with long-term versus short-term therapy, the fights that we have in the United States in terms of insurance companies it's really coming around to who needs what kind of therapy.

I. Whether something is development or not, in terms of choice of conceptual framework, is then whether or not you ask the question: Is this what the client needs? What do you think of this?

Dr. A.   Yes, I agree with that, absolutely. The problem with this again is economic. If you ask that question very seriously, you might not get many patients. If you stick with one theory, if you're stuck with one modality, one way of approaching people, then you might not get many patients. Does this patient really fit what I can do, is this what this patient needs?

I.   We are really now talking about an economic barrier to development.

Dr. A.   Yes, that is true.

I.   Do you think you could generalize somewhat this way and say that people who are more interested in developing tend to be more generalists. With generalists you get people coming at you from all over the place and then you're more threatened, I guess, in the sense that if you have a narrow conceptualist system, it kind of topples quicker; and some people would be attracted to that process, maybe of being able to get a lot of input and then keep going, and other people would be very threatened and want a narrower range of clients to work with. I don't know if I'm really overstating something, but I guess you would, for example, take work with lots of different kinds of people. And some way your way of working with people can accommodate all these.

Dr. A.   I still refer a lot of people to other kinds of therapy. If someone needs a behavioral approach or some specific technique, I send them to somebody else because I just don't do that.

I.   We're trying to extract some components of what is ideal development. These are kind of value statement.

Dr. A.   That's right

I.   We would like to hear your reaction to this. We are talking about the ability to learn from experience, which means openness to experience, openness to varied sources of influence. And also the ability to tolerate ambiguity; and may be the most important in our way of thinking, willingness to reflect on one's experiences—thinking about it and talking to other people. And the ability and willingness to confront, see, and recognize one's own resources and limitations. And also, seeking out new experiences, that means taking on new challenges. And as a consequence of this, to adapt, change, and revise one's thinking.

Dr. A.   Yes, and to use what you learn.

I.   Maybe pseudodevelopment would involve really lots of repetition and repeating of old solutions. You've got it down and just kind of keep doing it, and doing it; somehow fitting people into what you do.

Dr. A.   That's right.

I.   Is there something here that is more important than the others?

Dr. A.   No, they have to all go together, they all kind of interact. Looking back at my experience.... These are all things we have talked about.

I.   We have been talking about barriers already, mostly internal barriers. Maybe we can focus on the external barriers, maybe barriers within our profession? Are there barriers within our profession that prevent development?

Dr. A.   One of the places to look on the negative side is to look at the literature on burnout. If you consider burnout as a symptom, one of the ways I conceptualize it is that burnout would be a symptom of stopped development. There are career issues that cause people to burn out, and there are ways in which people are forced to burn out. There are internal things which burn people out in terms of their own dynamics and personality. There are external things that burn people out in terms of the community support system, extended family issues, fights with insurance companies. There are active kinds of things that burn people out, such as people who don't actively take care of themselves physically. All of those things arrest development. The systems that we have within our field often burn people out because so many systems don't give people room for continued learning or basic respect as professionals.

I.   What system?

Dr. A.   The way clinics and hospitals operate, the way schools operate

I.   Mental health centers may not be nurturing enough to the staff?

Dr. A.   That's right. Nurturing in a variety of ways.

I.   Do you think people need a lot of nurturing in different ways or else the burnout will occur?

Dr. A.   They need it; so many systems don't care because of the money. They just hire somebody, work them as hard as they can work them and then if they can't do it any more, they'll fire them and get somebody else. Oh, you'd be interested in this, you could teach it to your students. Somebody came up with the most clever idea, to force people to do short-term therapy. You don't have to talk about short-term and long-term therapy, all you do is require somebody to take three new patients a week. That is all it takes. Isn't that clever, a practitioner can't do any long-term therapy because of all the meetings, paperwork, consultation. So how do you develop within that structure? Something has to go. It is important to look at any system and whether it support and encourages development. It is vitally important to renew yourself.

I.   This has been very interesting. I see that our time is up. We appreciate that you have given us this opportunity to talk to you. Thank you.

REFERENCES

Ackerman, D. (1999). *Deep play*. New York: Random House.

Adelson, M. J. (1995). Clinical supervision with difficult-to-treat patients. *Bulletin of the Menninger Clinic, 59,* 32–59.

Adorno, T. W., Frenkel–Brunswik, E., Levinson, D. J., & Sanford, R. N. (1950). *The authoritarian personality*. New York: Harpers Brothers.

Ambühl, H., & Orlinsky, D. E. (1998). Therapieziele aus der Perspektive der PsychotherapeutInnen. [Psychotherapists' perspectives on their therapeutic goals]. In H. Ambühl & B. Strauss (Eds.), *Therapieziele* [Psychotherapists] (319–334). Göttingen, Germany: Hogrefe.

American Psychological Association. (2003). Guidelines on multicultural education, training, research, practice, and organizational change for psychologists. *American Psychologist, 58,* 377–402.

American Psychological Association Presidential Task Force on Evidence–Based Practice. (2006). Evidence–based practice in psychology. *American Psychologist, 61,* 271–285.

Anastasi, A., & Urbina, S. (1997). *Psychological testing* (7th ed.) Englewood Cliffs, NJ: Prentice–Hall.

Andersen, T. (1987). The reflecting team: dialogue and meta-dialogue in clinical work. *Family Process, 26,* 415–428,

Andersen, T. (1999). Veiledning fra et språk-—og samtale perspektiv [Supervision from a language and dialogical perspective]. In M. H. Rønnestad & S. Reichelt, (Eds.). *Psykoterapiveiledning* [The supervision of psychotherapy] (pp.151–162). Oslo, Norway: Tano Aschehoug,.

Anderson, H., & Goolishian, H. (1992). The client is the expert: a not-knowing approach to therapy. In. S. McNamee & K. J. Gergen (Eds.). *Therapy and social construction*. London: Sage.

Anderson, J. R., Reder, L. M., & Simon, H. A. (1996). Situated learning and education. *Educational Researcher, 25,* 5–11.

Anderson, J. R., Reder, L. M., & Simon, H. A. (1997). Rejoinder: Situative versus cognitive perspectives: Form versus substance. *Educational Researcher, 26,* 18–21.

Angus, L., Hayes, J., Andersen, T., Ladany, N., Castonguay, L., & Muran, C. (2010). Future directions. In L. Castonguay, C. Muran, L. Angus, J. Hayes, N. Ladany, & T. Anderson (Eds.), *Bringing psychotherapy research to life: Legacies from the Society for Psychotherapy Research* (pp. 353–363). Washington DC: American Psychological Association Press.

Applied and Preventive Psychology (2009). Special issue on Goldfrieds classical article on principles of change. Vol. 13.

Arredondo, P. (2005). Mis inspiraciones y legados [My inspirations and legacies]. In R. K. Conyne & F. Bemak (Eds.), *Journeys to professional excellence: Lessons from leading counselor educators and practitioners* (pp. 33–44). Alexandria, VA: American Counseling Association.

Ascher, D. L., & Butler, S. K. (2010). *Balanced moderation supervision.* Retrieved from http://counselingoutfitters.com/vistas/vistas10/Article_39.pdf

Bacal, H. H. (1998). *Optimal responsiveness: How therapists heal their patients.* Northvale, NJ: Aronson.

Bain, K. (2004). *What the best college teachers do.* Cambridge, MA: Harvard University Press.

Baldwin, S. A., Wampold, B., & Imel, Z. E. (2007). Untangling the alliance–outcome correlation: Exploring the relative importance of therapist and patient variability in the alliance. *Journal of Counseling and Clinical Psychology, 75,* 842–852.

Baltes, P. B., & Smith, J. (1990). Toward a psychology of wisdom and its ontogenesis. In R. E. Sternberg, (Ed.), *Wisdom: Its origins, and development* (pp. 87–120) ambridge, England: Cambridge University Press.

Bateman, A. W., Fonagy, P. (2006). *Mentalization based treatment for borderline personality disorder: A practical guide.* Oxford, UK: Oxford University Press.

Bateson, G. (1972). *Steps to an ecology of mind.* New York: Ballantine Books.

Bauman, W. F. (1972). Games counselor trainees play: Dealing with trainee resistance. *Counselor Education and Supervision, 11,* 251–256.

Bauman, Z. (2001). *The individualized society.* Cambridge, MA: Polity Press.

Beck, U. (2000). *Risk society: Towards a new modernity.* London: Sage.

Beck, U., & Beck-Gernsheim, E. (2002). *Individualization: Institutionalized individualism and its social and political consequences.* London: Sage.

Belenky, B. L., Clinchy, B., Goldberger, N., & Tarule, J. (1986). *Women's ways of knowing.* New York: Basic Books.

Bengtson, M. (2011). Den unges prosjekt: Kliniske intervjuer med ungdom [The youth's project: Clinical interviews with adolescents]. In A.v.d. Lippe & M. H. Rønnestad (Eds.), *Det kliniske intervjuet, bind II* (pp. 204–222). (The clinical interview: Vol. 2. Practice with different client groups). Oslo, Norway: Gyldendal Akademisk.

Bennett, J. M. (1993). Towards ethnorelativism: A developmental model of intercultural sensitivity. In R. M. Paige (Ed.), *Education for the intercultural experience.* Yarmouth, ME: Intercultural Press.

Bereiter, C. (2002). *Education and mind in the knowledge age.* Mahwah, NJ: Erlbaum.

Bergin, E., & Rønnestad, M. H. (2005). Different timetables for change: Understanding processes in reorganizations: A qualitative study in a psychiatric sector in Sweden. *Journal of Health Organisation and Management, 19*(4–5), 355–377.

Bernard, J. M. (1997).The discrimination model. In C. E. Watkins, Jr. (Ed.), *Handbook of psychotherapy supervision* (pp. 310–327). New York: Wiley.

Bernard, J. M., & Goodyear, R. K. (2009). *Fundamentals of clinical supervision* (4th ed.). Columbus, OH: Merrill.

Blocher, D. H. (1983) Supervision in counseling: II. Contemporary models of supervision: Toward a cognitive developmental approach to counseling supervision. *The Counseling Psychologist, 11,* 27–34.

Bohart, A. C., Elliott, R., Greenberg, L. S., & Watson, J. D. (2002). Empathy. In J. Norcross (Ed.), *Psychotherapy relationships that work: Therapist contributions and responsiveness to patients* (pp. 89–108). New York: Oxford University Press.

Bohart, A. C., & Tallman, K. (2010). Clients: The neglected common factor in psychotherapy. In B. L. Duncan, S. D. Miller, B. E. Wampold, & M. A. Hubble

(Eds.), *The heart and soul of change* (2nd ed.,pp. 83–111) Washington, DC: American Psychological Association.

Borders, L. D., & Brown, L. L. (2005). *The new handbook of counseling supervision.* Rahway, NJ: Lahaska Press.

Bordin, E. S. (1979). The generalizability of the psychoanalytic concept of the working alliance. *Psychotherapy: Theory, Research and Practice, 16,* 252–260.

Bordin, E. (1983). Supervision in counseling: Contemporary models of supervision: A working alliance based model of supervision. *Counseling Psychologist, 11,* 35–42.

Bordin, E. S., & Brooks, L. (1990). *Psychodynamic model of career choice and satisfaction: Career choice and development: Applying contemporary theories to practice* (2nd ed.). San Francisco, CA: Jossey-Bass.

Boreham, N. (1988). Models of diagnosis and their implications for adult professional education. *Studies in the Education of Adults, 20*(2), 95–108.

Bowlby, J. (1969). *Attachment.* New York: Basic Books.

Bowlby, J. (1973). *Separation: Anxiety and anger.* New York: Basic Books.

Bowlby, J. (1980). *Loss: Sadness and depression.* New York: Basic Books.

Bradham, K. M. (2008). *Empathy and burnout in nurses.* Unpublished doctoral dissertation, Institute for Clinical Social Work, Chicago.

Brown, D. (1989). Logical positivism and/or phenomenology. *Counselor Education and Supervision, 29,* 5–6.

Brown, J. S., Collins, A., & Duguid, P. (1989). Situated cognition and the culture of learning. *Educational Researcher, 18,* 32–42.

Bruner, J. (1990). *Acts of meaning.* Cambridge, MA: Harvard University Press.

Calleson, D. C., Jordan, C., & Seifer. S. (2005) Community–engaged scholarship: Is faculty work in communities a true academic enterprise? *Academic Medicine, 80,* 317–21.

Carifio, M. S., & Hess, A. K. (1987). Who is the ideal supervisor? *Professional Psychology: Research and Practice, 18,* 244–250.

Carlsson, J. (2011). *Becoming a psychodynamic psychotherapist. A study of the professional development during and the first years after training* (Unpublished doctoral dissertation). Karolinske Institutet, Stockholm, Sweden.

Carlsson J., Norberg J., Sandell R., & Schubert J. (2011). Searching for recognition: The professional development of psychodynamic psychotherapists during training and the first few years after it. *Psychothery Research, 21,* 141–153.

Carroll, M. (1996). *Counseling supervision: Theory, skills and practice.* London: Cassell.

Carroll, M., & Gilbert, M. C. (2005). *On being a supervisee: Creating learning partnerships.* London: Vulkani.

Cassidy, J., & Shaver, P. R. (Eds.). (2008). *Handbook of attachment.* New York: Guildford.

Castonguay, L. G., & Beutler, L. E. (Eds.). (2006). *Principles of therapeutic change that work: Integrating relationship, treatment, client, and therapist factors.* New York: Oxford University Press.

Castonguay, L. G., Boswell, J. F., Constantino, M. J. Goldfried, M. R., & Hill, C., E. (2010). Training implications of harmful effects of psychological treatments. *American Psychologist, 65,* 34–49.

Castonguay, L. G., Muran, J. C., Hayes, J., Ladany, N., & Anserson, T. (2010). *Bringing psychotherapy research to life: Understading change through the work of leading clinical researchers.* Washington, DC: American Psychological Association.

Chapin, J., & Ellis, M. V. (2002). *Effects of role induction workshops on supervisee anxiety.*

Paper presented at the annual meeting of the American Psychological Association, Chicago, IL.

Charmaz, K. (2005). *Grounded theory: Methods for the 21st century*. London: Sage.

Chi, M. T. H. (2006). Two approaches to the study of experts' characteristics. In K. A. Ericsson, N. Charness, P. Feltovich, & R. Hoffman (Eds.), *Cambridge handbook of expertise and expert performance* (pp. 121–30). New York: Cambridge University Press.

Chi, M. T. H., & Ceci, S. J. (1987). Content knowledge: Its role, representation and restructuring in memory development. In H. W. Reese (Ed.), *Advances in child development and behavior* (Vol. 20, pp. 91–142). New York: Academic Press.

Chi, M. T. H., Glaser, R., & Farr, M. J. (Eds.). (1988). *The nature of expertise*. Hillsdale, NJ: Erlbaum.

Chi, T., Glaser, R., & Farr, M. (1988) (Eds.). *The nature of expertise*. Hillsdale, NJ: Erlbaum.

Chi, M. T. H., & Greeno, J. G. (1987). Cognitive research relevant to education. *Psychology and Educational Policy, 517,* 39–57.

Cole, D. A., & White, K. (1993). Structure of peer impressions of children's competence: Validation of the peer nomination of multiple competencies. *Psychological Assessment, 5*(4), 449–456.

Collins, S., & Long, A. (2003). Too tired to care? The psychological effects of working with trauma. *Journal of Psychiatric and Mental Health Nursing, 10,* 17–27.

Colvin, G. (2010). *Talent is overrated*. New York: Portfolio Penguin Group.

Crenshaw; K.W. (1989). Demarginalizing the intersection of race and sex. *The University of Chicago Legal Forum, 16,* 139–167.

Crits–Christoph, P., Gibbons, M. B. C., Crits–Christoph, K., Narducci, J., Schamberger, M., & Gallop, R. (2006). Can therapists be trained to improve their alliances? A preliminary study of alliance-fostering psychotherapy. *Psychotherapy Research, 16*(3), 268–281.

Csikszentmihalyi, M. (1990). *Finding flow: The psychology of engagement with everyday life*. New York: Basic Books.

Csikszentmihalyi, M. (1996). *Creativity: Flow and the psychology of discovery and invention*. New York: Harper & Row.

Csikszentmihalyi, M. (2008). *Flow: The psychology of optimal experience*. New York: Harper Perennial Modern Classics.

Cushman, P. (1995). *Constructing the self, constructing America: A cultural history of psychotherapy*. Reading, MA: Addison-Wesley.

Davis, J. D., Elliott, R., Davis, M. L., Binns, M., Francis, V. M., Kelman, J. E., & Schroder, T. A. (1987). Development of a taxonomy of therapist difficulties: Initial report. *British Journal of Medical Psychology, 60,* 109–119.

Davis, J. D., Francis, V. M., Davis, M. L., & Schroder, T. A. (1987). *Development of a taxonomy of therapists' coping strategies: Initial report*. Unpublished manuscript.

Dawes, R. (1994). *House of cards: Psychology and psychotherapy built on myth*. New York: Free Press.

Deckard, G., Meterko, M., & Field, D. (1994). Physician burnout: An examination of personal, professional and organizational relationships. *Medical Care, 32*(7), 745–754.

Denzin, N. K. (1989). *The research act: A theoretical introduction to sociological methods*. New York: McGraw Hill.

Dewey, J. (1933). *How we think: A restatement of the relation of reflective thinking to the educative process*. Chicago, IL: Regnery.

Dlugos, R. F., & Friedlander, M. L. (2001). Passionately committed therapists: A qualitative study of their experiences. *Professional Psychology: Research and Practice, 32*, 298–394.

Dodge, J. (1982). Reducing supervisee anxiety: A cognitive behavioral approach. *Counselor Education and Supervision, 22*, 55–60.

Doehrman, M. (1976). Parallel processes in supervision and psychotherapy. *Bulletin of the Menninger Clinic, 40*, 3–104.

Dreyfus, H. L., & Dreyfus, S. E. (1986). *Mind over machine: the power of human intuition and expertise in the era of the computer.* New York: Free Press.

Dreyfus, H. L., & Dreyfus, S. E. (1988). Making a mind vs. modeling the brain: AI back at a branchpoint. In S. R. Graubard (Ed.), *The artificial intelligence debate* (pp. 15–43). Cambridge, MA: MIT Press.

Dreyfus, H. L. (n.d.). What is moral maturity? A phenomenological account of the development of ethical expertise. Retrieved from http://www.alpheus.org/TS_Open/SkillAcquisitionTableText.pdf.

Duncan, B. L., & Miller, S. D. (2000). *The heroic client: Doing client-directed, outcome-informed therapy.* San Francisco, CA: Jossey-Bass

Duncan, B. L., Miller, S. D., Wampold, B. E., & Hubble M. A. (Eds). (2010). *The heart and soul of change: Delivering what works in therapy* (2nd. ed.). Washington, DC: American Psychological Association.

Ekstein, R., & Wallerstein, R. S. (1972). *The teaching and learning of psychotherapy* (2nd ed.). New York: International Universities Press.

Ellis, M. V. (1991). Research in clinical supervision. Revitalizing a scientific agenda. *Counselor Education and Supervision, 30*, 238–251.

Ellis, M. V., Krengel, M., & Beck, M. (2002). Testing self–focused attention theory in clinical supervision: Effects of supervisee anxiety and performance. *Journal of Counseling Psychology 49*(1), 101.

Elsass, P. (2003). *Håndbog i kulturpsykologi: Et fag på tværs* [Handbook of cultural psychology: One profession across]. Copenhagen, Denmark: Gyldendal.

Engeström, Y. (2001). Expansive learning at work: Toward an activity theoretical reconceptualization. *Journal of Education and Work, 14*, 133–156.

Eraut, M. (1994). *Developing professional knowledge and competence.* London: Falmer Press.

Ericsson, K. A., Charness, N., Hoffman, R. R., & Feltovich, P. J. (2006). *The Cambridge handbook of expertise and expert performance.* New York: Cambridge University Press.

Ericsson, K.A., Prietula, M.J., & Cokely, E.T. (2007). The making of an expert. *Harvard Business Review, 85*(7–8), 114–121.

Erikson, E. H. (1959).*Identity and the life cycle.* New York: International Universities Press.

Erikson, E. H. (1968). *Identity, youth, and crisis.* New York: Norton.

Farber, B. A., & Golden, V. (1997). Psychological mindedness in psychotherapists. In M. McCallum & W. E. Piper (Eds.), *Psychological mindedness: A contemporary understanding* (pp. 211–235). Mahwah, NJ: Erlbaum.

Feltovich, P. J., Prietula, M. J., & Ericsson, K. A. (2006). Studies of expertise from psychological perspectives. In K. A., Ericsson, N. Charness, P. J. Feltovich, & R. R. Hoffman (Eds.), *The Cambridge handbook of expertise performance (*pp. 41–67). New York: Cambridge University Press.

Figley, C. R. (1995). Compassion fatigue: Toward a new understanding of the costs of caring. In B. H. Stamm (Ed.), *Secondary traumatic stress: Self–care issues for clinicians, researchers and educators* (pp. 3–28). Baltimore, MD: Sidran Press.

Figley, C. R. (2002). Compassion fatigue: Psychotherapists' chronic lack of self care, *Journal of Clinical Psychology, 58*, 1433–41.

Fleming, J. (1953). The role of supervision in psychiatric training. *Bulletin of the Menninger Clinic, 17*, 157–169.

Fonagy, P., & Bateman, A.W. (2006). Mechanisms of change in metalization-based treatment of BPD. *Journal of Clinical Psychology, 62*, 411–430.

Fouad, N. (2003). Career development: Journeys of counselors. *Journal of Career Development, 30*, 81–87.

Fouad, N. A., Grus, C. L., Hatcher, R. L., Kaslow, N. J., Hutchings, P. S., Madson, M. B., ... Crossman, R. E. (2009). Competency benchmarks: A model for understanding and measuring competence in professional psychology across training levels. *Training and Education in Professional Psychology, 3*(4), 5–26.

Frank, J. D. (1961). *Persuasion and healing.* Baltimore, MD: Johns Hopkins University Press.

Freeman, A. (2003). We're not as smart as we think we are. In J. A. Kottler & J. Carlson (Eds.), *Bad therapy: Master therapists share their worst failures* (pp. 123–130). New York: Bruner-Routledge.

Freud, S. & Breuer, J. (1892). Studies of Hysteria. In: J. Strachey (Ed.) *The standard edition of the complete psychological works by Sigmund Frued,* Vol. II. London: Hogarth Press and the Institute of Psychoanalysis.

Freudenberger, H. (1974). Staff burnout. *Journal of Social Work, 30*, 159–165.

Friedlander, M. L., Siegel, S. M., & Brenock, L. (1989). Parallel process in counseling and supervision: A case study. *Journal of Counseling Psychology, 36*, 149–157.

Friedman, D., & Kaslow, N. J. (1986). The development of professional identity in psychotherapists: Six stages in the supervision process. *The Clinical Supervisor, 4*, 29–49.

Froman-Reid, M (2011). *A qualitative study of vicarious trauma of counselors who work with sexual assault victims.* Pre-dissertation research project. Dept. of Educational Psychology, University of Minnesota, Minneapolis.

Furedy, F. (2004). *Therapy culture: Cultivating vulnerability in an uncertain age.* London: Routledge.

Gadamer, H. G. (1975). *Truth and method* (G. Barden & J. Cumming, Trans.). New York: Seabury.

Gagne, R. M. (1968). Contributions of learning to human development. *Psychological Review, 75*(3), 177.

Garfield, S. L. (1997). The therapist as a neglected variable in psychotherapy research. *Clinical Psychology: Science and Practice, 4*, 40–43.

Garfield, S. L. & Bergin, A. E. (1971). *Handbook of psychotherapy and behavior change: An empirical analysis* (2nd ed.). New York; Wiley.

Garfield, S. L. & Bergin, A. E. (1986). *Handbook of psychotherapy and behavior change* (3rd. ed.). New York; Wiley.

Geller, J. D., Norcross, J. C., & Orlinsky, D. E. (Eds.). (2005). *The psychotherapist's own psychotherapy: Patient and clinician perspectives.* New York: Oxford University Press.

Gelso, C. J. (2002). Real relationship: The "something more" of psychotherapy. *Journal of Contemporary Psychotherapy, 32*, 35–40.

Gelso, C. J. (2009). The real relationship in a post-modern world: Theoretical and empirical explorations. *Psychotherapy Research, 19,* 253–264.

Gelso, C. J. (2010). *The real relationship in psychotherapy: The hidden foundation of change.* Washington, DC: American Psychological Association Books.

Gilligan, C. (1982). *In a different voice.* Cambridge, MA: Harvard University Press.

Gladwell, M. (2008). *Outliers: The story of success.* New York: Little, Brown.

Glaser, B. G., & Strauss, A. L. (1967). *The discovery of grounded theory: Strategies for qualitative research.* Chicago, IL: Aldine.

Glaser, R., & Chi, M. T. H. (1988). Overview. In M. T. H. Chi, R. Glaser, & M. Farr (Eds.), *The nature of expertise* (pp. xv–xxviii). Hillsdale, NJ: Erlbaum.

Goffman, E. (1967). *Interaction ritual: Essays on face–to–face behavior.* Garden City, NY: Doubleday/ Anchor.

Goh, M. (2005). Cultural competence and master therapists: An inextricable relationship. *Journal of Mental Health Counseling, 27*(1), 71–81.

Goh, M., Koch, J., & Sanger, S. (2008). Cultural intelligence in counseling psychology: Applications for multicultural counseling competence. In S. Ang & L. Van Dyne (Eds.), *Handbook of cultural intelligence: Theory, measurement and application* (pp. 257–270). Armonk, NY: M. E. Sharpe.

Goh, M., Starkey, M., Skovholt, T. M., & Jennings, L. (2007). *In search of cultural competence in mental health practice: A study of expert multicultural therapists.* Paper presented at the 115th annual convention of the American Psychological Association, San Francisco, CA.

Goh, M., Sumner, A., Hetler, J., & the Cultural Providers Network (2010, August). *Practice–based evidence in mental health services to diverse communities.* Paper presented at the 118th annual convention of the American Psychological Association, San Diego, CA.

Goh, M., & Yang, A. (2011, July*). Leading in multicultural counseling competence: A study of culturally competent exemplars.* Paper presented at the 7th Biennial Conference of the International Academy of Intercultural Research, Singapore

Goin, M. K., & Kline, F. M. (1974). Supervision observed. *Journal of Nervous and Mental Disease. 158,* 203–213.

Goldberg, C. (1992). *The seasoned psychotherapist: Triumph over adversity.* New York: Norton.

Goldfried, M. R. (1980). Toward the delineation of therapeutic change principles. *American Psychologist, 35,* 991–999.

Goldfried, M. R. (Ed.). (2001). *How therapists change: Personal and professional reflections.* Washington, DC: American Psychological Association.

Goldfried, M. R. (2009). Searching for therapy change principles: Are we there yet? *Applied and Preventive Psychology, 13,* 32–34.

Goldfried, M. R. & Wolfe, B. E. (1998). Toward a more clinically valid approach to therapy research. *Journal of Consulting and Clinical Psychology, 66,* 143–150.

Goldman, L. (1982). Defining non-traditional research. *Counseling Psychologist, 10*(4), 91–93.

Goldman, L. (1989). Moving counseling research into the 21st century. *Counseling Psychologist, 17,* 81–85.

Goodyear, R. K., Wertheimer, A., Cypers, S., & Rosemond, M. (2003). Refining the map of counselor development journey: Response to Rønnestad and Skovholt. *Journal of Career Development, 30,* 73–80.

Gough, H. B., & Heilbrun, A. B. (1983). *The adjective check list manual*. Palo Alto, CA: Consulting Psychologist Press.

Grater, H. A. (1985). Stages in psychotherapy supervision: From therapy skills to skilled therapists. *Professional Psychology: Research and Practice, 16,* 605–610.

Gray, L. A., Ladany, N., Walker, J. A., & Ancis, J. R. (2001). Psychotherapy trainees'experience of counterproductive events in supervision. *Journal of Counseling Psychology, 48,* 371–383.

Gray, S. W., & Smith, M. (2009). The influence of diversity in clinical supervision: A framework for reflective conversations and questioning. *Clinical Supervisor, 28,* 155–179.

Gross, S. M. (2005). Student perspectives on clinical and counseling psychology practica. *Professional Psychology: Research and Practice, 36,* 299–306

Grotevant, H. D., & Cooper, C. R. (1986). Individuation in family relationships. *Human Development, 29,* 82–100.

Gysbers, N. C., Heppner, M. J., & Johnston, J. A. (1998). *Career counseling: Process, issues, and techniques*. Boston, MA: Allyn & Bacon.

Gysbers, N., & Moore, E. (1973). *Life career development: A model*. Columbia: University of Missouri.

Gysbers, N., & Rønnestad, M. H. (1974). Practicum supervision: Learning theory. In G. F. Farwell, N. R. Gamsky, & P. T. Mathieu-Coughlan (Eds.), *The counselor's handbook* (pp. 133–140). New York: Intext Education.

Guy, J. (1987). *The personal life of the psychotherapist*. New York: Wiley.

Harrington, K. (1988). *Personal characteristics of Diplomates defined as master therapists* (Unpublished doctoral dissertation). University of Minnesota, Minneapolis.

Hatcher, R. L., & Gillaspy, J. A. (2006). Development and validation of a revised short version of the working alliance inventory. *Psychotherapy Research, 16,* 12–25.

Havighurst, R. (1972). *Developmental tasks and education* (3rd ed.). New York: David McKay.

Heinonew, E., Lindfors, O., Laaksonen, M. A., & Knekt, P. (2012). Therapists' professional and personal charateristics as predictors of outcome in short- and long-term psychotherapy. *Journal of Affective Disorders, 138,* 301–312.

Henry, W. E. (1966). Some observations on the lives of healers. *Human Development, 9,* 47–56.

Henry, W. P., Schacht, T. E., & Strupp, H. H. (1990). Patient and therapist introject, interpersonal process and differential psychotherapy outcome. *Journal of Consulting and Clinical Psychology, 58,* 768–774.

Hernandez, P., & McDowell, T. (2010). Intersectionality, power, and relational safety in context: Key concepts in clinical supervision. *Training and Education in Professional Psychology, 4,* 29–35.

Herroid, D. J. (1989). *A model of the process of becoming a master counselor* (Unpublished doctoral dissertation). University of Minnesota, Minneapolis.

Hersoug, A. G., Høglend, P., Havik, O. E., Lippe, A. von der., & Monsen, J. T. (2009). Pretreatment patient characteristics related to the level and development of working alliance in long-term psychotherapy. *Psychotherapy Research, 19*(2), 172–180.

Hess, A. K. (1980). *Psychotherapy supervision: Theory, research and practice*. New York: Wiley.

Hess, A. K. (1986). Growth in supervision: Stages of supervisee and supervisor development. *The Clinical Supervisor, 4,* 51–67.

Hess, A. K. (1987). Psychotherapy supervision: Stages, Buber and a theory of relationship. *Professional Psychology: Theory, Research and Practice, 18,* 251–259.

Hess, S. A., Knox, S., Schultz, J.M., Hill, C. E., Sloan, L., Brandt, S., … Hoffman, M. A. (2008, July). Predoctoral interns' nondisclosure in supervision. *Psychotherapy Research, 18,* 400–411.

Hill, C. (2009). *Helping skills: Facilitating exploration, insight, and action* (3rd ed.). Washington DC: American Psychological Association.

Hill, C. E., Charles, D., & Reed, K. G. (1981). A longitudinal analysis of counseling skills during doctoral training in counseling psychology. *Journal of Counseling Psychology, 28,* 428–436.

Hill, C. E., Thompson, B., & Williams, E. N. (1997). A guide to conducting consensual qualitative research. *The Counseling Psychologist, 25*(4), 517–572.

Hirai, T. (2010). *Personal and professional characteristics of Japanese master therapists: A qualitative investigation on expertise in psychotherapy and counseling in Japan* (Unpublished doctoral dissertation). University of Minnesota, Minneapolis.

Hoffer, E. (1951). *The true believer.* New York: New American Library.

Hoffman, M. L. (2000). *Empathy and moral development: Implications for caring and justice.* New York: Cambridge University Press.

Hogan, R. A. (1964). Issues and approaches in supervision. *Psychotherapy: Theory, Research and Practice, 1,* 139–141.

Holland, J. L. (1973). *Making vocational choices: A theory of careers.* Englewood Cliffs, NJ: Prentice-Hall.

Holland, J. L. (1997). *Making vocational choices.* Odessa, FL: Psychological Assessment Resources.

Holland, J. L., & Austin, A. W. (1962). The prediction of the academic, artistic, scientific and social achievement of undergraduates of superior scholastic aptitude. *Journal of Educational Psychology, 53,* 132–143.

Holloway, E. L. (1995). *Clinical supervision: A systems approach.* Thousand Oaks, CA: Sage.

Holmquist, R. (1995). *Countertransference feelings in milieu therapy* (Unpublished doctoral dissertation). Umeå University, Sweden.

Holt, J. (2011, November 27). Two brains running: In the conflict between intuition and rational decision-making, which side wins? *New York Times Book Review Section,* pp. 16–17.

Horowitz, L. M., Wilson, K. R., Turan, B., Zolotsev, P., Constantino, M. J., & Henderson, L. (2006). How interpersonal motives clarify the meaning of interpersonal behaviour: A revised circumplex model. *Personality and Social Psychology Review, 10,* 67–86.

Horvath, A. O., & Bedi, R. P. (2002). The alliance. In J. Norcross (Ed.), *Psychotherapy relationships that work: Therapist contributions and responsiveness to patients* (pp. 37–70). New York: Oxford University Press.

Horvath, A. O., Del Re, A., Flückiger, C., & Symonds, D. B. (2011). Alliance in individual psychotherapy. In J. C. Norcross (Ed.), *Psychotherapy relationships that work* (2nd ed.). New York: Oxford University Press.

Hoshmand, L. L. S. (1989). Alternative research paradigms: A review and teaching proposal. *Counseling Psychologist, 17,* 3–79.

Howard, G. S. (1986). The scientist practitioner in counseling psychology: Toward a deeper integration of theory, research and practice. *Counseling Psychologist, 17,* 61–105.

Husserl, E. (1970). *The crisis of European sciences and transcendental phenomenology.* Evanston, IL: Northwestern University Press. (Original work published 1936)

Ickes, W. (2009). Empathic accuracy. In J. Decety & W. Ickes (Eds.), *The social neuroscience of empathy* (pp. 57–70). Cambridge, MA: MIT Press.

Imber, J. B. (Ed.). (2004). *Therapeutic culture: Triumph and defeat.* New Brunswick, NJ: Transaction.

Ingleby, D. (1985). Professionals as socializers: The psy complex. *Research in Law, Deviance and Social Control, 7,* 79–109.

Jablon, M. (1987). Psychotherapists' perceptions of their professional development. *Dissertation Abstracts International, 47,* 4302.

Jacobsen, C. H. (2007). A qualitative single case study of parallel processes. *Counselling and Psychotherapy Research, 7,* 26–33.

Jacobsen, C. H., & Nielsen, J. (2011, June 23–26). *Clinical supervision in Denmark: Results from the Danish DPCCQ study of supervision.* Paper presented at the Society for Psychotherapy Research International meeting, Bern, Switzerland.

Jennings, L. (1996). *The personal characteristics of master therapists* (Unpublished doctoral dissertation). University of Minnesota, Minneapolis.

Jennings, L., D'Rozario, V., Goh, M., Sovereign, A., Brogger, M., & Skovholt, T. (2008). Psychotherapy expertise in Singapore: A qualitative investigation. *Psychotherapy Research, 18*(5), 508–522.

Jennings, L., Gulden, A., Oien, M., Goh, M., D'Rozario, V. & Skovholt, T. M. (2012). Multicultural knowledge and skills of Singaporean master therapists. (Manuscript in preparation).

Jennings, L., & Skovholt, T. M. (1999). The cognitive, emotional, and relational characteristics of master therapists. *Journal of Counseling Psychology, 46*(1), 3–11.

Jennings, L., Sovereign, A., Bottorff, N., Mussell, M. P., & Vye, C. (2005). Nine ethical values of master therapists. *Journal of Mental Health Counseling, 27*(1), 32–47.

Kadushin, A. (1968). Games people play in supervision. *Social Work, 13*(3), 23–32.

Kadushin, A., & Harkness, D. (2002). *Supervision in social work* (4th ed.). New York: Columbia University Press.

Kahneman, D. (2003). A perspective on judgment and choice: Mapping bounded rationality. *American Psychologist, 58,* 697–720.

Kaplan, B. (1983). A trio of trials. In R. M. Lerner (Ed.). *Developmental Psychology: Historical and philosophical perspectives* (pp. 185–228). Hillsdal, N.J: Erlbaum.

Kell, B. L., & W. J. Mueller (1966). *Impact and change: A study of counseling relationships.* New York: Appleton–Century–Crofts.

Kim, B. S. K., & Lyons, H. Z. (2003). Experiential activities and multicultural counseling competence training. *Journal of Counseling and Development, 81,* 400–408.

Kleinman, A. (1988). *The illness narratives: Suffering, healing and the human condition.* New York: Basic Books.

Kohlberg, L. (1979). *The meaning and measurement of moral development.* Heinz Werner Memorial Lectures. Clark University, Worcester, MA.

Korman, M., & Stubblefield, R. L. (1971). Medical school evaluation and internship performance. *Journal of Medical Education, 46,* 670–673.

Kubany, A. (1957). Use of sociometric peer nominations in medical education research. *Journal of Applied Psychology, 41,* 389–394.

Kvale, S. (1983). The qualitative research interview—A phenomenological and a hermeneutical mode of understanding. *Journal of Phenomenological Psychology, 17,* 171–189.

Kvale, S. (1986a). Meanings of data and human technology. *Scandinavian Journal of Psychology, 17,* 171–189.

Kvale, S. (1986b). Psychoanalytic therapy as qualitative research. In P. D. Ashworth, A. Giorgi, & A. J. J. deKoning (Eds.), *Qualitative research in psychology* (pp. 155–184). Pittsburgh, PA: Duquesne University Press.

Kvale, S. (1987). Validity in the qualitative research interview. *Methods, 1,* 33–50.

Kwon, K., & Kim, C. (2007). Analysis on the characteristics of Korean master group counselor. *The Korean Journal of Counseling, 8,* 979–1010.

Ladany, N., & Bradley, L. J. (2010). *Counselor supervision.* New York: Routledge.

Ladany, N., Friedlander, M. L., & Nelson, M. L. (2005). *Critical events in psychotherapy supervision: An interpersonal approach.* Washington, DC: American Psychological Association.

Ladany, N., Hill, C. E., Corbett, M. M., & Nutt, E. A. (1996). Nature, extent, and importance of what psychotherapy trainees do not disclose to their supervisors. *Journal of Counseling Psychology, 43,* 10–24.

Ladany, N., Walker, J. A., & Melincoff, D. S. (2001). Supervisory style: Its relation to the supervisory working alliance and supervisor self-disclosure. *Counselor Education and Supervision, 40*(4), 263–275.

Laitila, A. (2004). *Dimensions of expertise in family therapeutic process* (Unpublished doctoral dissertation).University of Jyväskylä, Finland.

Lambert, M. J. (Ed.). (2004). *Bergin and Garfield's handbook of psychotherapy and behavior change* (5th ed.). New York: Wiley.

Lambert, M. J., & Ogles, B. M. (2004). The efficacy and effectiveness of psychotherapy. In M. J. Lambert (Ed.), *Bergin and Garfield's handbook of psychotherapy and behavior change* (5th ed., pp. 139–193). New York: Wiley

Lambert, M. J., & Shimokawa, K. (2011). Collecting client feedback. *Psychotherapy, 48*(1), 72–79.

LaRoche, M. L., & Christopher, M. S. (2008). Culture and empirically supported treatments: On the road to collision? *Culture and Psychology, 14,* 333–356.

Larson A. C. (2010). *Utbrenthet. En veiledende bibliography* [Burnout. An annotated bibliography]. Center for Professional Studies Oslo and Akershus University College.

Larsen, A. C., Ulleberg, P., & Rønnestad, M. H. (2010). Depersonalization reconsidered: An empirical analysis of the relationship between depersonalization and cynicism in an extended version of the Maslach Burnout Inventory. Unpublished manuscript, Center for Professional Studies Oslo and Akershus, Oslo.

Lave, J. (1988). *Cognition in practice: Mind, mathematics, and culture in everyday life.* Cambridge, England: Cambridge University Press.

Lave, J., & Wenger, E. (1991). *Situated learning: Legitimate peripheral participation.* Cambridge, England: Cambridge University Press.

Lazar, A., & Eisikovits, Z. (1997). Social work students' preferences regarding supervisory styles and supervisor's behavior. *The Clinical Supervisor, 16,* 25–37.

Leary, T. F. (1957). *Interpersonal diagnosis of personality.* New York: Ronald Press.

Lee, J., Lim, N., Yang, E. & Lee, S. (2011). Antecedents and consequences of three dimensions of burnout in psychotherapists: A meta-analysis. *Professional Psychology: Research and Practice, 42,* 252–258.

Leiter, M. P., & Maslach, C. (1988). The impact of interpersonal environment on burnout and organizational commitment. *Journal of Organizational Behavior, 9*(4), 297–308.

Lerner, R. M. (1986). *Concepts and theories of human development.* New York: Random House.

Lesche, C., & Madsen, E. S. (1976). *Psykoanalysens videnskabsteori* [Psychoanalysis of science]. Copenhagen, Denmark: Munksgaard.

Levant, R. F. (2005). *Report of the 2005 Presidential Task Force on evidence–based practice.* Washington, DC: American Psychological Association.

Levinson, D. J., Darrow, C. N., Klein, E. B., Levinson, M. A., & McKee, B. (1978). *The seasons of a man's life.* New York: Knopf.

Lewin K. (1997). Defining the "Field at a Given Time". In *Resolving social conflicts and field theory in social science.* Washington, DC: American Psychological Association. (Original work published 1943 in *Psychological Review. 50,* 292–310)

Lewin, K. (1951) *Field theory in social science, selected theoretical papers* (D. Cartwright, Ed.). New York: Harper & Row.

Liddle, B. (1986). Resistance in supervision: A response to perceived threats. *Counselor Education and Supervision, 26,* 117–127.

Lincoln, Y. S., & Guba, E. G. (1985). *Naturalistic inquiry.* Newbury Park, CA: Sage.

Littrell, J. M., Lee–Borden, N., & Lorenz, J. A. (1979). A developmental framework for counseling supervision. *Counselor Education and Supervision, 19,* 119–136.

Loganbill, C., Hardy, E., & Delworth, U. (1982). Supervision: A conceptual model. *The Counseling Psychologist, 10,* 3–42.

Lorentzen, S., Orlinsky, D. E. & Rønnestad, M. H. (2011. Sources of influence on the professional development of psychologists and psychiatrists in Norway and Germany. *European Journal of Psychotherapy & Counselling, 13,* 141–152..

Lorentzen, S., Orlinsky, D., & Rønnestad, M. H. (2010). Norske psykiatere som psykoterapeuter. [Norwegian psychiatrists and psychotherapists]. *Matrix, 27*(4), 275–287.

Løvlie–Schibbye, A. (2011). Læringsprosesser i veiledning belyst ved utvalgte relasjonsbegreper [Learning processes in supervision viewed from the perspective of selected relational concepts]. In M. H. Rønnestad & S. Reichelt (Eds.), *Veiledning i psykologisk arbeid* [Supervision of psychotherapeutic work] (pp. 67–78). Oslo, Norway: University Press.

Luborsky, L., McLellan, T.A., Woody, G.E., O'Brien, C. P., & Auerbach, A. (1985). Therapist success and its determinants. *Archives of General Psychiatry, 42,* 602–611.

Lurie, S. J., Nofziger, A. C., Meldrum, S., Mooney, C., & Epstein, R. M. (2006). Temporal and group-related trends in peer assessment amongst medical students. *Medical Education, 40,* 840–847.

Lutz, W., Leon, S. C., Martinovitch, Z., Lyons, J. S., & Stiles, W. B. (2007). Therapists effects in outpatient psychotherapy: A three–level growth curve approach. *Journal of Counseling Psychology, 54,* 32–39.

Maddi, S. R. (2006). Hardiness: The courage to grow from stresses. *The Journal of Positive Psychology, 1,* 160–168.

Madsen, O. J.(2010). *Den terapeutiske kultur* [The therapeutic culture]. Oslo, Norway: Universitetsforlaget.

Mahoney, M. J. (1997). Psychotherapists' personal problems and self–care patterns. *Professional Psychology: Research and Practice, 28*(1), 14–16.

Marcia, J. E. (1966). Development and validation of ego identity status. *Journal of Personality and Social Psychology, 3,* 551–559.

Maslach, C. (2003). *Burnout: the cost of caring.* Englewood Cliffs, NJ: Prentice-Hall. (Original work published 1982)

Maslach, C. (1993). Burnout: A multidimensional perspective. In W. B. Schaufeli, C. Maslach, & T. Marek (Eds.), *Professional burnout: Recent developments in theory and research* (pp. 19–32). Washington, DC: Taylor & Francis.

Maslach, C. (2003). Job burnout. *Current Directions in Psychological Science, 12*(5), 189–192.

Maslach, C., & Jackson, S. E. (1981). The measurement of experienced burnout. *Journal of Occupational Behaviour, 2,* 99–113.

Maslach, C., & Jackson, S. E. (1986). *Maslach burnout inventory: Manual* (2nd ed.). Palo Alto, CA: Consulting Psychologists Press.

Maslach, C., & Jackson, S. E. (1996). *Maslach burnout inventory* (3rd ed.). Palo Alto, CA: Consulting Psychologists Press.

Maslach, C., & Leiter, M. P. (1997). *The truth about burnout: How organizations cause personal stress and what to do about it.* San Francisco, CA: Jossey-Bass.

Maslach, C. & Leiter, M. P. (2008). Early predictors of job burnout and engagement. *Journal of Applied Psychology, 93*(3), 498–512.

Maslach, C., Schaufeli, W. B., & Leiter, M. P. (2001). Job burnout. *Annual Review of Psychology, 52,* 397–422.

Maslow, A. (1966). *The psychology of science.* New York: Harper & Row.

Masten, A. S., Best, K. M., & Garmezy, N. (1990). Resilience and development: Contributions from the study of children who overcome adversity. *Development and Psychopathology, 2*(4), 425–444. McCann, L.,& Pearlman, L. A. (1990). Vicarious traumatization: A framework for understanding the psychological effects of working with victims. *Journal of Traumatic Stress, 3,* 131–149.

McCarthy Veach, P., Bartels, D. M., & LeRoy, B. S. (2001). Ethical and professional challenges posed by patients with genetic concerns: A report of focus group discussions with genetic counselors, physicians, and nurses. *Journal of Genetic Counseling, 10,* 97–120.

Meier, D. E., Back, A. L., Morrison, R. S. (2001). The inner life of physicians and care of the seriously ill. *Journal of the American Medical Association, 286*(23), 3007–3014.

Melton, J. L., Nofzinger–Collins, D., Wynne, M. E., & Susman, M. (2005). Exploring the affective inner experiences of therapists in training: The qualitative interaction between session experience and session content. *Counselor Education and Supervision, 45*(2), 82–96.

Merriam, S. G. (2002). *Qualitative research in practice: examples for discussion and analysis.* San Francisco, CA: Jossey-Bass.

Miller, G. A. (1956). The magical number seven, plus or minus two: Some limits on our capacity for processing information. *Psychological Review, 63,* 81–97.

Miller, W. R., & C'de Baca, J. (2001). *Quantum change: When epiphanies and sudden insights transform ordinary lives.* New York: Guilford Press.

Moskowitz, S. A., & Rupert, P. A. (1983). Conflict resolution within the supervisory relationship. *Professional Psychology: Research and Practice, 14,* 632–641.

Mueller, W. J., & Kell, B. L. (1972). *Coping with conflict: Supervising counselors and psychotherapists.* New York: Appleton–Century–Crofts.

Mullenbach, M. (2000*). Emotional wellness and professional resiliency of master therapists* Unpublished doctoral dissertation, University of Minnesota, Minneapolis.

Mullenbach, M. A. (2000). *Master therapists: A study of professional resiliency and emotional wellness* (Unpublished doctoral dissertation). University of Minnesota, Minneapolis.

Najavits, L. M., & H. H. Strupp (1994). Differences in the effectiveness of psychodynamic therapists: A process–outcome study. *Psychotherapy: Theory, Research, Practice, Training, 31*(1), 114.

Neimeyer, G., & Resnikoff, A. (1982). Qualitative strategies in counseling research. *Counseling Psychologist, 10*(4), 75–85.

Nerdrum, P. (2011). Om empati [On empathy] In: A.v.d. Lippe, & M. H. Rønnestad (Eds.). *Det kliniske Intervjuet: Praksis med ulike klientgrupper, Bind II* [The clinical interview: Practice with different client groups vol. 2] (pp. 55–78). Oslo: Gyldendal Akademisk.

Nerdrum, P., & Rønnestad, M. H. (2002). Changes in therapists' conceptualization and practice of therapy following empathy training. *Clinical Supervisor, 22*, 37–61.

Neufeldt, S. A., Karno, M. P., & Nelson, M. L. (1996). A qualitative study of experts' conceptualizations of supervisee reflectivity. *Journal of Counseling Psychology, 43*(1), 3–9.

Nielsen, G. H., Skjerve, J. E., Jacobsen, C. H., Gullestad, S. E., Hansen, B. R., Reichelt, S., ... Torgersen, A. M. (2009). Mutual assumptions and facts about nondisclosure among clinical supervisors and students: A comparative analysis. *Nordic Psychology, 61*, 49–59.

Nigam, T., Cameron, P. M., & Leverette, J. S. (1997). Impasses in the supervisory process: A resident's perspective. *American Journal of Psychotherapy, 51*, 252–272.

Nissen–Lie, H. A., Monsen, J. T., & Rønnestad, M. H. (2010). Therapist predictors of early patient–rated working alliance: A multilevel approach. *Psychotherapy Research, 20*, 627–646.

Nonaka, I., & Takeuchi, H. (1995). *The knowledge-creating company: How Japanese companies create the dynamics of innovation*. New York: Oxford University Press.

Norcross, J. C. (Ed.). (2002). *Psychotherapy relationships that work: Therapist contributions and responsiveness to patient needs*. New York: Oxford University Press.

Norcross, J. C. (Ed.). (2011). Adapting the therapy relationship to the individual patient [Special issue]. *Journal of Clinical Psychology: In Session, 67.*

Norcross, J. C., & Guy, J. D. (2007). *Leaving it at the office: A guide to psychotherapist self–care.* New York: Guilford.

Norcross, J. C., & Lambert, M. J. (2011). Psychotherapy relationships that work. II. *Psychotherapy, 48*, 4–8.

Norcross, J. C., Vandenbos, G. R., & Freedheim, D. K. (Eds.). (2011). *History of psychotherapy: Continuity and change.* Washington, DC: American Psychological Association.

Norcross, J. C., & Wampold, B. E. (2011). What works for whom: Adapting psychotherapy to the person. *Journal of Clinical Psychology, 67*, 127–132.

Norman, E., Price, M. C., Duff, S. C., Mentzoni, R. A. (2007). Gradations of awareness in a modified learning task. *Consciousness and Cognition, 16, 809-837.*

Norton, S. M. (1992). Peer assessments of performance and ability: An exploratory meta-analysis of statistical artifacts and contextual moderators. *Journal of Business and Psychology, 6*, 387–399.

Oddli, H. W. (2012). *Technical aspects in the initial alliance formation: Qualitative analyses of experienced therapists' behavior and post-treatment reflections.* (Unpublished doctoral dissertation). Department of Psychology, University of Oslo, Norway.

Okiishi, J. C., Lambert, M. J., Eggett, D., Nielsen, L., Dayton, D. D., & Vermeersch, D. A. (2006). An analysis of therapist treatment effects: Toward providing feedback to individual therapists on their clients' psychotherapy outcome. *Journal of Clinical Psychology, 62,* 1157–1172.

Orlinsky, D. E. http://humdev.uchicago.edu/people/faculty/orlinsky.shtml

Orlinsky, D. E. (2010). Foreword. In B. L. Duncan, S. D. Miller, B. E. Wampold, & M. A. Hubble (Eds.), *The heart and soul of change: Delivering what works in therapy* (2nd ed.). Washington, DC: American Psychological Association.

Orlinsky, D. E. (2011, Sept. 2). *The psychotherapeutic relationship, personal life, and modern culture.* Honorary doctoral degree acceptance speech. University of Oslo, Norway.

Orlinsky, D. E., Ambühl, H., Rønnestad, M. H., Davis, J. D., Gerin, P., Davis, M. L., … Wiseman, H. (1999). The development of psychotherapists: Concepts, questions, and methods of a collaborative international study. *Psychotherapy Research, 9,* 127–153.

Orlinsky, D. E., Botermans, J.–F., & Rønnestad, M. H. (1998, June). *Psychotherapeutic talent is the skill that therapists have already when they start training: An empirical analysis.* Paper presented at the 29th annual meeting of the Society for Psychotherapy Research, Snowbird, UT.

Orlinsky, D. E., Botermans, J–F., & Rønnestad, M. H. (2001). Towards an empirically-grounded model of psychotherapy training: Five thousand therapists rate influences on their development. *Australian Psychologist, 36,* 139–148.

Orlinsky, D. E., Norcross, J. C., Rønnestad, M. H., & Wiseman, H. (2005). Outcomes and impacts of the psychotherapists' own psychotherapy: A research review. In J. Geller, J. Norcross, & D. E. Orlinsky (Eds.), *The psychotherapist's own psychotherapy: Patient and clinician perspectives* (pp. 214–230). New York: Oxford University Press.

Orlinsky, D. E., & Rønnestad, M. H. (2005). *How psychotherapists develop: A study of therapeutic work and professional growth.* Washington, DC: American Psychological Association.

Orlinsky, D. E., Rønnestad, M. H., Ambuehl, H., Willutzki, W., Botermans, J. F., Cierpka, M., … Davis, M. (1999). Psychotherapists' assessments of their development at different career levels. *Psychotherapy, 36*(3), 203–215.

Orlinsky, D. E., Rønnestad, M. H., & Willutzki, U. (2004). Fifty years of psychotherapy process-outcome research: Continuity and change. In M. Lambert (Ed.), *Bergin and Garfield's handbook of psychotherapy and behavior change* (5th ed., pp. 307–389). New York: Wiley.

Orlinsky, D. E., Rønnestad, M. H., & Willutzki, U. (2010). The SPR collaborative research program on the development of psychotherapists. In J. Norcross (Ed.), *History of psychotherapy: A century of change* (2nd ed.). Washington, DC: American Psychological Association. (Original work published 1992)

Orlinsky, D. E., Rønnestad, M. H., Willutzki, U., Wiseman, H., Botermans, J–F., & Collaborative Research Network (CRN). (2005). The prevalence and parameters of personal therapy in Europe and elsewhere. In J. D. Geller, J. C. Norcross, & D. E. Orlinsky (Eds.), *The psychotherapist's own psychotherapy: Patient and clinician perspectives* (pp. 177–191). New York: Oxford University Press.

Osborn, C. J., & Davis, T. E. (1996). The supervision contract: Making it perfectly clear. *The Clinical Supervisor, 14,* 121–134.

Osborn, C. J., Paez, S. B., & Carrabine, C. L. (2007). Reflections on shared practices in supervisory lineage. *The Clinical Supervisor, 26,* 119–139.

Owen, J., & Lindley, L. D. (2010). Therapists' cognitive complexity: Review of theoretical models and development of an integrated approach for training. *Training and Education in Professional Psychology, 4*(2), 128–137.

The Oxford English Dictionary. (1989). (2nd ed.). Progressive. In J. A. Simpson & E. S. C. Weiner (Eds., 20 vols.). Oxford, England: Clarendon Press.

Paavola, S., Lipponen, L., & Hakkarainen, K. (2004). Models of innovative knowledge communities and three metaphors of learning. *Review of Educational Research 74,* 557–576.

Palmer, P. (1998). *The courage to teach: Exploring the inner landscape of a teacher's life.* San Francisco, CA: Jossey-Bass.

Palmer, P. J. (2004). *A hidden wholeness: The journey toward an undivided life.* San Francisco, CA: Jossey-Bass.

Parsons, F. (1909). *Choosing a vocation.* Boston: Houghton Mifflin.

Patton, M. J. (1991). Qualitative research on college students: Philosophical and methodological comparisons with the quantitative approach. *Journal of College Student Development, 32,* 389–396.

Patton, M. J., & Kivlighan, D. M. Jr. (1997). Relevance of the supervisory alliance to the counseling alliance and to treatment adherence in counselor training. *Journal of Counseling Psychology, 44*(1), 108.

Patton, M. Q. (1990). *Qualitative research and evaluation methods* (2nd ed.). Thousand Oaks, CA: Sage.

Patton, M. Q. (2002). *Qualitative research and evaluation methods* (3rd ed.). Thousand Oaks, CA: Sage.

Patton, S. M. (1986). The training and development of counselors and psychotherapists: Toward a comprehensive developmental model. *Dissertation Abstracts International, 47,* 3538B.

Paulsen, J., & Peel, T. H. (2006). *Psykologistudenter i obligatorisk egenterapi—erfaringer og mulige innvirkninger på terapeutrollen: En kvalitativ undersøkelse* [Psychology students in mandatory personal therapy—Experiences and possible consequences for the therapist role: A qualitative study]. (Unpublished candidate in psychology thesis). University of Oslo, Norway.

Perry, W. G., Jr. (1981). Cognitive and ethical growth: The making of meaning. In W. Chickering & associates (Eds.), *The modern American college* (pp. 76–116). San Francisco, CA: Jossey-Bass.

Peters, T. J., & Waterman, R. H. (1982). *In Search of Excellence—Lessons from America's best-run companies.* London: HarperCollins.

Piaget, J. (1972). *The principles of genetic epistemology.* London: Routledge & Kegan Paul.

Pines, A., & Aronson, E. (1988). *Career burnout: Causes and cures.* New York: Free Press.

Polanyi, M. (2002). *Personal knowledge: Toward a post-critical philosophy.* London: Routledge

Polkinghorne, D. E. (1986). Conceptual validity in a nontheoretical human science. *Journal of Phenomenological Psychology, 17*(2), 129–149.

Porter, N. (2010). Feminist and multicultural underpinnings to supervision: An overview. *Women and Therapy, 33,* 1–6.

Raichelson, S. H., Herron, W. G., Primavera, L. H., & Ramirez, S. M. (1997). Incidence and effects of parallel process in psychotherapy supervision. *The Clinical Supervisor,* *15*, 37–48.

Regelson, W. (1989). Physician burnout. *Loss, Grief and Care, 3*(1–2), 39–49.

Reichelt, S., Gullestad, S. E., Hansen, B. R., Rønnestad, M. H., Torgersen, A. M., Jacobsen, C. H., ... Skjerve, J. E. (2009). Nondisclosure in group supervision: The supervisee perspective. *Nordic Psychology, 61,* 5–27.

Reichelt, S., & Rønnestad, M. H. (2011). Kontraktetablering i veiledning [Establishing contracts in supervision]. In M. H. Rønnestad & S. Reichelt (Eds.), *Veiledning i psykoterapeutisk arbeid* [Supervision of psychotherapeutic work] (pp. 29–41). Oslo, Norway: Universitetsforlaget.

Reichelt, S., & Skjerve, J. (2002). Correspondence between supervisors and trainees in their perception of supervision events. *Journal of Clinical Psychology, 58,* 759–772.

Rizq, R., & Target, M. (2010). "If that's what I need, it could be what someone else needs." Exploring the role of attachment and reflective function in counselling psychologists' accounts of how they use personal therapy in clinical practice: A mixed methods study. *British Journal of Guidance and Counselling 38*(4), 459–481.

Roald, A. E. (2010). *Psyspeak, psykologisk diskurs: En teoretisk fremstilling av formative krefter i psykologiske meningssystemer* [Psyspeak, psychological discourse: A theoretical presentation of formative psychological meaning systems]. Unpublished candidate in psychology thesis, University of Bergen, Norway.

Rodolfa, E. R., Bent, R. J., Eisman, E., Nelson, P. D., Rehm, L., & Ritchie, P. (2005). A cube model for competency development: Implications for psychology educators and regulators. *Professional Psychology: Research and Practice, 36,* 347–354.

Roe, A. (1977). *The psychology of occupations* .New York: Arno Press.

Rogers, C. R. (1957). The necessary and sufficient conditions of therapeutic personality change. *Journal of Consulting Psychology, 21,* 95–103.

Rogers, C. (1961). *On becoming a person.* Boston, MA: Houghton Mifflin.

Rokeach, M. (1960). *The open and closed mind.* Oxford, England: Basic Books.

Rønnestad, M. H. (1977). The effects of modelling, feedback and experiential methods on counselor empathy. *Counselor Education and Supervision, 16,* 194–200.

Rønnestad, M. H. (1982). Om psykoterapiveiledningens målsetting [On the objectives of psychotherapy supervision]. *Tidsskrift for Norsk Psykologforening,19,* 5–42.

Rønnestad, M. H. (1983). Psykoterapiveiledning: Henimot en begrepsavklaring [Psychotherapy supervision: Towards a conceptual clarification]. *Tidsskrift for Norsk Psykologforening, 20,* 19–23.

Rønnestad, M. H. (1985). En utviklingsmodell for veiledning i klinisk psykologisk arbeid [A developmental model of supervision in clinical work]. *Tidsskrift for Norsk Psykologforening* [Journal of the Norwegian Psychological Association], *22,* 175–181 [English abstract].

Rønnestad, M. H. (2008). Profesjonell utvikling [Professional development]. In A. Molander & L. I. Terum (Eds.), *Profesjonsstudier* [Professional studies] (pp. 279–294). Oslo, Norway: Universitetsforlaget.

Rønnestad, M. H. (2009). Evidensbasert psykologisk praksis [Evidence-based psychological practice]. In H. Grimen & L. I. Terum(Eds.). *Evidensbasert profesjonsutøvelse* [Evidence-based professional practice]. Oslo, Norway: Abstrakt forlag.

Rønnestad, M. H., & Orlinsky, D. E. (2000b). Psykoterapiveiledning til besvær: Når veiledning hemmer og ikke fremmer faglig utvikling [Nonoptimal supervision: When supervision inhibits professional development]. In A. Holte, G. H. Nielsen,

& M. H. Rønnestad (Eds.), *Psykoterapi og psykoterapiveiledning* [Psychotherapy and psychotherapy supervision] (pp. 291–321). Oslo, Norway: Gyldendal Akademisk.

Rønnestad, M. H., & Orlinsky, D. E. (2005a). Therapeutic work and professional development: Main findings and practical implications of a long–term international study. *Psychotherapy Bulletin, 40*(2), 27–32.

Rønnestad, M. H., & Orlinsky, D. E. (2005b). Clinical implications: Training, supervision and practice. In D. E. Orlinsky & M. H. Rønnestad (Eds.), *How psychotherapists develop: A study of therapeutic work and professional growth* (pp. 181–201).Washington, DC: American Psychological Association.

Rønnestad, M. H., & Orlinsky, D. E. (2006). Therapeutische Arbeit und berufliche Entwicklung: Hauptergebnisse und praktische Implikationen einer internationalen Langzeitstudie.[Therapeutic work and professional development]. *Psychotherapeut, 51,* 271–275. (Berlin)

Rønnestad, M. H., & Orlinsky, D. E. (2010, June 23–27). *Healing involvement and stressful involvement in early career therapists: Key factors in professional development.* Presentation at Society for Psychotherapy Research International Meeting, Asilomar, CA.

Rønnestad, M. H., Orlinsky D. E., Parks, B. K., & Davis. J. D. (1997). Supervisors of psychotherapy: Mapping experience level and supervisory confidence. *European Psychologist, 2*(3), 191–201.

Rønnestad, M. H., & Skovholt, T. M. (1991). En modell for profesjonell utvikling og stagnasjon hos terapeutere og rådgivere [A model of the professional development and stagnation of therapists and counselors] *Tidsskrift for Norsk Psykologforening* [Journal of the Norwegian Psychological Association], *28,* 555–567.

Rønnestad, M. H., & Skovholt, T. M. (1992a). *The evolving professional self: Stages and themes in therapist and counselor development.* Chichester, England: Wiley.

Rønnestad, M. H., & Skovholt, T. M. (1992b). Themes in therapist and counselor development. *Journal of Counseling and Development, 70,* 505–515.

Rønnestad, M. H., & Skovholt, T. M. (1993). Supervision of beginning and advanced graduate students of counseling and psychotherapy. *Journal of Counseling and Development, 71,* 396–405.

Rønnestad, M. H., & Skovholt, T. M. (2001). Learning arenas for professional development: Retrospective accounts of senior psychotherapists, *Professional Psychology: Research and Practice, 32,* 181–187.

Rønnestad, M. H., & Skovholt, T. M. (2003). The journey of the counselor and therapist: Research findings and perspectives on professional development. *Journal of Career Development, 30,* 5–44.

Rønnestad, M. H., & Skovholt, T. M. (2011). Om terapeuters profesjonelle utvikling og psykoterapiveiledning i et utviklingsperspektiv [Professional development and psychotherapy supervision in a developmental perspective]. In M. H. Rønnestad & S. Reichelt (Eds.), Veiledning av psykoterapeutisk praksis [Supervision of psychotherapeutic practice]. Oslo, Norway: Universitetsforlaget.

Rønnestad, M. H., & Tjersland, O. A. (2009). Å gå til psykolog [To see a psychologist]. In S. E. Gullestad, B. Killingmo, & S. Magnussen (Eds.), Klinikk og laboratorium [Clinic and laboratory] (pp. 267–283). Oslo: Universitetsforlaget.

Rønnestad, M. H., & Ulvik, O. S. (2011). *On helping discourses.* Unpublished manuscript.

Rønnestad, M. H., & Winje, D. (1984). Methods and focus in the supervision of psychotherapy. Unpublished manuscript. University of Oslo, Norway.

Rosenberg, T., & Pace, M. (2006). Burnout among mental health professionals: Special considerations for the marriage and family therapist. *Journal of Marital and Family Therapy, 32*, 8, 99.

Ross, A. O. (1992). *The sense of self: Research and theory.* New York: Springer.

Ryle, G. (1949/2000). *The concept of mind.* London: Penguin Books.

Sackett, P. (2004). *Saving the world solo.* Seattle, WA: Emotion Literacy Advocates.

Sackett, D. L., Strauss, S. E., Richardson, W. S., Rosenberg, W., & Haynes, R. B. (2000). *Evidence based medicine: How to practice and teach EBM* (2nd ed.). New York: Churchill Livingstone.

Safran, J. D., Muran, J. C., Samstag, L. W., & Stevens, C. (2002). Repairing alliance ruptures. In J. C. Norcross (Ed.), *Psychotherapy relationships that work: Therapist contributions and responsiveness to clients* (pp. 235–254). New York: Oxford University Press.

Salanova, M., Agut, S., & Peiró, J. M. (2005). Linking organizational resources and work engagement to employee performance and customer loyalty: the mediation of service climate. *Journal of Applied Psychology, 90*(6), 12–17.

Savickas, M. L. (2004). The theory and practice of career construction. In S. D. Brown & R. W. Lent (Eds.), *Career development and counseling: Putting theory and research to work* (pp. 42–70) Chichester, England: Wiley.

Scaramalia, M., & Bereiter, C. (1991). Higher levels of agency for children in knowledge building: A challenge for the design of new knowledge media. *Journal of the Learning Sciences, 1*, 37–68.

Schaufeli, W. B., & Enzmann, D. (1998). *The burnout companion to study and practice: A critical analysis.* London: Taylor & Francis.

Schaufeli, W. B., Leiter, M. P., & Maslach, C. (2009). Burnout: 35 years of research and practice. *Career Development International, 14*(3), 204–220.

Schneirly, T. C. (1957). The concept of development in comparative psychology. In. D. B. Harris (Ed.), *The concept of development* (chapter 12). Minneapolis: University of Minnesota Press.

Schön, D. A. (1983). *The reflective practitioner: How professionals think in action.* New York: Basic Books.

Schön, D. A. (1987). *Educating the reflective practitioner: Toward a new design for teaching and learning in the professions.* San Francisco, CA: Jossey-Bass.

Schroder, T. A., Wiseman, H., & Orlinsky, D. E. (2009). "You were always on my mind …": Therapists' intersession experiences in relation to their therapeutic practice, professional characteristics, and quality of life. *Psychotherapy Research, 19*, 42–53.

Searles, H. F. (1955). The informational value of the supervisor's emotional experiences. *Psychiatry: Journal for the Study of Interpersonal Processes, 18*, 135–146.

Segal, Z. V., Williams, J. M. G., & Teasdale, J. D. (2002). *Mindfulness–based cognitive therapy for depression: A new approach to preventing relapse.* New York: Guilford Press.

Seligman, M .E. P., & Csikszentmihalyi, M. (2000). Positive psychology: An introduction. *American Psychologist, 55*(1), 5–14.

Sexton, T. L., & Whiston, S. C. (1994). The status of the counseling relationship: An empirical review, theoretical implications, and research directions. *The Counseling Psychologist, 22*(1), 6–78.

Sfard, A. (1998). On two metaphors for learning and the dangers of choosing just one. *Educational Researcher, 27*, 4–13.

Shapiro, E. (1995). *Eye movement desensitization and reprocessing: Basic principles, protocols and procedures.* New York: Guilford Press.

Shavelson, R. J., Hubner, J. J., & Stanton, G. C. (1976). Self–concept: Validation of construct interpretations. *Review of Educational Research, 46,* 407–441.

Shontz, F. C. (1982). To study persons: Reactions to qualitative strategies in counseling research. *Counseling Psychologist, 10*(4), 91–93.

Shostrom, E. L. (Producer). (1965) *Three approaches to psychotherapy I, II, and III* [Film]. Orange, CA: Psychological Films.

Simon, R. C., & Hughes, C. C. (1995). *The culture–bound syndromes: Folk illnesses of psychiatric and anthropological interest.* Boston, MA: Reidel.

Skjerve, J.& Nielsen, G. H. (1999). Utdanning av kliniske veiledere. Erfaringer fra et utdanningsprogram ved Universitetet i Tromsø. *Tidsskrift for Norsk Psykologforening, 36,* 1151–1156.

Skjerve, J., Nielsen, G. H., Jacobsen, C. H., Gullestad, S. E., Hansen, B. R., Reichelt, S., Rønnestad, M. H., Torgersen, A. M. (2009). Nondisclosure in psychotherapy group supervision: The supervisor perspective. *Nordic Psychology, 61,* 28–48.

Skovholt, T. M. (1985). Optimal stages of therapist/counselor development. Unpublished manuscript.

Skovholt, T. M. (2001). *The resilient practitioner: Burnout prevention and self–care strategies for counselors, therapists, teaches and health professionals.* Needham Heights, MA: Allyn & Bacon.

Skovholt, T. M. (2005). The cycle of caring: A model of expertise in the helping professions. *Journal of Mental Health Counseling, 27,* 82–93.

Skovholt, T. M. (2008). Two versions of erosion in the helping professions: Caring burnout and meaning burnout. *New Therapist, 52,* 28–29.

Skovholt, T. M., Cognetta, P., Ye, G., & King, L. (1997). Violence prevention strategies of inner-city student experts. *Professional School Counseling, 1,* 35–38.

Skovholt, T. M., & D'Rozario, V. (2000). Portraits of outstanding and inadequate teachers in Singapore: The impact of emotional intelligence. *Teaching and Learning, 40*(1), 9–17.

Skovholt, T. M., & Jennings, L. (Eds.). (2004). *Master therapists: Exploring expertise in therapy and counseling.* Boston, MA: Allyn & Bacon.

Skovholt, T. M., Jennings, L., & Mullenbach, M. (2004). Portrait of the master therapist: Developmental model of the highly–functioning self. In T. M. Skovholt and L. Jennings (Eds.). *Master therapists: Exploring expertise in therapy and counseling.* Boston: Allyn & Bacon.

Skovholt, T. M., & McCarthy, P. M. (1988). Critical incidents in counselor development. *Journal of Counseling and Development, 67,* 69–72.

Skovholt, T. M., & Rønnestad, M. H. (1992). Themes in therapist and counselor development. *Journal of Counseling and Development, 70,* 505–515.

Skovholt, T. M., & Rønnestad, M. H. (1995). *The evolving professional self: Stages and themes in therapist and counselor development.* Chichester, England: Wiley. (Original work published 1992)

Skovholt, T. M., & Rønnestad, M. H. (2003). Struggles of the novice counselor and therapist. *Journal of Career Development, 30,* 45–58.

Skovholt, T. M., Rønnestad, M. H., & Jennings, L. (1997). Searching for expertise in counseling, psychotherapy, and professional psychology. *Educational Psychology Review, 9*(4), 361–370.

Skovholt, T., & Trotter–Mathison, M. (2011). The *resilient practitioner: Burnout prevention and self–care strategies for counselors, therapists, teachers, and health professionals* (2nd ed.). New York: Routledge.

Skovholt, T. M., Vaughan, M., & Jennings, L. (2011). Practitioner mastery and expertise. In T. M. Skovholt (Ed.), *Becoming a therapist: On the path to mastery* (237–284) New York: Wiley.

Smith, A. G. (2008). *Personal characteristics of master couple therapists.* (Unpublished doctoral dissertation). University of Alberta, Alberta, Canada.

Smith, D. P., & Orlinsky, D. E. (2004). Religious and spiritual experience among psychotherapists. *Psychotherapy: Theory, Research, Practice, Training, 41,* 144–151.

Smith, T. B., Rodriguez, M. D., & Bernal, G. (2011). Culture. *Journal of Clinical Psychology, 67*(2), 166–175.

Soderfeldt, M., Soderfeldt, B., & Wang, L. (1995). *Burnout in social work. Social Work, 40*(5), 638–646.

Sonnentag, S. (1998). Identifying high performers: Do peer nominations suffer from a likeability bias? *European Journal of Work and Organizational Psychology, 7*(4), 501–515.

Spokane, A. R. (1996). Holland's theory. In D. Brown, L. Brooks, & Associates (Eds.), *Career choice and development* (3rd ed., p.33–69). San Francisco, CA: Jossey-Bass.

Sprinthall, N. A. (1975). Fantasy and reality in research: How to move beyond the unproductive paradox. *Counselor Education and Supervision, 14,* 310–322.

Stevanovic, P., & Rupert, P. A. (2004). Career–sustaining behaviors, satisfactions and stresses of professional psychologists. *Psychotherapy: Theory, Research, Practice, Training, 41*(3), 301–309.

Stoltenberg , C. D. (1981), Approaching supervision from a developmental perspective: The counselor complexity model. *Journal of Counseling Psychology, 28,* 59–65.

Stoltenberg, C. D. (2005). Enhancing professional competence through developmental approaches to supervision. *American Psychologist, 60*(8), 857.

Stoltenberg, C. D., & Delworth, U. (1987). *Supervising counselors and therapists: A developmental approach.* San Francisco, CA: Jossey-Bass.

Stoltenberg, C. D., McNeill, B., & Delworth, U. (1998). *IDM supervision: An integrated developmental model for supervising counselors and therapists.* San Francisco, CA: Jossey-Bass. Strauss, A., & Corbin, J. (1990). *Basics of qualitative research: Grounded theory, procedures, and techniques.* Newbury Park, CA: Sage.

Strupp, H. (1996). The Tripartite Model and the *Consumer Reports* Study. *American Psychologist, 51, 1017-1024*

Strømme, H. (2010*). Confronting helplessness. A study of psychology students' acquisition of dynamic psychotherapeutic competence* (Unpublished doctoral dissertation). University of Oslo, Norway.

Sue, D. W., Arredondo, P., & McDavis, R. J. (1992). Multicultural counseling competencies and standards: A call to the profession. *Journal of Counseling & Development, 70*(4), 477–486.

Sue, D. W., & Sue. D. (2008). *Counseling the culturally diverse* (5th ed.). Hoboken, NJ: Wiley.

Sullivan, M. (2001). *Master therapist's construction of the therapeutic relationship* (Unpublished doctoral dissertation). University of Minnesota, Minneapolis, MN.

Sullivan, M., Skovholt, T. M., & Jennings, L. (2004). Master therapists' construction of the working alliance. In T. M. Skovholt & L. Jennings (Eds.), *Master therapists: Exploring expertise in therapy and counseling.* Boston, MA: Allyn & Bacon.

Super, D. E. (1949). *Appraising vocational fitness by means of psychological tests.* New York: Harper.

Super, D. E. (1953). A theory of vocational development. *American Psychologist, 8,* 405–414.

Super, D. E. (1980). A life-span, life-space approach to career development. *Journal of Vocational Behavior, 16,* 282–298.

Super, D., Savickas, M. L., & Super, C. M. (1996). The life-span, life-space approach to careers. In D. Brown & L. Brooks (Eds.), *Career choice and development* (3rd ed., pp. 121–178). San Francisco, CA: Jossey-Bass.

Sutter, E., McPherson, R. H., & Geeseman, R. (2002). Contracting in supervision. *Professional Psychology: Research and Practice, 33,* 495–498.

Tatsuya, H. (2010). *Personal and professional characteristics of Japanese master therapists: A qualitative investigation on expertise in psychotherapy and counseling in Japan* (Unpublished doctoral dissertation). University of Minnesota, Minneapolis.

Tellegen, A., & Atkinson, G. (1974). Openness to absorbing and self–altering experiences ("absorption"), a trait related to hypnotic susceptibility. *Journal of Abnormal Psychology, 83,* 268–277.

Thoma, S. J., Rest, R., & Barnett, R. (1986). Moral judgment, behavior, decision making, and attitudes. In R. Rest (Ed.), *Moral development: Advances in research and theory.* New York: Praeger.

Thomas, J. T. (2007). Informed consent through contradicting for supervision: Minimizing risks, enhancing benefits. *Professional Psychology: Research and Practice, 38,* 221–231.

Timulak, L. (2007). Identifying core categories of client-identified impact of helpful events in psychotherapy: A qualitative meta-analysis. *Psychotherapy Research, 17,* 305–314.

Torre, J. de la, & Appelbaum, A. (1974). Use and misuse of clichés in clinical supervision. *Archives of General Psychiatry, 31*(3), 302–306.

Toynbee, A. J. (1965). *A study of history* (Abridged ed., 2 vols.). New York: Dell.

Trotter–Mathison, M., Koch, J., Sanger, S., & Skovholt, T. (2010). *Voices from the field: Defining moments in counselor and therapist development.* New York: Routledge.

Tversky, A., & Kahneman, D. (1974). Judgements under uncertainty: Heuristics and biases. *Science, 185,* 1124–1131.

Tynjälä, P., Nuutinen, A., Eteläpelto, A., Kirjonen, J., & Remes, P. (1997). The acquisition of professional expertise—A challenge for educational research. *Scandinavian Journal of Educational Research, 41,* 475–494.

Ulvik, O.S. (2011). Forståelse av mangfold og makt [Conceptualizing variety and power]. In M. H. Rønnestad & S. Reichelt (Eds.), *Veiledning i psykoterapeutisk arbeid* [Supervision of psychotherapeutic work] (pp. 149–159). Oslo, Norway: Universitetsforlaget.

Vaillant, G. E. (1977). *Adaptation to life.* Boston, MA: Little, Brown.

Vygotsky, L.S. (1972). *Thought and language.* Cambridge, MA: MIT Press.

Vygotsky, L. S. (1978). *Mind in society: The development of higher psychological processes.* Cambridge, MA: Harvard University Press.

Wampold, B. E. (2001). *The great psychotherapy debate. Models, methods, and findings.* Mahwah, NJ: Erlbaum.

Wampold, B. E. (2010). *The basics of psychotherapy: An introduction to theory and practice.* Washington, DC: American Psychological Association.

Wampold, B. E. (2011). *Qualities and actions of effective therapists* [DVD]. Available from http://www.apa.org/videos/

Wampold, B., & Brown, J. (2005). Estimating variability in outcomes attributable to therapists: A naturalistic study of outcomes in managed care. *Journal of Consulting and Clinical Psychology, 73,* 914–923.

Wampold, B. E., & Weinberger, J. (2010). Carl Rogers: Idealistic pragmatist and psychotherapy research pioneer. In L. G. Castonguay, J. C. Muran, J. Hayes, N. Ladany, & T. Anderson (Eds.), *Bringing psychotherapy research to life* (pp. 17–27). Washington, DC: American Psychological Association.

Ward, L. G., Friedlander, M. L., Schoen, L. G., & Klein, J. G. (1985). Strategic self–presentation in supervision. *Journal of Counseling Psychology, 32*(1), 111–118.

Welch, S. (1975). Sampling by referral in a dispersed population. *The Public Opinion Quarterly, 39*(2), 237–245.

Wertsch, J. (1991). *Voices of the mind: A sociocultural approach to mediated action.* London: Harvester Wheatsheaf.

Wertsch, J. (1998). *Mind as action.* New York: Oxford University Press.

Whaley, A. L., & Davis, K. E. (2007). Cultural competence and evidence-based practice in mental health services. *American Psychologist, 62*(6), 563–574.

White, M., & Epston, D. (1990). *Narrative means to therapeutic ends.* New York: Norton.

Widick, C. P., Knefelkamp, L., & Parker, C. (1980). Student development. In U. Delworth, G. R. Hansen, & Associates (Eds.), *Student services: A handbook for the profession* (pp. 75–116). San Francisco: Jossey-Bass.

Williams, A. B. (2000). Contribution of supervisors' covert communication to the parallel process. *Dissertation Abstracts International Section A: Humanities & Social Sciences, Vol 61 (3-A), 1165.*

Williamson, E. G. (1939). *How to counsel students.* New York: McGraw–Hill

Winner, E. (2000). The origins and ends of giftedness. *American Psychologist, 55,* 159–169.

Wiseman, H., & Egozi, S. (2006). Personal therapy for Israeli school counselors: Prevalence, parameters, and professional difficulties and burnout. *Psychotherapy Research, 16*(3), 332–347.

Wolberg, L. R. (1967). *The technique of psychotherapy* (2nd ed.). New York: Grune & Stratton.

Wood, D. J., Bruner, J. S., & Ross, G. (1976). The role of tutoring in problem solving. *Journal of Child Psychology and Psychiatry, 17,* 9–100.

Worthen, V., & NcNeill, B. W. (1996). A phenomenological investigation of "good" supervision events. *Journal of Counseling Psychology, 43,* 25–34.

Worthington, E. L., & Roehlke, H. J. (1979). Effective supervision as perceived by beginning counselors-in-training. *Journal of Counseling Psychology, 26,* 64–73.

Wrenn, C. G. (1962). The culturally encapsulated counselor. *Harvard Educational Review, 32,* 444–449.

Yalom, I. D. (1980). *Existential therapy.* New York: Basic Books.

Yalom, I. D. (1995). *The theory and practice of group psychotherapy* (4th ed.). New York: Basic Books.

Yalom, I. D. (1996). *Lying on the couch.* New York: Harper Perennial. Yalom, I. D. (2002). *The gift of therapy: An open letter to a new generation of therapists and their patients.* New York: Harper Perennial.

Yalom, I. D. (2012). *Love's executioner and other tales of psychotherapy.* New York: Basic Books.

Yogev, S. (1982). Happiness in dual–career couples: Changing research, changing values. *Sex Roles, 8,* 593–605.

Yourman, D. B., & Farber, B. A. (1996). Nondisclosure and distortion in psychotherapy supervision. *Psychotherapy: Theory, Research, Practice, Training, 33*(4), 567.

Zunker, V. G. (1998). *Career counseling: Applied concepts of life planning* (5th ed.). Pacific Grove, CA: Brooks–Cole.

INDEX